SPREADING INDRA'S NET

D. T. Suzuki, Columbia University, 1953

SPREADING INDRA'S NET

THE COLUMBIA LECTURES OF D. T. SUZUKI

EDITED BY

RICHARD M. JAFFE, SHIGEMATSU SŌIKU, TOKIWA GISHIN, AND ELIZABETH MARY THOMAS

Columbia University Press *New York*

Columbia University Press
Publishers Since 1893
New York Chichester, West Sussex

Library of Congress Cataloging-in-Publication Data
Names: Suzuki, Daisetz Teitaro, 1870–1966 author | Jaffe, Richard M., 1954– editor | Sōiku, Shigematsu editor | Tokiwa, Gishin editor
Title: Spreading Indra's net : the Columbia lectures of D. T. Suzuki / edited by Richard M. Jaffe, Shigematsu Sōiku, Tokiwa Gishin, and Elizabeth Mary Thomas.
Description: New York : Columbia University Press, [2025] | Includes index.
Identifiers: LCCN 2024060964 (print) | LCCN 2024060965 (ebook) | ISBN 9780231192866 hardback | ISBN 9780231550000 ebook
Subjects: LCSH: Zen Buddhism
Classification: LCC BQ9266 .S953 2025 (print) | LCC BQ9266 (ebook) | DDC 294.3/927—dc23/eng/20250324

Frontispiece: Columbia University, 1953. D. T. Suzuki's calligraphy reads, "Sitting alone on Daiyū peak, Daisetsu." The quotation is a reference to Case 26 of the Blue Cliff Record. (Photograph courtesy of Matsugaoka Bunko.)

Cover design: Julia Kushnirsky
Cover image: Photograph courtesy of Matsugaoka Bunko

GPSR Authorized Representative: Easy Access System Europe, Mustamäe tee 50, 10621 Tallinn, Estonia, gpsr.requests@easproject.com

For Elizabeth Mary Thomas

Her efforts made this record of D. T. Suzuki's lectures possible.

CONTENTS

Abbreviations ix
Editorial Notes xi

Introduction: A Course with No Beginning 1

DAISETZ TEITARO SUZUKI'S COLUMBIA UNIVERSITY SEMINAR LECTURES, 1952–1953

I 67
II 93
III 115
IV 133
V 173
VI 235

Character Glossary 305
Acknowledgments 313
Notes 315
Bibliography 345
Index 351

ABBREVIATIONS

AFM	*Açvaghosha's Discourse on the Awakening of Faith in the Mahâyâna*
CUSM	Columbia University Seminars, 1952–1953 (manuscript)
EMT	Elizabeth Mary Thomas Seminar Notebooks
EZB, 1, 2, or 3	*Essays in Zen Buddhism*, First, Second, and Third Series*
IZ	*Introduction to Zen Buddhism**
LS	*Lankavatara Sutra*
LZ	*Living by Zen*
MCB	*Mysticism: Christian and Buddhist*
MZB	*Manual of Zen Buddhism**
S&T	Daisetz Teitaro Suzuki's *Columbia University Seminar Lectures*
SLS	*Studies in the Lankavatara Sutra*
SWS	*Selected Works of D. T. Suzuki*, Volumes 1–4
SZ	*Studies in Zen*
ZB	*Zen Buddhism: Selected Writings of D. T. Suzuki*
ZBJC	*Zen Buddhism and Its Influence on Japanese Culture*

Publication details for these works are in the bibliography.

*Page numbers given first for these works are for the post–World War II Rider or George Allen and Unwin editions published in the United Kingdom. Additional references in brackets are for the first editions, published in Japan.

EDITORIAL NOTES

- This edition of D. T. Suzuki's Columbia University Seminar Lectures, 1952–1953, is based upon the Japanese edition of the lectures, *Daisetz Teitaro Suzuki's Columbia University Seminar Lectures*, edited by Shigematsu Sōiku and Tokiwa Gishin (Kita-Kamakura: Matsugaoka Bunko, 2016).
- In reediting the lectures for this edition, I have used the 2016 Matsugoka edition while referring to a photocopy of the lectures typescript manuscript preserved at the Matsugaoka Bunko. That typescript, simply labeled "Columbia University Seminars 1952–1953," is divided into six chapters numbered with Roman numerals, I–VI. I have followed that structure, not attempting to divide the lectures into hypothetical "class sessions," as in the 2016 Matsugaoka Bunko edition. As explained in the introduction, we know that Suzuki taught this material at Columbia from the spring 1952 semester to the spring 1953 semester, but it is unclear how he divided the chapters into class sessions, how much of the written lectures he delivered in class, and on what dates he presented any given section.
- I have deleted or revised many of the footnotes provided by Shigematsu and Tokiwa for the 2016 Matsugoka edition,

having decided they were too detailed or, at times, unnecessary for Anglophone readers.

- Unchanged substantive endnotes from the 2016 Matsugaoka edition are marked with the initials of the editors, [S&T]. I note if I have modified the comment with my initials, RMJ.
- Footnotes in the text are, unless otherwise noted, Suzuki's original footnotes.
- Editors' notes are endnotes, numbered with arabic numerals, gathered at the end of the book.
- Shigematsu Sōiku and Tokiwa Gishin did a magnificent, Herculean job tracing almost every reference in the lectures to the original Chinese and Japanese Buddhist texts that Suzuki quotes throughout the manuscript. I have added line references for the SAT Daizōkyō and Chinese Buddhist Electronic Text Association (CBETA) editions of the texts cited. In addition, whenever possible, I have provided references to published English-language translations of those texts, including those by Suzuki himself. Although the translations are at times problematic, they allow those unable to read Buddhist Chinese to see the sources from which Suzuki is drawing his quotations in their surrounding context.
- In reediting the manuscript, I have deleted almost all interlinear comments from the typist/editor that were indicated by section marks, § . . . §. In several places interlinear comments helpful to the reader have been rendered as endnotes.
- Typed and handwritten insertions in the manuscript have been incorporated into the text.
- Text added to the main body of the text by me for clarity is noted with square brackets [. . .].
- Minor changes in punctuation have not been marked.

- American English spelling is used throughout, apart from quotations from sources using British orthography.
- Major departures from the typescript and problematic passages, missing text, etc., are discussed in the endnotes for each chapter.
- Romanization of Chinese and Japanese terms has been standardized using the Pinyin and modified Hepburn systems.
- Diacritical marks, when not in the original typescript, have been added to Sanskrit and Pāli words.

SPREADING INDRA'S NET

INTRODUCTION

A Course with No Beginning

RICHARD M. JAFFE

401 Low Library—a capacious classroom at Columbia University—was filled with students and curious faculty members on February 5, 1952. They had come to hear Daisetz Teitarō Suzuki (1870–1966), then approaching eighty-two years of age, teach the first class of his course, Chinese 128, Chinese Philosophy. Suzuki announced that he would be teaching about the "development of Buddhist thought in China and especially its culmination as contained in the Kegon (Hua-yen) formulation."[1] He began on Kegon/Huayan, the highly influential "Flower Garland" school of Chinese Buddhism, with these words: "This will be a course on a philosophy of timelessness and spacelessness, which have no beginning. Therefore the course will have no beginning."[2] To understand Kegon, Suzuki continued, one must see who was "at the back of Kegon"—that is, none other than the Buddha himself.[3] And to understand the Buddha, it was necessary to comprehend the nature of the Buddha's awakening, which is the basis of the Kegon philosophy.

With those words, Suzuki began nine semesters—five years—of teaching at Columbia and close to seven years of residence in New York City, from 1952 through 1958. For the very first semester, Chinese Philosophy was slated as a "graduate lecture course" and delivered on Tuesday and Thursday afternoons from 5:10 to 6:00 p.m.

The biweekly, midweek scheduling may explain why, as the semester progressed, the faculty presence diminished, leaving only graduate students in attendance.[4] For the fall 1952 semester the course was moved to a smaller seminar room, 716 Philosophy Hall, which held a large oval seminar table with chairs surrounding the table and along three of the walls. The new, more felicitous course time, Friday afternoons from 4:00–6:00 p.m., and then, for the spring 1953 and future semesters, Fridays, 5:10–7:00 p.m., proved more appealing for non-Columbia attendees who were drawn to the classes from all over the New York City area.

As word about Suzuki's course on Buddhism spread through New York's artistic, literary, and intellectual circles, the number of nonstudent attendees grew to include such cultural luminaries as Carolyn Brown, John Cage, Erich Fromm, Phillip Guston, Dorothy Norman, Ad Reinhardt, and many others. Arthur Danto, a philosophy professor at Columbia who attended the classes, recollects that the seminar room in Philosophy Hall was filled each week with students and a diverse group of auditors that at times approached forty in number.[5] Margaret Rioch, an American psychiatrist who studied Zen with Dr. Hubert Benoit in Paris, attended the seminar in 1952. She recalled students seated around the large seminar table with auditors in the chairs lining the walls.[6] Composer John Cage similarly recollected the chairs being filled and a few people standing in the doorway.[7] Lundsford P. Yandell, who attended the seminars in the mid-1950s, recalls three to four dozen attendees, including undergraduates, graduate students, therapists, and, like Yandell, "lay auditors, many long engaged in their own searching."[8]

Dr. Albert Stunkard, an occasional seminar participant who had met Suzuki in Japan in the late 1940s, recollected that Suzuki's classes were small, with attendees sitting in chairs facing him in a "small conference room." Suzuki would often spend considerable time explaining Chinese terms that he had written on the blackboard. John Cage, an enthusiastic attendee, described how Suzuki spent much of one seminar trying to come up with a translation for the Sino-Japanese term *yū* 幽, eventually settling on "unexplainable" as the closest he could come. Suzuki "laughed and then said, 'Isn't it strange that having come all the way from Japan I spend my time explaining to you that which is not to be explained?'"[9]

By the start of Suzuki's last semester at Columbia, his course was literally in *Vogue*, with the editors of that magazine noting in the "People Are Talking About" section, "PEOPLE ARE TALKING ABOUT . . . The Columbia University classes of the great Zen Buddhist teacher, Dr. Daisetz Suzuki, who sits in the centre of a mound of books, waving his spectacles, with ceremonial elegance while mingling the philosophical abstract with the familiar concrete: 'To discover one is a great achievement, to discover zero a great leap'; or, another time, 'Have no ulterior purpose in work, then you are free.'"[10]

For the next three semesters, Suzuki presented the sweeping, idiosyncratic survey of Buddhist philosophy in this book to an audience that included university students, faculty members, and an array of auditors drawn from different corners of the New York City intellectual world. Grounding his presentation on a set of Buddhist classic texts that included the *Dhammapada*, the *Awakening of Faith*, the Flower Garland Sutra, Chinese commentaries on the aforementioned texts, and various collections of Zen stories, Suzuki discussed with the attendees how the Buddha achieved the full awakening that freed him from all mundane suffering, as well as the Buddhist understanding of awakened mind, the nature of time, the etiology of delusion, and the importance of compassionate vow.

In the course, Suzuki expounds on how Buddha's awakening is fundamental Will—something much deeper than just the biological: becoming self-aware. "So this Will, instead of remaining blind and unconscious, wants to live and become conscious of itself. When this consciousness is realized this is enlightenment. So the enlightenment experience which Buddha realized after six years of moral and intellectual trials, this experience is no more than Will becoming conscious of itself. Will always tries to become conscious of itself, and this becoming conscious is enlightenment" (282).[11] Throughout the lectures composing *Spreading Indra's Net*, Suzuki pushes the students toward what he argues is the central point of Buddhism: the realization that "becoming itself is Being, this is suchness." Ultimately, Suzuki concludes, Zen is about realizing the "absolute subject," which he glosses as "all-beings-Mind" and Zen, while eschewing "words and concepts," provokes us to "move from mind to Mind" (303).

Spreading Indra's Net is an edited, annotated version of the typed manuscript, "Columbia University Seminars, 1952–1953," preserved in Suzuki's archive, the Matsugaoka Bunko (Pine Hill Library), in Kita-Kamakura, Japan. In this introduction, I refer to the published book you are reading as *Spreading Indra's Net.* I refer to the unpublished typed manuscript version of the lectures, the "Columbia University Seminars, 1952–1953," as the "Seminars Manuscript." The title of the book alludes to the metaphor of Indra's net that is used widely in Huayan/Kegon Buddhist literature. As depicted in the Flower Garland Sutra, above the god Indra's palace is spread an infinitely vast net that has a mirror at each node. Each mirror reflects and simultaneously is reflected in all the other mirrors, an image that illustrates one of the key doctrines of Flower Garland Buddhism: the mutual interdependence and interfusion of all phenomena.

Utilizing hints gleaned from the manuscript version of the revised lectures, Suzuki's letters and diary entries, and several conversations with Mihoko Okamura-Bekku (1935–2023), his assistant from the early 1950s until Suzuki's death in 1966, I had concluded that the manuscript for this book was transcribed and typed by the noted

Egyptologist Elizabeth Mary Thomas. (Henceforth, I will refer to Mihoko Okamura by her first name, so as not to confuse her with other members of the Okamura family, whom I will discuss passim below.) From fall 1952 until Suzuki's return to Japan in late 1958, Thomas had been a devoted student, participating in the Columbia seminars regularly, frequently meeting with Suzuki, and attending many of his public lectures. Like many of the other regular attendees, Thomas met with Suzuki outside of class, including visits at his residence in Butler Hall. According to Mihoko, after Suzuki had moved to her parents' home in January 1954, Thomas often would pick her and Suzuki up en route from Princeton to the Friday afternoon Columbia seminar. Mihoko and her younger sister Reiko became good friends with Thomas, whom, along with Suzuki, they often had visited in 1955–1956. Mihoko also told me in one of our conversations that after Thomas was diagnosed with cancer in 1985, she had given Mihoko some Suzuki seminar-related documents before moving from Princeton back to her family home in Mississippi.[12]

Thomas was an independent scholar and accomplished Egyptologist. Over the course of her education, which included an MA degree from the Oriental Institute at the University of Chicago, she had taken classes in Egyptology, classics, comparative religions, and Hinduism. She also had studied various forms of ancient Egyptian, as well as Greek, Hebrew, and a few European languages.[13] After working as a cryptologist in Washington, DC, during the Second World War, in 1949, Thomas joined the Bollingen Foundation-funded Egyptian Expedition, led by Natacha Rambova and the Egyptologist Alexandre Piankoff. After returning to the United States Thomas moved to Princeton, New Jersey, in 1951, where she could use the university's library resources for her research and have easy access to New York City. Thomas returned to Egypt to continue her archaeological work for part of 1953 and again in 1959–1960. Based on her extensive research on tombs in the Valley of the Kings in Thebes, Thomas, dissatisfied with the printing standards of most presses, self-published in 1966 the *Royal Necropoleis of Thebes.*[14] This work, now in a second edition, "remains the definitive study of Theban royal tombs."[15]

Thomas probably first met Suzuki in Princeton in spring 1952, as Suzuki was finishing his first semester of seminars at Columbia. Soon after that, she began corresponding with and visiting Suzuki in New York.[16] On October 10, 1953, Thomas began attending Suzuki's seminars regularly. She also, judging from entries in her notebooks, carefully read Suzuki's writings. As she got to know him better through their meetings outside of class, she also began helping with his writing projects, including extensive editing of chapters for *Zen and Japanese Culture*, the revised version of Suzuki's 1938 *Zen Buddhism and Its Influence on Japanese Culture.*[17] Even after Suzuki had moved back to Japan in 1959, Thomas continued to send him newspapers and periodicals he requested. In her letters to him, Thomas also expressed a strong desire to find some way to continue working for him, noting, "If I can fit at all into that work you want to do, please let me know, for that remains what I, too, want to do."[18]

Thomas's comments in the "Columbia Seminars Manuscript" suggest that she had taken careful class notes in Suzuki's seminars. After much unsuccessful searching, including a trip to her archive at the Institute of Egyptian Art and Archaeology at the University of Memphis, I mistakenly concluded that the notes were no longer extant. Just as this book went into production at Columbia University Press, however, I was alerted by a friend in Kyoto, Japan, that Thomas's spiral-bound, 7.5" x 5" notebooks—forty-one total, filled with notes taken in Suzuki's seminars between October 10, 1952, and May 10, 1957—were stored in the the late Mihoko Okamura's Kyoto residence and was allowed to borrow the documents. These forty-one notebooks provide the most complete extant record of Suzuki's Columbia seminars.

Thomas compiled the "Seminars Manuscript" that is the basis of *Spreading Indra's Net* from seven notebooks—a total of 1,111 pages—of extremely detailed, at times almost verbatim, notes taken in Suzuki's seminars between October 10, 1952, and May 15, 1953. As she typed those notes to create the "Seminars Manuscript," Thomas incorporated material taken from the class notes of such other graduate student seminar attendees as Arthur W. Sadler and Frances Cassard. She also added numerous dated clarifications and elaborations about the seminar material based on one-on-one meetings with Suzuki, his private talks to small groups in Princeton, his publications, and his numerous public lectures. She added references to a variety of sources named, or simply alluded to, by Suzuki in his lectures. In addition, throughout the "Seminars Manuscript" Thomas inserted interlinear queries, comments, and her own elaborations on the material for Suzuki's consideration. These insertions were bracketed by section marks, § . . . §.

Most of the material in the "Seminars Manuscript" was presented in Suzuki's seminars in the fall 1952 and spring 1953 semesters. Thomas missed the first seminar of the semester on October 3, 1952, but used notes borrowed from other students, including Sadler and Cassard, to fill in the missed lecture in the "Seminars Manuscript." She also incorporated into chapter I material from Sadler's notes that he took early in the spring 1952 semester. Thomas's letters to Mihoko indicate that she had nearly completed her draft manuscript, dubbed "1952–53," by November 1957 and gave it to Suzuki the next month.[19] Although the typescript is undated, references inserted into the lectures indicate that it was created after 1957.[20] In these letters to Mihoko, Thomas asked whether Suzuki had any comments on "1952–53." I have not found any documents indicating Suzuki's reactions to or plans for the manuscript.

In notebook VII of her class notes, Thomas wrote a draft introduction for what she hoped eventually might be a published version of the lectures manuscript she was compiling. She wrote that in the seminars, "Dr. Suzuki probably gave the fullest expression to his experience and his thought as a whole." Thomas continued, "To present, therefore, as nearly whole and as nearly in his own words as possible has been the constant aim of the compilers, for compilers we have been most of all; we have been only occasionally editors by necessity."[21] Based on her statements and the detailed nature of her notes, I believe that the edited version created by Thomas is the best record extant of the Suzuki Columbia seminars, which were crucial in stimulating interest in Zen Buddhism in the United States in the post–World War II era. Given Thomas's crucial role in preserving a record of Suzuki's seminars and compiling the manuscript, I have credited her as a coeditor and have dedicated this book to her.

Later in this introduction, I will review in more detail the many other varied records I've discovered that describe Suzuki's lectures by those who attended them. But first, let's look at Suzuki's life from the grander perspective that it deserves. Numerous brief biographical sketches have been written in recent years and offer more information about the timeline for his fascinating, almost century-long career. Below is some essential background concerning Suzuki's winding path to the classrooms in Lowe Library and Philosophy Hall at Columbia University in the 1950s.

Suzuki's five years at Columbia was not his first time at the university or in the United States.[22] Born in 1870—when the Gilded Age was getting underway—in Kanazawa, a former castle town on the Japan Sea, Suzuki had studied Buddhism, particularly Zen, since his high school days. His earliest years were not easy, as Suzuki was but six years old when his father, Ryōjun, died, leaving his mother, Masu, to support him and his four siblings. Although he graduated from the Ishikawa Prefectural Vocational School, his family's poverty forced eighteen-year-old Suzuki to withdraw from the Ishikawa Prefectural Higher Middle School after just three months. Remarkably, despite not earning a formal degree until the 1930s, he became a university teacher, thinker, and writer who influenced American, European, and Asian culture in major ways for much of the twentieth century.

In 1891, increasingly lured away from studies at what are now known as Waseda and Tokyo Universities, Suzuki began several decades absorbed in the study and practice of Rinzai Zen with two teachers, Imakita Kōsen and Shaku Sōen, at the Engakuji Buddhist monastery in Kita-Kamakura, approximately twenty-nine miles southwest of Tokyo. In 1895, he withdrew from being a nondegree student at Tokyo University to live and practice as a layman at Engakuji, which had become a thriving center for serious lay Zen practice. Suzuki would maintain a residence in Kita-Kamakura for much of his adult life, first on the Engakuji grounds and, toward the end of his life, at the Matsugaoka Bunko housing his library on the grounds of the nearby temple Tōkeiji, where Shaku Sōen had retired.

Thanks to contacts made by Sōen with the philosopher and publisher Paul Carus during the 1893 World Parliament of Religions, Suzuki came to the United States to work at Open Court Publishing, where the editors and owner, already concerned about harmonizing religion and science, had taken a deep interest in Buddhism.

So, at the turn of the century—from 1897 to 1908—the young Suzuki found himself working in, of all places, a Gilded Age mansion while living in a modest home nearby in La Salle, Illinois. There Carus's father-in-law, Edward Hegeler, had become a wealthy man running a zinc processing operation. Hegeler also found time to pursue his remarkable spread of interests in science, philosophy, and religion by founding Open Court Publishing and entrusting the venture to his son-in-law. While working for Open Court, Suzuki began translating a series of Chinese philosophical works and Buddhist texts. He also began writing extensively about Buddhism in English, focusing on explaining to an Anglophone audience the legitimacy and relevance of East Asian Mahayana Buddhism in the twentieth century. Suzuki fell under the spell of William James's approach to the study of religion and mysticism and found in James's 1902 book, *The Varieties of Religious Experience*, the key to understanding Zen and his own experiences in Zen practice. Although Suzuki's ideas evolved, James's perennialism and psychological approach to religion would remain touchstones for the rest of his long career.

His time in the United States led to another major change in Suzuki's life: while on a trip with Shaku Sōen to New York City, Suzuki met a Radcliffe College graduate named Beatrice Erskine Lane. And Beatrice, as Suzuki called her in his journals and other writings, would marry Suzuki in Japan in 1911, becoming not only his wife but also one of his closest intellectual collaborators until her death in 1939. In particular, Beatrice's connections with Theosophical circles and interest in the literature of the New Thought movement exposed Suzuki to ways of thinking about religion that deepened his William James-inflected perennialist predilections.[23]

Following his return to Japan in 1909, Suzuki continued to study Zen with Shaku Sōen. Suzuki worked closely with Sōen on the journal *Zendō* (Zen Way), participated in zazen (Zen meditation) retreats, and continued private practice interviews with his teacher. Akizuki Ryōmin, a certified Rinzai Zen teacher and close associate of Suzuki, surmises from his comments that at the time of Sōen's death in 1919, Suzuki was working with his teacher on advanced koan in the Rinzai training system.[24] Suzuki also began teaching at Gakushūin University in Tokyo and, beginning in 1921, at Otani University in Kyoto. Over the course of the next three decades, he taught at Otani while publishing extensively about Buddhism, particularly Zen, in English and Japanese. Working in partnership with Beatrice and several colleagues at Otani, Suzuki launched a pathbreaking journal, *Eastern Buddhist*, which was devoted to explaining East Asian Mahayana Buddhism to an English-language audience. Over the course of the twentieth century, *Eastern Buddhist* became one of the most important and main ways by which Americans, myself included, and Europeans learned about East Asian Buddhism well into the 1970s and beyond.

With generous financial support from a wealthy Kanazawa friend, Ataka Yakichi, Suzuki then published a series of books—*Essays on Zen Buddhism*; *Manual of Zen Buddhism*; *An Introduction to Zen Buddhism*—and important translations that would establish his reputation in Europe and America as one of the foremost authorities on Buddhism and Zen.

During the twenties and thirties, Suzuki also worked with Zen compatriots in Kyoto to find ways to accommodate non-Japanese seekers—such as Ruth Fuller Sasaki—who came to Japan to engage in Zen practice, which was an extraordinary venture at the time. His reputation growing and spreading, Suzuki started to receive invitations to participate in overseas teaching opportunities and international conferences concerned with Buddhist philosophy and spirituality.

After meeting Suzuki in 1930, scholar of Asian religions Kenneth Saunders and Charles Richard Crane, a wealthy inheritor of the Crane Brothers Manufacturing fortune, suggested that Crane's Institute of Current World Affairs, which he founded in New York City, sponsor lectures by Suzuki at Columbia and Union Theological Seminary. Foreshadowing Suzuki's later stay in the 1950s, Saunders recommended in a letter to the institute that Suzuki lecture on Japanese culture, religion, and meditation at those institutions.[25] Although the proposed lectures failed to materialize immediately, in 1936, en route home to Japan from a trip to the Congress of World Faiths in London that was funded by Crane, Suzuki traveled across the United States by train, from New York to California, delivering a series of lectures that would form the basis for one of his best known works, *Zen Buddhism and Its Influence on Japanese Culture* (republished in revised form in 1959 as *Zen and Japanese Culture*).

As Japan entered the era of the Fifteen Years' War, Suzuki took an increasingly nationalistic stance in his writings, particularly those aimed at a non-Japanese audience. As early as 1906, in his survey of Zen written for the *Journal of the Pāli Text Society*, Suzuki had echoed the growing consensus in Japan that made the historically questionable assertion that there was an essential connection between Zen Buddhism and *bushidō*, the "way of the samurai."[26] When, in response to criticism of the invasion of China, Japanese government organizations sponsored individuals to participate in their use of soft power to portray Japanese culture and international actions in a more favorable light to non-Japanese, Suzuki joined in those efforts. In 1935, he gave lectures to non-Japanese in Japan on behalf of the Society for International Cultural Relations (Kokusai Bunka Shinkōkai) that became the pamphlet *Buddhist Philosophy and Its Effects on the Life and Thought of the Japanese People*. In addition, Suzuki's aforementioned 1936 trip across the United States, although funded primarily by Charles Richard Crane, also was sponsored by the Foreign Ministry of Japan. In the book that grew out of those lectures, *Zen Buddhism and Its Influence on Japanese Culture*, Suzuki wrote at length about the supposedly inextricable connections among Zen, swordsmanship, haiku, tea ceremony, painting, and fearlessness in the face of death. When Hermann von Keyserling, a German philosopher who heard about Suzuki's work through Charles Richard Crane, wrote to Suzuki that the book would be of great appeal for the "New Germany," Suzuki expressed his pleasure to Crane, despite the ever more ominous situation in Germany.[27]

Although Suzuki continued to receive invitations in the late 1930s to participate in international conferences as a spokesperson for

Buddhism, his beloved Beatrice's mortal illness—she died in 1939—and the outbreak of the Pacific War prevented further travel to Europe and America until the late 1940s. Following Beatrice's death, as total war began in the Pacific theater, Suzuki, although continuing to teach at Otani University, spent ever more time at Engakuji, overseeing the start of planning and construction of the Matsugaoka Bunko. His writing concerning Buddhism continued through this period, although most of his publications were in Japanese. In particular, as Robert Sharf pointed out in his groundbreaking 1993 article, Suzuki gave voice to theories of Japanese uniqueness and essentialized depictions of Asian versus Western culture that dominated Japanese discourse at the time.[28] Suzuki was triumphalist in his descriptions of Japanese Buddhism in comparison to the tradition elsewhere in Asia. He claimed that indigenous Japanese spirituality was uniquely suitable for the flourishing of Buddhism, particularly Zen, while pejoratively noting that the Chinese had failed to seamlessly integrate Zen into daily life.

Nonetheless, Suzuki's writings and actions concerning the war in Asia were cautiously ambiguous. After the Nanking Massacre in 1938, despite the risks, Suzuki wrote to Nyogen Senzaki in the United States, asking his friend to send articles on the incident from the US press to him in Japan, suggesting that Senzaki insert clippings of the articles into his letters of response.[29] Although never an outspoken opponent of the war effort, the then seventy-year-old Suzuki did not directly vilify the enemies of Japan and rarely used words with jingoistic connotations like *Yamatodamashii* (Japanese spirit) and *kokutai* (national polity) in his own writings. Although it was risky, on the eve of the full outbreak of hostilities in the Pacific, Suzuki wrote dismissively in his letters about Japanese government rhetoric concerning the unity of "rite and rule" (*saisei itchi*) and the "New East Asian Order" (*Tōa shin chitsujo*).[30] Even his 1941 contribution to the officer corps' unofficial support organization journal,

Kaikōsha kiji (Kaikō Association Journal), is remarkable as much for its avoidance of any explicit mention of Japan's enemies, including China, as for its advocacy of fearlessness in the face of death.[31] Subsequent to Japan's crushing defeat, Suzuki quickly became unequivocal in his denunciation of the violence his country had unleashed in Asia, declaring just one month after surrender that "The war that began in Manchuria was purely an act of plundering imperialism."[32] As with so many of Suzuki's actions connected with the Fifteen Years' War, no doubt some see this as opportunism rather than an expression of his true feelings, now that it was safe to openly voice them.

Within a few years following the end of World War II, Suzuki resumed his participation in international conferences and, for the first time, began extended teaching overseas at universities in the United States. Following his participation in the Second East-West Philosophers' Conference at the University of Hawai'i, he taught at the University of Hawai'i and Claremont Colleges. It may have been Charles W. Morris, a philosopher at the University of Chicago, who met Suzuki at the East-West Philosophers' Conference and informed Chadbourne Gilpatric, a program officer for the humanities at the Rockefeller Foundation, about Suzuki's tantalizing work on Buddhism.[33] After interviewing Suzuki in March 1950, Rockefeller program officers decided to support his request for a $2,500 grant to fund a three-month speaking tour in the eastern United States.[34] Foundation officers arranged for Suzuki to be based at Union Theological Seminary, an institution closely tied with Columbia at the graduate level.

While at Union Theological in fall 1950 and winter 1951—drawing closer and closer to the time of his teaching at Columbia University and his delivery of the lectures captured in this book—Suzuki had a dizzyingly busy schedule of public lectures and meetings with a wide range of people interested in Zen. From September 1950 until May 1951, with logistical assistance from program officers at the

Rockefeller Foundation, he was an invited lecturer at numerous elite universities, colleges, and other institutions on the East Coast. In fact, predating the establishment of his Columbia seminars, in early March 1951, he gave three high-profile lectures on Kegon Buddhism, sponsored by the Taraknath Das Foundation, in Columbia's Butler Library that drew from 150 to 300 attendees.[35] It is fascinating that these three very academic lectures, which covered the development of Chinese Buddhism, Kegon philosophy, and the relationship between Kegon and Zen, pulled in such large American audiences. And it was there that Suzuki set out in broad strokes the subjects he would explore in his Columbia seminars.[36]

The Rockefeller Foundation continued to support Suzuki as he laid out a proposal to write an introduction to Kegon thought. In spring 1952, while at Claremont Colleges in southern California, and then back at Columbia, Suzuki carried on a series of exchanges with the foundation program officers, describing his intended book in some detail. Writing to the foundation on January 29, 1952, as he prepared to fly to New York, Suzuki mentioned that the lectures and classroom interactions concerning Kegon at Columbia would allow him to organize and clarify the preliminary work he had completed while at Claremont the previous autumn semester. He wrote that the presentation of this material was important because "it adds a great deal to the stock of knowledge the West has with regard to the East. Kegon philosophy has never been explored by any European scholars as far as I know and the knowledge of this philosophy helps the Western people to understand the Eastern way of thinking and feeling. Besides, the Kegon itself marks the culmination of Buddhist thought as developed in China. The Kegon is a kind of synthesis of Indian and Chinese thought." Suzuki added that this was a most difficult task, particularly because "the gap between the Western way of thinking and that of the East being in many cases fundamental, the rendering of some key terms is extremely difficult."[37] Writing and lecturing at a time when there were few English-language translations of important Chinese and Japanese Buddhist materials, Suzuki was faced with the daunting task of constructing appropriate ways to communicate extremely abstruse Sino-Japanese and Sanskrit Buddhist philosophical concepts.

Although some faculty members expressed interest in having Suzuki teach a seminar, Columbia's administration apparently failed to come up with funding for the course. Carrington Goodrich, a professor of Chinese and Japanese, appealed to the Rockefeller Foundation to support the Suzuki seminar, but it also declined to provide further funds. Suzuki, however, had a long history of finding financial support from friends and those inspired by his work on Buddhism. Over the course of his long career, such prosperous businessmen as his fellow Kanazawan, Ataka Yakichi, and Charles Richard Crane had sponsored Suzuki's research, travel, and teaching. When Rockefeller and Columbia both failed to support the proposed Columbia seminar, once again a member of the wide circle of acquaintances Suzuki had made in New York generously agreed to pay for Suzuki's teaching.

Suzuki's new benefactor came from the network of people associated with the neo-Freudian therapist Karen Horney, whom Suzuki met while in New York in 1951. Horney's psychoanalytic patients included Cornelius Crane, nephew of Charles Richard Crane, and Cornelius's ex-wife, Cathalene Parker Crane, both of whom, along with Horney, were interested in Zen and the work of Suzuki. (Horney, who frequently socialized with her therapeutic clients, seems to have had little regard for doctor-patient boundaries by twenty-first-century standards.) Although divorced in 1940, Cathalene and Cornelius remained close friends. According to Parker Crane, Cornelius had introduced Horney to the work of Suzuki in 1940, when he showed her *Zen Buddhism and Its Influence on Japanese Culture*, which was dedicated to his uncle, Charles Richard Crane.[38]

Cornelius attempted to contact Suzuki by letter in 1940 and Horney, who was intrigued by Suzuki's book, quoted from it in her 1945 work, *Our Inner Conflicts*.[39] When Cathalene told Horney that she had heard Suzuki at a Church of the Peace Union lecture in New York City, in January 1951, Horney arranged a dinner with Cornelius, Cathalene, Suzuki, and Richard DeMartino, a close student of Suzuki and his de facto assistant. The group continued to meet regularly in New York City and at Cornelius's family's summer estate, Castle Hill, in Ipswich, MA. They even planned a group trip to Japan, which eventually took place in the summer of 1952.

According to Suzuki's diary, as early as February 1951 he was discussing with Cornelius the need for salary support to continue teaching at Columbia in the 1952–1953 academic year. By the end of May, Cornelius worked out an arrangement with Carrington Goodrich to pay Suzuki's teaching salary, and in January 1952 Cornelius sent Columbia a check for $2,000 to cover the first semester of the course. Cornelius would continue to pay Columbia $4,000 each year for the course until Suzuki retired from the university in 1957.

Once the funding had been arranged with Cornelius Crane, Goodrich arranged for Suzuki to teach the seminar on Buddhism. Assisting in this effort were two Columbia philosophy professors who were involved with the interdepartmental PhD program in religion, Horace L. Friess and Herbert W. Schneider.[40] Initially Suzuki was appointed as visiting lecturer in Chinese, but by June 1952, he was reappointed as associate in religion, a position he continued to hold until he stepped down at the end of June 1957.

Contemporaneous accounts, including Thomas's, of the seminars reveal that Suzuki entertained numerous questions from the attendees. According to Sadler, Yandell, Albert Stunkard, and John Cage, an early and avid participant, Suzuki delivered his lectures in a soft voice while covering the blackboard with diagrams and

Sino-Japanese characters. In her draft introduction for "1952–1953," Thomas mentions how the lectures she compiled give a glimpse of Suzuki "as he tries out and sometimes coins English words that will give the feel, taste, and meaning of the Sanskrit, the Chinese, the Japanese—as he tries by every possible means and every feasible repetition to convey the unconveyable."[41] Yandell recalled Suzuki telling him that "The lectures take much time . . . but they make me think and stimulate me to careful preparation."[42]

In a 1950 interview, Chadbourne Gilpatric, one of the Rockefeller Foundation program officers, asked Suzuki whether he felt that he had effectively communicated his ideas through his books. He responded that he was "still, after many published efforts, dissatisfied with his expression and argument." According to Gilpatric, Suzuki elaborated that "he is more confident as time goes on that ultimate persuasion rests on face to face encounter since only in this way can the full personality make itself felt."[43]

John Cage in a 1991 documentary and his own memoir recalls how Suzuki put this emphasis on "face to face encounter" into practice even in the seminars, and the unconventional, desultory, and perplexing aspects of Suzuki's classes.

> It is very surprising that one would look forward to each one of those lectures. Because very frequently you would leave the lecture without any consciousness of having learned anything. So that nothing would have been pounded into your head. Or made even noticeable to you [laughs]. What he would do is, he would come into the room and he would look, I think he looked at each person. And he would smile, and there would be some kind of individual greeting to each person, and if, after he sat down, he didn't feel that he had accomplished everyone, he would look to see again, and take notice of that. And then having done that he

> would unwrap his books, which were around, and it was as though he were looking for something to say, no one was asking him questions. So he would look in his books and he'd either look and find something and say something—and it would make no sense, at least I wouldn't know how to respond to it—or he would put it aside without saying anything and take up another book. He might go through all his books and not find anything. And then he'd sit as though he was looking somewhere else for an idea of what to say, and finally he would speak, and for the most part he'd say something that you couldn't remember. Now and then there would be an idea, and then in that setting this idea would be very striking.[44]

Cage remembered on one occasion sitting in the classroom at Columbia with the windows open on a warm evening. As Suzuki lectured, a plane from LaGuardia heading west passed overhead, drowning out his soft voice. Suzuki, Cage writes, continued lecturing, although his voice was inaudible. After the plane had passed, he continued speaking, and no one asked him to fill in the gap in the lecture caused by the plane's noise.[45]

Albert Stunkard describes another memorable occasion. A young attendee stood up in the classroom to question something Suzuki had said. Watching the heated exchange that followed, Stunkard thought at the time with some envy and remorse that this was the sort of vigorous dharma exchange that he had yet to have with Suzuki. After class, however, when Stunkard asked about the meaning of the discussion, Suzuki responded that he himself was perplexed by the man's comments, leaving Stunkard relieved that after working with Suzuki for some time, he was not lacking some insight that the outspoken student had grasped quickly.[46]

Horace Friess, the Columbia philosophy professor who had helped arrange the seminar, attended a number of the classes during

Suzuki's first semester. He noted in a letter to the Rockefeller Foundation program officers that the lectures, although worthwhile, were difficult to follow, writing,

> The lecturer [Suzuki] has reached an age at which his oral communication is apt to be discursive and too oblivious of the requirements for classroom effectiveness. He is, however, dealing here with material that very few people able to use English know so that a permanent record should undoubtedly be made. Moreover it is extremely subtle material that cannot be grasped at a sitting, but requires repeated pondering for assimilation.[47]

Spreading Indra's Net conveys in detail Suzuki's career-culminating interpretation of how awakened/enlightened mind is conceived in Mahayana Buddhism. Suzuki endeavors to describe the nature of awakening and delusion from the perspective of his own Zen practice and more than a half-century of studying Buddhism. Over the course of the 1952–1953 lectures, Suzuki explains how awakening occurs, the codependent interplay of delusion and awakening, the Buddhist notion of time as it relates to enlightenment, the structure of mind as portrayed in the *Awakening of Faith in the Mahāyāna* (*Dasheng qixin lun*; hereafter abbreviated as *Awakening of Faith*), and the relationship among vow, compassion, wisdom, and awakening. Suzuki drew from four main sources in constructing this grand picture of enlightened mind: Huayan Buddhism, especially as interpreted by the third patriarch of the Huayan school in China, Fazang; the *Awakening of Faith* as interpreted by Fazang; Zen literature, particularly the "Record of the Transmission of the Lamp [Compiled in] the Jingde Era" and the *Record of Rinzai*; and his own understanding derived from more than six decades of Buddhist practice and study.[48]

One of the compelling aspects of the lectures for the attendees must have been the way Suzuki interlaced material from European and American writers, philosophers, theologians, and scientists with his disquisitions on Buddhist doctrine. As he lectured at Columbia, Suzuki was completing his book *Mysticism: Christian and Buddhist*, which was published in England in 1957. With that material much on his mind, Suzuki frequently presented Buddhist doctrinal and philosophical ideas about awakening in comparison with perspectives drawn from Meister Eckhart, Christina Rossetti, and his own interpretations of Christian theology. Like many who joined his seminars, Suzuki was a convinced perennialist much indebted to William James's view that religion, first and foremost, was about profound mystical experiences that were rare but similar for practitioners across religious boundaries.[49]

Some students who had come to hear about Zen Buddhism, however, found Suzuki's penchant for interlacing material from Eckhart and other Christian mystics with his disquisitions on Buddhist teachings off-putting. John Cage records one humorous exchange on this point in a seminar: "There was a lady in Suzuki's class who said once, 'I have great difficulty reading the sermons of Meister Eckhart, because of all the Christian imagery.' Dr. Suzuki said, 'That difficulty will disappear.' "[50] Japanese Zen teachers as well could be critical of Suzuki's freewheeling presentation of Zen. Hisamatsu Shin'ichi, lecturing at Harvard Divinity School in 1957, witnessed firsthand Suzuki responding to postlecture questions from audience members at Hisamatsu's own lectures. Although he valued Suzuki's ability to connect with Americans, Hisamatsu cautioned his Japanese interpreter, who had expressed admiration for Suzuki's off-the-cuff skill and wittiness, "Dr. Suzuki is unique, but we shouldn't try to imitate him. Others should be as strict and accurate as possible in speaking of Zen."[51]

With Existentialism coming into vogue among post–World War II intellectuals, Suzuki also drew upon H. J. Blackham's overview, *Six Existentialist Thinkers*, to compare aspects of Buddhist doctrine with the perspectives of Simone de Beauvoir, Karl Jaspers, Søren Kierkegaard, and Jean-Paul Sartre.[52] At times, working from memory, Suzuki would inaccurately quote non-Buddhist writers. For example, I and the editors of the Japanese translation of the lectures have been unable to locate in Voltaire's corpus Voltaire's supposed statement that is repeated in several places in *Spreading Indra's Net*, "To save is God's business. Let him alone, he will do his work" (166). However vague Suzuki's references might be, peppering his lectures with mentions of those figures, Christian texts, and his glosses of current philosophical buzzwords like Sartre's *pour-soi* (for itself) and *en-soi* (in-itself), as well as analyzing the much bandied-about concept "freedom," which Louis Menand has called the "slogan of the times" for the 1950s, enhanced the allure and relevance of the lectures for his American audience.[53]

In *Spreading Indra's Net*, Suzuki surveys different aspects of the Buddhist understanding of enlightenment. In chapter I, for example, he interprets Śākyamuni's awakening experience through the lens of his own Zen practice, emphasizing that "To understand Buddhism we have to be familiar with what enlightenment is; and when enlightenment is known, all other teachings whatever may be **negated**. Enlightenment is thus to be taken as the one thing which must be understood well and thoroughly" (71; emphasis as in the manuscript). Rejecting efforts to understand the Buddha's awakening from an exclusively intellectual or philosophical perspective, Suzuki views Śākyamuni's path in terms of his own practice as a young man. As described by Suzuki, Śākyamuni's effort to free himself from the endless cycle of birth and death, that is, *saṃsāra*, functioned as his koan. "As long as Buddha had this question in his mind, he could never come to its solution, for the question separated him from himself. The question stood externally before him; he could never solve the problem this way. Since the problem, the question, came out of his being, the solution must be in his being, too" (74). Having tried what Suzuki calls the intellectual approach and the ascetic approach to resolve his question, Śākyamuni pushed himself into a dead end from which there was no escape. Using a rather distinctive understanding of *samādhi*, one-pointed concentration of mind, Suzuki describes this:

> Now Buddha was in this state of being pushed into the last ditch, and he did not know how to get out of it. *Samādhi*, as we have seen, is the name of this state of mind where there is no seeking. And Buddha did not know where to seek, he was just lost; there was no seeking in any form and no moral discipline. He simply did not know what to do—this is really what is known as *samādhi*. (78)

Having pushed himself in desperation into this state of one-pointedness of mind, that is, "mental equilibrium" (78–79), the Buddha looked up and saw the morning star, triggering his awakening, in which "he and the question altogether vanished. Something that is neither question nor questioner, yet at the same time is both question and questioner—this he intuited" (80). Suzuki contends that Śākyamuni's awakening upon seeing the morning star was akin to the experience of such Zen practitioners as Kyōgen, who was awakened upon hearing a pebble strike a piece of bamboo, and Rakan Oshō, who achieved enlightenment when he saw the rising sun.[54]

Suzuki's description of Śākyamuni's awakening bears striking similarities to Suzuki's recollection of his own awakening (*satori*) experience while trying to resolve the *Mu* koan given by his Zen teacher, Shaku Sōen. Writing half a century later about his awakening in 1896 during a seven-day *sesshin* (meditation intensive), Suzuki recalled,

> This crisis or extremity came for me when it was finally settled that I should go to America to help Dr. Carus with his translation of the *Dao de ching.* I realized that the *Rōhatsu sesshin* that winter might be my last chance to go to *sesshin* and that if I did not solve my koan then I might never be able to do so. I must have put all my spiritual strength into that *sesshin.*
>
> Up till then I had always been conscious that *Mu* was in my mind. But so long as *I* was conscious of *Mu* it meant that I was somehow separate from *Mu,* and that is not a true samadhi. But towards the end of that *sesshin*, about the fifth day, I ceased to be conscious of *Mu.* I was one with *Mu,* identified with *Mu,* so that there was no longer the separateness implied by being conscious of *Mu.* This is the real state of samadhi.
>
> But this samadhi alone is not enough. You must come out of that state, be awakened from it, and that awakening is *Prajñā.* That moment of coming out of the samadhi and seeing it for what it is—that is satori. When I came out of that state of samadhi during that *sesshin* I said, "I see. This is it."
>
> I have no idea how long I was in that state of samadhi, but I was awakened from it by the sound of the bell. I went to *sanzen* with the Rōshi, and he asked me some of the *sassho* or test questions about *Mu.* I answered all of them except one, which I hesitated over, and at once he sent me out. But the next morning early I went to *sanzen* again, and this time I could answer it. I remember that night as I walked back from the monastery to my quarters in the Kigen'in temple, seeing the trees in the moonlight. They looked transparent and I was transparent too.[55]

Like Śākyamuni, Suzuki pushed himself into the corner he describes in the lectures as *samādhi*; emerging from that state, he finally resolved his koan and achieved his initial awakening.

Having examined how enlightenment occurs, Suzuki then turns to analyzing the nature of awakening, the relationship between the awakened mind and delusion, and the functioning of awakened mind as enlightened compassion. He bases his analyses on the *Awakening of Faith in the Mahayana* and the portrayal of the quest for awakening in the *Gandavyūha*, the long concluding chapter of the Flower Garland Sutra.[56] Suzuki delves into the nature of awakening and its implications from a variety of perspectives. In the process, he returns frequently to the initial awakening of Śākyamuni, as well as the enlightenment experiences of such paradigmatic Zen masters as Kyōgen and Rakan Oshō, to explain the nature of enlightenment in Buddhism.

The culminating perspective for *Spreading Indra's Net* is that of the Flower Garland Sutra, for, as Suzuki notes, "When Zen expresses itself in thought form, and when it tries to express itself in more and more advanced thought, it goes to this Kegon Sutra and thought system more than any other. In fact, the Kegon may be said to be the highest expression of Buddhist philosophy—and of Zen philosophy insofar as Zen is philosophical" (236).[57] Suzuki's presentation of the relationship of the fundamental mind that is the ontological foundation of all existence with delusion, and awakening is based on the *Awakening of Faith* and the Flower Garland Sutra, particularly as these texts were interpreted by Fazang, the third patriarch. The former text, which most contemporary scholars believe was composed in China in the first half of the sixth century CE, became one of the most influential treatises in the history of East Asian Buddhism.[58] In the *Awakening of Faith*, the author wrestles with the problem of how fundamentally pure mind, the only ultimately true existent, can give rise to defilement and the world of multiplicity. In answer to this question, the author posits that mind has two aspects, mind as suchness (C. *xin zhenru*) and mind that is subject to birth and death (C. *xin shengmie*), while identifying the latter aspect with storehouse consciousness (S. *ālayavijñāna*), adapting a concept from Yogācāra Buddhism. Storehouse consciousness is the aspect of mind that is subject to birth and death and that appears in the world of phenomena. In turn, storehouse consciousness has two aspects: enlightened (C. *jue*) and unenlightened (C. *bujue*).[59] As Suzuki explains the process, equating mind as suchness with "Will,"

> In the first Will is just beginning to move from the state of potentiality to the state of actuality. The initial sprout trying to get into definite form, this is birth. One Mind is absolute, we cannot distinguish anything in it. When it begins to move we have *shō* [birth]. Will moves to manifest, it does something—this is birth. Just willing to go out, but not yet showing itself in particular forms—this is *shō*. When this corresponds to the Buddhist *ālayavijñāna* it contains all those tendencies or potentialities that are to actualize themselves into the world. (197)

Suzuki's focus on the Flower Garland school and the *Awakening of Faith* as seen through the lens of Flower Garland scholar-monks was based on his long-standing interests in those sources. In 1900, during his first long residence in the United States, while working for Paul Carus at Open Court Publishing, Suzuki translated into English Śikṣānanda's version of the *Dasheng qixin lun* as the *Awakening of Faith in the Mahāyāna*, noting in particular the importance of the text for Fazang, who wrote several lengthy commentaries on the text.[60] Suzuki treated the *Awakening of Faith*, particularly seen through the lens of those commentaries, as "an aspect of Kegon thought as it came to be formulated by the Chinese mind" (236).

Suzuki did not question the canonical attribution of authorship to the Indian monk Aśvagohṣa in his 1900 translation. Despite growing debate over the validity of that attribution over the course of the twentieth century, in the 1950s lectures Suzuki never revisited it. Much to the frustration of his scholarly critics, for example, the Chinese intellectual Hu Shih, who insisted that one could only understand Chan/Zen Buddhism "in its historical context," Suzuki was not a stickler for historical accuracy.[61] As he comments in *Spreading Indra's Net* when discussing the veracity of several Zen stories, "History, historical fact, does not matter very much in my opinion; something like it may be more true than factual history" (79). Of crucial importance from Suzuki's perspective, as he argued in his response to Hu Shih's article, "Zen has its own life independent of history."[62]

As with the *Awakening of Faith*, Suzuki's interest in Flower Garland thought began much earlier in his career. He had written at length about portions of the Flower Garland Sutra beginning in 1932, when he published several essays concerning two of the most important and influential sections of the massive sutra, the *Gaṇḍavyūha* and *Daśabhūmika* chapters.[63] Suzuki renewed his work in the immediate postwar period, using key concepts found in the text to forge a less imperialistic notion of Japanese spirituality and during the Occupation, to contend that a complete grasp of the Flower Garland notion of the unobstructed interpenetration of all phenomena (*shishi wuai/jiji muge*) could serve as the basis for creating a harmonious, peaceful world.[64]

Suzuki's presentation of Buddhism in *Spreading Indra's Net* was based upon one of the most distinctively Chinese streams of the tradition. Proponents of the Flower Garland school systematized the ideas contained in the sprawling Flower Garland Sutra. The foundations were laid by a series of important scholar-monks that included

Fazang, whom Suzuki characterized as "the greatest" among the Flower Garland "philosophers," as well as Chengguan and Zongmi, who, both having studied Zen, helped synthesize Zen and Flower Garland thought.[65]

Of particular importance for Suzuki's work was the Flower Garland scholar-monks' transformation of the concepts of *śūnyatā* (emptiness; C. *kong*) and *dharma* (element of existence; C. *fa*) into the indigenous Chinese religio-philosophical ideas of *li* (principle) and *shi* (phenomenon/phenomena). Even more important for the development of Chinese Buddhism and Suzuki's understanding of enlightenment was the Flower Garland conceptualization of the relationship between principle and phenomena as being interpenetrating and nonobstructive, that is, the mutual nonobstruction of principle and phenomena (C. *lishi wuai*; J. *riji muge*) and the mutual interpenetration of all phenomena (C. *shishi wuai*; J. *jiji muge*). This Flower Garland conceptual dyad became the foundation for a more world-affirming perspective in Chinese Buddhism, for, as Robert Gimello notes in one of the best English-language studies of Flower Garland thought, "the assertion that *li* and *shih* are mutually nonobstructive has the culminating effect of validating and enhancing the worth of the phenomenal world. This it can do because it shows that each phenomenon is not only a thing or event but is also an emblematic instance of the most valuable Buddhist truths."[66] Although Suzuki does not utilize the Chinese technical terms for this interpenetration, which he calls "no-obstruction," "unobstruction," "interpenetration," and "interfusion" (172; 297; 300), these Flower Garland concepts undergird his perspective on the relationship between the Absolute and multiplicity.

> From the point of enlightenment experience is the way we have to think. And this world of multiplicities, just as it is—dog is dog, cat is cat, all individuals are retained just as they are—this aspect

> of Reality just as all things are is oneness. Manyness remains as manyness, not a particle of this manyness changes, yet this manyness just as it is is oneness. This is the most important thought needed to explain Reality. The idea of duality is so contaminating that it is very difficult for us to comprehend that one is many, many is one. (298–299)

There is no need, from this perspective, to flee the mundane, for it is suffused with the Absolute even while maintaining its multiplicity.[67]

In the lectures Suzuki accepts a monistic view of reality as given in the *Awakening of Faith*, according to which fundamental mind or suchness (C. *zhenru*/J. *shinnyo*), the Absolute, is equated with the matrix of the buddhas (S. *tathāgatagarbha*), which in turn is also identified with the storehouse consciousness (S. *ālayavijñāna*).[68] It is the matrix of the buddhas that endows all beings with buddha nature, while the storehouse consciousness is, in Suzuki's words, "a storehouse containing all possibilities, the container, where all things come out or are kept in their potentiality" (184). In light of this interpretation, even deluded mind is ultimately grounded in suchness. As Suzuki writes in chapter V,

> In itself Mind is substance, but as it appears to us in manifestation or form Mind can be understood from our side in its three aspects: substance, form, activity, or function. When Mind is understood in its suchness aspect, it is substance, and as substance it cannot be subjected to any relative way of thinking. When it asserts itself, when we try to understand it, when Mind tries to make itself understood to our mind, it negates itself. Mind somehow wants to express itself, and this expression is received by us as form and activity. As long as Mind remains as suchness, it does not change. When it expresses itself in form

> and activity, it subjects itself to birth-and-death. In one respect Mind is Absolute Suchness, eternally in its own Being, but when it expresses itself, it takes form or activity, and we have this world of birth-and-death, the world of becoming. (183–184)

Or, as Suzuki describes the emergence of storehouse consciousness from One Mind/Absolute Mind that is the ontological ground for all things,

> When One Mind has not turned itself into what it is not it is Absolute Mind. If Absolute Mind does not preserve its identity but asserts and negates itself, it becomes *ālaya-vijñāna*. In *ālaya-vijñāna* we have assertion and negation, a mixture of A and not-A. This mixing means it is A and at the same time not-A, this and at the same time that. But there is no mixing in the sense of mixing together: this mixing of enlightenment and ignorance in our way of talking is *ālaya*. Things going on in this world show *ālaya-vijñāna* in its *ālaya* or activity, we might say. (225)

Suzuki is presenting the view that Absolute Mind/tathāgatagarbha /*dharmakāya* is fundamentally pure but also can seem to be defiled, if viewed from the perspective of a deluded mind. The movement in the Absolute Mind gives rise to storehouse consciousness in its enlightened and unenlightened aspects, thus making experiential awakening possible.

In discussing the nature of awakening, Suzuki cleaves closely to his own translation of the *Awakening of Faith*, tracing step by step the four stages of awakening (*fanliu siwei*; J. *honru shi'i*): nonawakening, enlightenment in appearance, approximate enlightenment, and ultimate enlightenment. Following the text, Suzuki interprets the four stages, beginning with the arising of moral differentiation between good and evil ("nonawakening"); the initial perception that "the ego is not the real I" ("enlightenment in appearance"); metaphysical enlightenment regarding the arising and transcendence of subject and object ("approximate enlightenment"); and a complete understanding of suchness, that is, the Absolute ("ultimate enlightenment") (198–203). In describing ultimate enlightenment as it is theorized in the *Awakening of Faith*, he stresses the paradoxical relationship between delusion and awakening, Absolute Mind and ignorance.

> Original enlightenment, enlightenment *a priori*, is Absolute One Mind, pure original enlightenment in itself. But if original enlightenment stands still, enlightenment is impossible; Original Enlightenment mixed with Ignorance makes enlightenment possible. Just the tendency to move, the beginning of the will to move, is *shin* [truth], and in this *shin* we have ignorance or delusion, *mō*; we cannot say anything at all about it as long as ignorance does not assert itself. The possibilities of human enlightenment and the completely unenlightened in the first stage are possible only through this mixing of original Enlightenment with Ignorance, the result being that unconscious consciousness is finally enlightened. (204)

As the author of the *Awakening of Faith* remarks, full comprehension of the interplay between enlightenment and delusion can only be grasped by a buddha.

> The mind . . . that starts from the perfuming influence of ignorance which has no beginning cannot be comprehended by the intellect of common people (*pṛthagjana*), Śrāvakas ["Voice-Hearers], and Pratyekabuddhas [Solitary Buddhas].
>
> It is partially comprehended by those Bodhisattvas at the stage of knowledge and practice, who discipline themselves,

> practice contemplation, and become the Bodhisattvas of the Dharmakāya; even while those who have reached the highest stage of Bodhisattvahood cannot thoroughly comprehend it.
>
> The only one who can have a clear and consummate knowledge of it is the Tathāgata.[69]

Peter Gregory, in a classic essay concerning the problem of theodicy—the arising of ignorance from Original Mind—in the *Awakening of Faith*, saw within the contradictions inherent in the text the impetus in Zen Buddhism to approach the understanding presented in the *Awakening of Faith* with *mondō* (C. *wenda*), classic Zen encounter dialogues,

> because its resolution required breaking through the structures of thought in terms of which the problem had meaning. While such a position inevitably results in paradox when stated philosophically, it also opens up the possibility of a radical resolution through practice. It was just such a move that emerged out of the later Ch'an tradition as witnessed in the use of various devices (such as *hua t'ou* or *kōan*) to precipitate a spiritual crisis.[70]

By using the *mondō*, the stories of "questioning and answering" that pepper the book, Suzuki tries to nudge his readers and listeners to a fuller understanding of the abstruse concepts presented in the *Awakening of Faith* and the Flower Garland Sutra, while demonstrating how Buddhist philosophy is embedded in the Zen tradition. Throughout *Spreading Indra's Net*, Suzuki raises and unpacks the oftentimes paradoxical doctrinal explanations concerning time, being, delusion, and awakening, only to conclude with one or more Zen exchange to demonstrate how these doctrinal conundrums were given expression in Zen literature.

One of Suzuki's main concerns is clarifying the etiology from the *Awakening of Faith* detailing how the Absolute Mind that is the ontological foundation of all existence, completely quiescent, and identical to original enlightenment (C. *benjue*) gives rise to both ignorance and initial or first awakening (C. *shijue*). In Suzuki's words, due to the inexplicable arising of stirring of will within inherently awakened mind, ignorance and the possibility for the experience of awakening by an individual arise. With the manifestation of initial awakening and ignorance, the two dimensions of awakening, wisdom (S. *prajñā*) and compassion (S. *karuṇā*), come into existence as well.

> Enlightenment is noetic: a certain basis of knowledge is there, not in the way of ordinary experience but as pure intellect, pure reason, or original enlightenment. Yet enlightenment as it is in itself, being so neutral, uniform, unified that we may ascribe no special characteristics to it, this enlightenment divides into two, *prajñā* and *karuṇā*; and this division is the negation called *avidyā*, ignorance. But it must be remembered that ignorance is not just negative. When you are ignorant, you are enlightened. When I realize I am ignorant, this is another term for "the first awakening. (174)

According to Suzuki, it is when wisdom becomes aware of original enlightenment that initial awakening comes into existence. This "first awakening" is a "combination of enlightenment and ignorance." Following the *Awakening of Faith*, he explains,"When *prajñā* becomes conscious of original enlightenment in itself this is called the first awakening of enlightenment in the mind. The first awakening is original enlightenment: original enlightenment through this first awakening becomes conscious of itself." And

> in *prajñā* [wisdom] there is original enlightenment plus self-consciousness. *Prajñā* has in itself original enlightenment, and when *prajñā* becomes conscious of original enlightenment we call it the first awakening. The first awakening is a combination of enlightenment and ignorance, we might say: if there is no ignorance there can be no first awakening, original enlightenment would remain with itself forever. The first awakening constitutes both ignorance and enlightenment. (175–176)

First awakening can only exist in conjunction with ignorance. It is this first awakening, Suzuki writes, that manifests the two dimensions of awakening: the noetic, *prajñā* (wisdom), personified by the bodhisattva Mañjuśrī, which intuits the "unity" and "totality" of existence while comprehending "this absolute present that never remains" (141), the "static aspect of enlightenment"; and the conative, *karuṇā* (compassion), represented by the bodhisattva Samantabhadra, which is the "dynamic aspect" of awakening, that is, "becoming" (289).

> When we speak about ignorance there is duality in it. There is no duality in original enlightenment, but as soon as it asserts itself, ignorance and duality come up, the duality of *prajñā* and *karuṇā*. Thus original enlightenment by going through the medium of ignorance differentiates itself into *prajñā* and *karuṇā*. Out of *prajñā*, the noetic aspect, we have this intellect and reason; out of *karuṇā*, the conative, come love, compassion, will. (175)

In the final chapter of *Spreading Indra's Net*, Suzuki turns his full attention to the Flower Garland school, which he writes represents "the culmination of Buddhist thought as developed by the Chinese" (236), in particular focusing on the importance of compassion (S. *karuṇā*) and vow (S. *praṇidhāna*) in that stream of Buddhism. He builds on his extensive study of the last chapter of the Flower Garland Sutra, the *Gaṇḍavyūha*, begun in the 1930s, as well his deepening interest in Jōdo Shin Buddhist religiosity.[71] Suzuki places this examination of compassion in the broader context of his analysis of mind and enlightenment as presented in the *Awakening of Faith*, while illustrating the abstruse philosophical analysis with a wide range of Zen dialogues. Repeatedly in this chapter he stresses the interpenetration and nonobstruction of fundamental awakening and the mundane world in which ignorance, compassion, wisdom, unity, and multiplicity all coexist. "Manyness remains as manyness, not a particle of this manyness changes, yet this manyness, just as it is, is oneness. This is the most important thought needed to explain Reality" (299).

According to Suzuki, in the development of Buddhism in China and Japan, proponents of Zen have emphasized the wisdom, noetic aspect of the tradition, whereas Pure Land adherents have stressed the compassionate, conative component, personified by Amitābha (Amida) Buddha, who, through the power of his vows, rescues all sentient beings. Both qualities play a crucial role in Zen, he writes, with Mañjuśrī and Samantabhadra bodhisattvas representing wisdom and compassion, respectively (176). Nonetheless, Suzuki complained that talk by contemporaneous Japanese Zen masters about "seeking awakening while saving sentient beings" (*jōgu bodai geke shūjō*) was mere words, while their rote liturgical reiteration of the vow, "Sentient beings are numberless, I vow to save them," remained "too general and has no taste."[72]

Seeking a less abstract way to highlight these overlooked aspects of Zen practice, Suzuki emphasized that engaging with the world while embracing its perfect fullness is how Zen practice manifests compassion and vow. For Suzuki, the myth-historical accounts that Huineng, the Sixth Patriarch of Zen, was an illiterate lay worker polishing rice at the monastic establishment at Mount Huangmei and tales about Zen monks "farming, working in the mountains, splitting wood, performing all kinds of household activities in the monastery [such] as cooking and cleaning" (198) demonstrated how Zen clerics expressed compassionate vow through manual labor. Although the historicity of the claim that Baizhang Huaihai (749–814) founded the first independent Zen monastery and instituted the rule that "a day of no work is a day of no eating" is doubtful, Suzuki fully embraced such claims in his lectures.

> I think the best way to interpret Zen life is as *praṇidhāna.* It is significant that China emphasized daily life and manual labor, this coming out especially to me as I go over Zen texts. So this idea of returning to practical life is not new, for Zen started from the very beginning the practice of all forms of manual labor; and this manual labor has always been much encouraged. But full conscious development of this side of Zen was only made two or three hundred years after Bodhidharma, as Zen grew to become more conscious of this practical side. At the same time this literal way of expressing it developed to give literal expression to Zen experience. (267–268)

Suzuki stresses in the final chapter of *Spreading Indra's Net* how *praṇidhāna*, that is, "vow," functions as the worldly side of Zen practice, symbolized by the bodhisattva Samantabhadra, while the transcendent dimension of realization, wisdom, symbolized by the bodhisattva Mañjuśrī, inextricably suffuses mundane existence.

> Zen does not go out of this world. Zen works in this world, but is not limited by its relativity. Zen teaches one to live in the world of relativity, yet not to be of it. Being in it means following the life of Samantabhadra; transcending it means Mañjuśrī asserting himself. Life itself is not necessarily a combination of the two,

> but the integration of *prajñā* and *karuṇā* is necessary for a life of Zen. For this reason Zen doesn't despise working, manual work, the way all other people do. At the same time Zen sees something which is not altogether included in this worldly life, something which cannot be exhausted by getting up in the morning, eating, working, going to bed. And this something more that Zen sees is *prajñā*. *Prajñā* and *karuṇā* each complement the other, but in this complementing *karuṇā* is not separated from *prajñā*, nor *prajñā* from *karuṇā*. One is in many, and many is in one, immanent yet transcending, transcending yet not outside. (237)

We have known for many years that people from all corners of the New York intellectual world came to hear Suzuki lecture at Columbia, but until the publication of the material in this book have glimpsed only fragments of the seminars' content. Perhaps because Suzuki's salary was paid by Cornelius Crane, a non-Columbia-affiliated donor, the classes were open to non-Columbia auditors.[73] As examined above, much—probably most—of the material Suzuki discussed was new to many in the classroom. But as word about Suzuki's presentation of Zen, distinctive teaching style, and quiet, soothing presence spread, people from diverse segments of the intellectual community joined the seminars. Some came for just a class or two. Others found much of value in the classes and became regular attendees. By surveying the fragmentary accounts and extant class notes of some of the most fervent attendees, I have assembled a picture of how the broad-based audience responded to Suzuki's provocative classes.

New York City provided Suzuki with a fertile environment for his lectures. The vibrancy of intellectual life in the post–World War II city, which drew talented individuals from all over the United States, helped ensure that his lectures were filled with people who approached from many distinctive angles. In addition, since the early 1930s, New York had become home to numerous émigrés from Europe, including writers, artists, scientists, philosophers, and doctors who had fled Europe as the intellectual and cultural environment on the continent grew increasingly restricted with the rise of fascism. Such newcomers, for example, Hannah Arendt, Sari Dienes, Marcel Duchamps, Claude Lévi-Strauss, and Helen and Kurt Wolff, stimulated developments in numerous niches of New York cultural life, from academia to publishing. Word about Suzuki's classes spread among a large swath of the literary, artistic, religious, and intellectual elites, drawing an extremely diverse, accomplished group. Although I have not discovered a comprehensive list for any of Suzuki's seminars, by piecing together information from a variety of contemporaneous primary sources and scattered references in accounts concerning the New York cultural scene in the 1950s, I have put together a partial roster of those who attended at least some of the classes during Suzuki's five-year tenure at Columbia. Except for a few individuals, however, it is difficult to ascertain when, exactly, between 1952 and 1957 these well-known auditors came to Suzuki's classes. Nonetheless, surveying as best I can those who are known to have been present gives a good sense of how widely Suzuki cast his net of influence.

Individuals from several different intellectual, cultural, and religious spheres found their way to the classes. These networks of shared interest included the "downtown" artists, academics, psychoanalysts, writers, and spiritual seekers from a wide range of mainstream and nonmainstream traditions. Although these groups were distinct in focus, their memberships frequently overlapped, forging numerous connections between the distinctive circles. In particular, involvement with spiritual seeking in one form or another was typical of many individuals involved. As Matthew Hedstrom has noted, during first half of the twentieth century, religious book clubs and related reading lists had "legitimated a culture of spiritual seeking" among liberal Protestants, Catholics, and Jews. The inclusion in the selections of the Religious Book Club of such authors as Aldous Huxley and Gerald Heard, as well as the runaway popularity of Thomas Merton's autobiography, *Seven-Storey Mountain*, published in 1948, which sold 162,700 copies by April 1949, were indicators of how mainstream the notion of spiritual searching had become by the early 1950s.[74] Suzuki's lectures thus were sought after by many who shared in what the scholar Leigh Schmidt succinctly describes as a "progressive tradition" of American religiosity "in which the primacy of individual experience is joined to a whole web of spiritual practices and social commitments."[75]

When Suzuki arrived in New York City to teach in 1952, there already was in place a nucleus of individuals who knew him from his writings, attendance at his lectures there the previous year, or direct meetings with him, both in Japan in the post–Pacific War era or during one of his previous visits in the United States. The list of those who began meeting with Suzuki in the late 1940s to discuss Zen at his home in Kita-Kamakura includes Philip Kapleau, Richard DeMartino, Albert Stunkard, and Theodore Van Itallie. All of these men had gone to Japan to help with the International Military Tribunal for the Far East, conducting the war crimes trials or caring for the prisoners awaiting trial at Sugamo Prison. When Suzuki arrived in New York to teach in 1952, he was assisted by DeMartino, who, having followed Suzuki east from Japan to Hawaii, southern California, and New York, enrolled in a graduate program at Columbia. For more than a decade, DeMartino would remain one of Suzuki's most devoted students and assistants, reading Buddhist texts with him, arranging and attending many of his meetings with acquaintances, and going to his lectures. Steve Antinoff, who studied with DeMartino at Temple University, recalls DeMartino recounting many years later, "Hundreds of people met Suzuki and moved on. I met him and stopped."[76]

Although all these men worked for the Occupation forces in Japan and the International Military Tribunal for the Far East, in their published recollections of their time with Suzuki in the immediate postwar years, remarkably none mentions the war responsibility of the Japanese or questioning Suzuki about the war during their meetings. Stunkard even recounts spending time learning about Zen from Hiranuma Kiichiro, the former prime minister, in Sugamo Prison awaiting trial in 1947 and convicted of war crimes in 1948. During evenings spent in Hiranuma's cell, the prisoner tried to explain Zen to Stunkard and spoke of his time practicing with Suzuki's first Zen teacher, Imakita Kōsen. This piqued Stunkard's interest in Zen, leading him to seek out Suzuki. In his accounts of those days, however, he never brings up Hiranuma's role in the war or the question of Suzuki's activities during the war years.[77]

The two medical doctors in the group, Stunkard and Van Itallie, both attended Suzuki's lectures. Stunkard grew very close with Suzuki, bringing his teacher to his home to meet his parents and providing medical advice to him as needed. Stunkard's friend Van Itallie did his medical residency at St. Luke's Hospital in New York after returning from Japan, so he could easily have attended some of Suzuki's classes, as Stunkard mentioned in a 2003 documentary film interview with Michael Goldberg.[78] Both doctors helped Suzuki manage his high blood pressure and, on one occasion, dissuaded him from taking LSD to see if the drug was as mystically potent as many claimed at the time.[79] Kapleau, who attended at least some of the Columbia lectures, received Suzuki's assistance in his later effort to practice Zen in Japan. After years practicing there, Kapleau went on to found the Rochester Zen Center in 1966.

Psychoanalysts and their patients comprised another set of people interested in Suzuki's seminars and Zen Buddhism. By the early 1950s, analysis had become so trendy and widespread that the composer Morton Feldman advised Carolyn Brown, a dancer newly arrived in New York City in 1952, "The first thing you have to do is get yourself a shrink. Everybody who's somebody has an analyst."[80] Brown does not state whether she or Feldman had analysts, but both would soon, in the tow of John Cage, find their way to Suzuki's seminars, as did a number of therapists, for example, Erich Fromm; B. Joan Harte; Karen Horney; Akihisa Kondo, a Japanese analyst with a deep interest in Zen; and Albert Stunkard. Fromm and Horney, who were colleagues and former lovers, were among the émigré analysts increasingly interested in Suzuki's work. Fromm wrote that he attended some of Suzuki's Columbia seminars. Whether Horney was there is unclear, but as noted above, she was very close with Suzuki from 1951 until her untimely death from cancer in 1952. Although training as a psychiatrist at Johns Hopkins Hospital in the early 1950s, Stunkard found time to attend some of the seminars and bring Suzuki to meet his parents on Long Island.[81] Another group of ten to fifteen analysts attended a series of Sunday evening lectures on Zen given by Suzuki at the apartment of B. Joan Harte, a student at the American Institute of Psychoanalysis, the educational arm of Horney's Association for the Advancement of Psychoanalysis.[82]

Suzuki's lectures also drew a number of people involved with the Bollingen Foundation or working on the Bollingen book series published by Pantheon Books, a new publisher founded in 1942 by two German refugees, Kurt and Helen Wolff (née Mosel).[83] The foundation and the publication series had grown out of a collaboration between Olga Froebe-Kapteyn and Carl Jung, with the support of Paul and Mary Conover Mellon, who generously funded all the Bollingen-related endeavors. The foundation and the series also were connected closely with the Eranos Lectures that Froebe began convening in Switzerland in August 1933. The Second World War forced a hiatus in the lectures and curtailed Bollingen projects, but after the war all activities resumed.[84] A diverse group of lecturers spoke at the Eranos meetings, and the foundation supported a wide range of research through grants and its Bollingen Series. Related ventures centered on topics connected to Jung's extensive interests, including religion, alchemy, comparative mythology, archaeology, Egyptology, philosophy, literature, and psychology. Many members of this circle, for example, Mary Mellon and Nancy Wilson Ross, also were interested in spiritual seeking, which included Theosophy, the Gurdjieff work, and various forms of occultism, often framed by acceptance of the perennialist claim that the mystical experiences grounding every spiritual tradition were at their core the same. Suzuki was invited to attend the 1953 and 1954 Eranos meetings in Ascona, Switzerland, and word of his lectures at Columbia also circulated among members of the wider Bollingen circle. The group included Natacha Rambova, the widow of Rudolph Valentino, who had a strong interest in comparative religion as well as Theosophy-inspired myths of Atlantis. Rambova taught courses in comparative symbology in her New York apartment, drawing numerous figures, including the costume designer and translator of the *Mustard Seed Garden Manual of Painting*, Mai-mai Sze, and photographer Dorothy Norman, who would both attend Suzuki's lectures. John D. Barrett Jr., closely associated with the Bollingen circle, became associate editor of the Bollingen Series of books at Pantheon. He also was instrumental in arranging for Suzuki to publish *Zen and Japanese Culture*, one of his most well-known books, in the Bollingen Series in 1959.

In the wake of the war, with good portions of Europe and Asia in ruins, New York also became one of the most vibrant artistic centers globally, as émigré artists joined the many native-born practitioners of the creative disciplines who flocked to the city, particularly downtown in the Village. Members of the so-called "Loft Generation" were adventurous artistically, intellectually, and socially.[85] Forming a close-knit circle, such not-yet-famous artists, composers, dancers, and writers as Ellen and Walter Auerbach, Earle and

Carolyn Brown, John Cage, Sari Dienes, Phillip Guston, Jasper Johns, Ibram Lassaw, Jackson Mac Low, Willem and Elaine de Kooning, Phillip Pavia, Robert Rauschenberg, and many others mingled in downtown lofts, coffee shops, and bars. The Club on 8th Avenue, founded by Phillip Pavia in 1948, was an important hub for social gatherings and intellectual exchange on Wednesday and Friday evenings. The discussions and lectures offered covered a wide range of topics, including art, music, existentialism, and, notably, three lectures on Zen by Hasegawa Saburō and Matsumi Kanemitsu in November 1954.[86] The sculptor Ibram Lassaw recalled giving a talk to the members about Zen in which he read passages from Suzuki's books.[87] John Cage, an active member of the Club, also played a role in spreading word of the Columbia lectures and information about Zen among other members.

Members of this creative group became one of the largest contingents of auditors at Suzuki's seminars. Although we do not have detailed records of what they took away, a small number of the artists did mention their impressions. Both Kay Larson, in a biography of John Cage, and Ellen Pearlman, in her study of how Buddhism affected the American avant-garde, have used a wide variety of sources to determine who from this group attended Suzuki's seminars.[88] By synthesizing their work with memoirs and other accounts of the art scene in New York at the time, I have come up with the following list of impressive artists who were present for one or more of the sessions. Cage brought a number of his friends from the Club, including Carolyn Brown, Earle Brown, Phillip Guston, and Lois Long.[89] In addition, Ellen Auerbach, Robert Coe, Sari Dienes, Ibram Lassaw, Lois Larson, Jackson Mac Low, Dorothy Norman, Ad Reinhardt, and Mai-mai Sze found their way to the seminars.

Although the lectures were in part sponsored by Columbia's philosophy department, and though Suzuki lectured regularly to philosophers at numerous institutions of higher learning, few scholars of that discipline attended. Apart from Arthur Danto, Horace L. Friess, who taught both philosophy and religion courses at Columbia, told Chadbourne Gilpatric that he had attended a number of the lectures in the spring 1952 semester.[90] Danto also mentions that Abraham Kaplan, a professor visiting from UCLA, was one of the only other philosophers present. Kaplan, like Friess, was interested in religion as well as philosophy. He received a Rockefeller Foundation fellowship to explore philosophy in Asia and by the late 1950s had incorporated a good deal of material about "Eastern philosophy" into his popular course at UCLA and his book, the *New World of Philosophy*.[91] In addition, according to Suzuki's diaries, in the mid-1950s, Henry G. Bugbee Jr., a philosopher at Harvard University who first met Suzuki in 1951, occasionally would meet with him in New York, then accompany him to the Friday seminar.

Suzuki's lectures also drew listeners from the Japanese and Japanese American community in New York City, which had grown considerably since 1944. With the closure of the American concentration camps in which Japanese and Japanese Americans had been imprisoned, approximately 5,000 people of Japanese descent chose to move to the eastern United States, particularly New York City. There they bolstered the ranks of such largely Japanese American organizations as the New York Buddhist Church, on West Ninety-Fourth Street. The surrounding area of the Upper West Side became a hub of Japanese American life, with several Japanese Christian churches and the Nippon Club also in the area.[92]

Although the New York Buddhist Church never had more than 160 dues-paying members between 1948 and 1958, Japanese Americans in the region became a very important audience for Suzuki, as well as a vital source of community. Suzuki spoke with church members on at least three occasions in spring 1951. The following spring, as he began teaching his Columbia seminar, he also gave a series of Friday night lectures concerning True Pure Land (Jōdo Shin)

Buddhism at the American Buddhist Academy affiliated with the New York Buddhist Church.[93] Suzuki also met with members of the Buddhist Church for more informal conversations, and when the church was relocated to Riverside Drive in 1955, he delivered a speech for the dedication of the Shinran statue that Hirose Seiichi gifted to the temple as a goodwill gesture from Hiroshima, Japan.[94]

The Okamura family—Frank; his wife, Toshimi Nishikubo Okamura; and their two daughters, Mihoko and Reiko—moved to New York City after being released from the Manzanar Relocation Camp. They played an active role in the life of the New York Japanese community and provided support that helped make possible the more than eighty-year-old Suzuki's extended stay. Having lost his landscaping business in Los Angeles in 1942, when he was interned at Manzanar, Frank Okamura found work as a gardener at the Brooklyn Botanic Garden, where he became an important proponent of bonsai cultivation. Frank and Toshimi often entertained members of the New York Japanese community in their home on West Ninety-Fourth Street and would rent rooms in their brownstone building to visitors from Japan.[95]

Mihoko in particular, who was fifteen when she first heard Suzuki lecture in 1951, was drawn to him and his work. She leaves little doubt in her written reminiscences and conversations that her interactions with Suzuki were life changing. Once Suzuki was settled in New York in 1952, Mihoko visited him frequently at his residence in Butler Hall, especially following her high school graduation at the start of 1953, speaking with him in detail about Buddhism, typing manuscripts, fielding telephone calls, helping to host his numerous visitors, and accompanying him to an almost endless stream of lectures, dinners, and visits. In his diaries, Suzuki mentions frequently reading passages from Zen texts to Mihoko at the Butler Hall apartment and expresses amazement at the young woman's interest in such arcane stories. When Suzuki traveled to Europe to lecture at the

Eranos Conference in August 1953, Mihoko accompanied him as his assistant. As she grew close to Suzuki, her parents also befriended him, and in January 1954, Suzuki moved from his faculty apartment at Columbia to live in the Okamura home. Mihoko and her younger sister, Reiko, spent a good deal of time with Suzuki, often accompanying him on trips to Princeton, New Jersey, Ipswich, Massachusetts, and elsewhere in the New York area. When his lectures resumed in February 1953, Mihoko would often attend with him. In his diary, Suzuki notes that after attending the seminar on March 27, 1953, Mihoko "talked much about herself—her inner feeling, her lack of knowledge, her mind filled with superficialities, &c." and concludes that "Hers is not probably a scholarly mind. She wants to be sincere to herself."[96] When Suzuki returned to Japan in late 1958, Mihoko, then twenty-three years old, accompanied him, with her parents' blessing, and acted as his assistant, secretary, and close companion for the rest of Suzuki's life.[97] Although the close relationship between a teenager, and an octogenarian may understandably raise questions of impropriety, in the many conversations I had with Mihoko and others who knew her and Suzuki when she served as his assistant, I have never uncovered any evidence that their relationship was more than a platonic one of devoted teacher and disciple.

After Suzuki and Mihoko departed to Japan, Toshimi turned her penchant for hospitality into a business, operating the Japanese restaurant Aki Dining Room, just minutes from the Columbia University campus at 420 W. 119th Street.[98] According to Mihoko, some of the income from the restaurant was used to provide her with a degree of financial independence while she was working with Suzuki in Japan.[99]

In his book *The Making of American Buddhism*, Scott Mitchell has emphasized the indispensable role that domestic support like that provided by the Okamuras to Suzuki played in the creation and unfolding of Buddhism in America. As Mitchell stresses, although almost always overlooked, the acts of kindness that Suzuki, along with many other Japanese and American Buddhists, received in Japanese American households made the more visible work of disseminating Buddhism possible.[100] I find it difficult to imagine the more than eighty-year-old Suzuki staying in New York City for seven years without the support of the Okamuras and numerous other members of the community.

Suzuki began teaching his seminars as Americans were reengaging with numerous aspects of Japanese culture. With the end of the Occupation and the increasingly close Cold War alliance between Japan and the United States, Americans' fascination with Japan, submerged during the Pacific War, resurfaced. Such postwar Japanese films as *Rashomon*, *Gate of Hell* (*Jigokumon*), *Samurai*, *The Legend of Musashi* (*Miyamoto Musashi*), and *The Harp of Burma* (*Biruma no tategoto*) were all given special recognition by the Academy of Motion Pictures Arts and Sciences in the 1950s. The recognition of Japanese film, in turn, stimulated interest in the literature that was its source. In addition, private philanthropic organizations such as the Rockefeller and Ford Foundations devoted funds to enhance cultural exchange with Japan and expose Americans to the finest aspects of Japanese culture. As described above, Suzuki himself was one beneficiary. With the support of John D. Rockefeller 3rd, in 1953 a reinvigorated Japan Society sponsored a major exhibition of Japanese sculpture that opened in New York before touring Boston, Chicago, Seattle, and Washington, D.C. The preview of the exhibition on March 26, 1953, at which the Japanese Ambassador to the United States, Araki Eikichi, was the guest of honor, drew a crowd of six thousand to the Metropolitan Museum of Art.[101] The positive reception of Suzuki's seminars thus was part of a resurgence of American interest in Japan that grew in the 1950s.

The positive American reappraisal may explain in part why, as far as I can tell, none of the seminar participants questioned Suzuki about how he had responded to the recently concluded Pacific War and the Japanese violence in Asia. Soon after the end of the war, Suzuki had become outspokenly critical of Japan's aggression. Like many Japanese, having witnessed the horrors unleashed on his country with the atomic bombings at Hiroshima and Nagasaki, when Cold War tensions heightened in the early 1950s, Suzuki condemned the Soviet–US brinksmanship that threatened to plunge the world into a nuclear war.[102] As Suzuki became more well known in the United States, occasionally critics and interlocutors did mention the contradictions inherent in his valorization of *bushidō* in his writings. Historian of Asian art Alexander Soper, for example, wrote in his review of Suzuki's *Zen and Japanese Culture* that in light of the recent past, some readers would be uneasy about Suzuki's description of the *Hagakure*, a work of military strategy, in the context of the Japanese war in China and Suzuki's statement that "the enemy appears and makes himself a victim . . . This is the kind of sword that Christ is said to have brought among us."[103] According to Mihoko Okamura, Erich Fromm, in one early encounter with Suzuki, expressed puzzlement concerning the juxtaposition of Zen with the martial discipline of archery in Eugen Herrigel's book *Zen and the Art of Archery*, for which Suzuki had written the introduction. Mihoko reported that during one visit, Fromm angrily asked how Zen could have anything to do with weapons. In response, Suzuki retorted, "Who are you that is saying that?," at which point Fromm angrily departed. Several weeks later, however, he asked to see Suzuki again, stating that he had been pondering Suzuki's question for weeks. Mihoko reports that when Fromm visited this time, the meeting was cordial. The two men became close associates, and Fromm hosted Suzuki for several months at his villa in Cuernevaca,

Mexico, where they participated in a now-famous conference on Zen Buddhism and psychoanalysis organized by the Mexican Psychoanalytic Society.[104]

In the 1950s, most of the attendees at the seminars were hearing about Buddhist doctrine and practice for the first time. During the first half of the twentieth century interest in Buddhism and Zen had grown gradually in North America, but most people outside of Asian and Asian American communities remained relatively unfamiliar with the subject. In addition, English-language books about Buddhism and translations of Buddhist texts, particularly those aimed at nonacademic specialists, were relatively few. As a result, most of those attending Suzuki's Columbia seminars had little exposure to Buddhism and few resources to consult outside the seminars about the philosophical, dense Flower Garland and Zen material Suzuki presented. As noted above, even academics from related fields, for example Horace Friess, a specialist in philosophy and religious studies, found the lectures challenging, in part because of Suzuki's presentation style but also due to the complexity and unfamiliarity of the material.

Despite the novelty, some attendees, particularly those who came regularly, earnestly wrestled with Suzuki's presentation of Buddhism and applied what they learned in their life and work. Only a handful of the students left traceable records of their reactions, impressions, and deployment of Suzuki's teachings. Some who often attended, for example, Mihoko Okamura and Richard DeMartino, did not leave a detailed account. A few people at the 1952–1953 lectures, in particular Elizabeth Thomas and John Cage, did relate their reactions in the form of letters, interviews, autobiographical essays, and, in Thomas's case, her notebooks and the lectures manuscript itself. In addition, Ibram Lassaw left class notes for the lectures he attended in spring 1954 and spring 1955, but based on those outlines, clearly Suzuki was lecturing on different material from that which is contained in *Spreading Indra's Net*.

For the most enthusiastic seminar participants the allure was more than just the intellectual stimulation of Buddhist thought. The most devoted students were intrigued by Suzuki's calm, soft-spoken, slow-paced, contemplative teaching style, as the accounts of Cage, Ibram Lassaw, Dorothy Norman, Lunsford Yandell, and others all attest. They found the lectures compelling because of, as Yandell recalled, "the being of the man himself. No writings of his could convey his spirit—'the True Man.'" They sought to spend time with him outside class at dinners, taking him on outings in the environs of New York City, and assisting him with his numerous writing projects. A number of the devoted attendees, including John Cage, photographer Dorothy Norman, Mihoko Okamura, and Elizabeth Thomas, express some measure of personal crisis as their motivation for wanting to spend time with Suzuki inside and outside of the classroom. Dorothy Norman, for example, attended the seminars as she navigated the dissolution of her marriage, recalling, "He [Suzuki] explains that unless one is at a point of crisis when coming to Zen, it cannot have full significance. Only if the need to attain enlightenment is a matter of life and death will Zen reveal its true meaning. I have come upon Dr. Suzuki at exactly the right moment!"[105]

Mihoko Okamura told me on numerous occasions that when she first saw Suzuki lecture, probably at the March 1951 Kegon lectures at Columbia, she had never seen a person with such presence. When Suzuki returned to Columbia in 1952, Mihoko, then sixteen years old, sought him out, because she was feeling extremely depressed. On one memorable visit to Suzuki's apartment, she expressed being depressed and frustrated by not finding any people worth emulating. Much to her surprise, Suzuki took her hands, telling her to look at them while saying, "These are Buddha's hands." That oblique approach to her struggle left an impression that remained with her for the rest of her life. As she got to know Suzuki better, visiting him on her way home from school, she began helping him with typing, answering the telephone, conversing with him about his research, and cooking meals in the Butler Hall apartment.[106]

Although as a PhD student in philosophy at Yale Jacob Needleman had not attended the lectures, he, too, remembered how Suzuki's seemingly indirect response to someone seeking advice provided a bracing, beneficial shock. Needleman, who was delving into various spiritual teachings at the time, including the Gurdjieff movement, heard about Suzuki from Henry Greenwood Bugbee Jr., one of his undergraduate philosophy professors at Harvard. In the autumn of 1956, Needleman traveled to Manhattan to visit Suzuki, who tersely noted in his diary entry for October 16, "Needleman of Yale, a young man wanting to learn Zen." Needleman wrote many years later that his memories of the room were vague, but, echoing Mihoko's first impressions, "I remember only the face and figure of Suzuki himself—especially the eyebrows, which seemed to grow out from his forehead like enormous wings. He was old, slightly built like most Japanese; I vaguely remember a cardigan sweater and a bow tie. But what I do remember very clearly was his *presence*." After nibbling around the edges of a conversation, talking about Suzuki's impressions of the Gurdjieff movement, Needleman asked, "What is the self?" Suzuki responded, like a prototypical Zen teacher, "Who is asking the question?" Flummoxed and somewhat annoyed, Needleman blurted out, "I am asking it!" to which Suzuki responded, "Show me this *I*." Stunned into silence and disappointed in himself, Needleman stayed for tea, then headed back to New Haven, where for some time he continued to mull over his failure to respond. After some months, Needleman realized, "My God! This was what he was telling me! It was all intentional on his part! I was supposed to find this out by myself! It was not communicable in words, in thought! It was an event, not an idea! Who am I? This state was the answer!"[107] When I spoke to Needleman by telephone in 2021 about his visit to Suzuki, expressing my amazement that such a seemingly simple exchange had made such a deep impression on him, Needleman replied, "Richard, you have to understand. This was the 1950s. *No one* spoke to you like that."[108]

Elizabeth Thomas's interest in Suzuki's seminars and her reactions to his work provide another example of how the combination of existential concerns, spiritual searching, and intellectual curiosity drew people to the seminars. For the most avid attendees, contact with Suzuki offered both intellectual stimulation and spiritual solace. After hearing some of his lectures, Thomas wrote to him to express her feelings about what she had learned. Her letter reveals the intertwining of Thomas's intellectual and spiritual quests, as it captures the mixture of personal and intellectual motivations that led some of the most earnest students to the seminars.

> Dear Dr. Suzuki,
>
> Thank you very much for your letter and your willingness to talk with me again in the Fall. Meanwhile, I will continue to try to hear the sound and am glad to have your criticism. If you have any other suggestions, including that of particular books to read, I would like to have them, when, and if, your time allows.
>
> The difficulty you speak of is very difficult for the West, of course, and very real for me. The thinking, analytical approach has seemed natural for me, too—only it has never been enough in itself and I have always sought to go beyond Facts into Meaning. Frequently I have had the feeling of being between two worlds, without ability to go on to the second, yet with firm belief in its existence and firm determination not to return to the first,

> even if return were possible. Whether I can learn to go on and to prove one of those exceptions I don't know. Perhaps one day the pebble will hit the tree, but that is not my business?
>
> You are probably saying there is only one world, that the separation is due to illusion on my part, or lack of consciousness. I agree, of course. The "second world" is the same world, only with something added, Life itself, perhaps?[109]

Thomas makes clear that her interest in Suzuki's course was not just intellectual in nature. By the end of the second semester, January 16, 1953, she not only asked Suzuki for additional readings but also expressed interest in learning the "practical aspect of Zen."[110] When Thomas visited him in Butler Hall on January 7, 1953, he gave her detailed instructions for the Buddhist-Daoist practice of healing meditation (*nanso*; soft butter visualization) that had been transmitted by Hakuin Ekaku, one of the giants of Rinzai Zen.[111] Even after Suzuki's death, Thomas remained interested in various Zen organizations, maintaining correspondence with different Zen centers and financial donations to the San Francisco Zen Center until her death in 1985.

John Cage, the modernist experimental composer, was also a regular attendee at the lectures. He was an enthusiastic fan who regularly brought his artist, musician, composer, and dancer friends with him to hear Suzuki. Cage was not a stickler for chronological accuracy, which makes it hard to tie his numerous recollections of the seminar lectures to specific dates. For example, he mentions in one interview that he began attending Suzuki's seminars in 1947 or 1949, but in those years Suzuki was in Japan.[112] Cage recalls clearly the classroom in Philosophy Hall, where the seminars took place in fall 1952 and spring 1953, and the discussion of Kegon, so it is likely he began at that time.

Long before Suzuki's Columbia seminars, Cage had become interested in a variety of Indian and Chinese religious teachings, including Zen. While working as a piano dance accompanist at the Cornish School for Drama, Music, Dance, he met a coterie of Seattle-based artists and art critics who had begun investigating Sino-Japanese culture and religion. Mark Tobey, Morris Graves, and Nancy Wilson Ross were three prominent figures involved with the school who had been to Asia and experienced Buddhist practice in Japan. As Kay Larson points out in her superb Cage biography, Nancy Wilson Ross's 1938 lecture at the Cornish School, "Dada and Zen," "flew straight at Cage's heart."[113] According to Cage,

> One of the liveliest lectures I ever heard was given by Nancy Wilson Ross at the Cornish School in Seattle. It was called Zen Buddhism and Dada. It is possible to make a connection between the two, but neither Dada nor Zen is a fixed tangible. They change; and in quite different ways in different places and times, they invigorate action. What was Dada in the 1920s is now, with the exception of the work of Marcel Duchamp, just art. What I do, I do not wish blamed on Zen, though without my engagement with Zen (attendance at lectures by Alan Watts and D. T. Suzuki, reading of the literature) I doubt whether I would have done what I have done.[114]

Although Ross's lecture intrigued Cage, he did not immediately start reading about Zen. As his marriage to Xenia Kashevaroff fell apart in the mid-1940s, however, Cage felt unhappy personally and professionally. At that point, he turned to "Oriental philosophy," particularly Zen, rather than psychoanalysis to deal with his problems. As Cage recalled when speaking with Calvin Tomkins in 1964, after an unsatisfactory visit to a psychoanalyst in the late 1940s, he began immersing himself in "the philosophies of East and West" before discovering Zen Buddhism.[115] He began attending Suzuki's seminar at Columbia and engaging with Suzuki after class, hoping this would help him resolve his personal problems and realize alternative approaches to musical composition. According to Tomkins, Cage recalled that during his two years at Suzuki's seminars,

> "I had the impression that I was changing—you might say growing up," he [Cage] says. "I realized my previous understanding was that of a child." He saw that Zen, like psychoanalysis, was an attempt to open up the psyche from within to a more intense awareness (enlightenment or *satori*) of everyday life. Therefore he felt, it should be said that music should try to do externally what Zen and psychoanalysis attempted internally; it should not be concerned primarily with entertainment or communication or the symbolic expression of the artist's ideas and tastes, but, rather, should perform the specifically useful function of helping men and women attain a more intense awareness of their own lives, not only in the concert hall but during every waking moment.[116]

Cage did not write in a systematic manner about his understanding of Suzuki's lectures or how they affected his life and artistic work. Nonetheless, over the course of many interviews, he was articulate and philosophical concerning his own artistic process. Commenting on how he incorporated Suzuki's teachings into his artistic work, Cage said,

> Suzuki said Zen wants us to diminish that kind of activity of the ego and to increase the activity that accepts the rest of creation. And rather than taking the path that is prescribed in the formal practice of Zen Buddhism itself, namely, sitting cross-legged and breathing and such things, I decided that my proper discipline

> was the one to which I was already committed, namely the making of music. And that I would do it with a means that was as strict as sitting cross-legged, namely, the use of chance operations, and the shifting of my responsibility from the making of choices to that of asking questions.[117]

Cage emphasized in several interviews that Suzuki was not a typical verbose professor. I already have quoted his recollections of how Suzuki would greet each student in the classroom with a glance, a nod, or a word. Cage also recalled Suzuki being silent for intervals during the seminar, only occasionally making a statement. Like the experience students frequently have listening to a formal Zen practice lecture, that is, a *teishō*, Cage mentioned in several interviews how he often could not grasp the point of Suzuki's lectures or even remember much about them. At other times he needed to wrestle with the material before understanding it. Cage describes how with three lectures in particular, he was clueless about what Suzuki was saying, but after a week of mulling them over, while hunting mushrooms in the woods, understanding came to him.[118]

Suzuki's explanation of the interpenetration of all phenomena and the awakening of insentient beings (227; 255) made a particularly strong impression. When Cage took part in a symposium, "Time and Space Concepts in Art," held at the Pleiades Gallery in New York, he spoke about the importance of Suzuki's presentation of Kegon Buddhism for him.

> There was another lecture that Suzuki gave that I kept thinking of all the time. We have in the West this business of trying to find out, among a plurality of events in time and space, which one is the best. And then thinking of ourselves as separate from that and as desirably moving toward it. But in Kegan [*sic*] philosophy

> which Suzuki taught, each being whether sentient as we are, or nonsentient as sounds and rocks are, is the Buddha: and that doesn't mean anything spooky. It simply means that it is at the center of the universe. So that what you have in Kegan [*sic*] philosophy is an endless plurality of centers, each one world honored.[119]

The abstract expressionist sculptor Ibram Lassaw (1913–2003) was one of the artists who found his way to the lectures thanks to John Cage. Contained within Lassaw's diaries, which he referred to as "Day Books," are his notes for three semesters of Suzuki's seminars: spring 1954, spring 1955, and fall 1955.[120] (Suzuki was in Japan on leave in fall 1954.) Lassaw's notebooks, like Thomas's much more detailed ones, provide another week-by-week glimpse of the topics Suzuki covered and the flow of the lectures for 1954–1955.

Lassaw's notes show that Suzuki introduced the students to such texts as the *Laṅkāvatāra Sutra* (J. *Ryōgakyō*), the *Diamond Sutra* (J. *Kongōkyō*), and the *Prajñā Parāmitā Sutras* (J. *Hannyakyō*). As with the material in *Spreading Indra's Net*, Lassaw's notes record Suzuki speaking at length about the nature of awakened mind and buddhahood. On March 12, 1954, for example, Suzuki described Absolute Mind, saying that "in its absolute state, mind, the pure land, is devoid of worldly encumbrances, absolute reality is pure land."[121] He also spoke about various forms of Buddhist meditation practice. Lassaw records that on March 26, 1954, Suzuki lectured about zazen, recitation of the *nenbutsu*, and Shingon meditation, which, according to Lassaw, involves concentration on ○, the moon, or "the immensity of the infinitely expanding universe." Suzuki also told the class that the ultimate point of reciting the names of Buddha, for example, Amitābha, was "to go beyond any phrase / Word is to be forgotten / Recitation, reciting and reciter become one / Subject and object are to become non-existent."[122] On April 9, Suzuki expanded his meditation instructions, telling the class that they should wear nonconstrictive clothing and concentrate on the Sino-Japanese character for "one" or go to a high, treeless mountaintop, where they could see all four quarters and "feel the universe."[123]

Suzuki's classes remained an important touchstone for Lassaw the rest of his life. For example, he recorded in his notes for April 9, 1954, Suzuki saying, "The Buddha within ourselves is a far greater teacher than all external Buddhas that have ever lived / Do not be a slave to sutra teaching / The teacher is in ourselves / We must discover our own Buddha."[124] In interviews in 1968 and 1974, Lassaw echoed what was recorded in his class notes: "I still remember many of the things he said that are not in any of his books, just certain memorable phrases. One of them was, 'If in actual life you experience certain truths, and if all the Buddhas and all the patriarchs and all the sutras as one tell you you are wrong, then you must ignore the Buddhas, the patriarchs, and the sutras. And that was just it. I mean that jibed exactly with my experience in life up to that point.' "[125]

Like Thomas and Cage, Henry Bugbee, who had told Needleman about Suzuki, was another occasional seminar participant who grew enamored with Suzuki's interpretation of Buddhism and spent time visiting him. With a PhD from the University of California at Berkeley, Bugbee was teaching philosophy and comparative religion at Harvard when Suzuki came to lecture in 1951. Bugbee hosted Suzuki at his Harvard class for a lecture, dined with him, and met with him again several days later at Cornelius Crane's Castle Hill estate in Ipswich. Bugbee continued to meet Suzuki in New York and Ipswich in 1952–1953. When on leave from Harvard in spring 1954, Bugbee would occasionally trek from Cambridge to New York, where he would attend the Friday seminar, then dine and discuss his work with Suzuki. In March 1954, Bugbee gave his book manuscript, probably of *The Inward Morning*, to Suzuki, which they discussed on several occasions. In the introduction, Bugbee thanked Suzuki for reading the manuscript and for help in understanding Buddhism.

Bugbee's *The Inward Morning* is a difficult-to-characterize philosophical meditation written in journal form in 1953–1954, while Bugbee was the first recipient of a George Santayana Fellowship at Harvard. In his daily journal, he searches for the basis that empowers a person to "place his life in such a light that he can live his last moments in the most profound affirmation," arguing that it is "our capacity for the responsible realization of unqualified affirmation" that reveals the "measure of our understanding of reality."

> But the ambiguity of our situation is patent in the fact that the possibility of such affirmation can be systematically ignored or denied. Indeed systematic-thought is disposed to reflect the unification of complexes of discriminables; it is responsive in terms of uniformity; but how will it accommodate simplicity? Yet I suspect that the understanding of reality which I connect with the possibility of unqualified affirmation is more attuned to simplicity than to uniformity. This idea of reality understood in its simplicity might answer to the intent of the Buddhist thought with which I have been so much helped by Dr. Suzuki.[126]

In several places Bugbee refers to Suzuki's books, for example, *Living by Zen*, and echoes some of the material from the seminars. In particular, he emphasizes the importance of the experiences of wonder, awe, and unity, in which the distinction between the observer and the observed drops away. Reflecting on the nature of "ultimate" or "unconditional concern" that is the foundation of a true "religious attitude," Bugbee questions Reinhold Niebhur's insistence that all religious experience be grounded on an "objective basis," that is, God. Bugbee insists that true "religious attitude" does not depend on something like "a conception of God" as an object. Instead, "religious attitude is one of truly universal concern for things, of concern informed with the universality of finite things. I do not mean concern for 'things in general,' I mean, on the contrary, a concern which is concretely an experience of things in the vein of individuality, for this is precisely the vein in which they are experienced as universal."[127] In this interfusion of the individual and the universal are echoes of Suzuki's emphasis in his lectures on how, as cited above, from an enlightened perspective, which Bugbee is calling a "religious attitude," "Manyness remains as manyness, not a particle of this manyness changes, yet this manyness, just as it is, is oneness" (299).

Suzuki presented Buddhism in a decidedly intellectual, philosophical manner, which, for some of those seeking a practical solution to their existential problems, was unsatisfying. Not surprisingly, Suzuki's focus on awakening and viewing the world from an enlightened perspective piqued some students' interest in exploring more concrete aspects of Zen Buddhism. It is remarkable to me, as one who practiced Buddhism in the United States and Japan for many years, how little in *Spreading Indra's Net* Suzuki speaks about Zen meditation, monastic life, ritual, and other dimensions of Buddhist practice. This left some students asking for more in that regard. Thomas, for example, as quoted above, wanted Suzuki to teach her about the "more practical aspect of Zen." Later in the course, Ibram Lassaw recorded in his notes that Suzuki explained zazen to the seminar students in the spring 1954 semester, perhaps because Thomas and others expressed interest in that subject.

Philip Kapleau, who went on to found the Rochester Zen Center in 1966, first met Suzuki in Japan during the late 1940s and attended some of the seminars. In his classic book on Zen practice, *Three Pillars of Zen*, Kapleau reproduces a diary entry about his growing frustration with the lectures: "April 20, 1953: Attended S____'s Zen lecture today. As usual, could make little sense out of it . . . Why do I go on with these lectures? Can I ever get *satori* listening to philosophic explanations of *prajna* and *karuna* and why A isn't A and the rest of that? What the hell is satori anyway? Even after four of S____'s books and dozens of his lectures, still don't know. I must be awfully stupid."[128] Suzuki, however, as a layman, would only go so far in playing the role of a Zen master. He deferred to those who had been certified as Zen masters by their own teachers in Japan to conduct zazen and direct koan study. For example, in fall 1957 he helped arrange the visit of Hisamatsu Shin'ichi, who had come to the United States to lecture on Zen at Harvard Divinity School, and joined Hisamatsu at his lectures. When some attendees requested more practical instruction in Zen, Hisamatsu agreed to lead Zen practice at the nascent Cambridge Buddhist Association in the home of Elsie Mitchell. Suzuki again assisted Hisamatsu but did not take an active role overseeing the meditation practice at the association, even while lecturing to the group on occasion and serving as its titular president.

Delivered at a time when avant-garde art, Beat literature, spiritual searching, and engagement with East Asian cultures were effervescing just beneath the surface of mainstream culture, Suzuki's Columbia University seminars had broad, significant impact on New York and US religious, cultural, and intellectual life. The seminars became must-attend events for cultural and intellectual leaders in New York City in the 1950s. As Jane Iwamura has written in her book *Virtual Orientalism*, at least part of the attraction must have been that Suzuki fit the stereotype of the gentle, wise Zen teacher. The attendees quoted above spoke of him in the same manner, including comments on such superficialities as his striking eyebrows. Needleman, who kept a picture of Suzuki in his study until the end of his life, even suggested that I entitle one chapter of my biography of Suzuki "Suzuki's Eyebrows."

More than just the allure of the exotic was involved, however. Suzuki also was offering something dynamic to those who gathered in Philosophy Hall each week to hear him speak about Flower Garland philosophy and Zen. The fragmentary student accounts above demonstrate that many were searching for a new way to experience and think about the world. The presentation of material from the *Awakening of Faith* and the Flower Garland tradition provided a different perspective on mind, the world, and awakening. Suzuki, although criticized by many for facilely juxtaposing Zen teachings, Christian mystics, poetry, Einstein, and mathematics, tantalized his audience with those comparisons. Such ideas as the nondual nature of reality, monism, interpenetration of phenomena, sentience of the material world, and objectless compassion were generative for the artists, composers, philosophers, seekers, and analysts who found their way to the seminars.

Arthur Danto, the Columbia philosophy professor who attended some of Suzuki's classes, aptly compared the Columbia seminars to another pivotal intellectual event: Russian emigré Alexandre Kojève's lectures on Georg Wilhelm Friedrich Hegel's *Phenomenology of the Spirit*, which he delivered in Paris during the 1930s. "I think Suzuki's course played a role in New York much like Kojève's did in Paris. It helped redirect the way those who were thinkers actually thought."[129] Kojève's lectures, attended by Louis Althusser, Raymond Aron, Georges Bataille, Jacques Lacan, and Jean-Paul Sartre, among other prominent figures, proved inspirational because, as one intellectual historian has written, "Kojève captivated students with his ability to make connections. Using complex diagrams and graphs, he presented a reading of Hegel that drew from Einstein's physics, Bergson's intuitionism, Husserl's phenomenology, Heidegger's ontology, and Marx's politics. For the young French intellectuals, everything Kojève gave them seemed new."[130] In much the same way, Suzuki—weaving together Flower Garland Buddhist philosophy, tales of the Zen masters, writings of Christian mystics, existential philosophy, science, and mathematics—provided a springboard for those changing the trajectory of intellectual and cultural life in New York in the 1950s, all the while laying the cornerstone for the blossoming of Zen practice in America that was just around the corner.

DAISETZ TEITARO SUZUKI'S COLUMBIA UNIVERSITY SEMINAR LECTURES, 1952–1953

I

First we will see what Zen is from the etymological point of view. Its scholastic name in Sanskrit is *buddhahṛdaya,* "The Doctrine of the Buddha Heart." Popularly, the Japanese term "Zen" is generally used because the Japanese introduced this form of Buddhism to the West. Zen is shortened from *zenna,* the Japanese transliteration of the Chinese transliteration, *channa,* of Sanskrit *dhyāna,* literally "meditation" or "contemplation."[i] The Sanskrit root is *dhī,* "to perceive," "to reflect upon," "to fix the mind upon," while *dhī* may have some etymological connection with *dhṛ,* "to hold," "to keep," "to maintain." When used in a religious sense the definition usually given is "profound or abstract religious meditation." "Abstract" is really not correct, however, for in profound meditation on one special subject the meditator becomes identical, practically speaking, with the subject; and the result is concrete, rather than abstract.

In general, the Buddhist distinguishes four stages of this *dhyāna* as meditation:

---

i. Actually, *dhyāna* is not precisely meditation, but we may take one as roughly corresponding to the other. It is more nearly mental concentration, or discipline in tranquilization; my discussions include: IZ, 96, 100; EZB 2, 305 [283]; SZ, 38; four *dhyāna:* SLS, 367; as interpreted by Huineng: EZB 3, 31[15]; ZB, 167, 179.

1. Freeing the mind of sense impressions, particularly by meditation on the transiency or the becoming aspect of things, their impermanence. Reason may have a part here and also general observation of nature and life.
2. Concentration on one point, bringing emotional joy or ease. Intellect is still present.
3. Serenity replaces emotion, though joy remains, and concentration deepens. Intellect is replaced by intuition, nondiscrimination, suchness.
4. Serenity matures to perfect tranquility of mind, equanimity of heart. Wisdom, understanding, *prajñā*-intuition, totality are present.

These divisions are only convenient distinctions, with no sharp definition between. It is not possible to say where one stage ends or another begins. The concentrated state of mind is difficult to attain, but when the meditation stage is fully reached the mind feels more at home with itself and joy comes. When the emotion of joy is put away, intellectual tranquility is reached. But to be conscious of tranquility is to fail to attain it completely. The fourth stage is perfect lucidity and *dhyāna* itself. But Zen is not here.

The Buddhist also distinguishes eight *mokṣa,* methods of liberation or emancipation from purity as well as from impurity.[1] Attachment is the root of all our troubles, and nothing is pure or beautiful when analyzed—flowers, animals, humans all die and decay. The last stage of emancipation is the state of extinction, where everything is utterly analyzed away and no attachment whatever remains. But again, Zen is not here.

Samādhi, a troublesome term that will be discussed later on, is never really defined by scholars, though the Chinese, especially, tried hard to understand it. The seven different Chinese synonyms they gave it show finally where *samādhi* differs from Zen.[ii/2] These could actually be increased to any number, for *samādhi* is predicable in various ways. Though all are desirable, Zen is none of these things, the essence of Zen is not here. When these are all understood, however, the first step in the understanding of Zen has been carried out.

As for philosophy and the philosophy of Zen, Zen is not philosophical, and to talk of the philosophy of Zen seems to talk of what Zen is not. In a sense Zen is antiphilosophical, Zen has nothing to do with philosophy. However, where human life is concerned, Zen is concerned, and here Zen has no objection to philosophy. But it must be remembered that when we finish philosophical Zen, Zen itself remains; Zen is much more than philosophizing.

As Zen is not a philosophy in the general sense, it is not a religion as the term is ordinarily understood. Zen is an experience and, it being an experience, both philosophy and religion for Zen have to be based on this experience.[iii]

Without a philosophical basis we can know nothing of Zen, but philosophy alone is not Zen experience. Philosophy alone is in another sphere of human activity; it has nothing to do with experience in Zen. No matter how subtle the philosophy may be, it is only empty talk when experience itself is not present. If the philosopher is content with empty talk, that is all right and Zen has nothing more to say, but why not connect philosophy with life itself? The difference between philosophy and the philosophy of Zen is that the latter can only be based on experience; it can never be just intellection in abstract terms.

ii. These were listed and discussed briefly, as were the eight *mokṣa*, but I failed in each case to get enough down accurately to include here. [ET]

iii. It may be of use to insert here the present writer's definition, or understanding, of religion: the investigation, study, and experience of reality. In this sense of religion Zen is, of course, a religion par excellence. [ET]

The philosophy of Zen always has in mind the source from which it comes. In Christianity there is a difference between theology and philosophy, the former having its basis in faith. While Zen has no such God context as Christianity does, it may come to God in a different way. Its philosophy is analogous to Christian theology, for experience and faith correspond here to some extent. Christian faith is considered to come from outside ordinary experience and to be impossible to trace to intellect or the senses. But Zen thinkers believe faith must be a kind of experience, or it lacks certainty for them; one comes to be absolutely certain where he is walking, not uncertain. This is the kind of experience on which the philosophy of Zen is built. Philosophy and the philosophy of Zen have the same problems, one being reality as it actually is. Self in Zen's understanding of the term is reality and reality is the self, psychologically and metaphysically. When one is understood, the other will be understood as well.

When Zen had its beginning in India, all Indians were wanting to be liberated from the cycle of birth and death. The question of emancipation from birth-and-death—it is perhaps better as a single hyphenated term—moving into the whatness of self, *ātman*, was the beginning of Buddha's search. He thought that if he could take hold of *ātman* he would learn what *ātman* was and thus understand becoming and being, birth-and-death. If he could take hold of *ātman* he believed the central problem of escape from the round of birth-and-death would be all but solved.

In the beginning all Indian philosophers hypothesized *ātman* as something corresponding to an object graspable by the hand, or to an intellectual postulate. Then Buddha experienced *ātman*; and when he did he found *ātman* to be neither of these things—neither an object of sense nor an intellectual concept. But we have to use terms when we talk. It is impossible not to make *ātman* a kind of concept when we speak of it, but the experience is something else; and it is very difficult indeed to give expression to the experience that is enlightenment. It is necessary instead to make the experience possible, for it is from this experience that the philosophy of Zen comes and Zen itself comes.

Enlightenment is the basis of all Buddhist teachings, regardless of their date, both Hīnayāna and Mahāyāna, the "small and great vehicles." Later Buddhists thought that the earlier teaching was not large enough to carry all beings across the stream of *saṃsāra* or birth-and-death. Since all sentient and nonsentient beings are destined finally to attain enlightenment, the "great vehicle" claims to be better than the "small" one. But both Hīnayāna and Mahāyāna have enlightenment as their foundation, for the word "buddha" means "enlightened one," and Buddhism is necessarily first of all the teaching of enlightenment. Enlightenment has continued to be the most important element, as it was when it happened to Buddha, for Buddha was of course not Buddha until he was enlightened. It was by this experience that Gautama Siddhārtha became a buddha, an enlightened one. To understand Buddhism we have to be familiar with what enlightenment is; and when enlightenment is known, all other teachings whatever may be **negated**. Enlightenment is thus to be taken as the one thing that must be understood well and thoroughly.

The understanding of Zen and Zen philosophy begins, then, with an understanding of the enlightenment experience of Gautama Siddhārtha. According to Indian belief this buddha, like those who had preceded him, was a man who sought awareness for himself—through discipline in innumerable lives for an infinite number of *kalpas*—that he might help to awareness, or enlightenment, "all beings," *sarvasattva,* the Buddhist technical term that means "all that is," "all that exists," and that includes everything both sentient and nonsentient: every human, every animal, every plant, every river, every rock, every mountain, every component of this page and the ink upon it, every atom of the cosmos.

Gautama, like other Indians of his day, sought to free himself from the cycle of birth-and-death; he was unlike the others, however, in failing to find satisfaction in the orthodox methods of liberation. He left home at the age of nineteen or twenty-nine[iv] to study with Ālāra Kālāma and Uddaka Rāmaputta, two noted teachers of the orthodox Sāṃkhya school and of its dualistic interpretation of existence. He remained with them for two years and found that dualism could not give a satisfactory answer to his quest. Where there are two, one controls the other. Mutually controlling, conditioning, binding, restricting, there can never be any freedom in any sense. Buddha realized that it would be impossible for him to go through in this way the cycle of birth-and-death to emancipation, liberation, and freedom.

With us today freedom is more or less negative, for we take it to be freedom from.[v] With Buddha, however, it was positive. He wanted just to be free in himself, free in his own right, not free from any external bond whatsoever. This distinction is to be clearly made, I think. When we talk of "infinite" as opposed to "finite," we quite naturally tend to think "infinite" is a negative term, for we are bound by our senses. Infinite is a negation of things finite, but the very idea of things finite is based on the idea of the infinite. It is the positive idea of the infinite that makes us hunger to be free from finite things. When we try to become conscious of infinite, finite is already there and comes first into our consciousness. When we want to be free, we actually want emancipation from things finite. But we already have, unconsciously, the infinite in ourselves. The whole problem is to dig up this infinite that is so deeply buried at the base of consciousness, to rid ourselves of finite ideas in a conscious search for

iv. Historical facts as such will not be our concern in these lectures.

v. Freedom is treated at some length in my "Freedom of Knowledge in Chinese Buddhism," *Middle Way* 31, no. 1 (1956): 12–18; and see further below.

the infinite. But this finite so hems us in in every direction on every side that when we try to get into the infinite we find ourselves so hampered by finite ideas we are at a loss for the way to break through this fence—which causes all sorts of trouble.

When Buddha began to try, he began in the old traditional way, by making use of intellect. Intellect is double-edged, useful in its own sphere but harmful to one who does not wield it properly. Its main characteristic is its division of reality into two, subject and object, seer and seen. Always there must be two as long as intellection is concerned; intellect can never be master of itself, never free. Buddha found that intellect was not the thing that could unlock the cosmic riddle in which he was so deeply involved.

Next he turned to the ascetic practice of moral discipline, curbing one's egotistic impulses to make them work according to the ideal life. In our ordinary way of thinking the reason we cannot reach reality, or grasp truth itself, is that our ego impulses are so despotic we are subdued by them and our highest virtue is submerged under them. These ego impulses come, we generally conclude, from the assertion of our physical existence. We think that when this physical existence is controlled as fully as possible, this moral idea that we have may be able to assert itself. In those days they thought that weakening of the physical body gave moral discipline. If the body is made to obey what we think are moral ideas, we may be able to realize what we think is the highest good. This is the materialistic view, derived from senses that report the actual world in which we live to be material. But matter is not the final word; morals, like intellect, are on the relative plane and cannot lead to enlightenment. Like intellect, asceticism could only fail Buddha. When we think about this existence we are living now, we find that our daily lives are finally controlled by our own minds, our own ideas. The infinite does not exist to the physical senses; we can only experience through them the finite world. But we can impose the idea of the infinite over the material world and make the finite reveal itself in its fundamental aspect. Weakening of the body, however, does not necessarily weaken ego, for ego comes from our way of taking material existence as final.

Buddha became so weakened physically that he could not rise from his seat, but egotistic assertion was still present. He realized that he was becoming too devoid of strength to carry moral discipline on to the answer he sought. He realized that the body may die, but that another form of physical existence will follow as long as desire remains. When he found that merely weakening the body could only threaten his existence, without freeing him, he saw that the body is needed. The problem, therefore, is to continue this existence and yet to be free from this existence. This contradiction, this paradox, somehow must be solved by something that is free of, or behind, contradiction.

Of course, Buddha did not reason these things out at the time. He was still intellectually pursuing his end of ascetic discipline. This contradiction was still there because he was still on the plane of intellection, still dualistically involved in subject and object. How to continue existence, yet not be controlled by it? How to be in it, yet out of it? How to be free of the bondage of birth and death? How to grasp reality itself? As long as Buddha had this question in his mind, he could never come to its solution, for the question separated him from himself. The question stood externally before him; he could never solve the problem this way. Since the problem, the question, came out of his being, the solution must be in his being too.

While there is separation of question and questioner only an intellectual answer is possible, and such an answer inevitably ends in contradiction. This separating oneself as question and questioner, subject and object, is impossible in this kind of question. Intellect is clever enough to present us with this question of inquiry into inmost existence, but it is a cruel guide who leaves us with it, with no ability to take us to its bottom. Intellect does not know it separates its own work; it wants us to continue to rely on it as if it were the final thing. But the only way to answer the question is to go to the source from which the question came. Through intellect we first become aware, unconsciously, of something behind ordinary things; there is no question where the question has not been raised. But intellect can only bring it out. We have to go in beyond intellect for the answer. Due to the question we are able to go back, so intellect is that important. We have the question and we expect the answer from somewhere else, but the answer must be there where this question came from. Gautama, the person himself called Gautama, must be the answer. The question came out of him, it looks at it, it wants him to answer. Buddha's idea is this question; it cannot be separated from the questioner, or there can be no solution.

But how did the questioner come to ask the question? It is only possible to question when the questioner separates himself from reality, from himself. It is the privilege only of humans to question; there is no question for animals, who are themselves reality without standing away from it. At this point Zen teachers ask, "Who is the teacher of all the buddhas and patriarchs? Where do all these enlightened beings get the authority to teach?" Then the teachers answer their own question, "From dog and cat." Of course, this is a most profane answer from the religious point of view, quite sacrilegious to our ordinary understanding. But the trouble comes because we start to ask a question; we use the human privilege, we suffer, and we know animals are our teachers. Then we judge ourselves and are our own teachers after all. We know how to put ourselves out of reality and thereby torment ourselves. When we look back later and realize the way we came to ask all those questions, we are rather amused with ourselves, though it was a matter of life and death while we were going through the experience; for life is nothing but thought. It is our privilege to be tormented and blessed, happy and unhappy, not that of animals.

Separation is needed only to ask the question; then it keeps us from the solution. For the answer, the question, and the questioner must become one. When this oneness takes place, the answer comes, the question solves itself—this is the position taken by Buddhists. As long as we think the one who is bound is not the binder, we are tormented by separation. It is by meeting the binder that the question is answered, that the questioner ceases to be outside the question. When we return to the very beginning of things, before the very creation of the world, the thing is possible in one's own experience without logical abstraction. Logic is useful after the question is answered, but before this no answers given by intellect can be real answers. The Buddhist, therefore, strongly emphasizes the experience by which the answer comes. And Buddha's experience proves conclusively that it cannot be obtained by intellection or by moral discipline alone.

The question is really that of separation of subject and object. The real answer is found at the source, where question and questioner are the same. Ordinarily, question and answer are different things, but to the Zen philosopher questioning is answering. Instead of trying to see God outside of the questioner himself, where he can never be seen, the master asks the disciple, "Who are you?" If a master were asked, "Will Christ save us?" he would answer, "You are not yet saved." This is no answer from the ordinary point of view, but because one is not saved the question is asked. To "Is Buddha really enlightened?" and "What is enlightenment?" the master responds, "Where are *you* this very moment?"

And there was one who had a goose in a bottle; the goose grew, the bottle remained the same; the goose wanted to get out; how without breaking the bottle? We are in this existence; there is something in every one of us that wants to get out. The master called out, "O monk," and the monk answered at once, "Yes, Master, I am here." Then the master exclaimed, "There, the goose is out!" The binder is the releaser, rescuer, ourselves. We do not generally realize this, so we keep repeating the question. Here is the most practical side of Zen. Each of us has to find out that philosophizing never comes to an end, never helps anybody—except that today we like to argue about all these things, and thus it does help us in a way. And unless the question is asked no answer can be forthcoming.

This was the experience of Buddha. The answer came when he identified himself with the question. When he was no longer separated from himself, he experienced enlightenment. One day, as we have seen, he was too weak to stand. He thought, *If I die, who will solve this question?* He began to eat in order to be able to carry on his inquiries. But he had had two failures; now he did not know what to do—and the urge was stronger than ever. Neither of India's two ways had answered him, neither intellect nor moral discipline.

Now, unconsciously, he called upon being, being that had nothing that needed solving. Unconsciously, he poured his whole being into the question; he finally became the question itself, the undivided unknown. Not knowing what to do, his whole personality went into the question itself; his whole being and the question became one. He was the question; the question was himself. From this state of identity, *samādhi,* there emerged an outburst of consciousness. This is a strange thing; we can only say it takes place. It takes place because it takes place; it is just the fact. With the merging of question and questioner we may say there is no consciousness. We do not know how long this identification will last, an instant, an hour, perhaps days. Then the breaking out of enlightenment takes place.

Each of us has to see in himself how this really takes place. Of course, it raises all kinds of questions from the external point of view. How does this enlightenment come out of this identification or unconsciousness? The fact is that this comes out of what may be called the cosmic unconscious, where there is no separation of question and questioner. This rising of the unconscious may be thought a kind of memory or recollection, but really it is not.

Now Buddha was in this state of being pushed into the last ditch, and he did not know how to get out of it. *Samādhi,* as we have seen, is the name of this state of mind where there is no seeking. And Buddha did not know where to seek, he was just lost; there was no seeking in any form and no moral discipline. He simply did not know what to do—this is really what is known as *samādhi.*[vi]

Yogins try to get into this state of mental equilibrium, indifference, tranquility, uniformity, oneness, sameness, no duality, no dualistic thoughts, but ordinary yogins try to induce this state of mind artificially. When the mind is so concentrated on one thing—such as crystal gazing, looking at the first letter of the alphabet, and so on—when concentration comes to this point where all other thoughts are successfully discarded, this one single object remains; and when this single object vanishes from consciousness, a verging on unconsciousness takes place. Psychologically speaking, consciousness is so clean swept that nothing is left.

In Buddha's case, however, his attaining *samādhi* was not the result of artificial experience. He was simply cornered into this hole. He was just pushed into it, through no artificial way of coming to this point, by his desire to go beyond this existence, to take things back before the division into object and subject, by his urge, which he felt so strongly, to go beyond birth-and-death. He was strongly urged and was not able to satisfy his urge. It was impossible for him to go forward, to go back, or to stay where he was. The result was

vi. But in Buddhism *dhyāna* is the process that matures in its final stage into *samādhi,* the unity of subject and object, literally, becoming completely collected or unified. For a further comparison of *dhyāna* and *samādhi* see EZB 1, 80–83 [70–71].

much the same state of mind as that artificially induced by ordinary yogins. But it should be emphasized that there was no predesign on Buddha's part, it just happened.[vii] If complete identification is present, as it was in Buddha's case, it will be real *samādhi* and lead to enlightenment. If the identification is not perfect, it is not real *samādhi* and it cannot lead anywhere, really.

When Buddha was in this state of mental equilibrium, *samādhi,* he happened to look up and see the morning star.

A sense experience of this kind may occur. Kyōgen, as we shall see, heard a pebble strike a bamboo, while Rakan Oshō saw the rising sun.[3] Some sense stimulus is needed, it seems, to wake the mind from the total unconsciousness of *samādhi.* This stimulus causes a wave, as it were, to be produced on the calm ocean. Just a little tremulation takes place, yet however little, this tremulation changes the whole phase of mind, of consciousness. This was experienced by Buddha—or so we are told. Whether it was historically true does not matter very much. It shows that later Buddhists experienced such things and thought them to have been in Buddha's experience by analogy. History, historical fact, does not matter very much in my opinion; something like it may be more true than factual history.

Buddha saw the morning star and the beam went into his eyes, then along his nerves to the center of consciousness and caused a ripple in the ocean of absolute tranquility.

When this happened, the whole balance was upset. "Upset" may not be a very good term. Awareness, psychologically, took place in him, and this solved all the doubts that had assailed him since his

---

vii. This kind of unconscious state of mind is also possible to attain by certain medicines (drugs). But one main difference is that such artificially induced states may not open into enlightenment experience. Just to be in this state of equilibrium is not enough. It is merely preliminary equipping, or necessary qualification. Preliminary things, not exactly preparations, may come up naturally, but they do not necessarily break out into enlightenment experience. It was quite natural in Buddha's case, and everything went on as it should go on.

search for emancipation was begun. This awareness intellectually interpreted, this identity of question and questioner, psychologically may be called awakening, awareness, or the breaking up of equilibrium. Intellectually it is the union or perfect identity of question and questioner, object and subject—the dichotomy is altogether wiped out. When there is this wiping out, most people like to think it brings in nothingness; but if nothingness is left, it stands against something that is not nothingness, and the dichotomy is still there, going on and on forever. This will never do.

So when all dichotomy vanishes, a certain connection or link—not a good term—a kind of linkage, which Buddha did not know before, between subject and object is now perceived. This world of multiplicities remains as it is, things are left as they are in the multiplicity of existence, yet unity is there and is experienced. "Unity," however, is not a good term, either; a certain old way of dualistic thinking is in it, for unity necessarily presupposes an original diversity. Rather, this multiplicity is seen in its sameness, its identity. One is many, many is one, but this one is not to be abstracted from many. The many are left as they are, yet one is there. You are you, I am I, yet you are I, I am you, we are not-two. When we talk of this kind of unity, we may think it is a kind of abstraction from all multiplicitous objects, for this is the ordinary way of intellection. But in this intuitive experience nothing like this takes place.

When Buddha attained this consciousness, he and the question altogether vanished. Something that is neither question nor questioner, yet at the same time is both question and questioner—this he intuited.

It is difficult to express in words. Words, developed since the first awakening of consciousness among humans, I suppose, are just meant to communicate what we get through our senses. The world of subject and object is the basis of all words, that is to say, our primary experience. Words are very useful in their own way, but we get attached to them and forget to understand critically the use of words. Words can only fail to express what is experienced inwardly, for words and concepts were invented to handle the senses. We make instruments out of words; we turn the whole of our sense experience into an instrument. But then we try to attain by means of this instrument something else, something beyond it. Life itself being analyzed intellectually, we use words to maintain this life instead of building into the valley, into the meaning of life itself. We do not walk for the sake of walking, but for health, a destination, and so on. When we live we do not live without aim, we do not just live. We live to attain something, to fulfill desires, and so on. Yet life itself, its significance, is never made the object of desire.

On returning to his monastery after a walk in the mountains, Changsha Jingcen (Chōsa Keishin) was once asked by his chief disciple, "Where have you been?"

Master: "In going I felt green grasses covering the mountain paths." He just felt those green grasses. "Coming back I tried to follow the falling flowers filling the walk."[4] He did not say anything about an object of going to a certain place, or about where he had been. His walk was altogether devoid of external aim; he just walked and enjoyed the walk.

We may say that this is more or less like an animal. Human life generally has an object to attain. We hurry on, we invent things to make us hurry, without living. So living becomes a slave to a certain objective wish to be obtained. And when this is obtained another is set up. We are harassed all our life, instead of enjoying every moment of our lives. So in their own respect words are very fine. But real enlightenment takes place when awareness takes place, by looking at the morning star, for example. When the beam strikes the sense organs, the nerves take them into the nerve center, then into something beyond not yet defined, the center of consciousness, whether defined or not.

Buddha was so absorbed in the enlightenment experience that he stayed in it for a week, according to the [?] Sutra.[5] This seems a rather long time; perhaps it was actually one or two days; it does not matter for present purposes. As the sutra describes it, he felt as if all the heavenly stars were reflecting the surface as the ocean expanded in every direction infinitely. All the stars were expanding too, as this world of multiplicities cast shadows or reflections in his consciousness.

This, we may say, was a state of perfect passivity in a way. When subject faces object, subject is always conscious of the subject himself. Here the subject is conscious of this meeting between subject and object, but the subject reflects on the ocean—calm, infinitely expanding—and in this there is no consciousness of activity on the part of Buddha. This state he experienced; and all those who have gone through this experience know it to be perfect passivity. Stars are there, ocean is there, separate though one, not-two. The subject is not conscious of looking at objects as separate from himself and from each other; they are separate, yet one. This peculiar state may, of course, take place in different ways with different people.[6]

It is true that pure experience conceptualized becomes ordinary experience. But Zen philosophers talk of pure experience, experience itself, that cannot be abstracted from ordinary experience. If it is abstracted it becomes a concept and we take it as ordinary experience. As I have said, this pure experience goes through other experiences, and we have to experience it while ordinary experiences are going on. When we ask how, we already abstract. Pure experience can never be grasped intellectually, for nothing is going on when we take it out. As it goes on it is functioning continuously; as it moves on, as we leave it, it is functioning, operating there. Zen philosophy starts from this pure experience that can only be experienced, understood, as it goes on, as it functions continuously. Modern man, having no pure experience, wants to intellectualize.

Ancient man just gave a straightforward expression or, rather, utterance to his own experience, and we naturally have to go back to it. When this pure experience is really understood—I hope it will be as we go on—all those questions and answers of monks and masters will become quite clear.

After his experience Buddha spent a week, according to legend, contemplating what he had realized. He knew it would be difficult for most men to understand his enlightenment and he wondered whether it would be better for him to remain in retirement, not to try to teach. When he showed no sign of rising from his seat, Brahma, the high god, became worried. If Buddha did not come out into the world of manyness to give this experience, or help all beings come to the realization of it, then all beings would not profit; and the experience could help neither Buddha nor all beings. So Brahma dramatically appeared to Buddha to ask him to come into this world of multiplicities and propagate the experience. Buddha answered: "I may follow your advice, but who will be able to understand me? What will be the use? It may just waste my energy." But Brahma repeatedly asked him to try to teach, for some mind might understand; and Buddha finally consented. This is dramatically told in the sutras; we can interpret it in our own way.[viii]

Buddha's enlightenment would not have been possible if Buddha had been all alone; an absolute being with no beings beside him is not possible. Enlightenment was only possible to Buddha because other beings exist. Actually, when Buddha was enlightened, the whole world was enlightened. We are never alone; in a way we are all together. On the relative plane we speak of myself and others. On the absolute plane myself is myself and everything else; "myself" includes everything. We are so used to a world of differentiation. As a result, when we pass beyond this realm we carry along the

viii. See EZB 1, 118–120 [110–111], with further references.

concepts of this world, of this differentiation—and there is confusion. Even a quite logically clear mind finds itself involved in differentiation.

You cannot have enlightenment all by yourself, for your existence is conditioned by the existence of others. In Buddhism we talk of man and environment, for each person always goes with his environment. This is a close relationship, and the statement made by Buddhists is quite true: environment changes the character of being, being influences environment. This influence is due to the fact that something is common to both; otherwise there would be no influence whatever. One can never be added to another one unless there is a mutual relationship between the two. Two ones in the same field can be united, adding takes place between two mutually related numbers; feet can be added to feet, but not to eggs or men. On account of this, one is always not-one as well, as I will try to make clear later.

Buddha's enlightenment has two phases: one to Buddha as an individual, the other to his fellow beings. Enlightenment is characteristically double-edged; in fact, enlightenment cannot be enlightenment unless it has these two sides or phases: self, individual, private; other, social or universal, public. Everything has these two aspects, everything is actually a contradiction or paradox. In enlightenment this is not a choice, for this is the beginning of the two things, before choice begins to make itself felt. In enlightenment when we have this we must have that too. If we just have one, somebody must be suffering for lack of it, for society is so closely knit. I have the whole thing; at the same time you have the whole thing too. I am different from you, you are different from me, yet at the same time we both have enlightenment. You can never be free without helping others to freedom, so there is no absolute freedom. Everything is bound together, there is no real freedom. As far as I affirm, I put my hand down; that is free will.

Individually, enlightenment is Buddha's own possession. But if it were just Buddha's own and could not be shared, Buddha could have it even as a private possession. As long as enlightenment is restricted to Buddha as a private possession, it is *prajñā*. Buddha's *prajñā* intuited this reality, but at the same time it belongs to others. He has broken through the bondage of birth-and-death and at the same time all beings, sentient and nonsentient, have attained emancipation. This characteristic attaches itself to enlightenment, or enlightenment has this characteristic.

The Shin school of Buddhism tells of the same experience. When Amida Buddha vowed to save all beings, he said he must get enlightenment himself, or he could not save others.[ix] But he made this condition: "If all beings do not attain enlightenment at the same time I do, may I not attain." Thus there is definite mutual relationship between his and all beings' attaining. But our mutual relationship is always so close that one attaining can never be had without the other. Buddha attains enlightenment, therefore all beings have already attained enlightenment and are in the Pure Land itself.

With further regard to his private enlightenment experience, three expressions of it by Buddha may be quoted. First, the *Dhammapada*, verses 153–154:

Thro' many a birth in Samsara wandered I,
Seeking but not finding, the builder of this house.
Sorrowful is repeated birth.
O house-builder! you are seen. You shall build no house again.
All your rafters are broken, your ridge-pole is shattered.

---

ix. For Shin Buddhism and Amida, or Amitābha, the "Buddha of Infinite Light," see my "Development of the Pure Land Doctrine in Buddhism," *Eastern Buddhist* 3 (1925): 285–326. According to the Larger *Sukhāvatī-vyūha*, Amida was a king in one of his former incarnations. Due to the sermons of the Buddha Lokeśvara[raja] he became a homeless *śramaṇa* and later realized buddhahood.

To dissolution goes the mind.
The end of craving have I attained.[x]

When Buddha sees the builder, he becomes the master, not the slave, of the builder and knows that the material house will not again be built. Material existence is in a state of complete dissolution; that is, relative existence, *saṃsāra,* is dissolved, and absolute emptiness results. When the mind attains this state, the end of thirst—the literal meaning of *taṇhā,* "craving"—comes and will in the relative sense stops.

Real Will, which has created this world and our wish for something deeper—our wish to be free, to obtain the ego, the Absolute, the infinite—can never be suppressed. In fact, will can in no sense be suppressed, for to will to suppress the will is will itself. The Buddhist never tries to suppress or annihilate will to obtain relative emptiness or nothingness; this is a false interpretation of Buddhism and especially of the Buddhist enlightenment experience. This is clearly shown by Buddha's own activity after he was enlightened. Rather, it is especially to be noted that will is to be enlightened, not to be put an end to. Of course, Will, with a capital W, is not will in the ordinary sense, or in Schopenhauer's meaning of "will to live," which is actually just will on the biological plane. It is Will in the deepest possible sense, Will that is identical with life itself and with the totality of one's being.

But this does not give enough insight into the content of enlightenment. Buddha has seen the builder and has created himself, not just of this material body but of the whole universe, of the cosmos. He has come face to face with the creator, the Christian godhead. A much more illuminating description appears in the other two passages. First I will quote *The Majjhima Nikāya, gāthā* or verse 26:

x. *Dhammapada,* trans. Nārada Thera (Colombo: Daily News Press, 1946), 26.

I have conquered and I know all,
I am enlightened quite by myself and have none as teacher.
There is no one that is the same as I in the whole world where
  there are many deities.
I am the one who is really worth,
I am the most supreme teacher.
I am the only one who is fully enlightened.
I am tranquillized.
I am now in Nirvana.[xi]

With this, of course, is to be compared the legend of the great illumination that took place in all the ten quarters of the world at Buddha's birth and the lion-roaring cry with which he made his entry into the world: "Above the heavens, below the heavens, I alone am the honored one!" Relatively speaking it was, of course, impossible for this infant to make any ejaculation. But from another point of view he really made it, and not only the Buddha. Every one of us and every one of the things we see and every conceivable thing in the objective world all make this declaration—this is true from the Zen point of view, which transcends our ordinary way of thinking. This is a very important point, and a very important point of view that can be obtained with proper discipline. The ability to get out of the realm of

xi. Vinaya, Mahāvagga, in I. B. Horner, *The Book of the Discipline (Vinaya-Pitaka)*, 6 vols. (London: H. Milford Oxford University Press, 1938), 4: 11–12; Robert Chalmers, *Further Dialogues of the Buddha*, Sacred Books of the Buddhists, Vol. V (London: H. Milford, 1926), 121. With this may be compared another *gāthā*, 353, from Nārada, *Dhammapada*, 58.

> I have conquered all, I know all, in all conditions of life I am free from taint,
> I have left all, and through the destruction of thirst I am free. Having by
> myself attained specific knowledge, to whom can I point as my teacher?

It is possible that the two verses come from the same original source.

conceptualization has to be developed out of ourselves; it cannot be taught. First it is necessary to realize that Buddha's experience was not unique in the sense of being the only one of its kind; it was uniquely his in a personal or private way, just as for every one of us. From the Zen point of view each particle of the universe, or cosmos, no less than he, can potentially say: "I alone am the honored one." It is only necessary for the self or the infinite within each of us and within each particle to be experienced or realized.

This absolute, infinite I has conquered all by a conquering that is knowing—this is the important thing. Relatively, there are the one who is conquered and the one who conquers; but in the absolute conquest, no conqueror, no vanquished. With this conquest, this kind of experience, "I know All" takes place. Here omniscience equals omnipotence; they are not different, though this kind of knowledge, being infinite, cannot be proved according to laws of finite knowledge. Absolute myself has no teacher. If a teacher taught, he could only teach knowledge that could be proved or disproved by logic, for logic is only relative intellection. No one is the same as this absolute I in the whole world. It all depends on the point of view with which one surveys the world, the relative world full of deities, demons, gods. All values except this absolute I are relative; nothing or something comes into existence externally, not something that comes out of the certain existence that is itself value. This is what Buddha has experienced.

"I am the most supreme teacher," this naturally follows. "I am tranquil"—in a sense that is as dynamic as static. Nirvāṇa is not to be understood as a vacuum's nothingness. The place where this absolute conqueror–absolute knower stands, this is Nirvāṇa. This passage is very eloquent and quite expressive of the state Buddha attained at the time of enlightenment. With it may be compared *Dhammapada* 179:

Him whose conquest (of passion) is not turned into defeat,
Whose conquest no one in the world approaches,
Him, the trackless Buddha of infinite range—
By what way will you lead him?[xii]

It is not a conquest of passion, but of the relative world of subject and object. These are altogether conquered; therefore there is no chance for this kind of conquest to be turned into defeat, as in the conquests of this world. Here there is no question of fighting or of a fighting conqueror. There is no passion and no chance for any passion to conquer him again. Radhakrishnan attempts to interpret this from the moral viewpoint, but if it is understood morally what follows has no sense whatever: there is no way to meet up with this trackless Buddha of infinite range.[xiii] If Buddha had left a track when he attained enlightenment, it would serve as a pointer; we could find the way to him, to enlightenment. But this being infinite range, no finite search, no reasoning way to take hold of the enlightenment experience will be possible. Infinite range cannot be reached by anything of finitude.

Being trackless, this circle has its center everywhere; it has no one center as a finite circle has. Being everywhere, this center can be traced everywhere—and nowhere. The center is right here where we are now. But as soon as we become aware of the center, it disappears. So how can you find the track that will lead you, or us, to the center? It cannot be traced by any road of our finite minds, or of anything finite. Our conceptualization, sense perception, sense experience—all are finite. All this is what the stanza tries to express.

---

xii. Nārada, *Dhammapada*, 31.

xiii. *Dhammapada*, trans. S. Radhakrishnan (London: Oxford University Press, 1950), 119. [RMJ]

When we, and probably mathematicians also, speak of 1 we have in mind the equation: $1 = 1/2 + 1/4 + 1/8 \cdots n$. How can we have this infinite series of numbers making the finite 1? It is because of this that we can say finite and infinite are one—and the trackless Buddha is here in this room in this limited space and time. The very place in which Buddha came out of his mother—it may be India, America, anywhere—we think of as limited by space and time. But this very moment, as I move this finger, is not limited, yet when we speak about it there is finger, there is body, and so on. When we speak of an experience the very experience is lost. But when the experience is *prajñā*-intuition we intuit; the line is not conceived intellectually, yet moving along with the line itself, we know where the line is. Buddha was born twenty-five centuries ago in space and time, a fact that can be understood historically. But at the same time we can compress, we can have him born here in this room every moment. What is finite is infinite. Buddha with a track becomes the trackless. Here is a creative force or event, not terminating with Buddha's birth in India, but going on every moment everywhere.

When this stanza is understood in this way, then we know how impotent in themselves are the formulas taught by most Buddhists: the Eightfold Path, the Twelvefold Chain of Causation, the Four Noble Truths, and so on, given by Buddha to his disciples after his experience. The earlier Buddhists, especially, thought that these moral injunctions exhaust Buddha's enlightenment, that nothing more is to be found in it. But when compared with the understanding or interpretation given above, these formulas lose all their power; they have nothing creative in them. When the end of logic has reached all ends, nothing comes out of them. They do not express or interpret the real meaning of the experience Buddha had.

In the historical sense the earlier records of Buddha's experience are the best; they are also closer to him linguistically. But we know now that the earlier writers were unable to free themselves from the older orthodox trends of thought. Indeed, Buddha himself could not transcend the orthodox trend in expression. Early Buddhists try to explain Buddha's enlightenment experience to suit their own way of interpreting final enlightenment, without being able to penetrate into it. Metaphysically and philosophically later Buddhists, growing more and more, can see more deeply into the experience Buddha had. Once the way is opened to look into reality in a certain way we can follow it deeper and deeper, or more and more deeply. As experiences grow, the experience of them can grow and deepen. As the experience of Buddha grew in the minds of his followers, it grew in its own way and developed infinitely. Of course, Buddha's enlightenment experience was fully as deep as any that have succeeded it, but the experience may deepen for us. The attempt to explain it to others, to make it clear to others, may serve to deepen it, or may be one way that it deepens.

II

The bondage of birth-and-death from which Buddha sought freedom comes from a false conception of *ātman*, self, ego. Ego is generally supposed to be a kind of separate entity, as if it had a real existence. We try, as the Indians did, to locate it. They argued: "Where is the self? In the middle of the body, in the upper part, in the eye, ear, limbs? Where is it?" Of course, this self is impossible to find, no matter how thoroughly the body is dissected. Nowadays we think self must be in the complicated system of nerves in the brain. But all these materialistic interpretations of self cannot make us experience the real ego. We know we cannot find it in the body or in psychological function, yet something urges us to think that self *is* and we are constantly haunted by the desire to find this "I." When we think we are finally coming upon it, it eludes us. When we search for "I" we find there is no integrating principle that holds together all the different bodily functions, physical, emotional, mental.

The sun has light, light comes from the sun. We make constant use of "I" and its emanations, yet we cannot locate it. Whatever we do or think is prefixed with this constantly recurring prevalent notion, "I"; it cannot be a phantom or a dream. Our constant wishing to return to it without being able to, this is what causes all sorts of trouble. "I" as Buddha first thought of it is separate, removed from the real I, self, ego.

The burden of I separated from the absolute I, felt with particular keenness in the West, is vividly shown in the Christina Rossetti poem that I will quote in full:

WHO SHALL DELIVER ME?

God strengthen me to bear myself,
That heaviest weight of all to bear,
Inalienable weight of care.
All others are outside myself;
I lock my door and bar them out,
The turmoil, tedium, gad-about.
I lock my door upon myself,
And bar them out; but who shall wall
Self from myself, most loathed of all?
If I could once lay down myself,
And start self-purged upon the race
That all must run! Death runs apace.
If I could set aside myself,
And start with lightened heart upon
The road by all men overgone!
God harden me against myself,
This coward with pathetic voice
Who craves for ease and rest and joys:
Myself, arch-traitor to myself;
My hollowest friend, my deadliest foe,
My clog whatever road I go.
Yet One there is can curb myself,

Can roll the strangling load from me,
Break off the yoke and set me free.[i]

Looking on her real self as a heavy burden, she wants to put it out, which she can never do. It weighs so heavily because she wants to keep her real self away from her. She need not ask God to help her bear herself, for if she realizes it is she herself she will feel no weight. Self is a real thing, and it being real, we can take hold of it, though not by seeking it intellectually. The solution can only come when question and questioner become one. While this identification is not realized, the real self will be inalienable and the heaviest weight. With the realization the weight will not decrease, but the burden of it will go. The elephant goes around carrying weight and does not complain; neither do any of the elements, the planets, the other heavenly bodies, or the Earth. The Earth would most earnestly pray for lightening if it once saw itself as separate from Itself. Emancipation consists in being liberated from this separated I, not from the real I. The latter is not realized by intellection, but by *prajñā*-intuition.

If a man carries such a heavy burden, why does he not throw it down? This is impossible, for even when cast away the burden is still there. A disciple said to a Zen master, "When I have cast away all my burden, I have nothing to carry on." The master replied, "Throw it down." Then the disciple asked, "When I have nothing, what am I to do?" "Carry it away." It is still on you, even when you think it is thrown down, until it can be carried joyfully. As long as she does not realize the burden is herself even God cannot help Christina Rossetti get away from it. Her whole feeling is quite natural as long as she

i. *The Poetical Works of Christina G. Rossetti* (Boston: Little, Brown, & Co.: 1900), I: 283–284.

thinks the burden was added to her by somebody else. Buddha first thought of it as foreign to himself, not as coming from within. As long as the burden stands against, it can only be a foe. The root of the trouble is the consciousness of I on the plane of relativity only. Due to intellect every one of us is suffering under it, from our inability to lay hands on the absolute I, which refuses to be shut out the door, yet fails to show itself as long as we are on the plane of subject and object—and which always refuses to allow being locked in. This we all have to solve by ourselves. Hostility makes the duality and the burden. Carrying the burden is, in fact, a human privilege, though we are quite unknowing sometimes where our dignity lies. Sometimes it seems to be a heavy price, but it is really worthwhile.

Thinking, intellect splits "I" into two parts, I and not-I or relative I. This split has tragic results on one hand; on the other, it makes us seek for the absolute, ultimate I. Without it there would be no opportunity for us to identify the burden with the real self, to come to know I am Buddha and Buddha is myself. The West seems to want to bear the burden, the East to get free of it. The result is the same from one point of view, for we can never be free of it, we have to carry it, but it is not felt when one knows he is identical with it. In Buddhism the principle of separation or discrimination is to be transcended. The main thing is to be free from intellect, which holds in itself the contradiction it is unable in itself to solve. The West is troubled by the burden, the East has more to say of enlightenment—there is a difference of temperament. We are all different, and this difference makes this world. Why? Why all the difference of fish in the same water? Why do they taste so different too? Sometimes we have to take things as they are because they are so.

Long before the birth of Buddha, Indians had the idea of *karma*, cause and effect. The world is as it is because of what it has been, because of what has preceded. If the cause can be known, the bondage of birth-and-death will be broken. In Christian terms, the question would be, "Why did God create the world?" In the human way of things, it would not be necessary for God to negate himself. Human life requires the assertion of one's being; this is not possible absolutely, but it does not go through the process of negation. But for God to know himself he has to separate himself from himself; otherwise, this knowing of himself is not possible. Why did he want to know himself? We don't know really. He may have different ways of doing things, going on with the process of knowing. Why did God want to create the world? Why did he not stay in himself and not negate himself? All the problems we have in this world come from his creating it, or our making him create it. What is the use of his knowing himself? What good can it do? What purpose can it serve?

These questions can never be answered while we are on the plane of relativity, yet with the awakening of human consciousness, we have come to desire to know ourselves—from this comes all our troubles. As a Zen teacher in the fifteenth century said, because of Buddha's birth he himself had had to make inquiries about all kinds of things leading into enlightenment; if Buddha had not been enlightened, there would have been no such trouble; we would all have gone along like dogs, for example, without bothering. Unmon (Yunmen), a master of the early Five Dynasties period, once said when he was commemorating Buddha's birthday: "If I had heard him make that highly self-assertive statement attributed to him at birth, I would have struck him down with one blow of my stick and let the dogs eat the corpse."[1] This is a most irreverent remark from one viewpoint, but it is characteristic of Zen. Zen is not so pious; it is quite outspoken. And when we really know what Buddha experienced and we experience the same thing we can say, "What nonsense he proclaimed, as if enlightenment were the most desirable thing to have," and so on. If man had remained ignorant, he would never have had any desire to know anything. The waking of consciousness is the eating of the fruit of the tree of knowledge—hence all the problems of this world.

When I said God wished to know himself, it is really us wishing to know ourselves. In fact, God is in us, not without. And all the questions we ask about God are really asked of ourselves. But when I say that man wants to know himself, it is not man in the ordinary sense. It is Man, capital M, the absolute self that transcends itself, the everyday self. When we inquire about this relative self, we miss inquiring about the absolute self that is behind the relative self. In language we have to make this distinction and put one on one side, the other on the other. We think we know this relative self very well, but one day we suddenly realize that we do not after all know ourselves, that myself is altogether unknown to me. We carry on with this physical body, as if we know him perfectly well, but something someday makes us inquire. Then he suddenly turns stranger. This realization that we know nothing about this stranger who is I makes us very uneasy and is at the bottom of all the uneasiness we generally feel. It is fundamental anxiety. As I do not know where this self comes from or whither it goes, it becomes all the more strange to me.

The rise of consciousness is really the root of the trouble. No animals or plants raise any questions, they just go on. They may go hungry, but they do not ask why; they just take it as something natural. The questioning comes with consciousness; the whole world comes into something quite different. We create this world with the awakening of consciousness. Without it the world has no meaning. Consciousness is not passive; it cannot be a mere onlooker. It wants to work itself out in the practical world. It wants to interview personally the asker of all these questions, the Person in the absolute sense. It is never satisfied with a mechanical postulate. Frequently when Zen monks get enlightenment they exclaim, "I see you," "you" being the builder as Buddha expressed it.

About sixty years ago in Japan there was a great Zen teacher who had been a Confucian when he was young.[2] But he was not satisfied with this talk of moral principles and so on. He wanted, instead, to see the teacher behind the doctrine, Confucius himself. Since Confucians do not teach in this way, he went to a Zen monastery and asked for instruction, that he might see Confucius himself. After some years of discipline, he had his realization and exclaimed, "How long it has been since I saw you!"

Another great Zen teacher, of the ninth century, was killed by a gang of robbers.[3] This bothered a Zen student a great deal. He thought that an enlightened man who had behaved well would have had a happy life and a tranquil death. But after some years of study this student came to his realization, saw this master, and cried out to him, "Oh, you are still alive!"[4] The fundamental question will be answered when this kind of personal interview takes place, and the relative self realizes the absolute self, though of course this does not mean that either has ever been a separate, independent entity. When we talk like this it is simply easier to express it this way. Actually, the absolute self is never out of sight of the relative self. The latter is apt to separate itself from the former, but the absolute comes along with the relative when it can. Once the relative self has this intuition of the self it is to be cultivated, for this intuitional experience leads into life itself and no gap will be left between intuition and life. The whole life is to be devoted to this discipline, that perfect identification may take place. This is where Buddha's *praṇidhāna* begins.

If this enlightenment experience goes deep, really into the root of existence, it is something like Buddha's experience. But ordinarily it does not penetrate so far and requires constant re-experience. In the usual Buddhist explanation, our ignorance is so strong that many years of training are needed to get rid of it. The human personality may be represented thus:

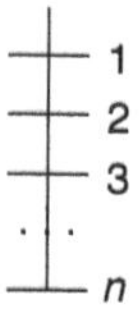

Perhaps the last line should be omitted, for there is really no base, no limit in infinity. But psychologically there are different layers, so the personality can be deepened with self-training. Actually there are no divisions; consciousness makes the beginning and the end. In itself relative consciousness has no meaning whatever unless absolute consciousness is behind it. Hence we really have here a beginningless beginning and an endless end. I don't think personality can ever purify itself completely—this is the endless end.[ii]

Before the rise of consciousness no individuality was possible. Since individuality is self-centered and self-assertive, we feel hostile to each other. As long as we live in this relative world there is no way to avoid this hostility, though this "I" in a practical way is against it. This separation, or hostility, is God separating himself to be himself. When self is asserted, other is also asserted, for self can never be by itself. We have altruistic impulses too. We try to correct ourselves, but we are too deeply involved in ordinary human affairs. When we have good, evil always comes along with it; this is life. As in the story of the two inseparable sisters, evil follows good as a shadow. According to the Indian myth the two are the goddess of fortune and the goddess of darkness.[5] We

ii. A philosopher says the beginningless beginning and the endless end are nothing and we exist from nothing to nothing. In the Middle Ages God took care of both nothings. Now consciousness has come in and wants to take care of itself; God is no more.

want Fortune alone, but Fortune herself refuses to go anywhere without her constant companion. In nature these things go on mechanically.

Absolute self, godhead, affirmation, good may be represented as A; not-A is then self, God, negation, evil. But A is never lost while going through affirmation and negation. Affirmation is negation, negation is affirmation, being is becoming, becoming is being. While negating itself A is ever longing to be back in itself. This is love, yearning for oneness. Despite the conflict of good and evil there is an undercurrent toward harmony or unification that is expressive of love, *karunā*. But contradiction makes up this life. Nature, on the other hand, has no malice, no evil intentions; she does all these things mechanically without conscious choice or decision. All this changes when man comes in; we read human thinking into nature, which has no such thing as cruelty or hate. We bring consciousness in and mere existence changes itself altogether, into meaningful existence.

Adam and Eve were innocent before they became conscious; then good and evil came in. We want to return to Paradise. Christ spoke of the need for childlikeness, and Wordsworth wrote of the child's closeness to immortality; in China a great man does not lose his child-heartedness. This wish to return to unconsciousness, ignorance, has, or may have, evil in it too. Psychologists call it infantilism, a mental disease. Biologically it may be a regression, it may go against evolution; but metaphysically we always want to go back consciously to the original state of unconsciousness. This does not mean going back in time sequence, though the past is actually never lost altogether. However, in my opinion psychologists are not deep-sighted enough when they say this is just a wish to escape conflict. Conflict will remain, and one will remain in the conflict, but it is possible to become not of the conflict.

A French existentialist says:[iii] "I remember having felt a great calm in reading Hegel in the impersonal setting of the Bibliothèque Nationale, in August 1940. But when I found myself again in the street, in my life, outside the system, under a real sky, the system was no longer any use to me: it was, under the pretext of the infinite, the consolations of death which it had offered me; and I still wanted to live in the midst of living men." Hegel's system from the theoretical point of view is so well-constructed that no loophole can be found in it anywhere, but it leaves no room for actualities, for the contingencies of this practical world.

In his discussion of Karl Jaspers, Blackham has this to say:

> Science is therefore the necessary ground and first stage of philosophy, but is not capable of achieving the unity and totality which reason cannot renounce. Science is concerned with determinate being and the philosopher beginning with science comes up against its limits, recognizes that he can neither think absolute being nor renounce the will to think it; he is forced to reflect: "it is thinkable that there may be an unthinkable." Philosophy cannot add anything to the objective knowledge of science. Philosophy begins with the philosopher's existence, with what he is, not with what he knows; he achieves and communicates not knowledge but himself. The unity and totality which philosophy recognizes that science can never achieve belong to the world in its transcendence (being-in-itself), to which the thinker has access only by means of his own transcendence (being-oneself) of the empirical world (being-there). The thinker participates in all three realms of being and by that means alone

iii. Simone de Beauvoir, *Pour un morale de l'ambiguité,* p. 221; quoted by H. J. Blackham, *Six Existentialist Thinkers* (London and New York: Routledge, 1951), p. 65, note 1 [Kindle edition].

> can approach the unity and totality to which his reason aspires, never by trying to reduce everything to the universally intelligible order of being-there. Nothing is more philosophical than science when it abjures metaphysics and is faithful in attention to its own empirical pursuits, for in its docility and persistence it is then near the authentic reality to which it aspires. But to say this is to shift the accent from science to the scientific worker, who is himself the authentic philosopher when he is going about his own business with understanding and purpose. Philosophy begins with science and cannot do without it, because there is no other world independent of the objective world which science explores. "Only one who has passionately given himself up to the exploration of the world can find access to philosophy." Philosophy which is dissociated from the world is lost.[iv]

Here Zen takes the side of experience, though Zen does not despise science. Science has its own ground and is "first stage of philosophy," but it cannot embrace totality; it can have no reason in a higher than ordinary sense. The philosopher "can never think absolute being, nor renounce the will to think it." Will cannot be stopped by intellectual limitations, for it knows there may be an unthinkable beyond. Philosophy begins with what the philosopher is, not with what he knows, scientifically or otherwise. "The thinker participates in all three realms of being"; by this means only can he reach what his being desires, not by reducing things to science. And what he desires to know is what he is. Philosophy cut off from the world is lost. The philosophers who do not dare to plunge themselves into the very abyss of emptiness simply look down into a bottom that is altogether unknown to them—and that they think, therefore, to be altogether

iv. Blackham, *Six Existentialist Thinkers*, 46–47.

unknowable.[v] This may be all right for philosophers. The Zen way of approaching the questions of being and of consciousness is shown below in the first *mondō,* which I will discuss rather fully.

The *mondō,* literally "questioning and answering," is a special feature that distinguishes Zen from all other forms of Buddhism and also, as far as I know, from all other religions. Zen expresses itself most characteristically in this *mondō.* It is not dialogue, it does not go along intellectual lines. It is just *mondō,* nothing else, just questioning and answering where just a kind of gesture or action often seems to be enough. In this connection the following passage from the *Laṅkāvatāra Sūtra* is of interest:

> Words are not known in all the Buddha-lands; words, Mahāmati, are an artificial creation. In some Buddha-lands ideas are indicated by looking steadily, in others by gestures, in still others by a frown, by the movement of the eyes, by laughing, by yawning, or by the clearing of the throat, or by recollection, or by trembling. Mahāmati, for instance, in the worlds of the Steady-Looking and in those of Exquisite Odours, and in the Buddha-land of Samantabhadra the Tathagata, Arhat, Fully-Enlightened One, the Bodhisattva-Mahāsattvas by steadily looking without a wink attain the recognition of all things as unborn and also various most excellent Samādhis. For this reason, Mahāmati, the validity of all things has nothing to do with the reality of words. It is observed, Mahāmati, even in this world that in the kingdom of such special beings as ants, bees, etc., they carry on their work without words.[vi]

---

v. Another part of the quotation from Blackham is also discussed in SZ, 200.

vi. Nanjō Bun'yū, ed., *Bonbun iri Ryōgakyō* [Sanskrit text] (Kyoto: Ōtani Daigaku, 1923), 105. See my translation, LS, 91–92.

A part of my commentary may be repeated here:

> If so we never need wonder at those Zen masters who merely raise a finger or utter an unintelligible cry in order to demonstrate the profoundest experience ever attainable by human consciousness. When there is nothing in my mind which can respond to or which is already awakened to take in what is flashed out from another mind, the latter may use the finest expression possible in our language, and yet my mind may remain perfectly blind to its truth. If, on the other hand, there is a chord of harmony between the two, a touch on either side will create a reverberation in the other.[vii]

In this respect Zen reminds us of animal life too. Animals do not use articulate language; they just cry, bark, crow, and so on. Zen corresponds to these peculiar ways of communicating, in a way, and from this we see that Zen is not intellectual at all, that Zen expresses itself in any possible way and through intellectual channels too, of course.

This *mondō* is not always carried on in the Zen or dharma hall, where sermons are frequently given. It is not necessarily related to such formal occasions, but it can take place anywhere the master and pupil meet, while they are working, and so on—on the farm or in the fields. The master will talk and work with the monks, and it is quite characteristic of Zen that the *mondō* often took place while they were engaged in labor to maintain the monastery. One begins with a question, the other answers. Either master or disciple may begin; and sometimes a *mondō* takes place between two masters, or two monks. It is short and epigrammatic. It is often quite enigmatic too, full of short laconic expressions that can be understood in many different ways, perhaps implying many different things. Puzzling as they are

---

vii. SLS, 107–108.

from the outside, short expressions can be rightly understood between those who understand, as I have said.

Rinzai (Linji, d. 867), a great Zen master in China and founder of the school that has his name, once was asked by a monk, "What was the idea, will, or intention of Bodhidharma's coming to China in the sixth century?"[6]

Bodhidharma is supposed to have gone into China in the sixth or seventh century of our era. He was the first patriarch of Zen in China. Now the question means this: According to Buddhist teachings everybody and everything, all beings, are in possession of buddha nature, truth, reality, self. If that is the case, what was the need for Bodhidharma to come from India to China to teach all beings that they are already in possession of it? What was the use? It was altogether unnecessary, his dangerous trip over the ocean. All these talks of ours are meaningless, really, but we like to do such talking—this is human life.

So the disciple asked why Bodhidharma came. This is one of the questions most frequently asked, especially among Zen followers in China. What is recorded in books does not necessarily record what actually took place in those days. The subjective attitude of the historian is not necessarily exact; even today certain errors still come in. Even in our courts, where every possible effort is made to be objective, the subjective comes in; we can never be just mechanical as long as we are human. How far to rely upon these books is another question. It is all right to use history as an intellectual exercise. That it objectively took place exactly as the records show—those historians I am afraid are not reading history quite right.

Superficially it seems a most innocent question. Yet it is quite important when we think of it; it is the most fundamental question—why are we here? What is the meaning of all these doings? What is the meaning of human existence? If God created the world, why do we go against him? If God created the world and the world goes according to his will, then how could the world go against God, even when one thinks we go against? God wanted it to go either way, for or against—how could this be possible? When we go against, something makes us contrite, we feel sinful, and so on. When he made the world he knew—if he was at all omniscient—that human beings were going to do things against him. Why create them? They do both bad and good. What is the meaning of *praṇidhāna,* prayers or vows?

All these questions are involved in the question of Bodhidharma's coming. It seems simple enough on the surface. Rinzai, the disciple's teacher, does not follow, however, the logical rules of logic; he has the same freedom God had when he created the world. Thus Rinzai's answer was just as free-minded as God himself: "If Bodhidharma had had any idea he would not be able to save even himself."

If Bodhidharma had any human desire when he came to China, if he had any such idea or intention, he could not save even himself. This was Rinzai's answer, or no-answer, to the question of his disciple. Another answer sometimes given to a similar question is: "Well, because you ask." If there is any answer at all, you are it. Instead of the answer coming out of you, you are it.

The disciple continues: "If Bodhidharma had no idea, how did the second patriarch get his answer?"

That is, what about the talk about passing the thing from one person to another, and so on? Bodhidharma is said to have transmitted his understanding to the second patriarch, the second to the third, and on down. If when Bodhidharma came to China he had no intention of propagating Buddhism, then how could anyone at all understand him and transmit the Self-consciousness or enlightenment or truth? If Bodhidharma came to China and he had no idea whatever, why was there a man called the second patriarch who claimed to understand the truth as experienced by Bodhidharma? If you understand it, it is easy enough, I suppose, to attain the truth.

When Buddha had an enlightenment experience and when Bodhidharma had an enlightenment experience, the two experiences were quite identical things. And when this identity is realized, we say that truth came from Buddha to Bodhidharma to everyone in China and the East and the world. When considered from this angle, transmission is made; the same experience has been experienced by, according to Buddhist terminology, Buddha, bodhisattvas, patriarchs, and so on. When this experience takes place, the one who experiences it becomes convinced of the experience being universal, absolute truth. This is called the transmission of this *dharma,* truth. But from another aspect there is no transmission whatever. There is no such thing at all in Zen; we just talk as if it were handed down from one to another. When enlightenment experience takes place, this is universal, fundamental, what everybody can experience and will experience. This conviction, that it is universal, comes along with the experience, the faith. But faith is also liable to be misunderstood.

Of course mystic experiences have occurred everywhere but are not expressed in the same terminology. My view is that the experience is fundamentally the same, that only the expressions of it are conditioned—by such things as the temperament and environment of the experiencer. These outward expressions are modified by circumstances, including all the past, and perhaps by racial psychology, natural environment, and all such things that help differentiate expressions of the experience, the experience itself being the same—Christian, Islamic, Hebrew, Confucian, Taoist, Buddhist, and the rest. Naturally, mind may have a great deal to do with obscuring the experience. The talker may mean one thing, the listener has his own background. When one speaks to people they try to understand according to their own "soil." The quality of the soil has a great deal to do with making a seed grow, or not grow. So the modern way of living has a great deal to do with making us not understand experiences that people have gone through. But Zen, as I will try to develop later on, has peculiar points not yet accessible to the West as far as I know. Zen may have its own limitations, backgrounds, and so on, but the West seems to be historically conditioned and not quite free, or not quite as free as Zen is, from certain restrictions.

Now the disciple's question to Rinzai is quite a natural one. If Bodhidharma had no special idea or desire to transmit *dharma* in coming to China, why the second patriarch? This question brings another: Why did we ever come to self-consciousness? Why did Adam and Eve eat the apple, in spite of God's warning? This is the very beginning of consciousness. Since we are conscious not only of ourselves but also of all the rest of creation, social consciousness starts here. Man makes use of such things as tools, we transform the world; we make use of these to change the world to suit certain projects we may have, all the result of consciousness, of personal relationships from social consciousness. "Why all this?"—that is the question of the disciple. All of these questions and answers seem harmless, but all of them have deep meaning.

Rinzai answered, "What is called 'attained' is really 'not-attained.' "

To attain is really not to attain, attaining is really not-attaining. When the second patriarch, or someone else, says he has not-truth, this having not-truth is having the truth. When we say things are, we mean things are not. Affirmation means negation. In the ordinary way, this answer by Rinzai is no answer at all. But just so it is an answer, for Zen is not to be handled in the ordinary way of things. God has no object, no purpose, no teleology. When he created the world there were no trees of knowledge, but trees of not-knowledge. Existence has no purpose; we are born purposely. Consciousness has no meaning. Who? What? How?—all these questions are nonsense, according to Rinzai.

The disciple questioned once more: "If there is no attainment of any kind, what does this not-attained mean?"

We quite readily understand the disciple's position. When Rinzai said there is no attainment whatever, there would have been no further question from the disciple if he had understood. He puts it off of himself, and therefore his question can never be answered. He has to answer himself, for the question comes out of himself, out of the place where there is really no question at all. He is heavily involved in logical contradiction. The meaning of reality reveals itself when it is revealed in its suchness. Until then the disciple has to go on questioning.

Rinzai comes down more nearly to the ordinary level to reply: "All your questionings are due to your mind ever running after things in all directions, without knowing where to stop itself. With all your wisdom, your cleverness, you are always in search of another head than the one you have. When you heard this, about Bodhidharma's attainment, if you had lighted your own light within, you would have had no question. You do not understand, you keep on questioning. If you would do as I have taught, you would find out that your mind and body are in no way different from those of Buddha, Bodhidharma, and the patriarchs. You would be in perfect peace yourself. This is called attaining the *dharma*."

This turning one's light within, not outside, may remind some of you of Christian experience, for Christians sometimes talk of the light going in, not out. But in fact there is no without in Zen, and no within. There is attainment, and by this attainment is expressed.

One path, one passage everybody walks, the one that God made for us to walk, according to Christians. There was revolt against Buddha while he was living, and because of it he is said to have gone down into hell.[7] If the world was created by God, is it possible for anything to go against him, to revolt? Or is this in the course of nature, a natural thing? But this is mixed up in the relative and absolute senses; going to hell is not bad from the dharma point of view. How is it possible on the ordinary plane? Bodhidharma never came to China, the second patriarch never went to India—on the absolute plane. During the Five Dynasties there was a monk traveling from one monastery to another. While he was making this long pilgrimage he fell over a stone and hurt his toe. It bled profusely and the bleeding made him realize what *dharma* is.[8] This is the same question we ask, the same question as the disciple's first.[9]

His third question is the same as asking, "When emptiness is all broken up, where can one safely stand?"[10] Well, emptiness itself is already where nobody finds anyplace to stand, and this emptiness is itself broken down; this makes it doubly difficult to get a place for rest. All these questions point in the same direction, and the answers will be all the same. An interesting thing is that Zen poses questions in this way. In the history of no other religion or philosophy have such questions been asked, especially this last one.

Another question practically comes to the same thing. A monk came to a monastery and said to the master, "I am a man so poverty-stricken, so empty, so poor; please give me something, please help me."

The master called him by name and the monk answered. Then the master said, "You have had so much fine liquor while you were in the village, yet you still claim you have never wet your lips." That is, you have plenty already, for when you say "emptiness" you already have something.[11]

When Rinzai was going around as an itinerant monk he was once walking toward a place called Hōrin. In his day, the T'ang dynasty, Zen was in its most prosperous condition, I suppose, when not only monks but also old ladies are mentioned. On his way to this monastery Rinzai happened to meet one of these old ladies. She asked where he was going.

Rinzai: "I am going to Hōrin."

Lady: "He is not at home."

Rinzai: "Where did he go?"

The lady walked away without answering.

Rinzai called her back. When she turned her head he said ["Who says he is away?"][12] This time nothing special is said, but just walking by, walking away—this is quite full of suggestions.

Another time Rinzai was going to visit a place called Myōke.[13] He was asked, "Old man, why are you going back and forth? What is the use? It profits nobody."

Rinzai: "That's right, it is just wearing out the sandals."

"What is the ultimate conclusion of all this?"

Rinzai: "This old fellow does not even know [the thread of a talk.]" We might say Rinzai means, "This old fellow does not even know Zen." This sounds innocent, but sometimes more takes place.

There was a strange-behaving, quite a queer-behaving Zen master. One day Rinzai was invited to dinner with him at a Zen devotee's house. Rinzai said, "Now it is said that one hair swallows the whole ocean and one seed of mustard contains the whole of Mt. Sumeru. Do you think this is a thing supernatural, or reality itself from the first?"

The other master upset the whole table; he kicked it down—he did not just push but kicked it down.

Rinzai: "How rough you are!"

"Here is there any rude one to talk about fineness, subtleness?"

Later Rinzai and he were again invited to dinner at another house. Rinzai asked, "What do you think of today's dinner in comparison with yesterday's?"

The master did the same thing again, [he] kicked the table down.

Rinzai: "This may be all right, you may be all right, perhaps, but how rough!"

"You are just a blind know-nothing fellow. Is there anything in Buddhism we can predicate as rough or fine?"[14] Reality itself transcends all these dichotomous predicates.

This may be all right in ordinary things, but kicking the table down seems to go a little too far. Such things are not just made the subject for intellectual discussion; something more is working behind these *mondō*, this behavior. The masters must be said not to be just working from any metaphysical or logical reasoning; they must have had something more than that—insight, intuition, just Zen faith in the Zen sense, not in the Western use of faith in contrast to knowing or to rationalization.

This strange master went about in the street ringing a bell and announcing; "If a man comes from brightness, I beat him away by brightness. If he comes from the dark side, I beat him away by the dark side. If he comes from the eight faces (double the four quarters, from all directions), I beat him back by means of the whirlwind. If he comes from the emptiness of sky (from a pure sky where there is nothing to take hold of) then I will beat him back with a flail." He went about like this. If a man comes with affirmation he meets with affirmation. If with negation he meets him with negation. If from all directions, an irregular way, he meets him with a whirlwind. If as a bolt from the blue, with a flail. There seems to be a certain sarcasm here, but it is not meant that way.

Rinzai, hearing of this master, sent an attendant to see him, to take hold of him, and say this, "If a man comes to you in no way you mention, what will you do?" All negatives are negated, all affirmatives are also negated. In this case see how he behaves, what he does.

The attendant did as he was told. He took hold of the master and asked what he would do if a man came from nowhere.

He pushed the attendant away and said, "Tomorrow a good dinner is to be given at Daihi-in Temple, I understand, to which all monks are invited."

When the attendant reported, Rinzai said, "Well, I have been suspecting him; now I see he is a real one."

I will give another example with "What is the idea of Bodhidharma coming from India?" This is the same as asking, "What is the essence of Buddhist teaching, of enlightenment?"

To this the master Zhaozhou replied, "The cypress tree in the courtyard." There was an evergreen tree growing in the courtyard, he looked at it.

Monk: "Don't try to tell me by means of objective method."

"No, I don't use objective method."

"If so, what is the quintessence of enlightenment?"

"The cypress tree in the courtyard."[15]

The monk is still in his metaphysical mind. So subject and object are separated in the monk's mind.[16]

When this *mondō* became well known, another master and disciple asked and answered in this way:

Second master [Fayan]: "Now I understand Zhaozhou has the cypress tree *mondō*. Is this really so?"[17]

[Huijiao said, "No." Fayan said, "Everyone who's been around says a monk asked him about the meaning of Chan and Zhaozhou said, 'The cypress tree in the yard'—how can you say no?" Huijiao said, "The late master really didn't say this; please don't slander him."]

[Chi]nese are not so much given to metaphysical speculation as the Indians. Confucianism has produced a practical system, not a metaphysical system. Laozi is quite metaphysical and mystical, but he does not develop into what may be called a system, as in India. China is always practical, and this practicality shows itself in Zen and in the *mondō*.

III

But my interpretation of the content of Buddha's enlightenment does not explain what enlightenment means. Relatively speaking, there are two things in Buddha's enlightenment: the psychological side, the way he felt, his conquest, his assertion of absolute will; and the epistemological, the noetic factor, omniscience. Omniscience does not mean knowledge of every particular thing, but basic, pure knowledge underlying all particular knowledge, pure experience underlying every particular experience—not the abstract, generalized experience that is conceptualization. In enlightenment, as we have seen, it is pure experience that runs through every particular experience and is not to be particularized.

This noetic aspect of enlightenment is *prajñā*, or *prajñā*-intuition—unity, totality. The Chinese say that *prajñā* is *dhyāna*, *dhyāna* is *prajñā*, they are not different—this is the Chinese Zen interpretation. According to Huineng's *Platform Sutra*, *prajñā* without *dhyāna* is not the real thing, and *dhyāna* without *prajñā* is not the real thing.[1] The ultimate stage of *dhyāna* is really *prajñā*; we cannot have one without the other. In life itself, according to the Chinese understanding, *prajñā* is *dhyāna*.[2] So Zen really means *dhyāna*; to be empty of the very process of *dhyāna* is *dhyāna*.

Of course, this *prajñā*-intuition is not the kind of intuition we generally speak of. Our ordinary intuitions are partial, not totalistic. *Prajñā*-intuition is of quite a different order, and we have no English term for it. Of intuition itself there are at least two kinds: sense intuition, always working on the relative plane, always limited to sense perception, always finite; operational intuition, always apprehending reality in its aspect of wholeness, of suchness, never limited by the senses or otherwise, always infinite in scope. *Prajñā*-intuition in a way is ordinary intuitions unified in a unification that has no limits. This existence of ours is not finite, it cannot be enclosed; but neither can totality ever be definitively grasped.[3]

Prajñā is complete in itself, without measure or extent; it is not concerned with space, time, karma, good, or bad. *Prajñā* has in itself nothing to be measured, though it can be penetrated to different degrees of depth by different men; divers of small ability cannot dive into the deeper beds of the ocean possible to those more skilled in diving. Intellect analyzes; it attempts to reduce everything to component parts, then it tries to understand each separately, and finally as parts added together. Analytic reasoning as a way of grasping reality is impossible, for analysis is always limited: analysis has to stop its work to see the result. It never takes in the totality of reality as it is, this being the function of *prajñā*. *Prajñā*-intuition grasps reality as it moves on eternally; it apprehends reality in its aspect of wholeness as it is, in its aspect of suchness, not in its parts, parts that can never actually equal the totality.

This wholeness of things is very elusive; we cannot say the whole ends here, or there. When we ordinarily speak of this wholeness, we think of things as having limits, but there are no limits in this comprehension by *prajñā*-intuition. Reality actually has no limitation. But to comprehend without limit something that the intellect cannot grasp is beyond intellect. Intellect, itself limited, can only limit itself when it tries to comprehend a thing. *Prajñā*, on the other hand, is "excessive." It takes a thing in its limitless aspect, without any bounds. *Prajñā*-intuition goes beyond sense perception—that of the five physical senses and the mind—to apprehend or intuit the infinite. *Prajñā* apprehends wholeness extending infinitely, yet *prajñā* can take this reality in. Most Buddhist scholars, especially the earlier, do not seem to understand what *prajñā* really means, and this is particularly true of Western scholars.

Buddhist philosophy rests, is based on, this *prajñā*-intuition, which is apprehension from the aspect of eternity, infinitely extending and eternally becoming. This expanding in space and going on to the end of time are both comprehended in *prajñā*-intuition, and both movements are two-directional: backward as well as forward; past as well as future. Of course backward-forward and past-future also include "here" and "now," to be taken up later in some detail. When *prajñā* is comprehended in this way, our own living is fused with this *prajñā*-intuition. Thus *prajñā*-intuition is not just intellectual understanding, it is an experience. This can be demonstrated from another point of view.

Buddhism has what is known as triple discipline: moral discipline; mental discipline, *dhyāna*, tranquilization, concentration of mind; *prajñā*-intuition. Of course, moral discipline is necessary as long as we are moral beings; mental discipline keeps our minds undisturbed selfishly and makes them better able to serve our ends. These two, however, are more or less negative and restraining. If they culminate it is in *prajñā*, in the intuitive grasp of things that characterizes the philosophy of Buddhist life. It becomes possible to apprehend the whole world in its state of suchness, reality, eternity. Suchness has no limiting concepts, like time or space; it cannot be understood intellectually. Suchness is apt to be understood statically, but it is really comprehension of things as they go on, dynamically. Intellect requires its own medium to work properly, the medium of negation in this case. By negating itself, reality is able to be understood. But *prajñā*-intuition ignores the medium of intellect; apprehending things as they are, as a whole, *prajñā*-intuition needs no medium of any kind.

The Noble Eightfold Path of Buddhism, [according to] *Dhammapada* 191, is as follows: right seeing, *sammādiṭṭhi*; right aspirations, *sammāsaṁkappo*; right speech, *sammāvācā;* right actions, *sammākammanto*; right living, *sammājīvo*; right exertion, *sammāvāyāmo*; right recollection, *sammāsati*; right meditation, *sammāsamādhi.*[4] "Right" is *sammā*, "rightful," "truthful," "ought to be so." Why is the beginning "seeing" and the end *samādhi*? According to my understanding, the enumeration of these eight items is not made in order of progress. It could begin with *samādhi* and end with seeing; it may be reversed all the way. The middle ones are not so essential from my point of view. *Samādhi* is used here instead of *dhyāna*, the outcome instead of the process of meditation. When *samādhi* is attained, for the first time we realize that what constitutes right seeing depends on *samādhi.* Actually, however, *sammāsamādhi* is a state of mind; it is not itself right seeing, or seeing things in the aspect of suchness. *Sammāsamādhi* is perfect identification, but this identification must break out into differentiation before we can really have right seeing. Though I say "before," there is no time sequence, no priority in time here. When we reach the real state of *samādhi* it is sure to break out into differentiation, which is right seeing.

When I see a flower in its real aspect of suchness, not only do I see the flower, but the flower also sees me. There must be mutual penetration, mutuality, of flower and self. The object is identified with the subject, the subject is identified with the object. When it is mutual, right identification, *sammāsamādhi,* takes place. Seeing objectively is not really right seeing. The identification must be mutual. With this mutual identification it is not possible to stay in a static state of *samādhi*, without movement. Identification must break forth into right seeing, that is, seeing things as they are. This breakout is *prajñā*-intuition, the basis of Buddhist philosophy. Always based on this *prajñā*-intuition, and always trying to see this *prajñā*-intuition in its purest way, it is possible to build up a real philosophy of Zen or of anything. Of course, Buddha's enlightenment experience was nothing but *prajñā*-intuition. Most scholars who try to explain Buddhism understand it as rational and thus fail to comprehend, really, what Buddhism teaches, or what it really ought to mean.

I have already spoken of *mondō* and of the *Laṅkāvatāra Sūtra* passage relating to the expressiveness of bodily or physical gestures and the like.[i] Here we are reminded that there are other means than words for communication, and it is such means that *prajñā*-intuition often uses. Sometimes just our glances, contracting the facial muscles, are enough to convey all that is behind. *Prajñā*-intuition is something like this. Just an ejaculation, without meaning in itself, is sometimes enough, something humans are not supposed to use when they are so far developed. Yet the Zen master goes back to original, primitive ways of communication, like those used by dogs, cats, and such animals. This cry, or ejaculation, is meant to cut off all the conceptual way of communicating. This developed in China, and this is why Zen is unique among religions—if Zen can be called a religion; it is certainly religious experience.

In this connection I have been asked whether *prajñā*-intuition implies clairvoyance. My answer is, "Absolutely no." In a sense you are there, I am here, clairvoyance may take place in a way, for I can see all the past and future. But there are no miraculous powers, as psychologists call them, in *prajñā*-intuition. Clairvoyance is not properly in Buddhism, though it may be a by-product in some cases by temperament, but without practical connection with Zen *prajñā*-intuition. Zen is not concerned with this clairvoyance; Zen is not

---

i. See my previous lecture, II, p. 50.

interested in this, though it may develop. There is a story about one of Buddha's disciples who made use of his supernatural powers to convert people to Buddhism. This was prohibited by Buddha when he learned of it.

I might say too that when Zen has this *prajñā*-intuition nothing is risked, nothing is endangered. When they embrace faith Western theologians go out into an unknown region where reason is of no help. They seem to understand, according to my way of thinking, that faith is against reason. When they make this choice, this decision means responsibility, and, as they do not know where they are going, there is a certain insecurity. They have a contrast between reason and faith, they do not know a bridge between reason and faith. For them everything in reason goes against faith, everything in faith against reason; faith cannot be reasoned out. Also, they talk about risking everything when they take something on faith. Zen followers object especially to this, for there is nothing to risk in Zen. In Zen faith is intuition, and intuition is faith. Will is enlightened, and on the path to which this enlightenment opens there is nothing to risk, nothing to endanger one who walks this road.

There exist speculative and practical reason, according to some thinkers. But this practical reason is not something that can be separated from the speculative, which is at the bottom of the practical; the practical cannot operate without it. If we try to reach *prajñā*-intuition, we cannot just follow the route of speculative reason—there is a leap, no doubt about it. But what makes speculative reason dissatisfied and want to transcend itself is no other than *prajñā*-intuition, so *prajñā*-intuition is at the base of speculative reason itself. Instead of going along the road paved by speculative reason and trying to reach faith or intuition, a road that is risky or not quite safe, we should reverse the order and try to see what works under this speculative reason, what makes it function. It is necessary to turn our steps backward. Speculative reason is not part of reality itself, so it has to come to a certain stop and hence is risky. But if we just turn back and look within we find intuition quietly lying there, making speculative reasoning possible.

In a recent discussion of Kierkegaard this risking comes in.[ii] Possibly reflecting on the future for himself, the author says: "The Incarnation is a paradox which can never be thought nor accepted by reason, and therefore the claim that it is the supreme truth imposes a limit on thought and throws the inquirer into a passion of uncertainty. If, by the grace of God, he sets reason and experience aside and joins himself to the paradox in the passion of faith, he is 'out upon the deep, over seventy thousand fathoms of water' and risks everything." The Incarnation is God becoming man. In Christianity human and divine natures do not mix.

This risking is something that escapes my understanding altogether. If he sets reason and experience aside and is led by God, why not let God take the risks? He is not following God yet; he contrives to leave faith out of speculative reasoning. In Zen experience this intuition is faith itself, so there is no object that is not known if we go rightly about it. Zen intuition, *prajñā*-intuition, takes reality in its totality, so there is no risk, no despair. This man speaks even of faithfulness. This idea of risking—really I do not understand it. Of course when theologians say they abandon reason they are actually still following reason.

Now in philosophy generally this enlightenment experience is considered to be something apart from our daily life and is so treated. Therefore, a philosopher may think out a deep system of thought without necessarily living that thought himself. What he has thought out and himself are two different things, set apart. But Zen has brought this enlightenment experience into our everyday affairs. What characterizes Zen is this fact, that this experience is not

ii. Blackham, *Six Existentialist Thinkers*, p. 4.

separate or apart from our everyday life. In Zen, philosophy and the one who contrives the system of thought are one. But it is difficult, indeed, to describe what this oneness is. In ordinary cases, here is a system of thought, and one tries to live up to it as something apart from the man himself. Then this thought goes ahead of the man; to identify himself with the thought he has to keep running after the thought all the time. But in Zen this thought is not the outcome of thinking. It comes out of one's enlightenment experience itself, and its foundation is thus in the person, not in thought separated from the person.

Since all Buddhist teachings start from Buddha's enlightenment experience, they come from his experience, not from his thinking. Zen has the experience, and Zen thinking comes out of the experience itself. Thus Zen living is thinking, and thinking is living. This fundamental thing that is enlightenment experience is very simple and direct; it can be grasped instantly, for it is not the result of gradual, slow, progressive thinking. Hence it is called intuition, prefaced by *prajñā*. It is simple, direct, instantaneous, sudden, unexpected; if it were a logical process, the result could be expected. But the thing flashes all through consciousness instantly, without going from one point to another, or through all points at once. The whole thing comes up instantly, without any regular process of thinking 1 to 2 to 3, and so on. It jumps, as it were, from zero to infinity, from infinity to zero. Thus zero is infinity, infinity is zero. Being intuition, it cannot be analyzed but is something fundamental beyond which we cannot go, [it being] beyond rationalization. This is what constitutes *prajñā*-intuition, the content of enlightenment experience. By it one gains what is most fundamental in an instant, the pure experience that goes through all particular experiences that are our daily life. When this fundamental experience is grasped, one lives it along with particular experiences without trying to apply it to each of them.

The experience is sudden, but after he is enlightened the Zen student still has to go on, psychologically, with many other stages to full maturation. As the enlightenment experience matures fully, as the process of maturing is completed, he does not just apply fundamental experience to each particular experience one by one, as certain principles learned in art or handiwork, for example, are then applied in particular cases. It is not that kind of maturing, not applying that formula to each particular experience, though it is something like it. Life is not to be divided into so many particular instants, but life goes through the particular as it goes on. Therefore, in maturing one cannot apply experience to case 1, then to case 2, etc. As life goes on without stopping at any particular thought moment, this consciousness of the experience, metaphysically, is all there. But as life is lived and as it goes on living, each moment I live my whole being; at each moment of speaking I am all there. But when consciousness tries to become conscious of this wholeness or totality, that very trying cuts living into two sections, and the real thing is lost. To go on living a whole life and yet to become conscious in an unconsciously conscious way—this is the way to maturity.

The thing is this: we live this absolute present, but at the same time there is no absolute present, for the present goes on.[iii] This going on lives into the future, and our life has no meaning without it. If this living on into the future is conceptualized, then this living is intellectually murdered. But how can we live without thinking of the future? This very moment is gone, and the coming moment is not yet come—we do not have to think of it. Actually, we live from one moment to another when we think of life this way. But when we actually live, we live from absolute moment to absolute moment. When the problem is put up to the philosopher, he has to analyze it and build up logic, dialectic, to explain this process or this

iii. To be discussed later.

experience. The philosopher must first have the experience, then present it in a way that is not rational, but that will satisfy our demand for reason in its absolute sense. As yet this has not been done.

I will give some stories from Zen history to help explain what I have tried to make intelligible to myself and to you too.

When Rakan Oshō (Luohan *heshang*) went to his teacher to be enlightened, his teacher struck him on his chest. This caused Rakan Oshō to come to realization, and he composed a verse full of colloquial expressions:

> It was in the seventh year of Xiantong [866 A.D.] that I for the first time took up the study of the Tao.
> Wherever I went I met words and did not understand them.
> A lump of doubt inside the mind was like a willow-basket.
> For three years, residing in the woods by the stream, I was altogether unhappy.
> When unexpectedly I happened to meet the Dharmarāja [Zen master] sitting on the rug,
> I advanced towards him earnestly asking him to dissolve my doubt.
> The master rose from the rug on which he sat deeply absorbed in meditation;
> He then baring his arm gave me a blow with his fist on my chest.
> This all of a sudden exploded my lump of doubt completely to pieces.
> Raising my head I for the first time perceived that the sun was circular.
> Since then I have been the happiest man in the world, with no fears, no worries;
> Day in day out, I pass my time in a most lively way.

Only I notice my inside filled with a sense of fullness and
satisfaction;
I do not go out any longer, hither and thither, with my begging
bowl for food.[iv/5]

This ball of doubt is a very special term. When you have some trouble that stays inside your body, it is something like a ball that goes around and around, without dissolving. It may be noted that monasteries are in quiet mountain spots, away from human habitation. This striking happens frequently in Zen. This verse shows that it is a very simple experience, but it goes on.

Kyōgen (C. Xiangyan Zhixian, ?–898) studied under Isan (Weishan Lingyou, 771–853).[v] When Isan saw this young man for the first time, he noticed at once that he had something that was quite promising and wanted to educate him to be a good master. Right away he questioned Kyōgen: "I will not make any inquiries about your learning or what you have memorized from the sutras. What I want you to tell me is this: when you have not yet come out of the body of your mother and when you have not had any discriminating consciousness, I would like to have you say a word (*yiju*)."

This is often asked without a preliminary remark. "Before you come to have existence as Kyōgen, before individual existence, when there is no-being, let me hear what you can say." This shows at once that Zen is not what is generally called religion; there is no piety, no worship, but just a practical question. Kyōgen could not answer, of course. He tried to several times after this, but each time Isan said,

iv. *The Transmission of the Lamp* (*Dentōroku*), fas. XI (T51, no. 2076, p. 288, c19–25). For a brief commentary see MCB, 34–5; D. T. Suzuki, "Eckhart and Buddhism," *Middle Way* 30 (1953): 52.

v. *The Transmission of the Lamp* (T51, no. 2076), fas. XI. And see SZ, 161.

"No." Finally Kyōgen asked Isan to explain it to him, but the latter refused, saying, "If I explain, that is my explanation; it has nothing to do with you." Kyōgen then went back to his room and got out all his notebooks to try to find something suitable to answer, but he could find no word, no phrase. Saying to himself that a painted piece of cake does not appease the hungry man, he burned all his notebooks and refused to study Buddhism anymore. He became an ordinary monk, not troubled anymore with spiritual questions. He left Isan and went to the tomb of a noted Zen master to take care of it. One day while he was cleaning the yard, he happened to sweep up a stone. It struck a bamboo and made a noise; this noise woke him up; he had his enlightenment experience and became aware of his unconscious consciousness that he had even before he was born. He went back to the monastery, burned incense, and expressed his gratitude to Isan: "Your great compassionate heart even goes beyond that of my own parents. If you had explained the thing to me, how could this experience have taken place?" And he composed a poem, the first two lines being:

> One blow has made me forget all my learning;
> There was no need for specific training and cultivation.[6]

No special description, no special cultivation is needed; each move I make, each act, each phase of my life, the ancient way is demonstrated, manifested, yet it is not just empty quietness. Wherever you go, you leave no steps, no track; it is a trackless track, as in *The Dhammapada*.[7] This "no track" in mortal terms is most highly praised by all who have mastered the path.

This is a good psychological study. You can see here how Kyōgen first tried to answer the question intellectually, by going through his notebooks, turning over all books on philosophy. But he could not find any answer in them. All intellectual queries availed not at all.

He wanted to be instructed by his teacher, but this would only have been the teacher's experience. You cannot get anything out of anybody but yourself. According to Whitehead, "Religion is the most personal affair between yourself and God."[8] When he could do nothing more, he abandoned the attempt, gave up, and went off to gain experience, he thought. But underneath he must have had an unconscious striving all the time, without its coming to the surface, in spite of his conscious way of thinking. This must have been maturing underneath his consciousness. Then his intuition like a match ignited dried grass. What was waiting in the unconscious for a chance to ignite exploded; then all was ablaze. Zen literature abounds in these interesting experiences.

We can see, therefore, that this experience goes along with our everyday experiences. Just sweeping the ground, a piece of stone striking, a man hearing the sound, but along with these experiences is something else that makes up the foundation of these experiences. It is not inside them; it is not particularized in that way; this unconscious experience diffuses and unconsciously soaks into our everyday experiences. Those particular experiences are infused with this basic experience; and certain Buddhists would say that it has always been in the unconscious, that it comes to the surface and at once is realized when the time is right or is mature. When one does not try, it comes up by itself. One feels that religious experience does not come out of oneself but from beyond: other power according to Buddhists, divine grace according to Christians. At the end of human efforts, when we come to the limit, a door opens from outside, not from our own conscious effort. This consciousness and unconsciousness have a great deal to do with it.

Of course, there is a contradiction here. If we do not consciously strive, we do not get anywhere. But when we are so intent on it, the very intensity hinders the unconscious thing in coming up. Each of us is the person himself doing this work. We are the observer and at the same time the one most intensely, personally concerned with it. That is the trouble.

Everyday experience is shown in this *mondō*:

A monk who later became a noted teacher once visited a Zen nunnery. He said to somebody, we are not told to whom, "If I find it suitable, or proper, I will stay here. Otherwise, I will overturn the chair"—that is, leave. He went into the meditation hall, where discussions generally take place, and the head nun came in.

Nun: "Do you come to enjoy the mountain, or for the sake of Buddhism?"

Monk: "I come for the sake of Buddhism."

Nun, after sitting down: "Where did you come from today?"

Monk: "From the *lukou* (entrance at the crossing)." This name has a connection with "mouth," so there is a play on words next.

Nun: "Why don't you shut up then?" There is nothing to talk about in Zen; if you want to talk, shut up first.

He could not answer. For the first time, he made bows to a master, or mistress.[9]

Here a later master comments: "Instead of this answer, I would have said, 'How could I be here then?' or 'How do I find myself here?' "[10] This enlightenment experience is beyond expression, since it is the oneness of question and questioner. If we say "man and thinker," here is a bifurcation, oneness is lost. And when oneness is lost there will be no enlightenment. Assertion implies negation. In explanation something must be expressed by mouth, by hand, etc. If nothing is to be said, if one is right in the midst of absolute oneness, nothing can be said—I am just here.

Realizing the nun's understanding was better than his, the monk in recognition of her superiority made bows to her and said, "What is this mountain?"—where the monastery was.

Nun: "No head is showing."

Monk: "Who is master of this mountain? Who is residing here?"

Nun: "Neither feminine nor masculine."

Monk, shouting: "Why do you not transform yourself?"

Nun: "I am not a spirit or a ghost. What transformations do you expect of me?"

These *mondō* sound quite innocent—where are you from, what is here, and so on. There are no religious abstractions, just ordinary conversation. But in these questionings and answerings, too short to be called dialogues, the great question is asked: What is this? or Whence comes my being? When the monk asked about the mountain, he was asking, "What is ultimate reality?" or something of the kind. When the nun replied, "No head is showing," she meant, "There is no limitation, there is nothing to be limited about." The top of the mountain can never be seen; it goes right up to the thirty-third hill, as Buddhists say. This answer is no answer, relatively speaking. Instead, it is absolute reality itself thrown out before this monk. Next he wanted to know the master of the mountain. When we talk of the Absolute, the intangible, there is nothing we can take hold of. But I am here, you are there, something must come out. He knows she, a nun, is master, or mistress. Hence he was really asking, "Who are you?" In her reply she was saying that reality has no sex, no masculine or feminine. Then he tried to call her down to the level of the relative, and she refused to be pulled down. After this he stayed at the monastery as gardener for three years.

Another example also has to do with a nun, this one on a pilgrimage, in about the ninth century. Like the monks, there must have been many nuns pilgrimaging from one monastery to another. The custom continued until the coming of the Communists, at least; I do not know how it is now. This nun came to a simple private shrine, as in modern China, kept by a priest, Gutei (C. Juzhi), not a Zen master, who had built his own little hut there.[11] She came in wearing the big head covering, a hat I suppose, that they generally wear when going around, and holding a stick or stock in her hand. He was meditating, and she went around his chair three times, the Indian way of paying one's respects to the presiding monk or priest.

Then she put the stick down and said, "If you say a word, I will take my hat off." This is another way of attacking the problem of reality, which is beyond words—yet we can't get into it without words. She said this three times, got no answer, and started to leave.

Then he said, "It is getting late, why not stay overnight?"

Nun: "If you could say a word, I would."

He could not, and she left. He thought, *I am a man, yet not a man*, and he wanted to go on a pilgrimage himself. That night, however, the mountain spirit said to him in a dream, "You just stay here. Someday a great master will come here and tell you what you need."

Ten days later the great teacher Heavenly Dragon (Tianlong, ninth century) visited his shrine in the expectation of spending the night, as was customary in those days, and then going on. The priest told him all about his experience with the nun and asked his instruction. The master held up one finger; the priest understood at once what this meant. Thus the priest was not just excited over his interview with the nun: he must have been seeking all the time, for otherwise just this interview would not have made his mind open.

From this time on the priest, now a master, just lifted one finger, without giving a sermon. When people came and asked the boy who stayed with him about his master, the boy just raised one finger like Gutei. One day he told the master about it, and when he raised the finger Gutei cut it off.[vi] The boy, we don't know how old he was, ran off crying. Gutei, calling him back, held up his finger. The boy tried to imitate the master, but his finger was not there; suddenly he understood what it meant.

---

vi. Of course, it is not possible to chop off a finger like this unless one is skilled, as a butcher for instance. The Chinese is so laconic. We aren't told how he managed it; he may have only hurt the finger.

When Gutei was dying, he said: "I have just one understanding from my teacher, that is, putting the finger up. And I have not been able to exhaust all the meaning attached to this finger, so full of deep meaning is it. There has been no finishing it."

But this was not the end, many later commentaries being written on this "one finger." One master remarked: "Even a fine feast will not be touched by a fully fed man." This is to say that just one finger may have something inexhaustible in it, but one may say that they need not make so much of it. However, Zen commentators generally do not try to explain the meaning of anything; they just make a kind of critical remark as a rule. Another [Xuansha] wrote: "If I see the master lift his finger, I will break it off." Another added: "What does Xuansha mean, anyway?"[12] That is, when you make an assertion, it goes along with a negation, a negation with an assertion, and so on without end. Another: "When Xuansha says that, does he approve or does he not approve? If he approves, why does he say he would break the finger off? If he disapproves, why did he say he could not exhaust the meaning of one finger all his life?"

This dilemma is common. If we say "This," it implies one of two things. When we take one, the other is left out, there is always this ambiguity; hence it is necessary to transcend both. Two things are left there, and one is there too. How settle it at once? What characterizes Zen is that it does not make this thing abstract.

But enlightenment actually stands upon two legs, *prajñā* and *karuṇā*, as we will see in some detail below. *Prajñā* is noetic and somewhat intellectual, while *karuṇā*, compassion, is conative. These two, *prajñā* and *karuṇā*, are the constituents, we might say, of Buddha's enlightenment. The Zen devotee is more along the line of *prajñā*. Other Buddhists, especially the Shin, emphasize strongly the *karuṇā* aspect of enlightenment. This Shin, or Pure Land, sect is actually a manifestation of *karuṇā*, while Zen comes from the *prajñā* aspect. In a way Hīnayāna Buddhism does not emphasize the *karuṇā* aspect as much as the *prajñā*, which strongly marks Hīnayāna too. But the Hīnayāna concept of *prajñā* is not so thoroughgoing as the Mahāyāna concept. Hīnayāna is more concerned with the relative aspect of existence, while Mahāyāna is rooted much more deeply, as we will see later.

When we talk about the identity of questioner with question, this may emphasize the *prajñā* aspect. But the one who realizes this identity is the questioner himself, the man himself. Self-identity is *prajñā*-intuition, but at the back of this *prajñā*-intuition man is the questioner. We have here enlightenment and there one who experiences enlightenment. Enlightenment belongs to the *prajñā* aspect, and the experience is the *karuṇā* aspect. Or, enlightenment is more metaphysical, and the experience is more psychological. We can say that *prajñā* and *karuṇā* constitute personality where thought and thinker are one. This personality experiences enlightenment, but this enlightenment is experienced in such a way that the one who experiences and the experience itself are not two. This is what is most difficult to understand. To understand it, the experience itself is needed. Just to rationalize this experience always ends in contradiction; it can never be solved as far as logic with language is concerned.

IV

What distinguishes Buddhism most from other religions is the notion of time. And this notion of time comes in especially in connection with this enlightenment experience. When Buddha lost himself in his question, he was no more, the question was no more. His mind was in a state of equilibrium, we may say. Now when this state of perfect identification, of self-identification, is reached, if we point it out and say, "There," there is no more there—it belongs to the past. This very moment, when this event—the beam of the star reaching the center of consciousness—takes place, is the absolute present, when there are no three divisions of periods or time, no past, present, future; in the experience itself we can't say before, now, after.

In this absolute moment, this timeless time, just one ripple, just one *nen*—the shortest possible division of time—one thought instant is waking, in this very moment, before we can say one ripple stirs, for when we say it stirs timelessness is over and time is begun. We use "before" and "after" here in a very confusing way. If it does not stir, it is not there; if we say it stirs, it is already gone. The moment between is the absolute present, and the moment of awareness of the absolute present is enlightenment, or *satori*, or *bodhi*. This use of language is really very confusing.

I have recently come to think more and more of using "absolute present" for this moment of awareness, instead of the statically fixed idea being connoted by "eternal now," "eternal existence," "tranquility," and other space-centered or ontological terms. Instead of expressing it in terms of space, it may be better to express it in terms of time. But actually absolute present includes both time and space, and it is not static. When I say "this very moment," it is pregnant with all the past and future, which are emerging from the absolute present; and it has a tendency to move in any direction. When it goes in one direction it is past, when in another it is future. There is no real present. The absolute present is the meeting of past and future, the center of all things, the very point where or when all creation starts, where or when God not exactly cried out, "Let there be light!" but where or when he was about to cry out—this moment is the absolute present. When he uttered the cry, all the past is concentrated there, all the future is ready to come out of it.

This absolute present is to be intuited, but when we say intuitively perceived, it is already too late. We ordinarily perceive in terms of space, since intellect, which belongs to the senses, always fragments; but *prajñā*, which is behind enlightenment experience, is totalistic—if there is such a word. Intellect takes in only part of the whole, but the totality of things, taken in by *prajñā*-intuition, is not finite. If it were finite, we would like to think of what is beyond. *Prajñā*-intuition is different in quality from sense intuition, as we know. *Prajñā*-intuition takes in all things infinitely expanding, infinitely stretching out. *Prajñā* indivisible is *satori*, the realization of *prajñā* by the individual is *satori*, and *satori* is the door by which we enter infinity. *Prajñā*-intuition, therefore, is open to the infinite, not closed. When I say "open to the infinite" this does not mean from point to point to infinity, but infinity as a whole, as one, united by *prajñā*—this cannot be overemphasized, for it is so foreign to the intellect-bound way of looking at things.

When this takes place, it is the same thing as intuiting the absolute present.

This infinity is not something negative. The infinite is not the finite negated; instead, the infinite is to be conceived as something positive. When I say "positive" you are apt to take it as limiting itself. It is hard to define. It is not to be grasped by means of process, it is not to be understood as an idea. For the infinite as it is, we will have to speak numerically later on, I'm afraid. The infinite as the object of *prajñā*-intuition is very difficult to express in words. Therefore, it is *prajñā*-intuition. What else can we say?

This existence as we have it here in this world is the intersection of finite and infinite:

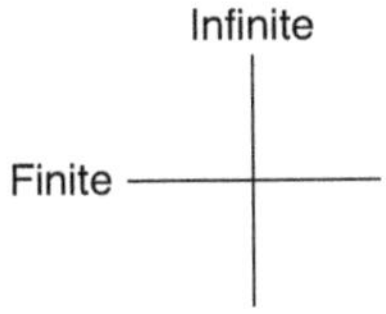

When we reflect on it, it turns into conceptualization. Where the lines cross there is no finite, no infinite. But when we reflect on it both are there; Indian philosophical systems try to explain this crossing point. The Indian mind is intellectual, it likes to use verbalism, so many words to explain just this *prajñā*-intuition that takes place in the absolute present. When Buddhism went to China, the Chinese mind was not satisfied with the Indian way. It wanted a more practical way, not coming out into concepts; it wanted to be this truth, this reality, in a most practical way and to have it in our daily life.

This is the reason the Zen *mondō* and *kōan* started. When it rains hard, the master may ask his disciple to stop the rain—of course nonsense unless one has chemical means, as today. This was the master's conundrum, just teasing, we may say. But the idea was not to be childish; great *prajñā*-intuition is behind it. The Chinese mind simply likes this way of demonstrating ultimate truth. In another *kōan*, a man over a precipice holding by his teeth to the limb of a tree, like a circus acrobat I suppose—his hands grasping nothing and his feet not touching ground—has a passerby ask him, "What is the teaching of Zen?" If he tries to speak, his mouth will open—this is somewhat like the dog with the bone on a bridge, except that here it is the man himself who will be coming down to earth. So he cannot open his mouth, but being kindhearted, he wants to answer. What can he do?[i]

Such things are not childish, I must emphasize, but they are peculiarly Chinese; they would probably not have been possible in India and Greece, for example. And as you know the *mondō*'s two or three questions and answers have no argument, no interchange of ideas. If any idea want[s] to develop it is cut short right away. We have seen that all kinds of things, including the stick, were used as a kind of contact in the attempt to demonstrate and thus experience.

Conceptually we may say "has come" or "will come," never "here now." The very moment we say, "It is here now," it is no more here. Yet we talk about "now" all the time; we have to start from something, even when we do not have it. In a way this start from what is not is no start. We are always going, or have always gone. No things are—this is quite important. When we begin to talk, thinking is carried on in time. As long as it is in time, our words will never convey the actual state of things as they are. When we become conscious of it, consciousness is also in time. When we try to reason about life, life is no more there. If we grasp it at all, it is conceptualized. Time itself cannot be caught in becoming. But life is a strange thing. As we live it as human beings we cannot help thinking and talking about it. In a way, human living is human thinking, for it so inevitably and inextricably enters into human living. If we live at all we must think.

i. See, further, IZ, 70 [62–63]; EZB 1, 275 [263]; ZB, 118; EZB 2, 217 [196].

This relationship between time and space is what constitutes this world, including human living. But space is really time, and time is really space—they are not two. Our eyes perceive, and this perception moves from one thing to another, which means space. But this means moving space is conceived and moving means here to there, past to future, so space is time. We conceive space as extended: —, while time moves on: |. The intersection, +, is where we are. Where or when—they are here indistinguishable—time and space cross is "here now." But when we say "here now" it is no more here. There can be no thought of time or of space without thinking of something moving on. This point of intersection can never be brought into our consciousness, which always moves on in time. When we say that question and questioner, object and subject, are one, this state can never be realized in time and space. In this actual world, there are always subject and object, past and future, time and space, and so on.

Some think this point of intersection, the absolute present, can never be experienced, but only postulated in our logic to enable us to carry on thinking. Where subject and object are no more, they say, it is impossible to experience. But as long as this "here now" is left to the logical way of explanation this "here now" will never be understood, and we will have to be questioning all the time. Of course, thinking inevitably has subject and object, hence this duality is inevitable in thinking and in everyday life. Yet we have to start from one that is not to be dualistically understood. We speak of time and space as if we were using two concepts to describe things as they move on in this world. But this is a great philosophical and religious question.

As long as we cannot go beyond thinking, dualistic reasoning, we can never experience enlightenment. Ordinarily, we say that because of thinking there is being, *cogito ergo sum.* This is all right as far as it goes, but unless something is there there can be no thinking. We are, therefore we think; we think, therefore we are—either will do. In fact, this thinking first brings out everything. Until we become conscious of things, things do not exist. However hard we try to escape ourselves, we are finally subjective; if we are not conscious, nothing will be in existence—for us. Just to be does not mean anything. Unless there is something of which we are conscious, there is no consciousness at all. The subjective is really the starting point of all things. For one to be, he must be thinking. When I think, the fact of being becomes known. To be is to be cognizant of. The whole world comes into existence when God takes cognizance of it, when he says, "It is good." Without divine apprehension or cognizance the world is nonexistent.

This is the same as saying that, if 1 is to believe [in itself], this 1 must become 2. 1 must divide itself into A and not-A, must negate itself, that is, must lose itself. But this losing, this negating does not have just a negative sense. Life is so imbued with the dualistic way of thinking that we try to put losing on the plane of the relative and ask how it is possible to have a negative and at the same time an affirmative, an affirmative and at the same time a negative, losing and not-losing. But when 1 is divided into 2, 1 is not lost; 1 is in 2. To be 1, that 1 must become conscious of itself, must be both subject and object, thus must be 2. Yet 1 retains its 1-ness in spite of this duality.

In this way self becomes conscious of self. When self is not divided, there is no self-consciousness whatever, for self-consciousness means separation, disintegration. Philosophy would insist that self-consciousness is experience, not a logical postulate. Experience is here and is primal, contradictory or not. "Here now," consciousness of the absolute world without losing one's identity, is a most strange experience from the ordinary viewpoint. When we try to experience it, those who are used just to the relative way of thinking say experience must be conscious of itself or it is not experience. There is no meaning in experience to animals, plants, and so on, though they experience all the time.

Philosophers and logicians are not experiencing enlightenment itself, yet at the back of their minds something makes them assume this experience and they have to talk as if they have it. But it is very difficult actually to realize there is such an experience without experiencing it. Philosophers ask for objective verification of mystic experience. However, this experience takes place before the division of object and subject, question and questioner, took place; Zen deals with things when object and subject have not yet separated themselves, when thinking has not yet come into existence. Thus no object and no objective verification are possible. Since there is no object, how can one verify objectively? Those who ask for objective proof try to put the experience on the ordinary plane, but it is not to be brought out into the world of relative experience. Mystics are quite right when they refuse to try to give so-called objective verification of their experiences.

Here now, the absolute present, becomes conscious of itself without losing itself. What is logically impossible takes place here. Before thought starts, rules of thought do not apply. Before thought starts, rules of thought are not yet in existence. When there is no thought, there are no rules of thought to apply; thus they are of no concern as far as this enlightenment experience is concerned. When there is no division of subject and object, no thought is possible. Therefore, what requires thought cannot apply to the time before the division took place.

When Buddhism talks of dealing with a world where subject and object have not separated themselves, this has nothing to do with time. And as far as Buddhist experience goes it has nothing to do with time. When they put it in a *mondō* and the language of time is used, the moment such things are uttered they are no more there.

Time begins with the division into subject and object; time prior to this division cannot be thought of. This is the question we all try to solve in our own way. We fail to arrive at a satisfactory solution, for we try to apply rules that cannot be applied. Self-consciousness is the starting point of time. We can speak of this crossing point, +, which is here now, as long as the lines cross. When the lines were not in existence, time and space did not exist; time and space cannot be applied to spaceless time or timeless space that has not yet made any division between subject and object. So any attempt to deal here with the two together, the two as one, is bound to fail. We must be on one side or the other.

This here now cannot be brought out into the field of intellection, for it is no more there if it is brought out. But no reasoning is possible without a postulate, and we postulate here and now without its actual existence as far as reason and intellect are concerned. When we say here or now, this world is already coming down onto this plane of relativity. When we begin to think we are already out of "here now" and down to the level of relativity. When we speak of self-consciousness, therefore, no consciousness in the ordinary sense is meant. Here it is used as a kind of analogy and is not to be understood in its psychological sense, where everything becomes relative. To be conscious and not-conscious, to be A and at the same time not-A, this is against the fundamental rules of ordinary thinking. But we must remember that logic itself is based on this contradiction. The measuring around too cannot measure itself: logic cannot measure its own limitations or falsehoods. Here something else is needed; we have to abandon logic altogether.

This self-consciousness, this identification of question and questioner, is its own judge; it does not rely on anybody else. It is not possible for logic to try to make this self-consciousness fall from its pedestal. The very foundation of thinking is where no thinking goes on. So in a way self-consciousness may be called pure consciousness, which is somewhat like pure experience. If I may say so, the experience starts, really, before we started. Then it tries to bring us into this timeless time, but this timelessness has to express itself in time by means of time. The experience brings us in through what I call *prajñā*-intuition, operational or actional intuition. Psychological experience it is, of course, but this psychology must go with metaphysics, or something that is not psychology results. I wonder if I can make it clear as I go on, at the end of these talks.

In enlightenment experience, question and questioner are identified, philosophy and philosopher are to be unified. In these things all religions have the same idea, I think. Christ wants one to pray in secret, in his closet, not showing how religious he is—in his own chamber, within himself, praying inwardly. We can say that questioning is becoming conscious of something, yet this something is not to be taken hold of, and the question is eternal. If one is conscious, one is able to immerse oneself in the world; if the world is taken in, then enlightenment will come out of it. Ordinary consciousness is knowing, knowing that is rather concerned with the past or present, but this knowing does not exhaust life. We realize the future by actually living into it—doing, creating, acting, which presupposes a world of multiplicities. This world of multiplicities in Buddhism is the occasion for *karuṇā,* absolute compassion, the conative aspect of enlightenment.

The noetic aspect, *prajñā,* consists in grasping this absolute present that never remains, that always moves on. By moving on, it creates this world of things, of multiplicities into which we are plunged. This absolute present is quite important, and this enlightenment experience is becoming conscious of the absolute present, which is the annihilation of time. Consciousness is time, and to be conscious of the absolute present turns itself into time. The enlightenment experience means the experiencing of contradiction, the grasping of timelessness in time, time in timelessness.

You may be thinking of the absolute present as something stationary, something that stays there. But the absolute present never remains the absolute present; it moves on because it is one. That is, its negation and affirmation are both there, no and yes are united. This bifurcation is our doing, acting, creating that is only possible in time. Living is the future realizing itself in the present. But the present is possible only when we actually live, when we actually act. There is a quotation by one of the Indian patriarchs that I often use:

The mind moveth with the ten thousand things:
Even when moving, it is serene.
Perceive its essence as it moveth on,
And neither joy nor sorrow there is.[ii/1]

When it moves it is living. When I catch it it is dead, not moving; science catches the dead, not the moving, the living. This moving is compared with the flowing of water: where this stream flows on there is movement. As mind becomes, you may grasp being, you may take hold of the fact that being is becoming. When this is understood, there is no fear, no anxiety, no care, no joy, no sorrow. But this does not mean actually no joy, happiness, or pain, nor does it mean nothingness. Life goes through the ten thousand conditions: joy, sorrow, and all such things. When it goes through one feels joy, sorrow, etc., and identification with these takes place. Scientifically seen there is joy, sorrow. As it moves on, there is no joy, no sorrow. When you experience this you are altogether *yū*. The experience of joy cannot be taken out and described in a systematic way; it is obscure and elusive when we want to catch it, or see it. When we say reality is there, it is there no more. The process is going through processing.

---

ii. Manura, the twenty-second patriarch; see EZB 1, 172 [159]. See below, chapter V.

To feel it is *yū*. This expresses in a most graphic way the essence of Zen philosophy. But it must be distinctly understood that no-joy and no-sorrow have nothing to do with nihilistic ideas. It does not mean turning into a piece of wood. It is, rather, the union of joy and sorrow that transcends both, and both together. It is not to be grasped, or expressed, in words.

The eternal now and the absolute present are the same, we may say. "Absolute present" is simply better, in my view, because it does not convey a static idea. The future is never here and the past is never lost—it also goes on. Then past changes into the world we have already lived. But this world is still there as we go on living into the future; history never ends, it always goes on into the future. But the past does not dictate the future, this we must remember, or this life is turned into a machine. Mechanically, the past may determine the future, but not life as we live it. As life is lived into the future it changes into the past; yet our work as creator goes on and the past can be changed. The psychoanalyst takes the past as determining the future, but in this case we do not live at all. We can remodel the past by changing our attitude toward it and making it the present. Intuition is always creative in one way or another. When *yū* is realized there is absolute freedom, then absolute joy.[2] All this is conceptualized as I speak, but we have to go on on this relative plane anyway; we cannot help it.

When we become conscious of such things, we know how to direct our course of life and live up to our potentialities, something that is impossible with most people and with animals. We are manufacturing our future as we go on creating all the time. This creation is original and creative each moment I live, never repetitious. This consciousness is the great difference. It is the great active, energetic agent, absolute consciousness. The enlightened and the unenlightened are not different as men, but awareness makes the difference. Ordinary men do not live a creative life at all in one sense. Though they create all the time, most people do not know how to appreciate. Animals, plants, and so on create in this ordinary way too.

Human dignity enters with knowledge, the whole world changes for the enlightened man, and he becomes more effective. When one is enlightened, he does not stand out from the rest of the world but embraces it. This one is no more there, for all the rest is there too. This very moment of enlightenment experience takes in the whole world and is totality. God has to deny himself to become conscious, but when he denies himself we can't say he is no more there. I would like to make this clear, but clear is no more there when I try; it is impossible to express what can't be expressed.

When we speak of death or birth we cut up the totality in which we are. We can say that there is no death, or that we live through death. There is no living either, but only the past continuing through the future. The individual just happens to be an individual. It is as if bubbles continually go up: when one disappears another comes. There is really no taking out or changing, but [something] only going on everywhere forever in the totality of related things. Death is only a concept that is actually going on here in this relative world. It is really impossible to express in language, but it may become somewhat clearer later on.

In both Hīnayāna and Mahāyāna there are three characteristics of what is called being or *dharma*—used here in the sense of reality—that show Buddhism to be different from other Indian teachings:

1. The constant change, physically speaking, that Buddhism calls the impermanence of things, or constant becoming.
2. Egolessness, or non-*ātman*, one of the things that distinguishes Buddhism from other religions.
3. Nirvāṇa, timelessness, we might say.

According to the *Dhammapada* and most other sutras, these three are apprehended by means of *prajñā*. Where we rationalize we come to understand that things are impermanent, that this causes unrest in the human mind, that nothing within or without is beyond change. But mere intellectual understanding, or reasoning, does not make us realize in ourselves that these things are so. Such understanding is conceptual, and the conceptual does not enter into the very core of our being; obviously we do not live according to real understanding of these concepts. While we are on this level, intellect may be clear enough to perceive the three [characteristics of being] quite readily, but life experiences do not go in the way of them. Mind and life go separate ways as long as perception is not that of *prajñā*; it is not *prajñā* living, only *dharma* living.

This first characteristic, the impermanence of things, also means egolessness. The second, ego, is ordinarily understood as something substantial that remains unchangeable permanently. If there is something called "ego" that goes through no changes whatever, that retains its own reality regardless of the passage of time, there will be no changing. But affirmation does not retain affirmation forever. When it tries to affirm itself, it negates. Negation means changing from one thing to another thing. If there is this constant change, we cannot have ego within us, that is, a personal soul which endures in spite of birth-and-death—and ego is assumed to be in existence in the external world, also. We may say that ego in this sense corresponds to God as God is ordinarily understood. When applied to the objective world, there is no God who retains existence outside the external world. The external world is constantly changing, so an unchangeable God is impossible in it. According to Buddhism, what does not change is nonego. When we talk of non-*ātman*, it means the nonexistence of being regardless of the change of the external world. Personally applied, it means there is no personal soul not subject to birth-and-death. All changes; therefore, there is no God who retains his existence personally, no soul who is not affected by this change of birth-and-death. Non-*ātman* is thus used in two senses.

When there is no God as we generally understand the word and when there is no soul—well, we like to live personally and when there is neither, Buddhists may be asked how constant change is possible of itself. Change is only possible if there is something not subject to change; this change must take place on something that is not subject to change.

What is this that is not subject to change? If God and the soul are denied, Buddhism finds itself in a contradiction difficult to get out of. But this Nirvāṇa is changing and not changing, this Nirvāṇa is changeless change. It goes on changing, yet it is not subject to this change. Yet Nirvāṇa is not something outside of this change. It changes, yet while changing it does not change—a contradiction our intellect cannot grasp. This notion of something not subject to change while changing is in all things. While we have a limited view we have to postulate something not subject to change and not apart from change itself.

But things go on changing from birthless birth to the end of time. In this case, we cannot have anything that does not change. We in a limited world talk of change and the changelessness outside it. But if change takes place endlessly and changelessly we cannot talk of something that does not change. If things go on infinitely without beginning or end we cannot talk of something that does not change. Being so limited, we cannot comprehend, as far as intellection is concerned, what is infinite. Intellect works with the limited. If we go beyond this field where intellect can work it is nonsense even to talk of permanence. So both permanence and impermanence refer to time.

But with timelessness as subject we have no room to admit the idea of permanence or of impermanence. Permanence assumes limitation, finiteness. When we go beyond this idea of finitude no such ideas as permanence or impermanence avail; we just cannot have any such ideas. The realm where neither come in is where Nirvāṇa is. Impermanence and nonego and Nirvāṇa—these three ideas condition one another, they are interrelated. Because of impermanence we have no ego, subjectively no psychological soul, objectively no God who stands against the created world. Where, or when, there are no such things we have Nirvāṇa.

Hence this Nirvāṇa is timelessness, we may say, something to which we can relegate no idea of either permanence or impermanence. This is the absolute present, the absolute now. To experience this that cannot be made a subject of intellectual discussion is what is needed. Intellect works where things are limited, where we can talk about time in space. If this time limit is broken through, intellect is of no avail and we have Nirvāṇa—and Nirvāṇa is the absolute present. When we say that this is where enlightenment is experienced, when we talk this way, we have already removed ourselves from this experience, but this is inevitable in our limited existence.

With further regard to the question and questioner becoming one, some questions always stand outside of the man who asks. Certain metaphysical, scientific questions always are beyond the questioner, standing outside of him. But some religious and spiritual questions are so vital that they come out of the person himself. For the most part philosophers and even religious people treat these as if they were outside the person and not concerning him. As long as they are so treated they can never be answered. To obtain emancipation from birth-and-death, in order that the most vital question may be answered, man must come back to the source from which the question came forth. This is no idle question to be treated as if it did not concern man at all. It actually concerns him in the most real sense possible. In many cases he puts himself into nothingness, as if he thinks nothingness will emancipate [him], but this is the intellectual way of understanding it, though he gets out of himself in the most common way. But to get really alone man must identify himself with the question. This man and his thought are one in this case. When thought is independent of him, it will never be his own, but it is something like a public possession. It must become his own in the most essential sense, not in the relative sense—like a book, a house, and so on. It must be possession in the absolute sense, that of identification. The thought must be the man, the man the thought.

When this takes place, this is the time when consciousness ceases to work—though this expression of it is not quite right. Consciousness does not stop its work, but this is the time—we have to use time expressions here, we cannot help it—consciousness is about to be itself. When it is itself consciousness limits itself. When it moves—a bad term—when consciousness starts to shape itself and be conscious of itself, this moment when consciousness is not itself, yet is about to be itself, this is the absolute present—when consciousness is not yet consciousness, that is, when subject and object have not yet separated as subject and object.

I do not know whether it is proper or not, but I like to say this: this consciousness is time and time is consciousness. When we have consciousness, time starts there. When we have no-consciousness we have no dualism. This is not no consciousness in the sense of going into a state of trance or temporarily losing consciousness, it is not that kind of no consciousness. Instead of no-consciousness, "general consciousness," "pure consciousness," or "zero consciousness" might be used. Consciousness when it starts is already 1, 2, 3, 4, . . .; it goes on in succession and the time element comes in. When I say "zero consciousness," this consciousness is the point where, or when, consciousness has not yet moved; that is, consciousness is in arriving, not actually there. To use "undifferentiated consciousness" would give the idea that consciousness is there, but it has not differentiated itself into consciousness. When we say "undifferentiated consciousness," all those things are implied. We must get out of the relative plane, but at the same time we cannot. Yet at the same time there are moments when this is experienced, when consciousness is zero.

Zero consciousness, that is, the absolute present, this is the time when dualism has not yet taken place, when man and his thought are not separate—enlightenment experience is here. In the beginning there was this separation. Christians say the world started from knowledge; Buddhists, from ignorance. We may think the two are quite opposed, but they are actually the same thing. Ignorance is not knowing, not understanding what zero consciousness is. And knowledge means that ignorance has already started its dualistic movement, that consciousness has begun its work. Thus ignorance and knowledge mean the same thing, though the words seem to contradict.

When consciousness has not yet started its work, that I call zero consciousness, and this zero consciousness is pure experience. This is what Buddhists have and what they call *wuxin* (Japanese *mushin,* literally "no-mind"); here is the Buddhist idea of *wunian* (*munen*), zero consciousness. In Sanskrit consciousness is *citta,* [??] means "no beginning," "no end."[3] Let us suppose consciousness to be represented by this line, extending infinitely in both directions: ——. It is cut into small pieces by time and 1, 2, 3, . . . start here: ++++. The smallest piece or division of time is called *nen* (or *nien* [*cittakṣaṇa*]) in Buddhist terminology. This *munen* means no *nen* is coming into birth, no *nen* is taking place yet.

Now this zero consciousness goes on with every number: 1, 2, 3 is actually 0 + 1, 0 + 2, 0 + 3, and so on. As we talk about it, this zero consciousness goes along with every division, each *nen* is accompanied by zero. So, $0 + 1 = 1$ does not change the relative relationship, but this relationship goes along with zero. This is something I would like to have you understand. We have to say this consciousness starts somewhere, but really it has no beginning, for it is not in the realm of biology, but in another realm. When we talk about *nen* we ordinarily think of something infinitely small, but my idea of *munen* is this: each moment of consciousness is lived by zero, and when this zero consciousness is consciously taken along with these moments of consciousness, that is *munen*. So *munen* is not separated from each moment of consciousness but goes along with each; yet as it goes on it does not go on.

When we talk about enlightenment experience, we may think it is something outside the flow of consciousness, but it is not that. Enlightenment experience goes along with all these particular moments of consciousness; they are all soaked thoroughly with zero consciousness. This *munen* is at the same time *nen*. When this is understood, Zen philosophy is grasped thoroughly.

We have to speak as if it had a start due to the limitations of language; we cannot start from a vacuum. Actually, however, being is nonbeing, nonbeing is being. Zero consciousness is zero consciousness, but zero consciousness is also in every particular conscious moment; it goes along with each—we cannot take it out and say, "Here is zero consciousness."

When we talk on the numbers—1, 2, 3, . . . —there are no such numbers independent of objects; numbers always go along with chairs, tables, and so on, numbers always go along with objects, though they are real, perhaps, as symbols. In the same way each moment of consciousness can be numbered, but this number itself does not exist. Something of the numerical is simply present when we talk about them. Of course, there is here no connection with the mathematical use of zero.

. . .-3 -2 -1 0 +1 +2 +3 . . . may also be expressed in this way:

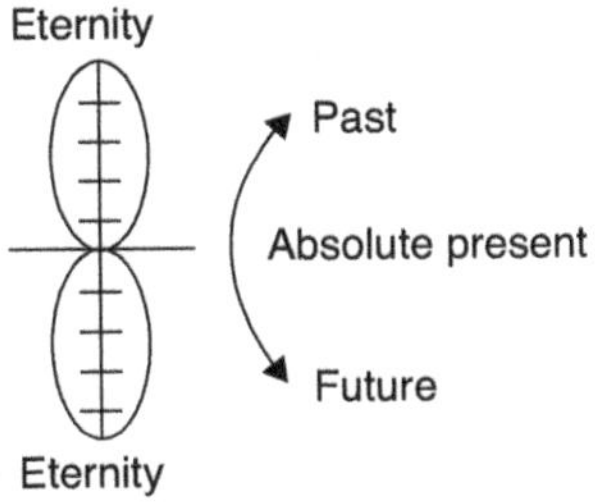

Zero is a definite point in mathematics, conceptually set up. I presume here that 1 is not just 1. These are regular numbers, yet at the same time they are zero—I don't know whether this use of zero is mathematically justified. We have this consciousness of *nen* going on, yet there is no rising of *nen:* this is zero consciousness, the absolute present. When we talk about time, it is generally represented by a vertical line. The trouble is that we have to say something, it has to be cut somewhere, while eternity has no ending.

The absolute present works in two ways. In the absolute moment all the past and future are here. This absolute present has come moving on from the past. Each moment is the absolute present and contains the past and future. Each moment is infinitely endowed with infinite possibilities: it has not exhausted itself. Consciousness works in the same way. This may be made a little clearer by reference to Eckhart. He speaks so much about this Now idea, for example:

> God is something that must transcend being. Anything which has being, date, or location does not belong to God, for he is above them all and although he is in all creatures, yet he is more than all of them.
>
> Some authorities maintain that the soul is in the emotions only but it is not so. Many great scholars make that error. The soul is whole and undivided, at once in the foot and the eye and

> every other member. Or take a section of time, it may be today or yesterday: the present Now-moment gathers all parts of time up into itself. That present Now in which God created the world is as near to this bit of time as any moment is and the Last Day is as near to it as yesterday.[iii]

This expresses what a Buddhist means by absolute now. I use Eckhart so that Buddha's experience will be made somewhat more intimate to you all.

God above them all, though in all creatures more than all—if there is a pantheistic idea here, one God outside is of the world, yet he puts himself in all things, yet he is more than all: there, but not they themselves; more, yet in, through, and so on, but not in the way a monotheistic God is. "God is neither being nor goodness. Goodness depends on being [limited being in this case], for if there were no being there would be no goodness, and thus being is purer than goodness. But God is neither good, better, nor best. To say that God is good is to falsify him as it would falsify the sun to call it dark."[iv] To say God is good is the same as saying he is bright. The sun is neither bright nor dark, God is neither good nor bad. It is very difficult to come to a final solution when morality enters. We cannot have good alone, we must always have evil with it. God is in both, yet is neither. Zero consciousness is neither 1-consciousness nor 2-consciousness, yet zero consciousness is in consciousness 1 and consciousness 2. This is what I like to emphasize.

Eckhart's use of will and thought is somewhat difficult and requires more explanation. Here is an example:

---

iii. Raymond Bernard Blakney, trs., *Meister Eckhart* (New York: Harper and Brothers, 1941), 218–9. [For all Eckhart quotations in these lectures see this translation. Several of these passages are also discussed in MCB. Suzuki cites page numbers for this edition.]

iv. Blakney, *Meister Eckhart*, 220.

> Willing, man conceives God in the garment of goodness. Thinking, man conceives God naked, stripped of both goodness and being. Goodness is a cloak under which he is hidden, and the will is content with God so clothed. If God were not good, my will would not want him. If one were to clothe his king in drab colors on the day of his coronation, his work would be badly done. Therefore I am not blessed by the fact of God's goodness. I shall never ask God to bless me out of his goodness, for he could not do it. I am blessed only by the fact that God can be known and that I can know him! Thus one authority says: "God's mind it is, on which all angelic being depends!" (p. 221)

Thought here is *prajñā.* Will is the starting of *praṇidhāna.* From the *prajñā* point of view, God is stripped of both goodness and being. If God were not good, my will, *praṇidhāna,* would not want him. I am only blessed by the fact that God can be known by *prajñā.*

> There is a difference between the soul's day and God's day but in the day most native to the soul, it perceives things from above all space and time, and finds them neither near nor far away. It is for this reason that I have said that in this day, all things are equal in rank. To say that God created the world yesterday or tomorrow would be foolishness, for God created the world and everything in it in the one present Now. Indeed, time that has been past for a thousand years is as present and near to God as the time that now is. The soul that lives in the present Now-moment is the soul in which the Father begets his only begotten Son and in that birth the soul is born again. It is still one birth, however often the soul is reborn in God, as the Father begets his only begotten Son.[v]

---

v. Blakney, *Meister Eckhart*, 214; 327, note 25(10), which cites as references Psalm 90:4; Augustine, *Confessions,* XI, 12–14; *Timaeus* 37.

There, you see Eckhart is quite explicit about it.

In this way Eckhart talks of God beyond time. Yesterday may mean thousands of years ago, or today, it does not matter. It is foolish to say beginning or ending in so many years. All was created in one present Now. Creation is taking place now, the past is as near as the present. The only begotten son is born when the Eternal Now is realized. Each time this is realized is the time the only begotten son is born. The idea of Christ is not just a historical event, but it is taking place everywhere, every day, every moment we realize this Now.

In another passage Eckhart talks about the soul that has, to use my term, thought and man united as one:

> that aristocratic agent of the soul, which ranks so high that it communes with God, face to face, as he is. This agent has nothing in common with anything else. It is unconscious of yesterday or the day before, and of tomorrow and the day after, for in eternity there is no yesterday nor any tomorrow, but only Now, as it was a thousand years ago and as it will be a thousand years hence, and is at this moment, and as it will be after death. This agent reaches God in his closet, or as the Scripture says: in him, above him and through him. "In him"—that is, in the Father. "Above him"—that is, above the Son. "Through him"—that is, through the Holy Spirit. (p. 153)

On such occasions the soul communes with God face to face. The man who has enlightenment experience is unconscious of yesterday, tomorrow, and so on, for in eternity there is no yesterday or tomorrow. I don't know Christian theology well enough to understand just how the idea of the trinity applies here; I think we may ignore it for our present purpose.

Eckhart refers to the absolute now-moment in another place where he speaks about two kinds of days. He quotes a passage from scripture, Eccl. 44:17, and interprets it quite freely. Buddhists have two ways of reading, the obvious meaning and the secret. The secret reading comes out of one's own private, cavalier reading like that of Eckhart here:

> "He pleased God in his days and was found just."
>
> Now notice. If we say "in his days," there are more days than one. There is the soul's day and God's day. A day, whether six or seven ago, or more than six thousand years ago, is just as near to the present as yesterday. Why? Because all time is contained in the present Now-moment. Time comes of the revolution of the heavens and day began with the first revolution. The soul's day falls within this time and consists of the natural light in which things are seen. God's day, however, is the complete day, comprising both day and night. It is the real Now-moment, which for the soul is eternity's day, on which the Father begets his only begotten Son and the soul is reborn in God. Whenever this birth occurs, it is the soul giving birth to the only begotten Son. Thus, the Virgin's Sons are more numerous than the children of ordinary women, for they are born beyond time in eternity. Still, however many the children [are] to which the soul gives birth in eternity, all together they are still only one Son, because it all happens beyond time, in the day of eternity. (p. 212)

Eckhart wants specifically to make something of these days. His day presupposes mine, the soul's day and God's day. Six days ago or six thousand years are as near as yesterday, for all time is contained in this present Now-moment. This is the absolute present. One week is as short as six thousand years because all time is contained in the present Now-moment. Days began with the first revolution of the heavenly bodies. Our day is in planetary time and comes from the revolution of the sun and the other heavenly bodies; God's day has nothing to do with this revolution and comprises both day and night. Here day is night, night is day—quite different from ordinary human time. God's day or God's Now-moment knows no past or future—it is the absolute present. God's day or God's Now-moment corresponds to eternity from the soul's point of view. But this Now-moment does not mean this [moment]: it is the shortest division of time—and the longest possible length of time to the soul, eternity.

According to Eckhart, the Now-moment, this absolute present, is eternity itself. His conception of the birth of Christ in the soul is quite different from the ordinary way of conceiving it. When he is born in the soul, this is the time God is born in us. This day that marks the birth of Christ is the day the absolute present is taken for eternity; that is, when time equals eternity, when time equals no-time, *munen* or *mushin*. In this respect Buddhism also differs from Christianity. Buddhism talks about mind essence, Christians about God, Christ, and so on. When we are free from all thoughts we experience the Now-moment, the absolute present. Eckhart is quite interesting in many ways. He takes from the Bible as he wishes and explains passages by his own real experience. He uses Now only.

Consciousness is time, and time means diversity. When there is just one uniformity of things, there is no time. Time is needed for 1 to become not-1, *munen*. When Buddhists talk of no-time, no-mind, no-thought, people think Buddhism is [a religion of] annihilation. But we use words quite unthinkingly. Nothing can ever exist as nothing. Absolute nothing is absolute now, not against anything; it stands by itself. Absolute Now does not belong to this relative sphere at all. No-consciousness, annihilation of consciousness, corresponds to the Now-moment, the absolute present. When this absolute present is grasped, then we know the absolute present is eternity, timelessness. Eternity is really timelessness, a term that is easier for us to grasp. When this Now-moment is understood to be eternity and eternity to be the Now-moment, or timelessness, this is the time the only begotten son is born in the soul. According to Eckhart, Christ is born every Now-moment, every absolute present, not only in the individual soul, but Christ is born in every soul whenever this experience, the union of Now with Eternity, takes place in any individual soul.

If the last two sentences of the last Eckhart quotation above are analyzed logically, all kinds of confusion come in and we get all mixed up. Children are born whenever the unity of Now and Eternity takes place. No matter how numerous, they are still only one son. In time 1 is 1, 2 is 2, 3 is 3. At the same time, time is timelessness. We could ask, "How do such things take place when there is no time?" All things go into time, they are born, die, and so on—according to us. But to Eckhart and other thinkers when time begins to come into existence all kinds of things take place, like birth and death. [And] this taking place of things is time.

The absolute present is time and timelessness at the same time. Therefore, time does not come in. All happens beyond time in the day of eternity. There is no difference between Eckhart, Aśvaghoṣa, and other Buddhists if they are properly understood. Eckhart speaks of God's and the soul's days. The former is not day, for it comprises day and night. Eckhart has the same eye looking inward and outward. When it turns outward, there are creatures and the soul; when it turns inward, God, timelessness, infinity. But all those different things, those differentiated objects, *dharma,* are only one thing. Eckhart puts it this way:

> Once in the cloister I said: "The true archetype of the soul is revealed when God alone and nothing else can be described or imagined." The soul has two eyes—one looking inwards and the other outwards. It is the inner eye of the soul that looks into essence and takes being directly from God. That is its true

> function. The soul's outward eye is directed toward creatures and perceives their external forms but when a person turns inwards and knows God in terms of his own awareness of him, in the roots of his being, he is then freed from all creation and is secure in the castle of truth. (p. 216)

We speak of inner and outer, as if there were divisions, but where is the dividing line? This body is not the boundary line; it belongs to the outer world. When the body is analyzed, or when it is discarded, when we think we have penetrated into consciousness, consciousness may try to retreat deeper and deeper into the core of consciousness. But as long as we say "inner" we are conscious of consciousness. There is no absolute inwardness, for always there is an inward within that inward line. If we go on like this, trying to seek self inwardly, in the depths of consciousness there sits "I" regardless of outwardness. But when we think we at last put our hands on "I," always another "I" remains. When we think we take hold of it, there is always another infinitely—so there is no real inward. The same thing is true of outward. Space is infinite; we can never come to the end of material existence. If the external is pursued in this way, the body itself is external to me. And this me is also external to me. So there is no outer or inner; there is just mental imagery.

Here is another place in which Eckhart speaks of the two eyes: "The eye with which I see God is the same eye with which God sees me. My eye and God's eye are one eye, and one vision or seeing, and one knowing and one loving" (pp. 206, 288). So after all the two eyes are one, which cannot be fixed anywhere, outer or inner, for what is outer is what is inner. This one eye is the absolute one eye, not the numerical one. This absolute eye, which is not inner or outer, is something like the absolute present, which cuts off all the past and future. But the absolute present has no point of beginning or end, it does not indicate any point. Yet we have to say something. Zero eye, zero consciousness—this is the start of all things.

Eckhart also speaks frequently of the castle, the agent in the soul, the soul's agent. The agent of the soul when used in the singular refers to original enlightenment in *prajñā*, we might say. In the plural, as if many were in the soul, it refers to creatures, the *karuṇā* aspect, where the ten thousand things are. When he speaks of the castle, it contains everything, yet they are all one and the same in the castle. The castle dissolves all differentiation and they become one. "Our Lord went into a little castle and was received by a virgin who was a wife."[vi] The virgin is God's day. Eckhart makes use of contradictory words, as does Buddhism: a virgin is a wife, a wife is a virgin; one is many, many are one. This is true in the little castle he enters, the core, the agent, the eye looking in, the absolute moment—all designate the same thing.

There is much more that I could quote in Eckhart, but I will stop here. It may be noted, however, that Eckhart does not go beyond thousands of years, while there are infinite numbers in the sutras.

So consciousness is time, time is consciousness. If I were a mathematician possibly I could give as good a definition as they do in a most roundabout way with numbers! Consciousness identifies, remembers, but also [does] something else. Psychologically, consciousness is only conscious of events going on; most materialists think things go on even where there is no consciousness, consciousness being just an accident we can get along without. My feeling is different. Consciousness is most living, most dynamic. We are apt to think it is static, but it is not so. Zero consciousness may be compared to the center in a circle that has no circumference: the center is everywhere in this kind of circle, so zero consciousness is everywhere and is not limited to this or that. Wherever, or whenever, we

---

vi. Blakney, *Meister Eckhart*, 207; cf. 107, 109, 210–1, 300–1.

make a point that is where zero consciousness, the absolute present, is. This is speaking rather abstractly, but in one's own psychological experience we may have this zero consciousness.

When enlightenment experience takes place the psychological reaction is something like this, as a Zen student says in one of the most popular stories about this experience: "The bucket I carry on my head has lost its bottom." There is no water in it anymore: "The white moon casts no shadow." This is from a woman. A man, who may or may not have known this story, also made allusion to the bucket after his experience: "The old bucket has lost its bottom." But not only its bottom: "The hoops also are all broken to pieces, and the staves." This absolute void he experienced, but it is not just pure emptiness.

According to a sutra, when one realizes enlightenment the whole of space itself breaks into pieces. This is quite expressive—not turning into emptiness, but space itself is broken into pieces, a certain dynamic feeling is there. At the time of his death one of the great Japanese Zen teachers expressed enlightenment experience in this way, "Space bites its own teeth."[vii/4] Empty space has teeth and those teeth bite or gnash; this is very expressive too.

Instead of a philosophical explanation Zen people give voice to these bare expressions, all of which are liable to be misunderstood. When a monk asks the question, for instance, of the idea of Bodhidharma's coming to China, his motive, what was in *his* consciousness, we might say, the master frequently replies, "Instead of asking about what does not concern you, what is your own present business? What do you have in your mind now?" That is, why don't you realize your enlightenment Now? When this is applied to our everyday experience, we have a Japanese term that is written in various ways and that means "thusness," "thus have I heard."

---

vii. Daitō Kokushi. For the entire verse see MZB, 148 [179].

Monks frequently ask the teacher, "How should we behave when birth-and-death come so close?" Birth-and-death come in so close on each other. We can't avoid them; how do we live in this valley of life? This is a great religious problem. But the master commonly replies, "When food is served, I eat; when tea is served, I drink." That is, I take things as they come; but this is not a child's taking—zero consciousness is behind it. And when asked, "Where is the Buddhist teaching here?" some teachers just extend the hand.

The experience of raising the head and realizing, for the first time, that the sun is really round is also a case of the suchness experience, for it represents the realization of the absolute present. And when Kyōgen swept the ground and a stone struck a bamboo, it made a sound he must have heard many times, yet this time he heard it in the real sense. We see things every day, but sometimes it happens that we really see these things, that we see in essence. And at this time suchness is experienced. On these occasions things we see we have not seen before, and we see things as we have not seen them before, for this time things see us as we see them. A mutual relationship between the seer and the seen takes place, a relationship never established until this time, when everything surrounding us is endowed with light. A kind of stream of sympathy is here, between seer and seen. There is a mutual sympathetic wave between the two, between subject and object. This is when we sometimes say the oneness of subject and object has taken place.

When we drink tea, for example, with zero consciousness, the relationship is just tea and yourself. Nobody else enters in. This tea, we might say, and yourself include the whole universe as one, not as this or that. A real relationship or sympathy is established. Through this special experience we really reach the basis of all particular experiences. What distinguishes Zen from other such mystical teachings is that in Zen every particular concrete object is taken up and made the subject of spiritual talk. Christian mystics make constant reference to Christ or God, while the Indian are most abstract; but tea and food form the subject of many such Zen *mondō*.

In the southern part of China, where bamboo grows quite luxuriantly, Duofu, a Zen teacher, lived in a mountain temple beside such a grove. When a student of Zen asked him, "What do you say about your bamboo grove?" he replied, "One or two are slanting," or grow slantingly. The student asked again, "What does that mean?" "Three or four bamboos are bent," or crooked.[viii/5] The description is quite literal, I suppose. Here they talk about bamboos, yet behind, though not really behind, it there is in these bamboos something that philosophers cannot understand, nor explain adequately through their concepts. This is where Zen teaching is unique.

When I say that enlightenment takes place when subject and object are united, that is, when subject becomes object and object becomes subject and there is no distinction to be made between these two, this is a rather epistemological way of presenting that of which enlightenment consists. Psychologically speaking, it begins with what we call a certain *impasse*, sometimes called *aporia*. Either *aporia* or *impasse*, it is the point at which one cannot go any further or step back or stay there.[6] This is the point, psychologically, when one wants to go on but can't and when one can't retrace one's steps either.

Zen students have many ways of expressing this state of mind. The one most popularly used is this: On a steep wall you keep yourself hanging over a precipice by the hands; you are hanging down over it, so you can't let go.[7] If you let the hands go you will fall; but when you finally have to go into a state of unconsciousness you do let go, then are at once revived. Letting go and reviving take place at the same time, simultaneously.[ix] It is once more going back to your former state of consciousness.

---

viii. EZB 2, 187 [166].
ix. EZB 2, 98 [82], 100 [84].

As long as there is an object before a subject the subject tries to take hold of the object, but this can never be taken hold of. It entices, allures, yet the subject cannot take hold, though it wishes to have it. When the subject exhausts itself and throws itself down, out of this exhaustion the reviving power comes, and you know where you are. This state of exhaustion is to be at least once experienced; otherwise, enlightenment will never be experienced.

But enlightenment experience is no complicated affair. It is most simple, being most fundamental. Yet it is not one of the particular experiences we go through every day. It goes through these particular experiences we undergo—these continue to take place, we cannot stop these. Really if fundamental experience is something complicated, needing some amount of analysis, it is not fundamental enlightenment experience. In a psychological event we may call the incident to mind sometime later: as I talk now this experience of letting my hands go is recorded back in my memory. But enlightenment experience, as Eckhart says, is in the naked state of being; we cannot say it lasts a moment, a minute, an instant. This is quite interesting.

The beginning may be understood in this way: if I strike something a spark comes off with the speed of lightning. In Zen literature we read of enlightenment experience compared with a spark from struck flint or with lightning.[8] Lightning that passes by before we can say "it lightens" might be taken as describing the quickness of the time experience in enlightenment, but here the question of time does not mean a question of time. When we strike, that very instant, this very moment is meant. When we speak of it it is no more there, for it is the absolute present, not belonging to the past and of course not to the future. It is not the quickness of time but the way the experience actually takes place. I remember a passage in the *Upanishads* where it is also likened to a flash of lightning:

> Of it [Brahma] there is this teaching.—
>
> That in the lightning which flashes forth, which makes one blink, and say
>
> "Ah!"—that "Ah!" refers to divinity.[x]

When one says, "Ah," it is already gone.

With regard to the spark coming out of flint, this spark is an interesting term in Eckhart. He makes frequent references to the spark in connection with the soul, *Fünkchen,* "little spark" being something that comes out of the soul, or the point where the soul gets enlightened with God.[xi/9] It cannot be described any better than this, I think.

In the hanging by the hands above the Chinese has this: after one has gone into the unconscious then one is revived again. But this "after" is not exact. When I strike, the spark comes out and vanishes—at the same time, simultaneously, not after. Therefore, enlightenment experience is a very realistic affair. How can such a simple experience have such momentous effect in one's life? Enlightenment experience takes place in the absolute moment, absolute now. But before one reaches this experience one has to go through, not exactly preparations but something akin to preparations. While going through them there are not preparations at all, but the most terrible experiences. While going through what are afterward called preparatory steps for attaining this object that is so uncertain of attainability, or nonattainability—these are really the most excruciating experiences.

But just because of these experiences, these hardships, the result of all these experiences, which finally bear fruit, is that

---

x. *Kena Upanishad,* 4.29(4). Robert Ernest Hume, *The Thirteen Principal Upanishads* (London: Oxford University Press, 1934), 339. EZB 1, 243, note † [230, note †].

xi. Blakney, *Meister Eckhart,* 210, 220.

enlightenment grows all the more significant according to the amount of labor spent on it. Thus the way Zen teachers frequently try their disciples does not come from malice or from ego motives, but to make them work hard and attain. In the Sung dynasty a master noted for the severity of his training was considered most cross-tempered, not willfully or pedantically cruel. Most pilgrimaging monks after some experiences with him went somewhere else, but one believed in him very much and stuck with him. When this monk was meditating in his room in the severest month, this master would come in and throw cold water on the floor, to freeze and add to the coldness of the air.[10] But however severely he handled his disciples, he had the most thoroughly penetrating insight into reality, and the same experience that must be experienced by the disciple himself. If the latter takes away from the master by strong, positive methods, the final result attained will be more appreciated by both disciple and master.

The thing is this: in one way the master thinks so highly of his experience, for it solves all kinds of problems and takes him through life quite happily, without his being troubled by worries and so on. As Eckhart says, the thing given to you is not as good as the thing torn from somewhere, or stolen from God. Striving, stealing, robbing is possibly a play on words, but "Taking the Kingdom of Heaven by force" is quite possibly analogous, though this is unusual on the part of Christians, I think. If God is willing, man takes it as a matter of course, without thinking much of it. When he gets it by cunning and effort he appreciates it more. It is something like this in Zen: using worldly terms, the teacher is unwilling to give to the disciple, but the teacher has to give because of what is in the disciple. If you put forth so much effort, what you get is worth so much. The master stays on the highest level possible and lets the disciple try to come up to him. There frequently is a kind of tug-of-war between master and disciple, though this is not the way tried by every master on every disciple. Psychologically, it is quite interesting.

When Rakan Oshō had his experience, when he looked at the sun and realized for the first time that it was really round, he really perceived this fact at the center of his consciousness.[11] Enlightenment experience does not always take place in the same way; it differs with different psychological structures. This Chinese monk went through many doubts and trials himself until he finally had his enlightenment. In the early morning on the mountain he saw the sun coming up. He thought a light coming out of his eye was going over to the sun, traveling so many thousand miles, while sunlight from the source was traveling so many thousand miles to his eye. The two meet; he realizes the sun is there. The meeting of the sun and himself, from out of this meeting a certain consciousness comes up that characterizes this enlightenment experience.

But some Shin devotee will say: "Amida made me attain long ago; he attained for me; he has his Pure Land somewhere." This is like Voltaire's "To save is God's business. Let him alone, he will do his work." The Christians take this as blasphemy, but I think Voltaire is quite right. We can't do anything; we cannot cross the gap unless God extends his hand to help. We must just stay and wait. But at the same time God will not come unless I try to invoke his help. We have to do something to try to bring about enlightenment, yet if we try to do something we cannot bring it about. This is the contradiction. We have to strive after it very hard, yet when we try very hard it goes farther and farther away—the very effort blocks. And just because I try very hard I know it goes farther away. But if I don't try I don't even know if it goes farther away or not.

The fact will be realized when the Shin devotee has his enlightenment. The time gap that can never be crossed is all canceled out in the devotee's enlightenment, and Amida comes and gets into his personality in person. All the devotee thinks or feels is Amida thinking, feeling; thus with Buddha's realization everybody, nonsentient and sentient, is saved. Now when any of us go through it all the world attains enlightenment. There is no need to do anything special. If we try to do something we will never be there. That which Buddha has experienced we will all experience like him.

Buddha saw the morning star, Rakan saw the rising sun, Kyōgen heard a pebble strike a bamboo—often there is a sense contact before enlightenment takes place. But feeling is really enough, without the five senses. It really depends on mental development. But metaphysically speaking, mental development is not actually necessary either. I consciousness, ego consciousness, must be in full development before enlightenment experience is possible, and this usually needs a sense basis for fullest development. There is a sutra about a dragon girl, about seven years old, who had enlightenment.[12] According to a noted sermon of Gensha, if Buddhism could not do anything with the blind, deaf, and dumb it would have no significance, it would be no miracle at all.[13] When a monk asked Unmon (Yunmen, d. 949) to explain this to him, the master first called out the monk's name. When he replied, "Yes, master," Unmon said, "You are not deaf." Next the disciple stepped back as Unmon was about to strike him and the latter said, "You are not blind;" then, "Do you understand?" "No, I don't." Unmon's final word was, "You are not mute."[14] But as far as sensibility goes the deaf, blind, and mute can have enlightenment.

In Zen *mondō,* when a master calls out a person's name and he answers, the master frequently continues, "What is this?" We may interpret this in terms of personality, and this is all right, for the person is very much emphasized too, as by Rinzai. But instead of talking about personality, which suggests something individual, the master is mainly pointing to the absolute present, which is free from such a complication. And in the *mondō* I quite often quote, "What was Bodhidharma's idea in coming to China from India, what motive did he have in proselytizing the Chinese?" the Zen master may answer, "What is your idea now, this very moment?" Instead of talking about some other event, what are you experiencing this very moment? In this moment, the absolute present, the past is all included, and the future is there. Time is about to move on, this very moment is to be grasped. When this is grasped, we understand if there is anything even before God created the world, we may say.

This enlightenment experience takes place in, and actually is, the absolute present, *sokkon* (C. *jijin*) in Zen terminology, "this very moment," the crossing point of time and space. But the absolute present is also the crossing point of time and timelessness:

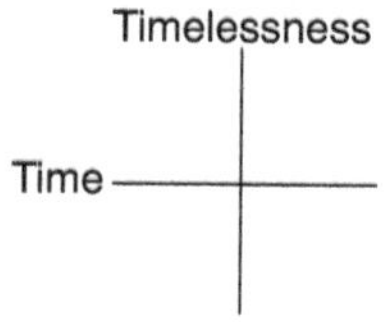

And when this point is understood, history will be understood and our life delineated in time will also be understood.

Sokkon represents time, "just now," while another Buddhist term refers to space, *shako*, "just so."[15] *Shako* does not specially signify this object or that; it is just *shako*, the most Zen can express as far as words are concerned, a specific Zen expression. It can be used as a time expression too, but it is usually connected with space, while *sokkon* is time, time and space being unified in the two expressions. We think now in terms of time and space, but either will do for the other actually, as we have demonstrated; I just distinguish them conventionally here.

So this absolute moment, absolute present, is *shako* and at the same time *sokkon*. With reference to this and the *Diamond Sūtra* there is quite a noted story that I will give only summarily here.[xii] Tokusan (780–865) was asked, "Since the past moment is impossible to take hold of and the present moment and the future also, in which mind do you wish to have refreshments?"—literally, "to punctuate the mind," *tenshin*; I do not know how the expression came about.[16] I should say too that the Sanskrit expresses it as past, future, present—this is noteworthy, I think—while we usually say past, present, future. The Indian mind comprehended past and future. And when past and future are there, the present has to be there—but the present is never there; when we say "present" it is already gone. So there is only absolute present, which is timelessness; there is no relative present. Out of this timelessness how does time come? When time comes absolute present is no more here. Thus the old lady who asks the question wants to see how the monk understands Zen.

We get hold of the absolute present when we are not in time. Therefore, we have to go out of time to grasp the absolute present. But when we are out of time we cannot talk of past, present, future anything. The thing is to get out and still be in: to be involved in it, yet to be out of it; to be conscious, yet not conscious; to be consciously unconscious or unconsciously conscious, either will do. The way we use logic, we cannot help hooking ourselves—and this hooking is quite fatal. As St. Augustine says, "I know when you do not ask; when you ask I am at a loss how to answer."[17] When one does not think of it, it is clear enough. When thinking is done away with, eternity is there. Yet when we are simply not thinking of anything, mind is there, and eternity cannot get in. I begin to think, division comes with past and future. There can be no absolute present when becoming is related to past and future. The absolute present as far as language is concerned is very difficult. We say the absolute

xii. For my translation see MZB, 38–50 [43–56B]. See also EZB 2, 44–46 [30–33]; MCB, 62ff, 97; LZ, 78–80.

present is out of the time flow, that we cannot catch it. But the time flow is the absolute present. When you have it, nothing is easier. When you have it not, nothing is more impossible.

Tokusan did not know how to answer, quite naturally; unable to fulfill his bargain and feed his hungry stomach, he went on. The absolute present is *sokkon* and at the same time *shako.* In this absolute present all past history is contained and all future history that is to develop. So the absolute present corresponds to emptiness, zero, and in this zero is infinity.

Past and present are to be found in this absolute present; all possible future and past are there. In Buddhist texts emptiness, or mind or original enlightenment, contains or implies merit, as many merits as the sands of the Gangā—this expression of so much sand is met almost everywhere in Buddhist texts. There are so many numberless objects, *guṇa*—mass and energy in physics—an infinite number of *guṇa* contained in emptiness, or original enlightenment. The present moves on and as it moves on the absolute present is there and infinite *guṇa* evolve out, or emanate. This emanation itself is reality; becoming is being, being is becoming. And in this present moment from which past and future history begins—going up, down, any way—infinite possibilities are realizing themselves.

I use "realize" since we think of it as if something were to be realized, but it is altogether purposeless; there is no track, no circumference whatever. This is the gist of Zen. Purposeless *praṇidhāna*, continuous, no interruption whatever, no limitation, no intermission, no track, altogether purposeless, for purpose belongs to time.[18] When time is taken away, there is no purpose whatever, for this purpose is time.

This seems quite confusing, I am afraid, for this is so different from the way most people ordinarily think that it is a kind of revolutionary idea, but this way of understanding reality could have a great deal to do with reducing conflict in the world. Although we cannot stop conflict, I often think of the energy spent on killing each other. If it could be devoted to the study of science, or to an institution for this kind of metaphysical study, so valuable to the enhancement of culture—but they do not seem to take this kind of thing seriously. Spiritual men have a certain melancholy.

An example of spacelessness and timelessness is given by Vimalakīrti.[xiii] His small room, not even so large as this one perhaps, contained not only all the people of Vaiśālī but also all sentient and nonsentient inhabitants of the whole universe. And yet this room was not found too small for them, while they remained as they were without any crowding or squeezing in. Spatial measurement is definitely symbolized here, yet he is not speaking just of space. *Shako* is no respecter of space or time. This story also represents timelessness, "just now" and "just so."

Another interesting incident in this sutra is as follows; Śāriputra was not so enlightened as the other occupants of this room. When celestial beings scattered flowers, these stuck to him as they fell. The more he tried to brush them off the more they stuck, or adhered. When he asked for the reason he was told, "Because your mind is still full of attachment the flowers attach themselves to you. There are no flowers on anyone but you; your attachment draws them to you."[19]

So the quality of attachment attracts the flowers. Mutual attractability will also be illustrated in the converse way in *pariṇāmana* and *praṇidhāna*.[20] There is always this mutual attraction taking place; revulsion or hate is the reverse side of mutual attraction. Otherwise we could never live together like this.

---

xiii. ZBJC, 181; EZB 1, 98 [86–87]; ZB, 45.

No obstruction, unobstruction, describes actual things as they are. Things go through to others without hindrance. Things melt, things pass through other things, there is perfect flowing through from one to another. *Sō, so-o*, can take place because of mutual attraction, *sō* being "idea," "conception," "thought," another fine word that is not to be understood in the ideational way.

V

Enlightenment is the subject of the **Mahāyānaśraddhotpādaśāstra*, an important treatise generally ascribed to Aśvaghoṣa.[i/1] Aśvaghoṣa—literally "Horse making a noise"—summarizes here the principal teachings of the Mahāyāna, as distinguished from the earlier Hīnayāna, form of Buddhism and speaks of original enlightenment, ignorance, and what he considers to be the four stages of enlightenment: ignorance or nonenlightenment, enlightenment in appearance, approximate enlightenment, enlightenment itself.[2]

First I will discuss briefly original enlightenment and its opposite and equal, ignorance.

The essence or ground of Buddha's experience is enlightenment, and this enlightenment is beyond words. It cannot be expressed, it is devoid of knowledge and will. We cannot predicate anything about

---

i. In AFM, I have translated the Chinese version of this work, the original Sanskrit manuscript being as yet undisclosed; here such disputed matters as its origin and date are discussed rather fully. In these lectures we simply consider the śāstra to be genuine, but cf. p. xxxix of my LS. I think that Aśvaghoṣa was earlier than Nāgārjuna and conclude (p. 17 of the AFM) that Aśvaghoṣa "lived at the time extending from the latter half of the first century before Christ to about 50 or 80 A.D. . . . At the very most his time cannot be placed later than the first century of the Christian era."

this original enlightenment, for it is also devoid of all characteristics. In itself, as many philosophers East and West will say, it is the ground, essence, core, basis of reality, the Christian godhead—from which flow *prajñā* and *karuṇā.* And as *prajñā* and *karuṇā* come out of original enlightenment, this coming out is enlightenment negating itself. This negating is called ignorance, *avidyā,* and Aśvaghoṣa speaks of it as follows: "Though all modes of consciousness and mentation are mere products of ignorance, ignorance in its ultimate nature is identical and not-identical with enlightenment *a priori*; and therefore ignorance in one sense is destructible, while in the other sense it is indestructible."[ii] Enlightenment is noetic: a certain basis of knowledge is there, not in the way of ordinary experience but as pure intellect, pure reason, or original enlightenment. Yet enlightenment as it is in itself, being so neutral, uniform, unified that we may ascribe no special characteristics to it, this enlightenment divides into two, *prajñā* and *karuṇā*; and this division is the negation called *avidyā*, ignorance. But it must be remembered that ignorance is not just negative. When you are ignorant, you are enlightened. When I realize I am ignorant, this is another term for "the first awakening" (*shijue*). To become aware of the positive you must first become aware of the negative. Ignorance is present all the time. When you know it is ignorance, it is enlightenment. This kind of ignorance is not ignorance. One remains unenlightened unless he himself becomes aware of his unenlightened state of mind; before he does this it is not possible to become enlightened—and sometimes conditions are such that he never awakens to enlightenment. If he is disturbed he is enlightened. "Disturbed" may not be strong enough; one is not so acutely conscious as a rule; one does not look at it for some reason. We are apt to think that there is a state of ignorance that is not enlightenment. We make a distinction between

ii. AFM, 67.

the two when we begin to talk. But actually this distinction is neither ignorance nor enlightenment. The whole thing moves on: this is the central point. It is hard to grasp, but when grasped the whole thing is here.

So there is negative enlightenment, and this is where all kinds of contradictions come out. To explain the process is not the process. If it is brought down to the level of our intellect, we have to say "process" or something of the kind. There is nothing to say about it as long as it remains in itself. We have to resort to language when we speak about original enlightenment—and ignorance always sets in. Ignorance is enlightenment itself in the same way that godhead is devoid of all differentiation; from godhead come God and creation. It is the same with enlightenment.

When we speak about ignorance there is duality in it. There is no duality in original enlightenment, but as soon as it asserts itself, ignorance and duality come up, the duality of *prajñā* and *karuṇā.* Thus original enlightenment by going through the medium of ignorance differentiates itself into *prajñā* and *karuṇā.* Out of *prajñā,* the noetic aspect, we have this intellect and reason; out of *karuṇā,* the conative, come love, compassion, will.

This duality of *prajñā* and *karuṇā* is complicated. Original enlightenment is pure oneness, sameness. When it divides to assert itself, ignorance comes in; and by means of ignorance *prajñā* and *karuṇā* enter. This separation of original enlightenment into *prajñā* and *karuṇā* has been called ignorance. And it is this separation that makes it possible for *prajñā* to be awakened to its own essence. *Prajñā* comes in on the relative plane, but it also retains original enlightenment of the absolute plane. When *prajñā* becomes conscious of original enlightenment in itself, this is called the first awakening of enlightenment in the mind. The first awakening is original enlightenment: original enlightenment through this first awakening becomes conscious of itself.

The relation of *karuṇā* to *prajñā* and *prajñā* to *karuṇā* will take some time to make clear. *Karuṇā* is the religious part of Zen, *prajñā* is the metaphysical part. Eckhart's eye looking out is the concrete not-self, *karuṇā*, while the eye looking in is self-knowledge, *prajñā*. Yet the two are one, turning this way and that way. Love is there in original enlightenment, as is will. Here will does not have the meaning in which it is generally used, but its most fundamental sense, "to move." Something just starting to move is will. When moved it is already not-will. *Karuṇā* implies the difference between love of others and love of self, love of others being compassion. Some people individually have more of *karuṇā*, less of *prajñā*; others have more of *prajñā*, less of *karuṇā*. *Prajñā* is present in Zen and seems more prominent, but at the bottom is *karuṇā*. The bodhisattva idea is very important in Zen, and Zen has two bodhisattvas, one to represent *prajñā*, one to represent *karuṇā*: Manjuśrī and Samantabhadra. Without clear insight self-love is contaminated; it should be self-love, for it is murkiness without insight.

In *prajñā* there is original enlightenment plus self-consciousness. *Prajñā* has in itself original enlightenment, and when *prajñā* becomes conscious of original enlightenment we call it the first awakening. The first awakening is a combination of enlightenment and ignorance, we might say: if there is no ignorance there can be no first awakening, original enlightenment would remain with itself forever. The first awakening constitutes both ignorance and enlightenment.

What is metaphysically negative, or divided, is psychologically positive, for it permits the possibility of the enlightenment experience. At the same time the division of one into two is sin, to use Christian terminology, the coming down into matter or manifestation. Thus our very existence is sin from this point of view, and we might say we are all sinners. But the Christian sense of sin has a moral connotation and there are no such ideas here; rather, relative existence itself is sin if taken in the sense of division, or separation.

To use a simple illustration, it is this way: when I don't talk all is clear, and *prajñā* comes out of a negative state to the power of realization. When I begin to talk all kinds of things are mixed up. As long as the enlightened man's realization is not quite enlightened, it is ignorance; he must have gotten psychological disturbance somewhere.

The thing is that our senses are so confused. The central disturbance we begin to feel may grow fainter and fainter. But in some people the inner disturbance is kept up and grows stronger. This kind of man cannot stay quietly in the world. In Buddha's day he went to the mountain. Circumstances differ, and there are so many different ways to deal with this fundamental disturbance, by each individual in himself and also by each group of individuals historically. Certain special trends or patterns are seen in groups, and individuals in groups also have different experiences. Some fundamental patterns most of us follow, but special cases are all different—this is what stimulates our study of religious phenomena, our psychological study of religious consciousness. Psychologically speaking, when we go the limit, *yang* into *yin, yin* into *yang,* there is a mutual interrelationship between *yang* and *yin* that takes place in the first awakening of *prajñā.* There is mutual relationship from one to the other, constantly moving. The *Yijing* is really the doctrine of interrelationship of the ten thousand things.[3]

Now this is where *karuṇā* comes in, the ignorance, the compassion aspect of enlightenment. Compassion presupposes duality, which comes out as *karuṇā*, while the *prajñā* aspect of the duality has no duality. This probably sounds confusing; I will try to make it clearer. To compare Buddhist doctrine with Eckhart is very interesting in many ways. When Aśvaghoṣa talks about the first awakening it seems far from Christianity. God in the Christian sense is never used in Buddhism. When Buddhists talk at all about doctrine they use enlightenment, which is more noetic than God. Godhead is not so personal as God, but it goes out to God. There is a personal element in Buddhism, but it does not come out so prominently as in Christianity. Personality is kept in its real place, not so conspicuous as in Christianity, which speaks of a personal God from the first.

Eckhart mentions two factors, agents, or powers of the soul: intellect or reason and will.[iii] He puts intellect above will as being more important. This corresponds to the Buddhist idea of having *prajñā* first; *karuṇā* is a negation of *prajñā*, we might say, and of course corresponds to will. I do not think it is logical to put *karuṇā*, or will, first. It does not seem to appeal as much as having intellect first and will second. But actually, we cannot separate them that way. From the purely metaphysical point of view it does not seem proper, and it does not appeal to me as much as intellect and will as one. Intellect is will, will is intellect. But it is convenient to distinguish the two when we talk; it makes our way of thinking clearer. Intellect takes truth, will takes goodness. If will is toward the godhead, God assumes goodness. If intellect is toward the godhead, God appears as truth. So *prajñā* is comparable to intellect, *karuṇā* to will. It is convenient for us to use this dualistic way of expression.

Eckhart speaks of two eyes,[iv] the soul looking inward toward unity and outward toward multiplicity. Inwardly it looks into essence and takes its being directly from God, as its true function. Multiplicity is outward, [and the eye is] directed toward creatures. Being a Christian, he talks so much about creatures; the Buddhist would say *dharma*, which corresponds in this case to creatures, as consisting of multiplicity, not quite *dharma*'s totality. Sometimes Buddhism uses *sarvadharma* for all beings, all things, all creatures. This applies to animals, humans, and so on, as does *sarvasattva*, also used for "the ten thousand things" of Buddhism. Creatures, of course, suggest a

iii. Blakney, *Meister Eckhart*, 221.
iv. Blakney, *Meister Eckhart*, 216, 288.

creator, but Buddhism has no creator in the Christian sense. In this sense there is no Christian correspondence to *sarvasattva*.

According to Eckhart, "The soul's outward eye is directed toward creatures and perceives their external forms." When a person turns inward and becomes aware of God, he "is secure in the castle of truth." The eye looking inward takes in the oneness of things, the other looking outward, their multiplicity.[v] In another place[vi] he says, "The eye with which I see God is the same eye with which God sees me"—a passage frequently quoted by Eckhart readers. When he speaks first of two eyes, the two are really one: the same eye by which I see God, God sees me. My eye and God's are one and the same: one in seeing, one in knowing, one in loving. This one eye is the same as the two, the two eyes are one.

This may be reading my thought into Eckhart. In Christianity creator and creature are so divided that one cannot turn into the other. The creator never becomes creature; creature can never become creator. In Buddhism creatures are creator, and creator is creatures. This is the fundamental distinction between Buddhism and Christianity. So creatures are actually their own creators. This distinction is usually kept in Eckhart, but sometimes it is ignored.

Aśvaghoṣa's knowledge as the first awakening by enlightenment of *prajñā* beginning to stir may be compared with this passage of Eckhart:

> Truly, as St. Augustine says: "God is nearer to the soul than the soul is to itself." God and the soul are so nearly [related] to each other that there is really no distinction between them. By the same [kind] of knowledge by which God knows himself, that is detached or dispassionate knowledge, the soul receives its being

v. Blakney, *Meister Eckhart*, 216.
vi. Blakney, *Meister Eckhart*, 288.

> from God. For that reason God is closer to the soul than the soul is to itself and therefore, God is in the soul's core—God and all the Godhead.[vii]

This first awakening of *prajñā* corresponds to this knowledge that is detached and dispassionate, by which God knows himself. The time the soul comes into existence is the time the soul has this knowledge by which God knows himself. The first awakening of *prajñā* is original enlightenment. Original enlightenment by negating itself, by turning itself into ignorance, knows itself. This knowledge, if we may call it knowledge, by which enlightenment knows itself, this first awakening is *prajñā*, which receives the knowledge from God. Hence God is closer to the soul than the soul to itself. This means: when the soul is on the relative plane the knowledge it has of itself is relative; when it is knowledge of God himself it is self-consciousness, which is not on the relative plane. God is the soul's core or ground here. God and all the godhead, original enlightenment and ignorance, everything is there. Metaphysically speaking, the soul is as close to soul as God. Relatively speaking, the soul is God.

Eckhart might have been Aśvaghoṣa, or a Buddhist like him, if he had been born in India, but he was born a Christian in Germany, so he uses Christian terms. Frequently he speaks of the birth beyond you yourself, before you were born, the exact Buddhist term. I do not know how most Christians take this; they would reject my idea of it at once, I suppose. But if we replace many of Eckhart's terms by Buddhist [terms] all these things become clear. This would result in a better understanding of Christian books, though not in the orthodox way. Be yourself before birth; know yourself as God knows himself.

---

vii. Blakney, *Meister Eckhart*, 214–215.

Aśvaghoṣa's *Awakening of Faith* was translated into Chinese rather early, around the middle of the sixth century at least,[viii/4] and it sums up the gist of Mahāyāna teachings. Especially after a commentary was written on it by a great Chinese Buddhist philosopher of the early Tang dynasty, Fazang, it was made into a kind of textbook for Mahāyāna students in China and Japan. All later students of Aśvaghoṣa generally depend upon this commentary. Thus this treatise has been very much associated with Buddhist philosophy, and it is made use of by Zen masters to explain their teachings more philosophically or metaphysically.

In fact, the *Awakening* seems to be in a way an attempt to systematize the *Laṅkāvatāra-sūtra,* which was already in China when Bodhidharma arrived there in the sixth century and which was used effectively by him.[ix] *Laṅkāvatāra* means "entrance to Laṅkā," Ceylon, which Buddha is supposed to have visited, though this may be a fiction only. Although this sutra had so much to do with Zen's development, later Zen people emphasized, instead, the *Prajñāpāramitā-sūtra,* the doctrine of Emptiness or *śūnyatā*. In fact, Zen is sometimes said to be the practical application of *śūnyatā* to our daily life. The fourth patriarch of Zen in China and his chief disciple tried to combine *śūnyatā* and Zen. As a result, perhaps, Zen came to be very closely associated with the Kegon Sutra, which colors with particular strength the Fayan (Hōgen) school of Zen of Korea.

Thus the *Awakening* is very important in the study of Mahāyāna Buddhism generally, as well as in that of Zen. I will now try to give a very short account of it to show its differences from and its close approach to Eckhart, and to attempt to make clearer to you what is actually meant by enlightenment experience.

---

viii. AFM, 36–41.

ix. For this sūtra see my SLS and my translation, LS. In the latter, xxixff., the closeness of the śāstra and the sūtra, in both time and doctrine, is discussed.

The purpose of the discourse is to expound what Aśvaghoṣa calls Dharma, in this case absolute being, not just thing, object, or doctrine. He calls the Dharma *sarvasattva* or *sarvasattvacitta*, "all beings" or "mind of all beings"; and this is the Dharma that is the subject of his treatise.[5] This *citta* (*xin*, *shin* in Chinese and Japanese), mind, has a double sense, one being absolute, the other relative. When this mind is used in the absolute sense, according to Aśvaghoṣa, it contains or takes in everything, not only things of this world but also things transcending this world. That is, it includes everything belonging both to this relative world and to the transcendental world, to this world and to what goes out of this world, thus being all-inclusive. And by this Mind he explains what is known as Mahāyāna:

> "What is the Mahāyāna? It is the soul of all sentient beings (*sarvasattva*), that constitutes all things in the world, phenomenal and supra-phenomenal; and through this soul we can disclose what the Mahāyāna signifies."[x]
>
> Because the soul in itself, involving the quintessence of the Mahāyāna, is suchness (*tathatā*), but it becomes [in its relative or transitory aspect, through the law of causation] birth-and-death (*saṃsāra*) in which are revealed the quintessence, the attributes, and the activity of the Mahāyāna.
>
> This Mahāyāna has a triple significance.
>
> The first is the greatness of quintessence. Because the quintessence of the Mahāyāna as suchness exists in all things, remains unchanged in the pure as well as in the defiled, is always one and

x. *Citta, hṛdaya, hsin, shin.* In this translation "soul" denotes the absolute aspect of suchness and "mind" its relative aspect, wherever this distinction is noticeable. But now I believe it is better to use Mind, capital M, instead of soul.

the same (*samatā*), neither increases nor decreases, and is void of distinction.

The second is the greatness of attributes.[xi]

Here we have the Tathāgata's womb (*tathāgatagarbha*) which in exuberance contains immeasurable and innumerable merits (*puṇya*) as its characteristics.

The third is the greatness of activity, for it [Mahāyāna] produces all kinds of good work in the world, phenomenal and supra-phenomenal. [Hence the name *Mahāyāna* (great vehicle).][xii]

This Mind, being absolute, is pure emptiness, sameness, oneness, we might say, yet this Mind is also what causes birth-and-death, in Buddhist terminology. It is rather complicated, but will perhaps become clearer in this diagram.

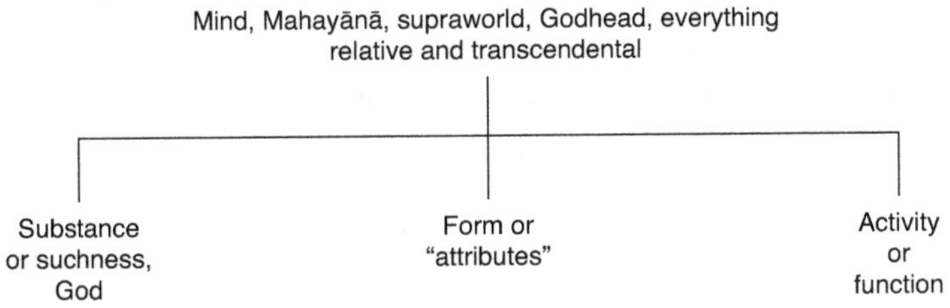

In itself Mind is substance, but as it appears to us in manifestation or form Mind can be understood from our side in its three aspects: substance, form or activity, and function. When Mind is understood in its suchness aspect, it is substance, and as substance it cannot be subjected to any relative way of thinking. When it asserts itself, when we try to understand it, when Mind tries to make itself

xi. Or "form."

xii. This triad may be compared with Spinoza's conception of substance, attributes, modes; and with the first principles of the Vaiśeshika philosophy: substance, *dravya*; qualities, *guṇa*; action, *karma*. AFM, 53–54.

understood to our mind, it negates itself. Mind somehow wants to express itself, and this expression is received by us as form and activity. As long as Mind remains as suchness, it does not change. When it expresses itself in form and activity, it subjects itself to birth-and-death. In one respect Mind is absolute suchness, eternally in its own being, but when it expresses itself, it takes form or activity, and we have this world of birth-and-death, the world of becoming.

So we can say when Mind becomes conceivable, or intelligible, to human intelligence we take it in three ways. However, these three are not Mind in its own absolute being but in its relative aspect. Yet even when it is in its relative aspect it is still absolute, beyond words; we cannot really make anything out of it. Things considered from the substance aspect have suchness, sameness, no increase, no decrease; things remain as they are. This Mind contains all possibilities—Buddhist philosophers say all virtues or qualities. In this respect it is what is called *ālaya-vijñāna,* a storehouse containing all possibilities, the container, where all things come out or are kept in their potentiality. In that it manifests in the form of *yū*: Tathāgatagarbha, the womb of Buddha, the mother body, the container, where all things come out or are kept in their potentiality.[6] When these things come out into relative existence we have all kinds of things good and bad—"good" and "bad" being used here, as always in Buddhism, as philosophic rather than moral terms.

This Mind can be conceived as suchness, or as birth-and-death; that is, as Absolute Mind and as relative mind. But Mind, with a capital M, goes beyond suchness and birth-and-death. It corresponds to Eckhart's conception of godhead, where suchness corresponds to God—though sometimes Eckhart uses "God" for godhead—God corresponding to Mind as suchness. Here Eckhart becomes more individualistic from the Buddhist viewpoint.

Mind as birth-and-death is becoming, but not just mere becoming. In it it has also something not subject to change. Aśvaghoṣa's absolute mind is: 1) suchness—being, God; 2) birth-and-death—becoming, soul. Mind as suchness contains everything, mind as birth-and-death contains everything of this world. As each of these two aspects, or gates as Confucius has it, contains all things belonging to the two worlds, we can say that Mind as suchness is mind as birth-and-death and mind as birth-and-death is Mind as suchness. They are mutually going from one end to the other, without a barrier dividing them; it is easy to go from one side to the other, they are not separable.

From this Mind as suchness—that is, God—that includes everything we can talk about, eternity, immortality, or such things. But this Mind is actually beyond our words or ideas; it cannot be symbolized or represented as an idea. Language is only provisional, as it is called by Aśvaghoṣa, and has no reality in itself. Therefore, suchness cannot be spoken of as having form; it cannot be translated into idea, for idea is not reality. Reality that becomes comprehensible through idea is not reality. Language is needed to go between reality and intellect, but we are really committing this fault of perverting reality all the time. We take idea as reality all the time and forget reality itself. So language is often a hindrance in the understanding of ultimate eeality. But still words are needed, even if only to prove words are not real things. We need to take things as they are, for they are all of sameness and suchness. This is what is difficult to understand.

When Aśvaghoṣa is explaining it like this it seems to be full of contradictions. He affirms something in one sense; then it changes into something else, and he denies it. Eckhart does the same thing, one sermon may contradict another. But this is inevitable. As long as we try to argue with a basis on words and ideas we always have to quarrel. But when we know what is behind these ideas then we seem to agree very well. Let me give two quotations from Eckhart to illustrate:

> I have often said before that there is an agent in the soul, untouched by time and flesh, which proceeds out of the Spirit and which remains forever in the Spirit and is completely spiritual. In this agent, God is perpetually verdant and flowering with all the joy and glory that is in him. Here is joy so hearty, such inconceivably great joy that no one can ever fully tell it, for in this agent the eternal Father is ceaselessly begetting his eternal Son and the agent is parturient with God's offspring and is itself the Son, by the Father's unique power. (p. 209)

> God blossoms and is verdant in this agent of which I speak, with all the Godhead and spirit of God and there he begets his only begotten Son as truly as if it were in himself. For he lives really in this agent, the Spirit together with the Father giving birth to the Son and in that light, he is the Son and the Truth. If you can only see with my heart, you may well understand what I am saying, for it is true and the Truth itself bespeaks my word. (p. 211)

When Eckhart speaks about an agent in the soul, he has this agent untouched by time and corporeal reality; yet if it is not touched by time and flesh we cannot predicate anything of this soul or agent. But he speaks about these things or beings as perpetually flowering, verdant, glowing—all of which belong to time and flesh. And the agent has nothing to do with time and form, so he cannot say it has to do with joy, glowing, and so on. This idea of God flowering is very interesting. In spite of his lack of time and flesh he is always flowering, verdant, always "in verdure newly clad." Earth is covered by this verdure, in spite of its being free from time and flesh.

And in this agent, which is untouched by time and flesh, the eternal father is ceaselessly begetting his eternal son. The agent is itself parturient with the son and is itself the son. Here we may compare Aśvaghoṣa and the activity in the Mind: substance, form, activity coming out of it. Mind begets an eternal son, or sons. This creating is done by a unique father. It cannot be duplicated, it is only possible by this father, and yet, from whence is this power? [It is from] this suchness in this father, not only in the phenomenal relative world but also in suchness's world. All these things take place in the Mind of suchness. God blossoming and verdant in this agent begets the only begotten son as truly as if begotten in himself. The begetting is not done outside, it is done in himself, for he really lives in this agent.

"If you can only see with my heart, you may well understand what I am saying." When he speaks with his own words Eckhart contradicts himself, but if we could see with his heart we might well understand what he says. Since he knows how lacking in communicability language is, he appeals to this. Intellectually speaking, there is no way of demonstrating the truth of anything. If it is demonstrated, what is the use of talking? He shows how difficult it is to make himself intelligible, but he tries his best.

> Look and see: this little castle in the soul is exalted so high above every road [of approach], with such simplicity and uniformity, that the aristocratic agent of which I have been telling you is not worthy to look into it, even once for a moment. No, nor are the other agents, of which I have also spoken, ever able to peek in to where God glows and burns like a fire with all his abundance and rapture. So altogether one and uniform is this little castle, so high above all ways and agencies, that none can ever lead to it—indeed—not even God himself. (p. 211)

The castle is exalted so high that there is no way to approach it. "Simplicity" is "pureness" to the Buddhist, "uniformity" is "sameness." The aristocratic agent is not worthy to look into it; nor are the other previously mentioned agents, intelligence and will. Eckhart has one supreme agent, light, or spark—"spark" being quite a characteristic term for Eckhart, as we have seen—that is absolute intelligence or reason. But pure reason, intelligence, will alone are not able to peek in where God lives and burns like fire.[xiii]

God is simplicity itself, but he burns, or glows, in activity. When we examine these statements intellectually, from the rational point of view, they are full of contradictions. But they have the same expressions great Zen masters frequently use. For example, compare "Even Buddhas cannot look into it" with this Eckhart passage:

> It is the truth as God lives, God himself cannot even peek into it for a moment—or steal into it—in so far as he has particular selfhood and the properties of a person. This is a good point to notice, for the onefold One has neither a manner nor properties. And therefore, if God is to steal into it [the little castle in the soul] it [the adventure] will cost him all his divine names and person-like properties; He would have to forgo all these if he is to gain entrance. Except as he is the onefold One, without ways or properties—neither the Father nor the Holy Spirit in this [personal] sense, yet something that is neither this nor that—See!—it is only as he is One and onefold that he may enter into that One which I have called the Little Castle of the soul. Otherwise he cannot get in by any means or be at home there, for in part the soul is like God—otherwise it would not be possible. (p. 211)

Altogether one is this castle, high above, not even to be approached by God himself. Even God can have selfhood. When we say this or that we differentiate; and when we make a little step toward differentiation all is lost, God is no more there, the castle is

xiii. Blakney, *Meister Eckhart*, 210, last paragraph, and further references in n. 8, p. 326.

no more there. Eckhart calls this selfhood or personlike. The "onefold One" is a good thing to note. When God tries to get into the castle, he forfeits all his divine names and personlike properties, these not being applicable here at all; the ordinarily personlike is like this relative self. He has to forgo all these if he is to gain entrance—from the human viewpoint, as we make him try to enter here. Except as he is onefold One, neither Father nor Spirit, neither this nor that, otherwise he cannot get in by any means. Only as he is one and onefold of soul may he enter into absolute mind, suchness, the little castle of the soul. As you see, when we go over these things closely we find that Eckhart, like Aśvaghoṣa, denies in one place, affirms in another.

Form cannot be conceived by the human mind; there are no words and no conceptions for substance, which is fundamental to all being. Psychology can surmise about it, the very point where psychological phenomena begin; it is the limit of our psychology and our own beginning [in self-investigation]. In modern psychology they do not discriminate so much between form and activity. Substance is something basic; it cannot be expressed at all, except through cognition by experience. Modern psychology cuts out both mind and substance; it approaches from the side of form and activity. Now psychology deals from outside, mind and substance with the inside. Of course, mind and substance are underneath our being all the time, and we must remember this. Substance is following when we go along with form and activity; Substance is underneath even if we are unconscious of it. To illustrate I will give you a *mondō* about one of the great leaders of Zen, Sekitō (Shitou):

One day when he saw Yakusan (Yaoshan) practicing meditation, sitting quietly somewhere, Sekitō asked, "What are you doing here?"

Yakusan: "I am not doing anything."

Sekitō: "If so, then you are sitting idly."

Yakusan: "Even idle sitting is doing something."

Sekitō: "You say you are doing nothing, but what is that which is doing nothing?" This is important.

Yakusan: "Even if you call up thousands of wise men, they cannot tell you that."

At this Sekitō heartily endorsed Yakusan's understanding of Zen. Then Sekitō composed a verse, an important one:

> Since of old we have been living together without knowing the name;
> Hand in hand, as the wheel turns, we thus go.
> Since ancient times even wise men of the highest grade failed to know what it is;
> How then can ordinary people expect to have a clear understanding of it in a casual way?

We just went on as we willed, we just lived—suchness is here. This that even ancient wise men could say nothing about is indeed difficult for ordinary people to comprehend. You must apply yourself most seriously, not in a haphazard way, or you cannot get it.

Later Sekitō happened to make this remark to his congregation: "Neither words nor actions are of any avail." That is, neither speaking nor acting is in relationship with reality; it is beyond words, gestures.

Yakusan replied: "Even when there are no words, no actions, they are of no avail." When we do not use words, actions, and so on we are not in relationship with reality either. Whether we affirm or not we cannot get at it, we cannot touch reality.

Sekitō: "Here in my place there is not room even for the point of a needle to enter." There is no room in reality to put even the point of a needle.

Yakusan: "Here in my place it is like planting a flower on the rock."

To this Sekitō gave his full approval.[xiv]

Now these are quite important statements made by each Zen master. One said that even a needle's point cannot enter; the other that it was like planting a flower on rock. Reality, absolute mind, is so inaccessible; whether we affirm or negate, we can never reach it. It is beyond everything and anything; yet there is no one thing that is not reality itself—absolute mind manifests everywhere, even in the point of a needle. Reality fills this world. Another way of saying it is "like planting a flower on the rock." When the master says it in this way he does not appeal to reason but describes a state of mind, enlightenment, and the experience itself. Unless you have this experience, unless you can see with Eckhart's heart, unless you have this heart a needle's point and a flower on rock will be totally nonsensical. Brought onto the intellectual plane, affirmation and negation will not do it; it is a perfect state of suchness or emptiness. In this state planting a flower on rock becomes quite intelligible.

Planted in earth, a plant is expected to flower. It is a vain attempt on rock, altogether purposeless we may say. We on earth expect a plant to bear fruit; the work is to be quite significant. When things are done purposelessly we think it is useless work, beyond utility. But this is what Zen expects of all of us, this kind of "useless" life to live. This *mondō* shows the difference between the Zen way of expressing this experience and the Christian way, or the philosopher's way. This story, I think, is quite fine. In it they do not ask about anything religious or metaphysical; there is nothing of soul, suchness, God, or anything of the kind. They just—well, how shall we describe this kind of *mondō*? Suchness is of both worlds. Mind incarnates itself in substance, and it is necessary for substance to be in form and activity for enlightenment, as we shall see.

---

xiv. SZ, 142-143.

In Zen *mondō* generally one side is trying to beat the other down in a way, or to be argumentative in the Zen manner. But sometimes one helps the other in order to complete what is begun, this being the kind of complementary *mondō* that characterizes the school of Isan (Weishan, 771–853). In this example Isan and his chief disciple, Kyōzan (Yangshan, 807–883), cooperate to help each other very much.[xv]

While they were picking tea leaves for the use of the monastery, Isan said, "All day we have been picking tea leaves. I hear your voice, but I do not see your form. Why don't you show me your original form?" This may sound very disorganized when picking tea. I have not seen the fundamental body of yours, what makes you you, your original reality as you are. Why don't you let me see it?

Kyōzan shook the tea plant without saying anything. These plants are not very tall, no more than six feet even when allowed to grow by themselves; they are generally cut lower for easy picking.

Isan: "Well, you have got the activity, but not the substance." Shaking the tea plant is not the disciple's original form, not the body itself. It is just function or activity.

Kyōzan: "O master, what would you do then?" What is your way of demonstrating the substance itself?

The master was silent for a while. Then Kyōzan spoke again. "You have just got the body, but not the activity."

Isan: "I spare you twenty blows." You deserve twenty blows, but this time I will spare you.

Not refuting but complementing, both try in this way to show what is substance, what is activity. They are saying: substance is activity, activity is substance; enlightenment cannot be conceived statically but dynamically. Being is becoming, becoming is being, but they do not indulge in this abstract way of stating it. They use

xv. EZB 1, 303 [289]; MCB, 28.

concrete terms, or means. These gestures, movements, seem somewhat more appealing than mere dialectics.

Another time Isan was having a nap when Kyōzan came in. The master, sensing his entrance, turned to face the wall, thus showing his back to the disciple. Kyōzan said, "Why do you do that?"

Isan, getting up, said, "A while ago I had a dream. I want you to find out what that was."

Kyōzan, without saying anything, just brought a basin filled with water and let the master wash his face.

A little while later another disciple, Kyōgen (?~898), came in. Isan said to him, "While I was having a nap I had a dream. Can you guess what it was? Kyōzan guessed it right; I wonder if you can too."[7]

Kyōgen, without answering, brought a cup of tea for the master to drink.

Then Isan said, "Well, I have disciples who go even beyond Śāriputra and Maudgalyāyana!" Mine are far ahead of these because they read my dream quite correctly.[xvi]

Now these things do not take place except in Zen, I think. Once Isan used a pitcher—they generally have a pitcher, for they are supposed to wash their hands frequently, to keep free from germs I suppose. He was handing the pitcher to Kyōzan, who wanted to take it, but Isan withdrew his arm and said, "What is this?"

Kyōzan, unable to get the pitcher, said, "O master, what do you see [this is]?" as Isan drew his arm back.

Isan: "If this is anything, what do you want from me?" If it is a what, why do you ask me to pass it over to you?

Kyōzan: "That may be so, but in this worldly way it is quite proper for the disciple to fill the pitcher for the master."

Isan then gave the pitcher to Kyōzan.

xvi IZ, 114–115.

In the beginning Isan must have wanted the disciple to fill the pitcher he was about to hand over. This just passing a pitcher between master and disciple is an ordinary thing, but even in trivial matters, which we experience in daily life, something profound can be discovered.

While at another time the master and the disciple [Kyōzan] were walking, the master pointing at a cypress said, "What is that?"

Disciple: "That is just a cypress tree."

Master, turning back and pointing to a farmer who happened to be there: "In that case, this fellow as well as a Zen master can be at the head of five hundred monks."

It is not necessary for Zen students to go through Zen discipline to find out a cypress tree is a cypress tree. If they do not go further than that, then the farmer, who is supposed to be ignorant of Zen, can just as well be at the head of five hundred monks. Just mere affirmation or negation—is this a book, or not?—seem [to be] quite innocent affirmations or negations; still something deep is underneath when they are analyzed.

In the classroom we may engage in such discussions, but they take place anywhere in Zen. When the same master and the disciple happened to meet, the master asked: "Where do you come from?"

Disciple: "I come from the rice field."

Master: "Is the rice ready to be harvested?" Is it fully ripe, ready for harvesting?

Disciple: "Yes, the ears are ready, they are fully ripe."

Master: "Do they look green or yellow, or do they look neither yellow nor green?" Now rice becomes the subject. When yellow it is ready to be cropped; it is not quite ripe if green.

Disciple: "O master, what is at your back?" The disciple does not answer directly.

Master: "What do you see?"

The disciple took from the field a spike of rice, lifted it up, and said, "Are you asking about this?" Instead of talking of greenness or yellowness, he just showed an ear so there would be no question of green or yellow—reality itself is present before every one of us. This is not exactly a *mondō*; it is nothing but action, we might say. But throughout this kind of pantomime we can see something going on behind.[8]

This reality, this One Mind, divides itself into the aspects of suchness and of birth-and-death. As One Mind comes out into this scheme of two aspects or phases of One Mind—literally the two gates of Confucius—Aśvaghoṣa has this bifurcation. One has to be quite careful not to misunderstand this division. It will be better to say simply: in itself this Absolute One Mind shows no kind of movement or will. When it shows this movement it divides itself. In this initial state, when it does not express itself as movement yet, Mind shows a certain tendency to move, and this tendency can be distinguished in Absolute Mind. It does not move, but a sign is there. This One Mind, God in Eckhart, is Absolute Mind when it just remains in itself. It is absolute will when it chooses to move. Before it moves, something is trying to move yet not showing itself as movement—a certain thing must be going on to express will this way or that way. And this potential movement is *isshin*, "one Mind," not yet showing itself in any form of movement. But although this *isshin* does not yet show itself in movement, we can distinguish two things in it: the tendency to manifest itself in itself; the tendency to stay, to remain absolutely quiet. This initial movement that does not show itself as movement cannot be divided into two. This One Mind has no differentiation; we cannot say definitely this or that. There is changeableness on one side, unchangeableness on the other. It is unmoving, yet about to move:

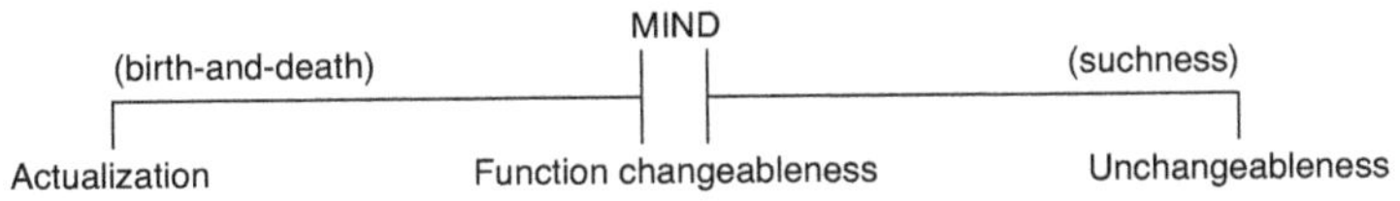

When One Mind actualizes [itself in particularities,] each particular thing contains emptiness. At the same time this Mind functions.

When it has no substance [in particularities], it reflects the unchangeableness of the other [side, that is, suchness]. One Mind is absolutely neutral. It is not nonexistence, but when we think it exists it is no more there. Our thought system requires us to postulate something, but it remains undifferentiated, empty, quiescent. From this Absolute Mind, One Mind, there is a beginning when we cannot say this or that, the beginningless beginning. Movement manifests itself into different forms, and when Mind manifests into movement there is a change into unchangeableness and changeableness.

This actualization side or aspect manifests itself and functions are there, but individually there is no substance describable as such. This is the state called emptiness in which the unchangeable aspect of One Mind empty of substantiality is. When One Mind manifests [itself], actualizes [itself], or whatever one calls it, this is delusion in Buddhist terminology, though not as this word is ordinarily understood.

This manifestation of the objective world can be described as having four aspects, forms, or stages of change or movement:

1. Birth, Sanskrit *jāti*, Chinese *sheng*; Japanese *shō*. But the commentator on Aśvaghoṣa, Fazang, says that *shō* is coming into existence, that it really means the initial state of birth, that it is not yet out into any form of existence, birth being only about to take place. When it has come into definite form it is the second aspect of existence.
2. The state of standing still or unchanging, *sthiti*, C. *zhu*; J. *jū*.
3. Decay, change, *jarā*, C. *yi*; J. *i*.
4. Death, passing away, *anityatā* ("impermanency"), C. *mie*; J. *metsu*.

In the first will is just beginning to move from the state of potentiality to the state of actuality. The initial sprout trying to get into definite form, this is birth. One Mind is absolute; we cannot distinguish anything in it. When it begins to move we have *shō.* Will moves to manifest, it does something—this is birth. Just willing to go out, but not yet showing itself in particular forms—this is *shō.* When this corresponds to the Buddhist *ālayavijñāna* it contains all those tendencies or potentialities that are to actualize themselves into the world. *Shō* is the initial movement that cannot yet be detected as movement; we cannot yet definitely say, "Here is birth." It is the instinct of birth, we might say. *Shō* is not recognizable by the senses. When it is at the stage of maturation then it is *jū.*

The second form or aspect is really the world detected by the senses. This will moving in has not yet expressed itself in form, but it is potentially there, about to move, has not moved yet. When it really moves, it divides into two. It just wants to become two first. When it really manifests there is knowledge, perception, awareness. Before it takes definite form there is something moving, this being more apparent than the first phase of birth, or not so subtle as the first. When this first stage is passed, it has definite form recognizable as such: subject and object are divided. The process goes on, it is a state of constant becoming. All four things or stages are distinguished.

The third, decay, *yi,* has no special connection with the ideas used to distinguish the first two; Fazang just borrows four stages to express himself, as quite frequently in Chinese. This decay is not to be taken in the ordinary sense. *Yi* is discrimination, we might say. By means of discrimination we get attached (C. *zhiqu*; J. *shūshu*), we cling to particular forms. This is more emotional, while [J.] *keimyōji* (C. *jimingzi*) is more intellectual, conceptual.[9] When the world of subject and object takes place and goes on continually our minds get attached and take this world as eternally so. We get emotionally attached and intellectually attached, we take concepts as realities with trouble resulting.

The fourth is *metsu,* impermanence, death. When these concepts go on we commit good or bad deeds, *karma.* This third stage is the karmic aspect of existence; all kinds of karmic activities are here. When all these deeds are committed what is committed does not just die away; it produces effects, fruition takes place. If we have the idea of causation, good deeds have good results, bad have bad results in this world of causation. By these aspects or stages Aśvaghoṣa tries to explain our existence.

Now that you have a clear understanding of Aśvaghoṣa's scheme of One Mind, we can come back to his four kinds, or stages, of enlightenment: ignorance or nonenlightenment, enlightenment in appearance, approximate enlightenment, perfect enlightenment.[10] I will begin with three quotations from Aśvaghoṣa:

> The multitude of people (*bahujana*) are said to be lacking in enlightenment, because ignorance (*avidyā*) prevails there from all eternity, because there is a constant succession of confused subjective states (*smṛti*) from which they have never been emancipated.
>
> But when they transcend their subjectivity, they can then recognize that all states of mentation, viz., their appearance, presence, change, and disappearance [in the field of consciousness] have no [genuine] reality. They are neither in a temporal nor in a spatial relation with the one soul, for they are not self-existent.[xvii]

> When you understand this, you also understand that enlightenment *a posteriori* cannot be manufactured, for it is no other thing than enlightenment *a priori* [which is uncreated and must be discovered].[xviii]

---

xvii. The older [Paramārtha] translation reads: "The four states of mentation are simultaneous [they belong together in time, that is, they are in uninterrupted succession], but have no self-existence, because enlightenment *a priori* always remains in its sameness." Bracketed phrases are Suzuki's insertions [RMJ].

xviii. AFM, 66. The bracketed phrase is Suzuki's insertion [RMJ].

> Common people (*pṛthagjana*) who, becoming conscious of errors that occur in a succession of their mental states, abstain from making conclusions may be spoken of as enlightened; but in reality theirs is non-enlightenment.[xix]

> By the so-called non-enlightenment, we mean that as the true Dharma [i.e., suchness] is from all eternity not truthfully recognized in its oneness, there issues forth an unenlightened mind and then subjectivity (*smṛti*). But this subjectivity has no self-existence independent of enlightenment *a priori.*[xx]

This karma that is good, bad, or neutral, we always get the result of it. When we think we ought to do this, that a bad thought ought to be put out of mind, a good thought let in, this is a kind of field of enlightenment. When we become conscious of the law of causation, of good, bad, neutral, we realize what is good, what is bad. When we try to take the good and avoid the bad, this is a kind of enlightenment. When we are aware of a thought beginning to move in consciousness, when we become conscious of evil and try to avoid it, to destroy this thought and cultivate what comes after, this is a semblance of enlightenment, but not the real enlightenment: this is a kind of moral awakening. Most people are ignorant, and this ignorance is nonenlightenment. Most people are not to be classed, even when they have some kind of self-awareness, as enlightened. This ignorance of theirs is entirely different from original enlightenment, for no bifurcation into subject and object is possible.

---

xix. AFM, 63. *Pṛthagjana* has a technical sense in Buddhism: one who is ignorant of the doctrine of non-*ātman* and commits all those actions that lead into constant transmigration.

xx. AFM, 70. Brackets as in the original typescript [RMJ].

The second stage of enlightenment is described as follows: "Śrāvakas,[xxi] Pratyekabuddhas,[xxii] and those Bodhisattvas[xxiii] who have just entered their course, recognizing the difference between subjectivity and the transcending of subjectivity both in essence and attributes, have become emancipated from the coarse form of particularization. This is called enlightenment in appearance."[xxiv] This is not real, not genuine enlightenment. Though it somewhat resembles it, it is actually the similitude of enlightenment, as Aśvaghoṣa says. It is enlightenment on the intellectual plane, when one is just becoming conscious of nonego, when we are just beginning to realize that ego is not the real I. This stage of consciousness is merely intellectual. This stage is static and ontological, with its bifurcation of subject and object, its taking things in by intellection. It is beginning to get beyond good and bad, right and wrong, for it is not the real thing and must be transcended. We cannot exactly say that it is moral enlightenment, though the moral also contains intellection. It becomes conscious of good and bad, stopping the bad, taking the good. Good-bad, subject-object are our way of recognizing the relative world of bifurcation. We must transcend this, for otherwise we cannot reach enlightenment, the realm beyond this world

xxi. Beings who have become wise, have faith in the Tathāgata, consequently apply themselves to his commandments, wish to follow the dictates of an authoritative voice, and apply themselves to acquire the four great truths for the sake of their own complete Nirvāṇa.

xxii. Also beings who have become wise, have faith in the Tathāgata, and apply themselves to his commandments; but they are desirous of the science without a master, of self-restraint and tranquility. They apply themselves to the commandment of the Tathāgata to learn to understand causes and effects—the twelve chains of relation—again for the sake of their own Nirvāṇa.

xxiii. Beings desirous of the knowledge of the all- knowing, the knowledge of Buddha, the knowledge of the self-born one, and the science without a master, they apply themselves to the commandment of the Tathagāta to learn to understand the knowledge, powers, and freedom from hesitation of the Tathāgata for the sake of all beings, out of compassion.

xxiv. AFM, 63–64.

of dichotomy. Most of us have this second kind of enlightenment. In accordance with bifurcation we conceive our existence. But this is simply the resemblance to enlightenment, enlightenment on the intellectual plane when one is just becoming conscious of nonego.

With reference to this intellectual enlightenment, I might add that there is a quickening of the moral sense itself in this stage. But why do we want to go to good and not to bad? Original enlightenment is absolutely undifferentiated, but it has more good in itself, though there is no real distinction between good and bad in original enlightenment. There is really no good or bad in ultimate enlightenment, but if enlightenment is carried out in daily life the enlightened man's life is always good. Even those who have nonenlightenment, those not conscious of the presence of enlightenment in themselves, unconsciously move toward good, relatively, in a moral sense. Consciousness never wants to move toward bad, but always toward good. The enlightened man never murders, for example; the unenlightened only thinks he does, thus making him murder, as it were. Compare the well-known passages of the *Bhagavad-Gītā*, the Upaniṣads, and Emerson's poem.

There was a Japanese master who did not specially observe Buddha's moral precepts, two hundred fifty of which are ordinarily observed by monks. A disciple who followed a master who gave much importance to these precepts, who was always thinking of them and their possible violation—this disciple asked the Japanese master if he followed them. The latter is enlightened and is naturally in accord with these precepts without thinking specially of them.

The third state of enlightenment is emotional, metaphysical, philosophical, partial, or fragmentary enlightenment. When we become conscious of this world of subject and object we begin to inquire how this happens and goes on. This metaphysical enlightenment is deeper than mere intellectual enlightenment, but it still has not reached the stage where real consciousness is. In this third stage there is no division of anything anywhere. But it is still far from ultimate, supreme enlightenment. Aśvaghoṣa says of it: "Bodhisattvas of the Dharmakāya,[xxv] having recognized that subjectivity, and the transcending of subjectivity have no reality of their own [that is, are relative], have become emancipated from the intermediate form of particularization. This is called approximate enlightenment."[xxvi]

The fourth is real, ultimate enlightenment: "Those who have transcended the stage of Bodhisattvahood and attained the ultimate goal, possess a consciousness which is consistent and harmonious; they have recognized the origin from which consciousness [or mentation] starts."[xxvii]

This will truly be called enlightenment.

> Having transcended the attributes of enlightenment and the subtlest form of particularization, they [that is, buddhas] have gained a perfect and eternal insight into the very nature of the soul [that is, suchness], because the latter now presents itself to them in its absolute and immutable form. Therefore they are called Tathāgatas, and theirs is perfect enlightenment; and therefore it is said in the Sutra that those who have an insight into the nonreality of all subjectivity, attain to the wisdom of the Tathāgata.[xxviii]

> In the preceding statement we referred to the origin from which consciousness [or mentation] starts according to the popular expression. In truth there is no such thing as the origin of

xxv. Those who have recognized the all-pervading Dharmakāya but who have not as yet been able to perfectly identify themselves with it.

xxvi. AFM, 64.

xxvii. Consciousness, that is, mentation or mental activity, is transient, it takes place in time, and must not be confused with soul, or suchness, or eternal wisdom.

xxviii. LS.

> consciousness [or mentation]; for consciousness [being purely subjective] has no absolute [but only a phenomenal] existence. How can we then speak of its origin?[xxix]

When this supreme enlightenment is attained there is neither subject nor object nor anything of becoming. This stage is conative. It is the perfect state of suchness, sameness, pureness, emptiness, *munen*—the state of perfect *munen.* This attainment, so to speak, is really not-attainment, so it is supreme enlightenment, there being no enlightenment. And just because it is no enlightenment it is supreme enlightenment. It is different from metaphysical enlightenment, where there is still a little spark, movement, or consciousness, we might say. Aśvaghoṣa says that there is still something a little subtle in the third stage. To get rid of it and reach supreme enlightenment, even this little something of awareness needs removing. In this fourth stage enlightenment reaches original enlightenment; supreme enlightenment becomes identical with original enlightenment.

First there is the coarser form of the tendency to move, the rough form. When something moves in One Mind, when there is potentiality to move, it divides into *shin*, truth, and *mō*, delusion, though not delusion in the ordinary sense. When this One Mind begins to think of moving, just its initial stage of will, real enlightenment must come from this—then we have real, ultimate enlightenment. Original enlightenment, enlightenment *a priori,* is Absolute One Mind, pure original enlightenment in itself. But if original enlightenment stands still, enlightenment is impossible; original enlightenment mixed with ignorance makes enlightenment possible. Just the tendency to move, the beginning of the will to move, is *shin*, and in this *shin* we have ignorance or delusion, *mō*; we cannot say anything at all about

---

xxix. AFM, 64–65.

it as long as ignorance does not assert itself. The possibilities of human enlightenment and the completely unenlightened in the first stage are possible only through this mixing of original enlightenment with ignorance, the result being that unconscious consciousness is finally enlightened. I will illustrate by a *mondō*:

A master asked a monk: "What day is this?"

Monk: "I do not know." This answer may mean two things: he does not want to make a differentiation; or he simply does not know, on the relative plane.

Master: "I know."

Monk: "What day is this?"

Master: "It is cloudy." If the master had said the fifteenth, for example, it would have been intellectual enlightenment.

As I have said, Aśvaghoṣa starts from One Mind, Absolute Mind. And this Absolute Mind divides itself into two: suchness, birth-and-death or *saṃsāra*. This world of birth-and-death, *saṃsāra*, is this world of particulars in which we are all living now, the world of multiplicities, of the senses—this world that comes out of One Mind. This One Mind is the part that is difficult to grasp. When grasped it receives enlightenment. One Mind is sameness, uniformness itself, now divided into suchness and *saṃsāra*. Aśvaghoṣa does not try to argue about these things; he simply states them as a matter of fact.[xxx]

The world of *saṃsāra*, of the senses, is where all forms of becoming take place. Here, where we have subject and object, we have a line dividing subject and object. The five senses act as a kind of boundary line between the subjective and objective worlds, an imaginary, conventional line that we use for talking. When we withdraw from the line and look within our own consciousness we find that these five senses are synthesized or unified by another "sense," *manovijñāna*, literally "mental perception," *ishiki* in Japanese. We may

xxx. AFM, 55–61.

represent the entire scheme Aśvaghoṣa proposes by the following diagram:

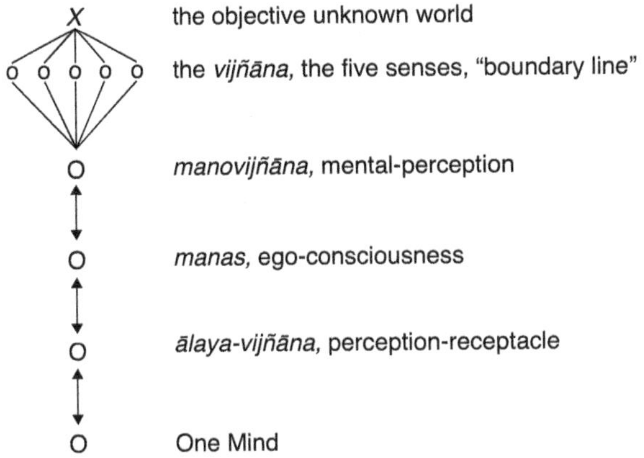

Omitting the objective world and One Mind, this diagram may be represented in another way.

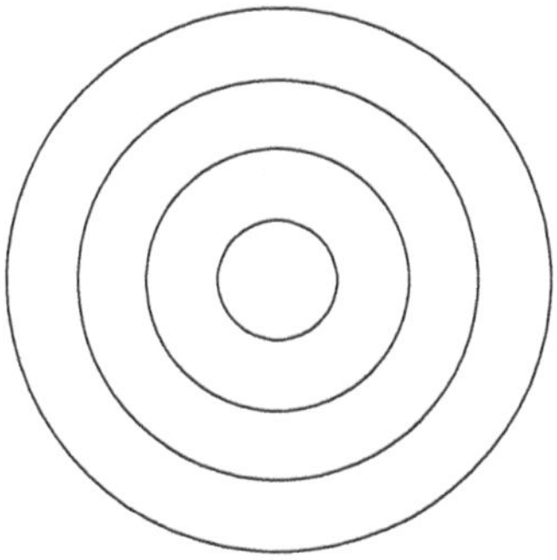

Here we look down into *ālaya,* the senses forming the outer circle. Everything is received from the outer world, by the senses, then integrated by *manovijñāna, manovijñāna* being behind the recognition of whatever the senses take in. A light wave taken in by the eye, for example, is perceived as color by *manovijñāna*, not by the eye itself. Space-time and causation, supposed to be existent in the objective world, cannot be experienced by the five senses, but *manovijñāna* is behind them, making them into the one structure made possible by *manas*,[11] which is behind *manovijñāna*. All sense, *manovijñāna*, experiences and data are possible because of this ego center, *manas*, although *manovijñāna* takes all of them as happening to itself. The system of the senses is only possible through *manas*, ego-consciousness itself. Sense data coordinated through *manovijñāna* to *manas* make the ordinary world possible.

In this *manas* we can distinguish two kinds of sense consciousness: one works outwardly, as it were, the other inwardly. The first is the consciousness that works on data from the outside world, the sense data that are coordinated by *manovijñāna* each time *manas* says, "This is my experience, it has taken place in me." The second is the unconscious consciousness of *manas* looking back into *ālaya-vijñāna* and taking *ālaya-vijñāna* for its real self. The first is conscious and self-conscious because its consciousness is intermittent; the second is unconscious because its consciousness is constant. Constant consciousness, that is, unconsciousness of self, is almost the same as unconsciousness. *Manas* doesn't realize it comes from *ālaya* because this stream of consciousness here is constant. *Manas* is thus the meeting place of intermittent self and constant self.

According to Buddhist psychology, *ālaya-vijñāna* is the storehouse or reservoir of all experiences that we have, good or bad. Here are all the memories, all the seeds, all the potentialities. But *ālaya* is still not the place where Aśvaghoṣa supposed supreme enlightenment to take place. We may say that subtle consciousness is here for him, though the Yogācāra school, this group of Buddhist psychologists, takes *ālaya* as ultimate reality.

If we express this unconscious consciousness, [mentioned] above, in terms of enlightenment as expressed by Aśvaghoṣa, nonenlightenment belongs, of course, to the area of the senses. Intellectual enlightenment takes place on the fringe of *manovijñāna*, while metaphysical, fragmentary enlightenment takes place where *manovijñāna* and *manas* work together, not exactly in *manas*. For the location of supreme enlightenment Aśvaghoṣa goes further up, or down. For him this *ālaya-vijñāna* is to be transcended to One Mind, Absolute Mind, the last stage, where all the different forms of *vijñāna* are included. Here is *munen* (*wunian*), full-sized emptiness, full-sized enlightenment.

This is the way it is when we turn back from the sense line, but ordinarily we look ahead without turning back. We can really say that the objective world is an unknown quantity, *x*. Of this unknown quantity we record whatever affects our senses. The senses take from this unknown as far as they can, but these senses cannot exhaust this quantity, though most people think that they do exhaust it. There is much else, and the unknown quantity still remains unknown. It can never be exhausted by the senses and science, these can never reach its end. Ordinarily the sense world is considered to be all there is, but this is not true, though we cannot take hold of this other world directly. Sense is able to chip off only so much of the unknown quantity, but the unknown quantity is still there; we can never take up the whole and examine it.

But this unknown quantity is there just because we divide this world into subject and object. Subject comes first if we have to choose one, so it is always present in spite of the material world. When we come to the bottom of subject we come to the unconscious consciousness that is *ālaya-vijñāna*. When unconscious consciousness is broken through, there is no absolute reality. At the bottom of subject, there always remains a very subtle residue, which makes possible our conception of unconscious consciousness. But this unconscious consciousness is to be broken through for supreme enlightenment; and when it is broken through we have godhead in the very act or "Let there be light!"

When we have supreme enlightenment we have One Mind. And when we have One Mind we do not have bifurcation of subject and object. As long as we have the world of subject and object, they have to be talked about outwardly, in the world: subject-object, in unconscious consciousness—conscious unconsciousness designate the stage where we are. But when we come to this One Mind and nothing else, when we reach absolute enlightenment, we cannot say anything about it. It is called the state of *munen,* a most important term, very difficult to comprehend.

Nen (*nian*) is a unit of consciousness, consciousness being constituted of so many *nen,* the shortest wave of consciousness in the conception of Buddhist psychology. The Sanskrit term for *nen* is *citta-kṣaṇa,* mind in the sense of consciousness plus the shortest possible division of time, a thought-instant.

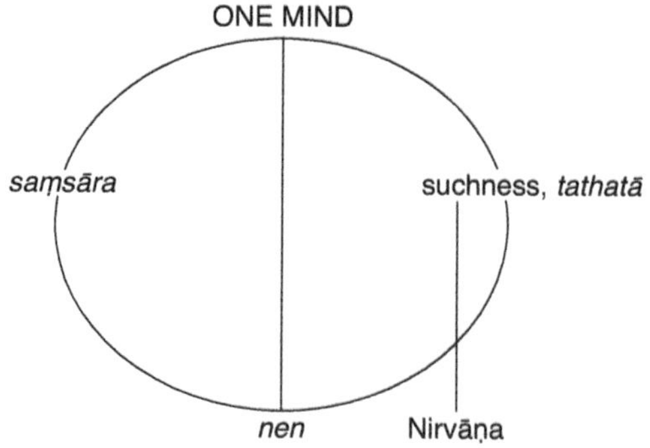

In this diagram the central line is the rising of *nen* in the absolute emptiness of One Mind. As soon as it rises, the world comes into existence, for this rising of one *citta-kshaṇa* is bifurcation. When this has not taken place but is about to take place, this very moment is called *munen,* literally "no thought-instant," though this does not give its real meaning. When one *nen* has not come up, no cleavage into two has taken place. When one *nen* comes up there is cleavage into two. Before the division takes place, before one *nen* moves, when no *nen* has yet come up to cleave but when one *nen* is about to rise—this is *munen.* And when we have consciousness of this *munen* we have supreme enlightenment. And this *munen* is, we may say, the state of absolute present or absolute now. In terms of time, everything goes on along the timeline.

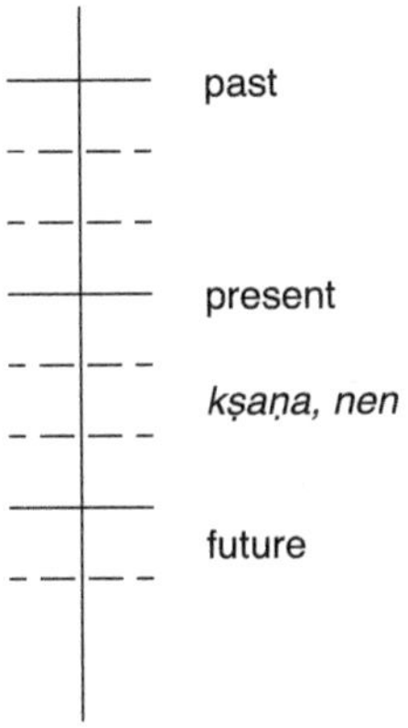

The present can be moved to any point, but when I say "now" it is no more now. When the present is not moving there is no past, present, or future. It is absolute present, when time begins to think, *Shall I go on, or not?* This absolute present is an important point and one not easy to grasp; but when the absolute present is grasped we have supreme enlightenment, distinguished from metaphysical, fragmentary, partial. This partial enlightenment, so-called, is very near supreme enlightenment, but something has not yet been brought in. When put into language, however, "the arrow has gone three thousand miles away."[12] Actually, however, these should be called four kinds, not four stages of enlightenment, for one does not necessarily lead to another; they are simply different in kind. Ultimate enlightenment does not necessarily come after the other three, though sometimes one may lead to another, sometimes we may go on from one to another.

This *munen* is used very much in Zen. Most people think it is a state of utter unconsciousness, where consciousness is all wiped out. But this conception of it is still on the relative plane, to be passed through before real enlightenment is possible. We have to say that this *nen* moves on, then there is dichotomy and this world we have. But when all these opposites have not taken place there is *munen,* from which all things come. The void of Christianity is really fullness. When nothing is taken to be on the plane of relativity an emptiness that is fullness is a logical impossibility. But we are to understand in Aśvaghoṣa's *munen* that the world came from nothingness that is really fullness, though of course not physically as scientists would take it. One Mind contains everything and produces everything. It contains all things as if not containing anything. It does everything as if doing nothing—this is an important point in Zen philosophy.

This *munen* is not "not having any thought or consciousness." It is simply *munen,* nothing else. *Nen* is a conscious instant, or we may call it a conscious quantum. Then this *nen* does not start to work and *nen* becomes *munen* [no conscious instant], no absence of consciousness quantum. When this *nen* goes on, one *nen* after another rises and goes on—this is the state of our everyday consciousness. Consciousness consists in going on without stopping. "No conscious instant" does not mean the stopping of any conscious instant; *prajñā*-intuition takes place or goes on all the time. But ultimate enlightenment consists in realizing this *munen.*

Now the potential tendency to move, for lack of a better term, begins to activate itself. This very movement is in a state of potentiality, one very difficult to describe. It is one conscious instant, one thought-moment, according to Aśvaghoṣa. It starts to move, it is about to change—this is a rather coarse way of comparing: this nothingness goes into somethingness, something is created out of nothing. Something like this may be used for it. One thought-instant is about to move into activity. *Munen* is about to turn itself into one thought-moment. It is neither moving nor not-moving—this is when enlightenment takes place. This Aśvaghoṣa calls original enlightenment:

> Now we speak of enlightenment *a posteriori;* because there is enlightenment *a priori* [original enlightenment], there is non-enlightenment, and because there is non-enlightenment we can speak of enlightenment *a posteriori.*[xxxi]

> . . . enlightenment *a posteriori* cannot be manufactured, for it is no other thing than enlightenment *a priori* [which is uncreated and must be discovered].[xxxii]

> Though all modes of consciousness and mentation are mere products of ignorance, ignorance in its ultimate nature is identical and non-identical with enlightenment *a priori*; and therefore ignorance in one sense is destructible, while in the other sense it is indestructible.[xxxiii]

> Now suchness is a pure dharma free from defilement. It acquires, however, a quality of defilement owing to the perfuming power of ignorance. On the other hand, ignorance has nothing to do with purity. Nevertheless, we speak of its being able to do the work of purity, because it in its turn is perfumed by suchness.[xxxiv]

xxxi. AFM, 62–63.
xxxii. AFM, 66.
xxxiii. AFM, 67.
xxxiv. AFM, 84–85.

Aśvaghoṣa speaks about ignorance in the relative and absolute senses and about its being identical with original enlightenment. Ignorance does not really belong to enlightenment but is preparation for enlightenment, as I have said. Original enlightenment corresponds to One Mind. There is a movement in original enlightenment, but to talk about this movement is rather confusing, as we have seen. It is not active, but there is a certain tendency, a potentiality, that is about to start. Potentiality is not quite actual movement, but we associate with it a certain amount of activity. From our way of talking about these things such confusion is inevitable, I think, for shortcomings of language are met everywhere. This original enlightenment moves out of its self-nature, which does not remain as it is. We may call it original ignorance, fundamental ignorance. Original enlightenment holds in itself this germ or potentiality of fundamental ignorance. When this combination begins to separate itself this *munen* begins to stir, one *nen* begins to move out of *munen, munen* begins to go into the activity of one conscious instant—this is when ultimate enlightenment takes place. Being so, it is very difficult to express in language. It can be illustrated this way:

This negation, not-A_1, is inevitable in affirmation. Absolute Mind does not really contain two, but when we speak of it two come out. We cannot really say anything about Absolute Mind itself. We have to go through A_1, which directly comes from Absolute Mind, before we can get to Absolute Mind at all. In this relative world all consists of Absolute Mind, A, but the thing is to become conscious of it. Unenlightened man does not bother about all these things; neither does the enlightened, yet the latter somehow reaches up to A. The difficulty comes in in consciousness—what else can we say?

When fundamental ignorance comes out, not-A_1 is ignorance and *isshin* is Absolute Mind. I have put A up above, (A_1 + not-A_1) down below, but the movement is back and forth. Speaking always involves a contradiction. To get one wedge out another must be put there,

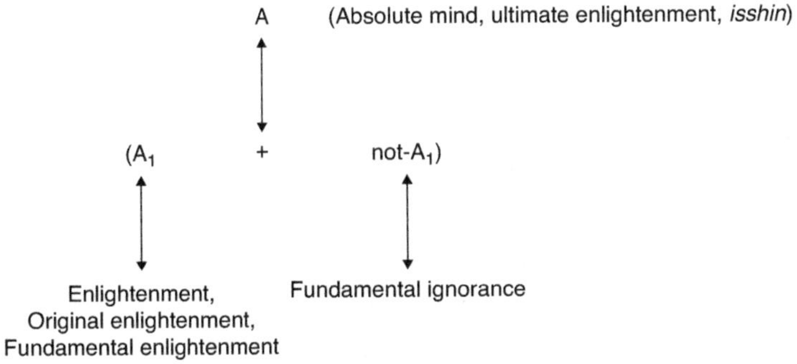

infinitely going on. To get out of this deficiency of language we have to use language. So we find noncontradiction in contradiction.

But I will now try to illustrate further what enlightenment is in the Zen way of demonstrating it, how Zen tries to give you what enlightenment is, without appealing to all these intellectual discourses of metaphysical talk. Different masters use different methodologies, for there is no consistent method, the masters differing in personality, intellect, and so on. Naturally the way they respond to a question differs. Several *mondō* have to do with this *nen*, and I will begin with one of them.

A monk asked Touzi, "How about when one *nen* does not rise?" That is, no sort of stirring takes place in one's consciousness. "Is this proper or not?" This is the attainment of mind the monk has.

Master: "It is a fault as big as Mount Sumeru."[13] This is a great mountain, around which all worlds are supposed to be situated, the highest, broadest mountain we can conceive.

The monk's question—not a ripple stirs in consciousness, no *nen* rises, consciousness is clean-swept—is the preliminary state for enlightenment. To this the master says, "Your fault is as big as Mount Sumeru." Those who know understand right at once the meaning.[xxxv]

xxxv. ZB, 225.

In another, "When I do not bring anything, is it all right or not?" is the same question in different wording: there is no subject or object about which I can ask your teaching; my mind is in perfect equilibrium.

Master: "Throw it down!"[14]

When there is nothing there is nothing to throw down. But this very point, when you are conscious of nothing, throw it away. Do not realize that nothing, do not think it worthy to express itself. His question shows the monk is still in a state of unenlightenment. He wants to reason about words, to hang on to the words the master has used. Another answer to this same question shows the satire, the sarcastic witticism, found in many *mondō*: "If so, carry it away!" If there is nothing to throw down, carry it away. This seems sarcastic, but the monk, who heard, came to enlightenment.[15]

Here is an example taken at random; it may not be easy to understand, but I will try to make it easier.

Shobi (Chuwei of Qianzhou) asked the monk Kyōzan Ejaku: "What is your name?"

Kyōzan: "Ejaku (Huiji)." Literally, *e* (*hui*) means "transcendental wisdom"; it is the Chinese word for the Sanskrit *prajñā*. *Jaku* (*chi*) is "peace," "tranquility." So Ejaku is the peace of transcendental wisdom, or of the originally pure.

Shobi: "What is *e*? What is *jaku*?" This divides the monk into a kind of dichotomy, subject and object: what is what? His name is divided into two; he is asked what the parts are.

Kyōzan: "Right before you." This is important.

Shobi: "Still there is a before-and-after relation." The Chinese has simply, "Before and after," no more.—You yourselves should think of all these things before I explain.

Kyōzan: "Let us put aside this before-and-after relation for a while." That is, we won't talk about this relation. "O master, what do you see?" This is important.

Shobi: "Have a cup of tea." This ends the *mondō*.[16]

Shobi first asks the monk his name. He knows it perfectly well and does not ask it for the sake of information, but for the sake of starting Zen talk. The totality of existence is divided into subject and object. What is the subjective world? What is the objective world? this Shobi asks. "Right before you"—the answer is a *kōan* (*gong'an*). He does not answer relatively, and he does not waste time in discussion. He just says, "Right before you." You all see me right before you; not *e*, not *jaku*—everything is right before you. Do not divide this unbroken vessel into pieces.[xxxvi]

In a way, "What is *e*? What is *jaku*?" is the same as asking, "What is One Mind?" But in supreme enlightenment there is no vestige of any kind of consciousness. When you say this or that you have missed it; even a little consciousness left and it is missed.

"Before-and-after"—the conception of space still sticks to you. Let us put aside spatial relationship altogether. Do you see anything spatial that can be divided into two? What do you see? The concluding statement is, "Have a cup of tea." If Shobi had said, "I see this" or "I do not see that," another series would have been required. So, "Have a cup of tea," then it is settled; [the way for solving] the most complicated question of division is just "Have a cup of tea," socially.

This is one way that is not so quarrelsome; the next one is different. There was quite a noted Zen master called Chin the Elder, a fine man who opened Rinzai's eyes to Zen. Once he happened to be standing at the top of the corridor steps when a monk who did not know him came up and asked, "Where is Chin, the old venerable master?" He asked by mistake; Chin was also known as "the old venerable master."

Chin took off one of his sandals and before making any remark struck the monk with it. Naturally the monk ran away. Chin called

---

xxxvi. *Zoku Dentōroku*, fas. 11. SZ, 171; *MW*, vol. 28, no. 2 (August 1953): 49.

after him, "O old venerable monk!" When the monk turned back Chin said, "There he goes," pointing at the monk. That is, Chin seems to be running away as the monk himself.[17]

When the question was asked it was a separation from the real wanting to know. So the question is unnecessary. But language is the key to the puzzle. While we stick to language bifurcation can never be erased, we can never come to enlightenment. We might say that the monk's asking this question divides himself into two. To remind him of this division, Chin strikes him, as if to say, "Here is undivided reality." The monk does not understand and runs away. Then Chin calls out. Unless there is an inner relationship between the two the call will never make him turn back. His turning shows the complete oneness of the two, and this oneness is what Chin wanted the monk to understand, so he said, "This Chin goes." The monk might be the world itself. When he responds, he has everything he has been after. But Chin was somewhat rough with monks.

Buddhism starts with enlightenment experience, and *satori* is naturally emphasized by Zen as its very foundation or cornerstone. This enlightenment is something not to be expressed by language, but communication is also impossible without language. Yet language is to be used with great caution; we are not to cling to language itself, for such clinging is very bad, it makes enlightenment impossible. The experience is also beyond both intellect and ethics, the experience cannot be reached by either intellect or ethics. To realize supreme enlightenment, etiology has to be crushed.

When this enlightenment takes place, Absolute One Mind is realized. One Mind does not stay in a state of absolute tranquilization, nothingness, emptiness. It holds in itself all tendencies and potentialities; it is about to move, a latent tendency not yet expressed in activity. When this movement has taken place, we are back, as it were, in this world of subject and object. When we have this will to move, from the point of view of enlightenment we have the most fundamental will we can come across. And One Mind is will in this most fundamental sense, the tendency to move and divide itself. Fundamental will, which has not yet come out into intellection, is the very basis of intellection and of *prajñā* and *karuṇā,* the two fundamental pillars on which the whole of Zen, in fact Buddhist, structure rests.

This will perhaps explain how enlightenment takes place, in a more or less metaphysical way. But in Buddhist philosophy they don't use "absolute" and "transcendent," or other such terms. Instead they have "pure" and "impure," they talk very much about pureness and sameness. This is not "pure" as the word is ordinarily understood, of course, but absolute pureness, One Mind or original enlightenment being pure. When they have defilement in opposition to purity, defilement is differentiation into two, not the usual sense of "dirty." What was one is now two, this is the defilement. No moral or ethical significance is implied anywhere; these are simply the metaphysical terms they use.

Thus it is possible to speak of pure consciousness. Ordinarily consciousness is carried on on the relative plane, for there must be opposites to make us conscious of anything. Yet pure consciousness underlies all our consciousness, all phenomena taking place in relative consciousness. We can speak of pure consciousness and of consciousness generally. When this pure consciousness begins to turn into relative consciousness, then this enlightenment takes place, or the awakening of awareness to it takes place. Pure consciousness is unconscious. This pure consciousness moving into consciousness is the beginning of the conscious instant. The moment it moves on, consciousness takes place.

When relative consciousness moves on to pure consciousness, this one *nen,* one thought-consciousness quantum, loses itself and becomes *munen,* no-consciousness moment or -quantum or -instant. So this movement reverses when we talk about it; we cannot speak of it from the side of pure consciousness. When this movement takes place, enlightenment takes place. When original enlightenment begins to turn into ignorance, it turns into consciousness and enlightenment, and this world. As I said, we can start from the world of relativity, of particulars, and go back to the state of pure consciousness, or we can start from pure consciousness. Then enlightenment, which is the turning about, *parāvṛtti,* is experienced.

Original enlightenment corresponds to One Mind, but when we talk about Absolute Mind or ultimate enlightenment we are liable to posit two things. Something corresponding to this idea of original enlightenment or Absolute Mind is there and can be conscious; this is allowed in this world of relativity, but we must go beyond, without transcending, this world of relativity to the transcendental world. Language we use to explain concepts. We make use of relative terms, but relative terms are not meant for the transcendental world. Ultimate enlightenment and One Mind are not in the realm of relativity, where we carry on our daily life. As I have said, when we assert anything about this One Mind we naturally negate it. Affirmation is carried out by means of negation. When this takes place, what we call *parāvṛtti* takes place. When we move from the plane of relativity to the transcendental plane, there is a kind of going home, a turning back, known as *parāvṛtti.* This Sanskrit term is used regularly to indicate turning back. This turning takes place in something on which the world of relativity depends. There is a certain fundamental turning about, almost corresponding to what religious psychologists call conversion. It has the same root and literally an intensive meaning, "a complete turning about." Originally it may mean the same thing as "returning" or "staying there."

We can say, and psychologically speaking it may be better understood this way, that when consciousness begins to start, then to become conscious of this moment of starting, to become aware of this, is enlightenment. Another way to express this phenomenon is to turn away from individual consciousness to get identified with pure consciousness. But one has to be careful [not to think that] consciousness is there—we must not think of pure consciousness as if it were one of the facts of relative consciousness. Pure consciousness is something that runs through relative, individual consciousness. Therefore, this Pure Consciousness cannot be picked up from the flow of daily consciousness. This is a most important point not to confuse.

Pure Consciousness is in relative, individual consciousness, and at the same time it is not one of those facts of consciousness that make up our ordinary consciousness. Another way of saying it is that consciousness comes out of unconsciousness, and in this moment of coming out we become aware of the fact. This awareness, or our awakening to this awareness, cannot be described, cannot be brought out into the world of verbal symbolism. Any language we may use has certain defects because of the very nature of language, inherently incapable of giving a clue to these experiences I have described. We cannot know the experiences themselves by language. Language is just meant for us to orient ourselves in the relative, material world, and to communicate to each other what we have experienced in this world of particulars. When we leave this world of particulars and go to the realm that transcends this world, language is naturally found full of shortcomings. But nevertheless we must use language and inevitably make all kinds of errors. To avoid this, Zen people appeal to their own way of communicating experience.[18]

If you strike something in this world it may be broken away; but in perfect emptiness you do not strike anything or leave any track. When the butcher knows how to use the knife and moves it along, flesh and bone part of themselves. In this case there is perfect emptiness, so nothing is struck and no tracks are left.

When mind is used like this, Mind remains unconscious; Mind remains not touched by anything. When mind is in this state the whole Mind in totality is Buddha himself, and Buddha himself is Mind. There is no differentiation between Mind and Buddha. When you have this realization you have the *Dao*. This is more or less along the metaphysical line and somewhat intellectual. This is another way of moving from the transcendental realm to the practical, relative world we all live in. But the world in which we live is really not separated from the transcendental realm. They are the same, yet we have to make the distinction—that is the way of language.

There is an interesting *mondō* connected with the most important sutra in Mahāyāna Buddhism, the Kegon (*Huayan*; *Avataṃsaka*, "What Garlands the Buddha"). When Buddha goes into *samādhi*, then gets this enlightenment, the whole world changes—the Kegon Sutra starts from this enlightenment. Buddha comes out as sitting under the Bodhi tree, where he attains enlightenment. When enlightenment comes upon him, at the same time the whole universe changes to something beyond description, to the most wonderful scene imagination can ever come to—though it is not proper to call it imagination. I have my own theory that I may come to later. There is no way to describe Buddha's inner consciousness, so the author of the sutra makes everything around him change into precious stones, the most perfect objects in this world, possibly the only way he can describe this state of inner consciousness.

Not only things on earth change. The clouds we see in this world also turn into something wonderful. "Wonderful" is a poor term here, but we have to use it. These clouds are really wonderful, like those we see from an airplane that reflect the rising sun: the colors change so rapidly, so magnificently, our language is not sufficient to describe them. Probably they were seen in those days from mountains. For the description of these clouds changing colors in infinite variety, their shining in different colors, the author exhausts his literary abilities and imagery: this blue-colored shining cloud, this violet-colored, and all other kinds.

Now the sutra starts like this, in depicting a world of supernatural beauty unknown to this world. A Zen master called Chin, usually also known as reverend or venerable elder, was once beginning the Kegon when a monk asked him, "What sutra are your reading?"

The venerable elder, without directly answering, just went on reading, "Great shining cloud, violet-colored shining moon," and so on. Then after a while he pointed out clouds in the actual world, clouds seen at the time I suppose, and asked the monk, "What are those clouds there?"

Monk: "The southern sky is covered with black, dark clouds." Possibly they were looking at the southern half of the sky.

Chin: "It is likely that we will have rain today."[19]

This venerable elder's not answering the monk directly, just going on reading the sutra, was already answering the monk's question. If he had said, "I am reading the Kegon Sutra," he would have made an assertion of that of which we cannot make any assertion. To say "Absolute One Mind" makes it no more the Absolute One Mind. The best way to answer is to go on reading the sutra. This was enough, but the venerable elder was softhearted enough to point to the sky and ask about the clouds. Then to [the monk's response] "very dark" he said, "It may rain." You may think this does not come to anything. But when you think of how impossible it is for ordinary language to describe the scenes taking place in the realm of enlightenment, the only thing to do is to refer to it this way.

We may reverse the order, for things in this world are directly related to those in the other, as I have said. In this case things start from the other end, then come here. We would start from the black clouds, then get to the luminance floating in the realm of enlightenment. Either way of approach is all right. This shortcoming of language Zen masters try to avoid as they try to present reality as it is. We have to shift background altogether. This kind of expression makes us all confused when we come across such a statement as we have here.

One Mind does not remain in itself, but being itself it keeps to itself, holding, not losing itself. That is, One Mind does not keep up its own existence as it is, it becomes; and when it asserts it also negates. This is an important notion, as we have seen: Absolute A splits itself into affirmation and negation, into A_1 and not-A_1. And something we are apt to forget I like to emphasize: when we say One Mind does not remain forever in itself, when we say this, the time concept comes in. [One might think this way:] So many eras ago there was something that sought to change itself, to become A_1 and not-A_1. Thinking is time; without time we can't think. In fact, however, there is no time: it is just the way we think of it; there is really no time relation at all.

Absolute Mind does not keep to itself; it changes from what is to what is not. It becomes instead of staying as it is. This relative way of thinking brings in time. This life as we live it is really this constant becoming, from what is not. This is constantly taking place. This self-being, self-nature, One Mind, does not stay—it changes from what is to what is not. Epistemologically it asserts, but from the physical sense it moves or becomes; they mean the same thing. Yet really becoming is being, being is becoming—this is another important notion we have always to keep in mind. So what is is what is not, what is not is what is. Negation is assertion, assertion is negation. This is contradiction; dialectic is important to understand what reality is. This world of becoming is being itself. As it becomes, it is. So "to be" means "to become," and "to be" is "not to be." This dualistic way of thinking of ours it is necessary to unravel if any mystery of Buddhist, especially of Zen, thought becomes, not intelligible, which belongs to the intellectual category, but graspable, if this Zen thought is to be grasped.

But we are so possessed of intellectualization, and we often ask why this Absolute Mind subjects itself to change and turns into what it is not. Intellectually we can ask why this takes place, but intellectually we can never answer this question. Intellect always keeps the question confronting itself, so the question and the questioner are kept separate. The dichotomy of the question and the questioner is attacked objectively. Yet this question can never be solved until the question becomes the questioner himself, until they are not split, until question and questioner are identified, thoroughly merged into each other. When they are merged we can understand the why, the significance of becoming. As long as becoming is watched from outside, the question will never be solved. As long as intellect is in opposition, we are always divided; a split of one kind or another is inevitable and in the very nature of intellect.

If intellect wants to get out of the dilemma it must destroy itself, it must cease to be itself, it must not be intellect anymore. Then the question itself vanishes. To answer, intellect must become no-intellect. No more intellect, now the question no more exists as far as intellect is concerned—this point I emphasize. Intellect goes on forever intellectualizing; and there is no answer to why being is becoming, becoming is being, and why One Mind wants to change from what it is to what it is not.

This identification of question and questioner can take place only when the question itself is lost, when the question turns into the questioner and the questioner turns into the question. The question ceases to be something objective, something that is to be analyzed. The question becomes subjective, it is not to be analyzed, it is now the questioner himself. To be the questioner himself means to be One Mind. And when One Mind by asserting itself negates itself, when this is about to take place, this moment of becoming, this moment of change, of assertion or negation—it does not matter which we say—this moment is to be seized, to be grasped. This grasping is done by what I call *prajñā*-intuition. Then there is no more intellectualization, there is no more relative knowledge.

When One Mind, *isshin,* does not remain in itself and wants to assert itself by negating itself, we are apt to think this took place historically and the world in which we live is the historical outcome of this change:

A

↕

(A_1 + not-A_1), this world of particulars, manyness

But this in fact is taking place as a whole every instant, and this world as it is is also A itself. When we realize this we can give an explanation of this world of conflict. Conflict already happens when A does not remain in itself. This is the beginning of the conflict, which is going on every minute. This world is a world of continuous *saṃsāra.* Yet at the same time Nirvāna is *saṃsāra, saṃsāra* is Nirvāṇa, being is becoming, becoming is being. So this world is nothing else but Nirvāṇa itself. A is original enlightenment. Ignorance moves in the body of original enlightenment, and original enlightenment splits itself into enlightenment and ignorance, this world of particulars. So this world is ignorance and this world is enlightenment: they are different, so they conflict, so there is conflict. Becoming means conflict. So conflict will be going on.

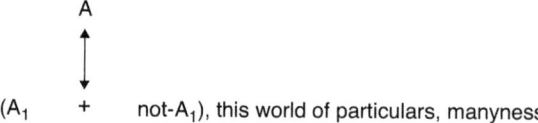

We talk of particulars and manyness as if they were something substantial, but they are really events, happenings. This world is nothing but an infinite series of conflicting events, happenings, becomings. When we talk of particulars, phenomena, individuals, we are apt to think of them as substantially existing. The actual state of things taking place in this world, these things are all happenings—this corresponding to the Buddhist idea of karma, or karma corresponds to event, happening.

So this world is to be conceived in terms of happening, or conflict. When we talk about it we have to fix a point of reference somewhere. We are apt to think of this point as something substantial, but it is not—we just put something there. And this event or this happening is karma. This whole world is alive. When One Mind has not turned itself into what it is not, it is Absolute Mind. If Absolute Mind does not preserve its identity but asserts and negates itself, it becomes *ālaya-vijñāna*. In *ālaya-vijñāna* we have assertion and negation, a mixture of A and not-A. This mixing means it is A and at the same time not-A, this and at the same time that. But there is no mixing in the sense of mixing together: this mixing of enlightenment and ignorance in our way of talking is *ālaya*. Things going on in this world show *ālaya-vijñāna* in its *ālaya* or activity, we might say.

These active workings of *ālaya* leave seeds, possible *ālaya* and actual *ālaya*. Whatever happens, they go on in the actual realm of *ālaya,* depositing seeds in the *ālaya* of possibilities. But the *ālaya* of seeds and the *ālaya* of actualities or realities are not two. That is, there is the thing called *ālaya* of actualities and the *ālaya* of possibilities. But there is not one *ālaya* to be called actual *ālaya* and another to be called potential *ālaya:* actual *ālaya* is possible *ālaya. Ālaya* is in opposition all the time, depositing seeds all the time. So actual working and going to seed are the same thing:

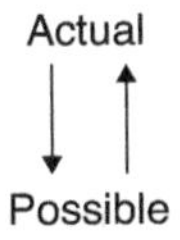

Ālaya is in actual opposition, and from this cause comes effect; or, *ālaya* being in opposition, the effect comes. We think that way, but in actual life cause and effect are one. That is the Buddhist idea of causation, of karma as causation. Karma is cause and at the same time effect. Cause is effect, effect is cause. Present is future, future is past. What is is what is not. This dialectic is so confusing to the ordinary way of thinking we carry on in daily life, but a Zen *mondō* may help you to understand. Those who have visited China know there is a tree, *hakuju* (*baishu*), that does not look like an ordinary pine; it is more like a cypress. In monasteries the subject of thought frequently turns to this tree, as it does in this case.

Monk: "Has the cypress tree buddha nature?" Buddha nature is *buddhatā*. The Buddhist idea is that not only human beings are endowed with buddha nature but also nonsentient and material things. So naturally the cypress tree must be endowed with buddha nature, as the monk has been taught. In fact the monk's question is not just asking for information; it is not necessary to ask the master this, as if it were something quite new. He deliberately asks; this means that he wants to get something from the master, that it is not just an innocent, information-seeking question, as the master understood quite well.

But the master answered in the ordinary way, "Yes, buddha nature is also present in the cypress tree."

The monk wanted to know more. The next question is quite in a way to the point; it also betrays what was in mind when the first question was asked: "When does this cypress attain buddhahood then?" When does it realize this? This, we see, betrays the fact that the monk has something in mind, that he is not just asking for plain instruction.

Master: "It attains its buddhahood when the sky falls down to earth." *Kokū* (*xukong*), "the [empty] air," "[empty] space," "the [empty] sky," is "sky" here. The master knew what the monk was after, from the very beginning.

Monk, still persisting: "When does the sky fall down to earth?"

Master: "When the cypress tree attains enlightenment, this is when the sky falls to earth."[20] If the master had not been really conversant with the subject he might have been caught.

You might say the sky will never fall, so you might consider that the cypress never attains, but this is not the idea at the root of the monk's question. The monk wanted to get the master involved in intellection. Really the cypress remains a plant in the courtyard, an evergreen; it goes on quite differently from a human being. As far as intellectual argument goes, if the cypress has buddha nature it must manifest it in one way or another. And it will not have it as far as intellection goes. But they talk on the absolute plane, in this absolute plane where buddha nature is considered to be possessed by all, including brick, stone, worm—everything shines with light from buddha nature. From this point of view everything is Buddha. But when we argue on the intellectual plane the cypress will never attain enlightenment. To make the monk come away from the intellectual plane, in which he wants to involve the master, the master refuses to be drawn down. Relative means are impossible, yet buddha nature is only impossible on the intellectual plane. So actual *ālaya* is the same as possible *ālaya.* The cypress tree is on the actual plane and when we say the sky falls, this is possible *ālaya.* And these two realms intellect conceives are one on the plane of the absolute. The master keeps himself on the absolute realm, so he does not get things mixed. Here differentiation is change, change is differentiation, *ālaya* is not two but one.

When things are going on in this world this is *ālaya* in its actual working, on its own ground, waiting for germination, actualization. So possible *ālaya* is actual *ālaya:* this world is actualizing itself all the time. This germination of seed into actuality, this germination can take place only when there is another idea, the Buddhist *innen* in Japanese. When *innen* materializes, actualization takes place. *In* is *hetu* in Sanskrit, "impulse," "motive," "cause." *En* is *pratyaya,* "idea," ground," "motive," "instrument," "assistant," with Buddhists "a cooperating cause." *Innen* is thus "cause and occasion," or primary and secondary causes or conditions. The Buddhist causation theory is the same as that of Kant.

Now the question is what is meant by these causes or conditions. What are these conditions that make germination possible? *Ālaya* is filled with germs or seeds waiting for conditions for ripening. If *ālaya* is just a storehouse of germs and seeds waiting for actualization, such actualization is only possible when conditions are mature. There is inactivity until the conditions come about. What are the conditions that make them grow? Where do they come from?

This is the way to understand it. There is not just one germ, but all kinds and an infinite number of germs. They are moving all the time; these are the conditions: there is no remaining inactive, they are working on each other all the time, infinitely working. Infinite events or happenings are the conditions. All these conditions vary infinitely, and as they vary infinitely in a vague way—this must make the germs turn into actualization. Conditions do not come from anywhere else; they all grow out of themselves, *jūjū mujin.*[21] *Jūjū* is one tier over another, infinitely, layer upon layer, inexhaustibly, infinitely piling up, infinitely influencing one another without resorting to any external agency.

We carry *ālaya* around with us all the time. In its actualization it becomes individual. I do not know whether or not the realm of *ālaya* is to be compared to Platonic ideas, but you might say that *ālaya* is the collective unconscious in Jungian terminology, or rather, the cosmic unconscious, as I like to say, because the collective unconscious includes only humans. But what distinguishes Zen from all these philosophies is that they talk as if all things take place in time. In Zen all these things take place right here now. Real enlightenment is not beyond this world but *right here.* It takes infinite time to reach infinity, but when infinity is right here there is no talk about time. This is the absolute now, the absolute present.

This world is really, as we move on, infinitely constructing [itself]. Something takes place here, this is really taking place, yet at the same time these things are our own intellectual projection. The absolute present is all there is; there is nothing more, nothing less. But to comprehend the absolute present we must use intellect. Intellect is meant to achieve a practical, teleological purpose. Without teleology intellect has no meaning whatever—this is the way I feel about it. There is really no actualization whatever. When we talk about it we try to describe it in the intellectual field, yet as it is in the absolute present nothing is going on. But when we say this the absolute present is taken away and we see the historical present. But while this is going on there is nothing but absolute present. I don't deny intellect: it is also in the present now. But we cannot make absolute now stay as it is: One Absolute Mind does not keep its own nature. Yet we want to have time get into this timelessness, and all kinds of involvements come out.

There is a *mondō* where a monk asked a great Zen master, "Where in this world of particulars, in this triple world of Indra, before creation, where are you?" That is, before we had this world, all ten thousand things arranged as they are, before this took place, where are you? At this very moment, is there anything about which we can state whether it is or not? This very moment, is there anything about which we can make an assertion or negation? Is there anything about which we can call "creating" at this very moment? That is to say, "Instead of talking about assertion, negation, being, nonbeing—what is this present moment?" "We cannot say past, present, or future. This very present moment is not to be described or stated in any way that is past, present, or future; it is not to be stated in time, for it is timelessness itself."

Sokkon (jijin), "the present moment," is the absolute present; the absolute present is *sokkon*. The monk wanted to know what this absolute present is. We talk about One Mind, and so on, as if in time, and neglect the very moment in which the absolute present is taking place. The Zen monk concentrates on this very moment. What is this moment? It is the eternal now, the absolute present, an important topic of Zen interest. Going through these metaphysical discussions is not really to the point.

To "What is Zen?" a master replied, "It is like boiling oil over a blazing fire." So if you want to approach it you cannot approach it. It is not a mere fire, but when you have oil burning it is all the more unapproachable. In China oil was used very much in cooking, so the idea probably came from daily experience.

Another master asked a monk, "Are you a newcomer?" This just appears to be an innocent question.

Monk: "Yes, I am a newcomer."

Master: "Throw down all such complications!" There is no connection at all, you might say. Ordinarily the master followed this by, "Do you understand?"

Monk: "I do not." It is quite natural that he did not.

Master: "One who confesses he is guilty, go away." When he makes an assertion about anything the monk already goes away, or confesses his guilt. The very assertion commits intellectual, metaphysical crime.

The monk started to go out. The master called him back. "Come back. Where do you come from? I really want to know."

Monk: "I come from the west of the river." This was a straightforward answer, I suppose.

Master: "Does your teacher who resides in the west of the river—he must be behind you—is he [not] very much afraid of your making random remarks?" This is another complication. Your master is following and watching your answers, [to] see that you do not talk nonsense.

The monk did not answer.

Innen is time cutting into timelessness. Possible *ālaya* has to turn into actual *ālaya*; and we go through this enlightenment experience ourselves. All these things come together, but you have to wait until they come just right. It ripens when it ripens. Somehow it comes, or ripens. Actually to tell how the combination combines is not possible; we can just say in a general way, it goes on all the time. Nobody can just predict. When we become conscious of the thing, before this thing comes out into consciousness, so many things go on unconsciously. We just wait till the unconscious opens, or comes out. Cause has no meaning until it becomes itself the effect.

While A remains A there is no causation whatever. But A does not remain A. It can be grasped only by intuition; intuition takes place. When I go there it is no more this, no more that—intuition takes place. Causation is only possible when this and that are there together. Ordinarily we have as "intuition" this looking at that. But it is not in that way that I use intuition. As long as we get out of ourselves we will be intellectual. When we are back in ourselves we will be intuitive. When you have the yearning, intuition will come by itself.

In an essay on Jean-Paul Sartre, Blackham says this:

> In its nature, then, consciousness by being always consciousness of something refers to itself and constitutes itself apart as not something else. This distinction, being consciousness aware of itself and not a distinction made by an onlooker (as between that inkstand and the pen), already constitutes the consciousness as personal, for personality in the first place is being which exists for itself in the sense of being present to itself. But this consciousness is consciousness not merely of difference but also of the nature of the difference, a perception however rudimentary of the object as a plenitude and of itself as a lack. My consciousness of myself thus already implies a projection of myself towards my possibility, what I lack in order to be myself identified with myself; and this is the structure of desire and the movement

> towards fulfilment. The ideal project which defines our existence and is the meaning of human presence in the world is the nisus towards some form or unity of the *pour-soi* with the *en-soi* in a totality which saves both. That is in principle impossible. Man aspires to be god, but god is a self-contradiction. Nevertheless, this absolute value is the lure which governs our lives.[xxxvii]

"Consciousness aware of itself," One Mind becomes conscious of itself; when One Mind does not remain in itself it means it wants to be conscious of itself. This means to make itself what it is not, to make itself not-itself, for otherwise there can be no consciousness. He is all right, this far. But if there is a plenitude there will be no consciousness at all; consciousness takes place only when there is a lack. I am not in possession of possibility. If I am, there will be no hankering. This becoming conscious of myself means becoming conscious of some possibility. It may be subtle. When he becomes conscious of himself he feels something lacking in his becoming himself. He seeks to get subject identified with object, not in individuality but in totality. One Mind asserting itself, turning into what it is not, already this lack, turning into possibility. This is ignorance. And when ignorance turns back to the very source, there is Absolute Mind before it becomes conscious of itself.

"This is in principle impossible." The principle is his own making, he makes it impossible. When Absolute Mind went out of itself it showed a lack. But going out is really going in. When we realize going out is nothing but going in, when this is understood, there is no principle that makes this idea impossible. This is the way I like to read it.

I think creation is God making up his own lack; his lack is creation. Man aspires to be God, yet God is going on all the time. I would like

---

xxxvii. Blackham, *Six Existentialist Thinkers*, 112.

to have each one of us stand where this goes on. When one knows this, all problems on the relative plane may be dealt with quite readily. This is the way I think it ought to be.

As for any purpose God may have in this creation, God himself knows about that. Indian philosophy talks so much about God's "sport." To be earnest is all right, but if we are too earnest patience breaks and we all get psychoses.

Some time ago I gave you a *gāthā* supposedly composed by the twenty-second Indian patriarch, Manura. It summarizes Buddhist philosophy very well, and I like it very much:

> The mind moveth with the ten thousand things:
> Even when moving, it is serene.
> Perceive its essence as it moveth on.
> And neither joy nor sorrow there is.[xxxviii]

Mind revolves in accord with the ten thousand conditions. And as Mind moves on, the point of movement is very *yū* [*you;* serene]. It revolves, moves on, flows on, becomes. I think this *gāthā* summarizes Buddhist and Zen thought. Another thing I might add: intuition is in accord with this stream or flow. As things flow on, or become, with this becoming, which intuition expresses, then you know all this [to be our] self-nature, we might say, *svabhāva.*

xxxviii. See also chapter iv, footnote ii and endnote 1.

VI

Absolute Mind, or Original Enlightenment, has two aspects, as I have said, *prajñā* and *karuṇā.* In a way, it may be said that Zen emphasizes the *prajñā* aspect, that of philosophy and intellect, more than the conative *karuṇā.* But Zen actually has not as much to do with philosophy and intellect as other Buddhist systems have. As Zen does not separate, it has no need for simplification, which is an assumption of the complexity brought about by division. And as Zen starts with experience, it has nothing to do with systematization. But the human mind is so made that it cannot help expressing itself; in fact, without it expressing itself there is no human consciousness. Yet when it tries to express itself this means we are out of the experience into the realm of thought, where systematization necessarily takes place. Here, however, Zen systematization has nothing to do with simplification, for it is the intellectualization, or systematization, of experience itself of which Zen is the product; this experience is the important thing and is to be clearly understood as the basis, and the only basis, of Zen. As Zen is not philosophy, we cannot talk of philosophical simplification, for there is nothing philosophical to simplify. You must understand this to get the real essence of Zen. We have to express ourselves in thought, but Zen expression and simplification are not the simplification of thought separate from experience; they are the direct expression of Zen experience itself.

The Kegon (*Avataṃsaka*) Sutra is the culmination of Buddhist thought as developed by the Chinese; one is overawed by its grand survey of the world from the metaphysical viewpoint. When Zen expresses itself in thought form, and when it tries to express itself in more and more advanced thought, it goes to this Kegon Sutra and thought system more than any other. In fact, the Kegon may be said to be the highest expression of Buddhist philosophy—and of Zen philosophy insofar as Zen is philosophical. Aśvaghoṣa's *Awakening of Faith* is an aspect of Kegon thought as it came to be formulated by the Chinese mind. His treatise is also, as we have seen, the philosophy of Zen and the religion of Zen. Like it too, Kegon's original enlightenment or Absolute Mind has the two aspects of *prajñā* and *karuṇā*, giving us this personalized trinity:

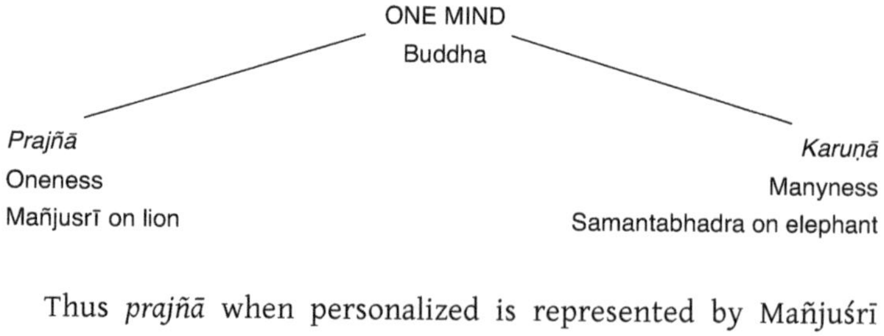

Thus *prajñā* when personalized is represented by Mañjuśrī (Monju; Wenshu), riding on a lion; *karuṇā* by Samantabhadra (Fugen; Puxian), on an elephant. The lion is supposed to drive away all animals, this world of particulars, for Mañjuśrī wanted to clear himself of all relative knowledge.

The *Prajñāpāramitā-sūtra* goes with him, the *Hannya* (*Panruo*), "Wisdom Personified" in Japanese. Samantabhadra manifests in this world of multiplicities and tries to save all beings through various means of enlightenment. The Kegon Sutra also goes into this world of manynesses, where apparently separate existences are shown by Kegon to be intricately interwoven.

Zen does not go out of this world. Zen works in this world but is not limited by its relativity. Zen teaches one to live in the world of relativity, yet not to be of it. Being in it means following the life of Samantabhadra; transcending it means Mañjuśrī asserting himself. Life itself is not necessarily a combination of the two, but the integration of *prajñā* and *karuṇā* is necessary for a life of Zen. For this reason Zen doesn't despise working, manual work, the way all other people do. At the same time Zen sees something that is not altogether included in this worldly life, something that cannot be exhausted by getting up in the morning, eating, working, going to bed. And this something more that Zen sees is *prajñā*. *Prajñā* and *karuṇā* each complement the other, but in this complementing *karuṇā* is not separated from *prajñā*, nor *prajñā* from *karuṇā*. One is in many, and many is in one, immanent yet transcending, transcending yet not outside. This is the Zen attitude, and it can be illustrated by the legend, if not also the true history, of the founder of Zen in China, Huineng (Enō, 638–713), the Sixth Patriarch.

Huineng is represented as coming to the monastery of the fifth patriarch, Hongren, from southern China in the Tang dynasty. In the southern part of China the mountains are directed south and north. The region was not developed, cultured, or civilized as well as the middle section; the people living in the south were not considered to be in the same category as those in the high culture of middle China. Huineng himself was not learned, as were some other monks in the monastery. In fact, he was not a monk, not ordained into the regular Buddhist monkhood. He was outside of the meditation hall and simply attached to the monastery, working for it. The monks read sutras and did meditation, but Huineng worked in the backyard of the monastery, or so we are told.

We don't know whether this is historically true or not: Zen people like to have him not so learned, not taken in as a regular member of the monastery. In less than a hundred years after Huineng, Baizhang (720–814) founded the first Zen monastery.[i] From this time on this monastery and others founded by Zen masters were no longer governed by Buddhist masters or Buddhist rules generally. Zen now had its own way of training: farming, working in the mountains, splitting wood, performing all kinds of household activities in the monastery [such] as cooking and cleaning. The monks also did carpentry and leveled the road. Of course, this was quite different from the way of the Indian monks, philosophers, and spiritual leaders, who despised manual work as below their dignity. Zen did not think it degraded; Zen's spirituality went along with its secular work.

Thus Huineng refined or polished rice. He was not even allowed to come to the classroom where his teacher lectured, nor to go into the zendō (*chantang*). But he was able to get enlightenment far more readily than the others, for he was not hampered by learning. Instead of sharpening the edge of intuition, intellect obscures the mind. Huineng, a great Zen genius, penetrated into the secrets of Zen. His teacher recognized his Zen attainment, while other followers, pursuing Zen in the regular way, were left behind—or so we are told. The question is not whether Huineng was ignorant. He was made ignorant; Zen was not handed over to intellection or learning, but to a simple ignorant man—this is the important point.

Huineng wrote no books, but his few disciples each took notes when he gave his sermons, and these were collected into a document called in Japanese *Rokuso dangyō*, the *Platform Sutra of the Sixth Patriarch.*[ii] This was passed secretly from one disciple to another and

---

i. EZB 2, 305, note 4 [283, note 4]
ii. SZ, 29–33.

much esteemed after Huineng's death; it has become a very important document in the study of Zen.

Huineng was the sixth patriarch in China, but he is really the first patriarch of Zen, and his sutra contains the essence of Zen. Additions were made to the text as it passed from one disciple to another, and several copies of it existed. Perhaps the name, *Platform Sutra,* was given to it because he delivered his sermons from a platform. No such public teaching was ever given by Buddhist teachers before him. Learned monks had wanted to study Zen by reasoning and intellection. But Huineng spoke directly to the general public, and his talks, including the early ones, are in a very easy style, without the difficulties in understanding of all the ornate, artificially composed classical works of the same period. Of his teachings, the most important one that was further developed in the history of Zen has already been discussed to some extent: *wuxin* (*mushin*) or *wunian* (*munen*), mindlessness or thoughtlessness. The latter is a better word for it but has other connotations that are not good. There is no rule saying whether *wunian* or *wuxin* is to be used.

Kierkegaard likes to say *munen* [the instant] is where infinity enters into finitude, where finitude enters into infinity—this is where *munen* takes place. It is godhead before he inserted himself, when nothing can be predicated about him. Eckhart's idea of the virgin who is a wife, a paradox that runs through many of his sermons, is the contradiction in which he weaves much of his thought, the contradiction of infinity and finitude. These two are so intimately identified that we cannot say where they are—finite is infinite, infinite is finite. Only in thought can we divide one from the other. Even a hair in space is to be joined between finite and infinite.

There is such a big gap between the two ideas that we despair of crossing from infinite to finite and from finite to infinite. This despair is the psychology of sin, the inability to cross from one side to the other. We are all psychologically in sin. Kierkegaard said the opposite of sin is not goodness—it is faith. This is important, and I would like to give you my interpretation of sin and faith.

When we become conscious of finitude we feel sin, in the Buddhist sense of sin as the division already spoken of. Therefore, sin is inseparable from our individual existences. When God created the world God sinned against himself. In my view, as God willed to turn this way or that way, he committed sin. And this sin is taken over by most Christians. We are children of this world, so we are all born sinners; we can never get away from it. If this idea of sin is guilt in its relative sense, its opposite may be guiltlessness or virtue. But these terms belong to moral categories that do not constitute spiritual life, which is faith. When we feel sin, when we become conscious of sinfulness—in this moment we have faith, which is the reverse side of sin. In "God acting is wisdom," acting is wisdom; then there is no sin. Sin is in our relative sense, our relative way of looking at things.

Sin doesn't turn to faith. It *is* faith to understand sin as faith. We should take sin as it is and yet as something that can be replaced by something not sin. This is the way to regard sin. Therefore, there is no risky plunge into faith, which is already a culmination. When we turn to the other side of sin we know it is faith. That is to say, we know existence—and then we know faith.

This kind of sin is not sin as it is spiritually or relatively understood. Sin is usually connected with morality, which is relative. When morality is transcended we have spiritual life; as long as morality is present we can never have a good life. The urge to do something is present, and this is sin. To go on without strain, without making an effort, with no tension, is impossible while we remain only in this relative world; if we feel some kind of oppression, then we are still in a state of sin.

If we throw sin away, then we have faith. Sin itself stands on faith. If we had no faith we would have no existence. If we feel sinful we have no faith. Existence is faith, and faith is original enlightenment. Faith is not intellectual, it is *prajñā*-intuition. Of course, orthodox Protestantism would not approve of this. Existence is duality. It is not-duality when this sin does not exist. When we make a dialectic of sin, this is the philosopher's business. Zen and spiritually minded persons are not worried about their own destruction; they plunge into life and find that existence is faith, that is, affirmation, though not just the relative affirmation that implies negation.

The enlightened person is sinful outwardly, relatively speaking, but not subjectively or inwardly. Outwardly, it is not a different sinfulness from that of other, unenlightened people. Kierkegaard speaks of this too. To feel despair is to feel singleness. After absolute enlightenment there is no more despair. The enlightenment experience has no sense of despair in it; it is the opposite of despair. The enlightened man may feel despair in looking at other people, on account of other beings not being conscious of this enlightened state of mind, but not on account of himself. And once you have real, absolute enlightenment it cannot be lost. This physical existence ceases to be as it was before, but not in the sense of disappearing into nothingness. Relative mind sees this book as a book; enlightened mind sees it as a book, yet at the same time as a not-book. Enlightened man knows it is a book and at the same time a not-book. Enlightened man knows it is a book, and at the same time there is something more than this. It is not limited, we may say. Whenever there is limit, despair comes out of it. When you know, or experience the fact, that this book has some other value as its inherent right, then no despair can come out of it.

I have often been asked what basis there is in Zen and in enlightenment experience for morals or ethics, for doing this rather than that. In the relative world we have to choose the right or left horn, as a Zen *mondō* gives it.[iii] But Zen comes before division took place. Zen's question is, "Where does the choosing come from?" We may say it has nothing to do with practical life, that is, with practical life in choosing in accordance with moral responsibility—by "practical" I mean "actional," not "practical" as opposed to "theoretical."

In this practical life of the world, where always there are two, this is the way it is:

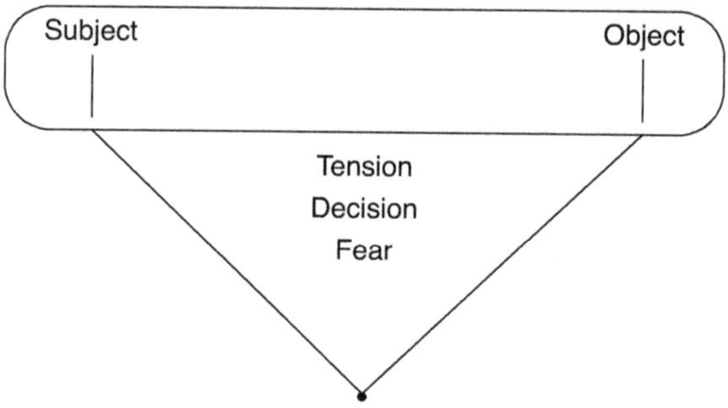

This relative world is dualistically minded, with which Zen is not concerned. Tension itself is there, decision itself is there, fear itself is there. But where do they come from? And where do subject and object come from? Zen wants us to grasp this point, indicated below, where subject and object are one, where they originate.

When Zen talks about this aspect of life, it is very hard to find a good English term for it. For when Zen comes to ethics it cannot be

iii. See also D. T. Suzuki, "Ethics and Zen Buddhism," in *Moral Principles of Action—Man's Ethical Imperative*, ed. Ruth Nanda Anshen, Science of Culture Series, 6 (New York: Harper and Brothers, 1952), 606–615.

called ethics—it is simply the practical side of Zen. "Ethics," "morality," "supernatural," "spiritual," "divine," "religious life"—I do not like to use these terms, for Zen denies "divine" or "spiritual," as these terms are constantly used in the West. As far as we are social beings, we must be moral; morality is required in community life. Buddha lived and worked in compliance with all beings on the plane of relativity, where morals and ethics apply. As long as we regard ourselves as relative beings, naturally morality comes in.

But when it comes to Zen, Zen has this to say: those who violate the precepts do not go to hell, while those who have led the most virtuous lives do not enter Nirvāṇa, they are not born in the Pure Land. But this does not mean to encourage us to do something bad. From the enlightenment standpoint, judgment by society has nothing to do with it—this is to be clearly understood. Shin expresses the idea in the same way: the good man goes to the Pure Land, the bad man goes to the Pure Land all the more. But they by no means go because they are good or bad. Goodness and badness have nothing to do with this going; this going is above these opposites. The Zen master referred to above does not try to observe moral conduct; his conduct is itself moral. And Tanka, the master who burned a wooden image of Buddha to warm himself on a cold night, may be judged sacrilegious by society; his act has nothing good or bad in it in his own judgment.[1]

The thing is—not to be concerned so much with morals. Just get enlightenment, that is the main thing. For the unenlightened, Zen always has this advice: get enlightened! Just get away from these differentiations, just get into enlightenment experience and see what will follow. In Buddhist terms it will then be trackless life, trackless living. *The Dhammapada* term is *apada,* "nothing left behind"—literally, "without feet," "footless," "trackless," "leaving no footprint," "having no desires." If there is a track, we can follow it and take hold; what cannot be grasped is trackless, unobtainable relatively.

Another Buddhist term frequently used in this connection is *anantagocara,* infinite or limitless field. *Gocara* is a field where a cow is permitted to walk about. It is generally translated into Chinese by *kyō* (C. *jing*). A field where cows may roam, the frame of consciousness in which a person lives, the general response he makes to whatever stimulus he gets from outside, his general way of responding, his general pattern—this is *kyō.*

When this is predicated by *ananta*—"no boundary," "no end," "no limits"—there is infinite range, where the cow is permitted to go, where man can roam without being hindered by anything. His consciousness has become so broad, infinitely expanding, coinciding with the cosmic unconscious. Ordinary consciousness is limited. It is expanded so boundlessly by enlightenment that it knows no limit. "Free in perception" is the translation by Radhakrishnan, but it actually means "field." "Infinite perception" sounds more intellectual, while "infinite range of consciousness" is more fundamental; it goes deeper into the roots of consciousness; it is not superficial.

This infinite *gocara* is a circle that has no circumference, and thus no track. This is where the Zen master and Zen people find their *gocara,* their field, their range, their abode; being infinite, their light has no track.

Since this *gocara* is limitless, there is no path leading to this area. If it were limited it would have a track leading in. And to reach this infinitely expanding field of the Buddha's mind you cannot have any limited passageway by which to reach the inwardness of Buddhist life. If you approach by a special path, he cannot be caught. He reaches so infinitely, the tracks cannot be found—he goes so deep. As there is no approach, so infinitely does he expand, he can be approached anywhere. No track means the track is everywhere; being without limit, his track is everywhere; every track leads us to him—this is an important point to understand in the Zen way of looking at life; this is also the gist of enlightenment experience.

There is no good way to express in words what the Zen master tries to say: there is no limit, therefore the track is everywhere; the circle has no circumference, therefore its center is everywhere. When a circle is limited, it has just one center. When it is not limited, its center is everywhere. So this *anantagocara,* this limitless field, is a most expressive term. The idea behind it is that its center is nowhere and everywhere. The tracks are everywhere since there is no track; there is no track, so the tracks are everywhere—this is important. And so is the approach, to be made by no special, no limited path or passageway.

Now we come back to ethics. This *mondō* may explain it, I hope. It does not speak of Zen ethics, it does not mention spiritual life, or worldly life, or divine life—yet this *mondō* is quite interesting.

Somebody asks: What is the garage, house, shrine, temple, anything? What is an abode, building, anything in which to put this self, body, physical existence? What is this existence, what is this body? The place where one stays, the house, tent, anything will do. "What is this existence?"

Master: "Just this," or just such, *tada shako* in Japanese, *zhi zhege* in Chinese.

So Zen does not try to define anything. What is the agent, the soul living within this body? Who is the person living in this physical body? What is the moving force in or behind it? And so on. It is "just this"—this is quite interesting.

Another master gave this answer: "What? What?" This means, "Now who is this man?" "I walk this way, what is this?"

In the *mondō* another question follows: "When a visitor comes, what will you do?"

Master: "Have a cup of tea."

Well, this does not satisfy all of you, I am quite sure. Zen does not try to interpret ethics in any dialectical way. It just says, "What? What?" In this world of multiplicities, interrelations come about here; what do you do? Just "have a cup of tea." This is the gist of Zen. When you understand this you understand Zen, and you will understand the circle without circumference whose center is everywhere.[2] "Have a cup of tea" is also the center. The universe moves around this. You can say nothing of this, it just is so. There is here no tension, no decision, no fear. It just is so. So far I have tried to present Zen morals and ethics according to my way of thinking. When it is boiled down, it comes to "just this." History, our living—in this very moment all the past is included, all the future is here. In this present moment there is no morality.

Enlightenment erases insulated ego—and there is no room for relative emptiness thereafter. There is no such thing as every moment from then on, for one is eternally living. There is no today or tomorrow, so there is no room for compassion. There is no complete unity [to attain]. If you are beyond the opposites, there is still further to go because if you are beyond there is something to be beyond. Psychologically, "yes" is in every moment. But at the same time this "yes" has a "no" in it. Metaphysically, we are all enlightened, so the question is psychological always:

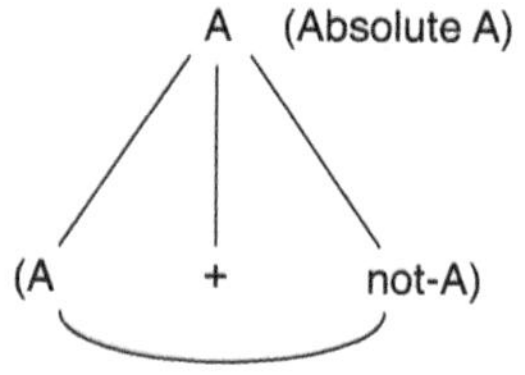

I said above that the enlightened man may feel despair when he sees that other people are unconscious of enlightenment. Then this teaching of *praṇidhāna* is awakened. According to Aśvaghoṣa, One

Mind divides, as we know, into suchness and birth-and-death. Under suchness is original enlightenment and under original enlightenment *avidyā*, ignorance, out of which *prajñā* and *karuṇā* come. *Prajñā* corresponds to suchness and *karuṇā* produces *praṇidhāna.*

This *praṇidhāna* is quite an important conception in Buddhism and in Zen Buddhism. It almost monopolizes Shin, the Pure Land sect, but it does not appear here as it does in Zen, where it comes out in the doctrine of work. In Zen philosophy and talk Zen generally emphasizes the *prajñā* more than the *karuṇā* aspect of enlightenment. But this *prajñā* [*karuṇā*] aspect is demonstrated by Zen in practice in this world of particulars, where things are so differentiated, this world of multiplicities, of ten thousand things, where the principle of discrimination is carried out.[3] *Karuṇā* is not seen as much as *prajñā* in Zen teaching, but it is clearly emphasized in the Zen way of manifesting *praṇidhāna* in daily life, in the monks' employing themselves in all worldly work and affairs. This is most conspicuous with Zen masters too. In India they did not come to the actual work but kept themselves in a retired place where they spent their time in meditation; they were not so connected with worldly affairs.

Pūrvapraṇidhāna or *praṇidhāna*, Japanese *hongan* (*benyuan*), is very difficult to translate into an English term. With some qualification, it is "vow," "strong desire" or wish, and "prayer"; and it has, besides, its own meaning. It is better to keep *praṇidhāna*, or original, primary, fundamental *praṇidhāna* when it is prefixed by *pūrva*, separate from the conative, *karuṇā* aspect of enlightenment. *Praṇidhāna* is not just prayer or wish, for it is more than a strong desire to do something. Prefixed by *pūrva, praṇidhāna* is "primal will," and it is contained in original enlightenment, in Absolute Mind itself. Yet this idea of *praṇidhāna* also expresses itself in our everyday life, and *praṇidhāna* is the religion of Zen.

Praṇidhāna has no teleology, and prayer doesn't exhaust its meaning. Also, prayer wants something to be accomplished, while *praṇidhāna* has nothing to be accomplished. It may think of attaining a certain end, but there is no eschatology at all in it. If we take a_1 a_2 a_3 . . . infinity, this infinity is not something we attain by going through every one of these steps. Every a_1 is itself infinite. When we think we are going one after another, infinity is already here at the first one. We generally think of progress as going on this way: → → → →, but actually infinity was when we started. To utter *praṇidhāna* is not volitional at all. It comes out of mouth or hand. Each *praṇidhāna* we utter is faith, as each sin we commit is an act of faith.

What Zen emphasizes most is to know, to experience, to become conscious of something that thinks, feels, works. When I say this "something," we may designate it as eternal self, *ātman*, permanence, reality, suchness, ultimate reality, transcendental self, self-nature—the Sanskrit term is very expressive, *bhūtakoṭi. Bhūta* is *jitsu* (C. *shi*), "reality." *Koṭi* is *sai* (*ji*), "end" or "ultimate." *Jitsu sai* (*shiji*) originally comes from Buddhism, "reality limit," that is, ultimate reality, the idea being the last reality.

But the trouble is when we use these terms, especially "self"; this suggests something that exists as an entity, a hypostasis, that lies behind, underneath. "Substance" has the same meaning. All these terms bring some tangible object to mind. Thus Zen tries very hard to make us realize what is what by gestures, out of the ordinary use of words, and so on: it wants us to become actually conscious of this thing, not in the usual way of trying to see something substantial with the senses. In ordinary conversation it is all right to be exact about what something means, but Zen tries to keep away from these associations we are apt to get into. When this is really understood, you come to what *praṇidhāna* really means. I will give a *mondō* to make this as clear as possible.

Once when a Zen master saw a monk coming from the village—those Zen monasteries are generally in the mountains—he asked, "Did you see an *ushi* (*niu*)?"[iv]

Monk: "Yes, I saw it."

Master: "Did you see the right horn or the left horn?"

The monk, not expecting this question, was silent. The master asked this question purposely: it is not necessary to mention each side, or the right and left horns, if you see an *ushi.* You just see the *ushi.* This question purposely divides the *ushi* into two.

The master answered himself, "Seeing has neither right nor left horn."

The seeing monk was unable to answer.[4]

There is no dualism in seeing, seeing is seeing. When we say, "I see an object," this separates subject and object. In the act of seeing itself there is no division. The division into seer and seen is the trouble we generally have. The master wanted to let the monk realize that there is no such dichotomy in seeing. But just to say "I" already deviates from the fact itself. The Zen idea is to upset, to get down into the baseless basis. If all comes from one, eternal regression will take place—we will finally get beyond intellect. There is no basis, no substance, no self—from this everything starts, from this all comes out.

---

iv. Chinese *niu*, Japanese *gyū*, *go*, or *ushi*, a name for all the bovine family without distinction of sex; it may be mother or father. In the Shin sect *oya* is used for both father and mother, not just for one of them. We use "parent" and "parents," but *oya* is both, singly and conjointly. The father represents justice, rightness; the mother, love, compassion—*oya* is both, physically and spiritually. The Christian God is father, never mother. This is significant, I think, especially that in Japan there is no dividing into two. The West has generally developed along the dualistic way. *Oya* is both qualities possessed by both, a kind of abstraction of fatherhood and motherhood, an abstraction not existing in Western European languages—I do not know about Greek or Latin. *Ushi*, not quite a cow, is this animal. Perhaps we call it a cow without emphasis of sex distinction.

Another monk was taking leave of the same master when the master asked, "Where do you go?"

Monk: "To Wutai Shan." This is the great place in China noted as the special shrine of Mañjuśrī, that of Samantabhadra being Emei Shan. This Wutai is well known in India too, and as far as Tibet; many pilgrims go there to worship the representation of *prajñā* with which Zen is much concerned. So the monk was going to visit this shrine.

The master held out his right index finger. "When you see Mañjuśrī of Wutai, you come back, and we will see. I will see Mañjuśrī on this finger as well as you."

The monk did not know what to answer. The master held one finger out, as if it were ultimate reality, from which all comes out.[5]

On another occasion this master tried to get away from this oneness; even this is to be avoided, for we may cling to it. He said, "When you go to visit a different monastery, do not tell people I, your old master, am here. If you say this it will be abusing me." It is not proper to say this old master is in this monastery: it will be slandering me.

Monk: "Oh, no, I will not talk about that."

Master: "You tell me this, where am I?" If you say so, where am I?

Monk: "I will raise one finger, as if you are here." This may correspond to the one erected by the master before.

Master: "Well, you are already slandering me."[6]

One finger does not mean the same thing each time the finger is raised. Sometimes it will do very well, at others not at all. The Zen master wants to keep our mind from cherishing ideas, from becoming inflexible, from cherishing anything else. Once he wanted to see one finger as containing all that is; on another occasion even this was already deviating. Zen wants us to be conscious of something that moves, feels, thinks, and so on. But Zen is scrupulously careful not to commit itself to one fixed idea of self. Therefore, words are not to be taken as standard, but meaning is represented by the words. When this meaning is grasped, it will be clear behind the words.

A Zen master, Shishuang Xingkong, was asked by a monk, "What is the essence of Buddhism?" What is Zen?

Master: "Suppose a man is at the bottom of a well. If you can save him without using an inch of rope, then I will tell you what Zen is."

Monk: "I come from the southern part of China and the masters there too talk of Zen in some such way." The monk was just superficially playing with words, not realizing what was behind them, so he said that many masters also talk like this.

Master to attendant: "This corpse, which has no life whatever, pull him out right away!"[7]

In connection with this, I might say that this attendant who was told to pull the corpse-like man out grew later into a great Zen master, Yangshan. Later he asked Danyuan, another master, "How can one get a man out of a well without using an inch of rope?"

Master: "You idiot! Who is in the well?"[8]

The monks all assume that there is a man in the well. This master asked if the man was in the well. It is the self that is not possible to grasp by ideation. This monk understood something, apparently, but was not quite satisfied with his understanding. He went to another master, Weishan, and asked the same question.

Weishan: "O Huiji!" (the name of the monk at this time).

Monk: "Yes, master!"

Weishan: "There, he is out!"[9]

When one is addressed one responds to it, something responds that comes out of the sense gate, self. But if we think this self can become an object of sense we make great error. When the monk understood Zen thoroughly, he mentioned these incidents and said to his disciples: " 'Who is in the well?' I got the name with this answer.

When I answered Weishan, Weishan said, 'He is out!' When I heard this, I got the ground."[v/10]

Who is in the well? You think there is somebody behind the senses, but there is no such self. Weishan actually called him up, and he answered, and this self walked out. When he got the name, something tentative, he knew where to look, perhaps; he had something to which to direct thought. Next he began to grasp this self; he got the ground, or substance. "Who is this?" is still on the relative plane, we might say. Next, there is an actual demonstration—not quite the right way to say it, but I know no better way to explain. This calling out one's name and responding is frequently used; when the response is given, the master says, "There he is."

This way of introducing the monk to the realization of what is behind sense is quite a natural way of making the monk come to the realization. There is a variation, we might say, in this *mondō*:

A layman asked a master, "Are you a Zen master?"

Master: "Well, I have never studied Zen."

The master sat quietly, saying nothing. After a while the master called out to him.

Man: "Yes!"

The master pointed at a palm in the courtyard. The man did not know what to say.[11]

We can see what the Zen master means. "Is there such a thing as Zen?" "Zen," the Zen master says, "is nonsense." So he sat quietly. The man did not understand. So the master called out to the man. The man answered, still without understanding. The master then pointed to the palm. The man still did not understand. Zen is most vividly displayed here; in a most lively way it is demonstrated, or practiced.

v. EZB 2, 219–220 [198].

This master one day called out to a monk, "Bring a chair over here."[12]

The monk brought the chair to the master.

Master: "Well, take it back again."

The monk took it back.

Master: "O monk!"

Monk: Yes, master!"

Master: "What is on the other side of the chair?"

Monk: "A pillow."

Master: "What is on this side?"

Monk: "Nothing, nothing is there."

Master: "O Ejaku!"

Monk: "Yes, master!"

Master: "What is this?"

The monk was silent.

Master: "You go away."[13]

All these things are meant to force the monk to take hold of something behind sense experience, for when we say this or that it is no more there. In this case it is expressed more or less in terms of space, or of a kind of psychology. It may also be demonstrated in terms of time.

The first buddha to appear on earth was Dīpaṃkara, Buddha of light burning, "Let there be light!" Buddha. A monk asked, "What did we have before the appearance of this light-burning Buddha?"—the light originator or time beginner.

Master: "You look after the disappearance of this buddha."

That is, to know what is before is to know what is after. When you know before, you know after. Time goes in the sequence of this and that. We have knowledge when we know something follows, in the nature of time.

Monk: "What is after it appears?"

Master: "What is before the buddha." To know after is to know before, to know before is to know after. After is before, before is after. Past is future, future is past. When we know one we know both.

Monk: "What is the very time this buddha appears, now?"—no past, no future, but this present moment—"What do we have when Buddha is actually here?" That is, "What is now?" Not going over the sequence of time infinitely in either direction, this is absolute now.[vi/14]

When I try to explain such a *mondō* I have to use all conceptual terms, which the master refuses to use. He just says, "Have a cup of tea."[15] He does not say the future refers to the past, the past refers to the future, and so on. The absolute present is just "Have a cup of tea." In these *mondō* the master tries in every possible way not to commit himself to hypotheses and so on. But these things are more or less on the epistemological side, for Zen *mondō* emphasize this side much more than *praṇidhāna.*

Praṇidhāna is emphasized in this way more in Shin, which developed in Japan, and more generally in the Pure Land sect. As I said before, in Zen *praṇidhāna* is asserted in the practical side of living: living itself is emphasized. Chinese people are very practical, not so visionary as the Indian. When this imaginative, fanciful Buddhism was taken to China, the Chinese turned it in the most practical direction. Buddhism became a highly workable religion; it did not indulge so much in dialectics as the Indian, the Yogācāra School for example, which sees Buddhist philosophy as a highly philosophical, epistemological system. But in China Chinese people created Zen out of those highly abstract ways of presenting the truth of Buddhism. Zen is the most practical way possible. In Zen our daily work is so

---

vi. For this *mondō* see Suzuki Daisetsu, "The Role of Buddhist Thought in the History of Far Eastern Culture" (unpublished in English), 20.

emphatically asserted, instead of the more visionary aspects, as you will see.

Of course, something in the Christian term "prayer" corresponds to *praṇidhāna,* but prayer will be quite misleading if we are not very careful. *Praṇidhāna* is the most thoroughgoing wish to be of service to others, nonsentient and sentient. This is where Buddhist cosmology is so different from that of almost any other religion. The objects of *praṇidhāna* are not just those with feelings like human beings or animals; rocks, rivers, and so on are also objects of Buddha's fervent desire to save. Further, if the Christian analogy of prayer is carried out, this *praṇidhāna*—prayer without an object, we might say—will have an object. When this object is obtained, *praṇidhāna,* if like prayer, will have performed its function. But *praṇidhāna* is really of infinite range and has no definite end to attain. From the relative point of view we would ask, "If there is no definite end to obtain, what is the use or purpose of *praṇidhāna*?" If all such notions as purposes to be accomplished some day, millions of years, or thousands—it makes no difference—are done away with, what then? But Buddhist prayer, however earnestly given, has no definite end to obtain; it is simply the infinite working of *praṇidhāna.*

This, therefore, is *praṇidhāna*, in great contrast to the ordinary conception of prayer. Objectively speaking, Buddhist *praṇidhāna* covers everything, sentient and nonsentient; its objects are infinite and inexhaustible. Therefore, *praṇidhāna* leads to infinite working, a conception of *praṇidhāna* that is altogether beyond the range of our relative understanding. From the absolute point of view, *praṇidhāna* does not think of obtaining ends. In itself, when it is interpreted not objectively but subjectively, innerly, from *praṇidhāna* itself as it comes out of the infinite range of consciousness it cannot be said to have any object, or aim. It only appears to have definite aim from the relative point of view.

In Christianity morality is so inseparably blended with spirituality that spirituality cannot be conceived without morality. Strictly speaking, however, spirituality transcends morality; we cannot go up to spirituality from morality. There is in spirit absolute freedom, while moral life is always limited; certain moral ends are to be obtained. There are certain moral objects, topics, subjects of morality, cardinal virtues, for example. But all these things work in the relative world, in relative life; they have to do with relationships to physical environment.

Spiritual life, on the other hand, does not limit itself; it works in the field where we can talk of infinite range of consciousness. In this infinite range of consciousness we cannot talk of any restrictions whatever. If it restricts itself it ceases to be the absolute field. As it knows no limits, it is perfectly free. Therefore, *praṇidhāna* goes out purposely, beyond etiology. When religious life is really in operation, whatever good one may practice, one has no consciousness of good. The man is not thinking of a special work of goodness. If it is good, it is good; if it is bad, it is bad. He does not consider such things; he just goes out of infinitely expanding consciousness, as we have already seen. When an act gets into this world, there is good, bad, moral responsibility. But as the act itself comes out, there is no such limited consideration here.

When certain acts bear fruit, or go out into this relative world, then we can talk of moral evaluation. Otherwise, there is no consideration of moral value. If there is moral value, the act has an object and ceases to be free. Most moralists fail to understand Buddhism here. Their vista is so limited that they cannot go out of the moral world in which they seek to live their life.

Zen *praṇidhāna* is like this; also, Buddhist philosophers, regardless of sect, equally hold this meaning of Buddhist *praṇidhāna*, or prayer in the Buddhist sense. The following story was once told of a

Zen master who lived about seven hundred years ago in Japan.[vii] His name was Myō-e Shōnin (1173–1232), and he was also a great philosopher and a student of Kegon philosophy. He sometimes sat cross-legged in the posture of meditation in a tree, as one of the Chinese Zen masters, popularly known as Niaoke, Bird's Nest, used to do.[viii] Once he was asked by one of his followers if he ever prayed for somebody or to obtain something, and whether he would specially pray for this man, whether he would make a special offering to Buddha on behalf of this person. He said, "No, I never make a special prayer. I cannot do this. I offer *praṇidhāna* every morning and every evening for the sake of all beings, of which you are one. There is no need to have one special, definite person or happening in view. My *praṇidhāna* is universal."

He means when he talks of "universal" that his prayer has no definitely limited object. His prayer comes out of his infinite range of consciousness and goes out to no special purpose. Such prayer might be considered not effective at all. But to put this kind of objective to this kind of prayer is already misleading. What comes out in the way it does is already *praṇidhāna.* He has no *praṇidhāna* for the special welfare of Buddha or anybody, so his *praṇidhāna* covers all beings, nonsentient as well as sentient. And as this *praṇidhāna* has no special object to obtain, so there is no special God or Buddha to whom to offer. This is a kind of self-expression of *prajñā* itself, we might say: God offering *praṇidhāna* to himself in Christian terms. Of course, this is the height of silliness from the relative viewpoint: to himself with no special object. But this is actually what God is doing every

vii. Daisetz Teitaro Suzuki, "The Shin Sect of Buddhism," *Eastern Buddhist* 7-3/4 (July 1939): 281.

viii. EZB 3, 367 and plate XXXIII [376 and plate XXXI].

moment; we are just not conscious of it. Becoming conscious of it is what we gain from our enlightenment experience.

One most interesting saying used in Zen very much is: *Daiyū genzen kisoku wo sonsezu*, literally, "Great act (operation, activity) being manifested, rules are not regarded."[16] "Great" in such cases means limitless, absolute, *mahā*. *Mahā* does not necessarily mean large in magnitude or measure, but it is unlimited, having no limit. *Yū* [*yong*] is the functional aspect of [enlightenment]. Our life never stands just statically; it moves on. Becoming is metaphysical, but *yū* is quite a meaningful word. When things can be utilized, utility is accomplished, as the *yū* of this hand or finger. But at the same time *yū* has no utilitarian object. It has both of these meanings in Chinese and is important, I think: purposeless, nonetiological; purposeful, etiological.

When God declares that there is light, God has no object in creating this world. If he has an object, the world will come to an end one day; but he conceives it as infinitely going on. When he said, "Let there be light!" he just came out of the infinitely extending range of divine consciousness that is working in every one of us and is attained in enlightenment. This is *daiyū*, especially in the Rinzai [Linji] School. It is infinite range without limit. Zen has no secrets, no esotericism; everything is open, revealed; all is open before us, nothing is hidden.

So this divine working coming out of divine consciousness is seen, or revealed, right before us. There is no esoteric meaning anywhere; everything is there. From another point of view, we can say this divine working is the absolute present. If past or present, it is gone already; if future, it is in anticipation. It is in full revelation only in the absolute present. *Daiyū genzen*—pointing to full revelation.

Freely translated, this term means, as Christians would say, "Love God, do what you will." In really original, creative work, God's creation, there are no outside restrictions. It all comes out of oneself when the real thing is carried out. No outside inhibitions are observed.

Another term used in connection with *praṇidhāna* is: *Rōshite kō nashi*, "Laboring and no consequence," result, effect, merit, fruit, no work done.[17] *Rō* is working to accomplish something personal. [*kō-*] *Nashi* means nothing coming out of it, no moral value coming out of it. This is often compared to a man filling a deep well with snow. The well has no limit: whatever snow is put in melts instantly; there is infinite range. [As to] *Kō* [*gong*], there is no creativity whatever; sometimes we put [things] into something that has no bottom. So, however much we put in, nothing is left. It is like piling things up in a basket.

But *daiyū* [*dayong*] in the beginning has an inner working. It actually comes out of divine consciousness, and we share this divine consciousness: we all have both human and divine consciousness. Even our unconsciousness has relative meaning. "Unconsciousness" here does not mean unconsciousness in opposition to ordinary consciousness. When I talk about unconsciousness it is absolute divine consciousness, no-mindness, no-thought. There is no good English term for this *mushin* [*wuxin*] or *munen* [*wunian*]; the terms themselves are better. Unconsciousness is used, then, not in its relative sense, but in the sense of divine consciousness or unconsciousness—they are the same thing, either will do.

When I say this activity comes out of divine unconsciousness I separate, but there is actually no division between the activity and the consciousness working—our language simply requires such a differentiation. Really when we divide things intellectually we are apt to take those things as existing separately from the original thing from which they came. Divine unconsciousness, relatively speaking, is working all the time; and we can't really say anything about it. When we take it as working relatively, it is empty, it is not working. At the same time it has constant becoming, constant creativity from the human viewpoint, coming out of divine consciousness—this is *daiyū*. This is the human way of talking, where differentiation is needed, but we must never forget that they are undifferentiated really. It may be better to say in its unity and totality, in its working, it is operating and not-operating. It looks as if it is purposely working on the utilitarian plane, but at the same time it has nothing to do with such things. When we use all these terms we seem to understand, more or less, but it is to be purely grasped. When it comes out, we think it has come up.

Genzen [C. *xianqian*] means revealing itself, just revealing itself in the absolute present; it has no eschatological sense connected with it. If it has, then there something is caught that belongs to the future, our anticipation. At the same time, this anticipation has no fruit to bear. When things are anticipated, this anticipation has no end; it continues as anticipation, we might say. It is related to the absolute present, not to the future.

The eternal future is future that knows no end; and the past is not something that has gone forever—it is in the absolute present. The absolute present is the reservoir of all possibilities, all potentialities—out of this the infinite future extends, or comes out. So the absolute present implies past and future. And when the absolute present is understood there is divine consciousness or divine unconsciousness, which is shared by every one of us and not only us, also the nonsentient and animals.

Praṇidhāna, therefore, is purposeful and at the same time purposeless. It works, and at the same time it does not work. It has a utilitarian object to obtain and at the same time it has none whatever. This *praṇidhāna* that has no fixed utilitarian object is working in the absolute present, that is, constant creativity.

A man once asked a Zen master, "You are a great enlightened man. Do you ever go to hell?"

Master: "Yes, I go right down to hell."

Man: "How is this possible?"

Master: "Just to save people like you."[18]

He means that we are all living in hell right now and at the same time we are in heaven, but we are not conscious of this heaven. We think of the two as opposite, but we are living in both at this moment. The questioner, like us, likes to divide—"Do you ever go to hell?" "Just to save people like you"—those who try to see from just one point in the relative world. There is no absolute world, except the relative world. Hell is heaven, heaven is hell. There is nothing to be afraid of in hell, or to long for in heaven. We live both right now. This is Zen *praṇidhāna.*

Christ was crucified and went to hell to save mankind only, not animals and the nonsentient. He shares what every man is and bears him with himself in a kind of vicarious atonement. But it is quite individual in this Buddhist case, I think. You believe in me, and I save *you* as the individual who is you. I go to hell to meet *you,* I go to hell to save *you.*

But in fact, there is no saving. One cannot save another. We are not to have concern about salvation. Let God do, we do our best, it is his business, as Voltaire said. This may be illustrated by a man, Shōma, who was quite an ignoramus, if there is such a thing.[19] He went around plowing and doing other such manual work that is not supposed to be very ennobling. But he had a very deep understanding of Shin teachings. His reputation went far, and many people came to see him. One day a man from very far came; his journey took many days. He saw this "ignorant" man at work pounding rice—he had never seen a man pounding or refining rice before. He asked him most earnestly the way to the Pure Land, to salvation. Shōma paid no attention, just went on pounding rice. The man repeated his supplication several times; Shōma did not turn his head.

The employer of Shōma felt sorry for the man and finally asked Shōma not to be so indifferent, to be somewhat sympathetic. But Shōma went on pounding rice. After some time the man, not being able to get an answer, was about to leave. For the last appeal he said, "You have not been able to tell me, so I must leave now."

Then Shōma at last said, "As to showing the way to salvation, that is not my business; it is under God and his business. I do not know anything about it, I can do nothing for you."

This remark ignited the gunpowder, but the explosion itself took place in the man. It would not have taken place unless he had been mature, ready for the explosion. It just happened to ignite; it was not Shōma's doing at all. From the self-power of gunpowder itself came the explosion.

A significant saying among the Japanese is *okage de genki desu*, literally "[I'm well] owing to your shadow." This is the common [reply to the] greeting, "How are you?" *Okage* is literally "love of Buddha." When we think kindly of others, the thought expands and covers the object of our thought. The thought casts a shadow that is your shelter: you are protected under it. I am not quite conscious of this shadow, but the shadow helps me. Shadows are cast by thoughts near and far. We help each other without our being conscious of it. This is really a very nice, and meaningful, expression when we look into it.

What we call a feast, or feeding day, for hungry ghosts takes place in the Zen monastery in summer. It is a rite performed to feed the hungry ghosts with which the world is filled. Buddhists, to help themselves spiritually, offer food to feed the whole universe. But when a ghost sees a bowl filled with rice and tries to eat, the rice turns to flame, so he goes hungry. The ghosts are not dead. All are living, we are all hungry ghosts. We partake in this ritual, and we pray to share the food with everybody else, not just the hungry ghosts. We pray to share whatever food we have now with all others. This shows the universal infinitely expanding relationship, with animals as well as with humans. I think this hungry ghost feeding ritual is conditioned more or less in observance of conventional ritual going on with other Buddhist rituals, and that it is a kind of Zen expression of *praṇidhāna.*

A master was asked, "What will you be afraid of when you are dead?"

We are apt to ask such idle questions all the time. We might say, "Considering my own future is my affair." We are so troubled with others we forget ourselves. This man is like one of us. His question involves the question of soul or spirit, but just in their ordinary sense here, about nothing living in us at present and [something] living somewhere else after our death. We often talk this way without meaning much. Actually I don't know whether it is correct to use "spirit" here. Zen is most profane. The Zen master says, "I go to hell in order to save you." So the use is vulgar. There is really no spiritual quality in this case.

Master: "I will turn into an ass in one of the villages, and I will become a horse in another village."[20] This does not necessarily mean he becomes ass and horse in two places at the same time—just that he may be an ass sometime somewhere and a horse sometime somewhere. Another master answered the same question this way: "I will become one of the donkeys kept in the village." In such short statements it is sometimes very difficult to get into the meaning. To the Zen master there is no death, no birth. Life is here. He refuses to be drawn out; he sticks to living itself. He becomes a donkey, an ass, a horse.

There is a most interesting point in these answers. Zen monasteries were generally in the mountains, the villages far down below. The monks work at the monastery, as does the master, but they are too many to support themselves entirely and they have to appeal to the villagers' goodwill. Sometimes there are more than five hundred, perhaps fifteen hundred, monks, though the Chinese are not quite exact in such matters of numbers and five hundred or fifteen hundred may simply mean "many." They are fond of saying five hundred and fifteen hundred; apparently they do not use any other numbers of monks than these. However, even three or four hundred is quite a large number to feed in a mountain monastery alone. So they are very dependent on the village, and the keeping of the monastery very much depends on the villagers who give to it. The villagers are willing to help these monks try to achieve enlightenment: there is mutual help. But the master's idea is to show his gratitude, to help the village farmers who have helped the monks. Hence the master becomes a donkey, for example, and helps the village in payment. This is the practical way of Zen; they do not just indulge in argument, discourse, and so on. This practical way is the Zen master's *praṇidhāna*, not that he necessarily turns into a donkey, ass, or horse, but just to show in this life that in the future he would help practically too, and not only spiritually. This helping the village corresponds to the *praṇidhāna* of the Pure Land sect, though Zen does not have its words of *praṇidhāna*. Zen's way is to practice *praṇidhāna* by exerting oneself in the daily way of living. Everywhere in Zen literature we see this practical way that is the *praṇidhāna* of Zen men and masters who were never averse to manual labor.

We can understand that the monk would want to know the meaning of the reply he received. He asked, "What does that mean?"

Master: "When I want to ride, I ride. When I want to get down, I get down."

This refers to his actual riding, I suppose; it does not seem to go well with his first answer, which has nothing to do with riding or getting down. This has to do with his present life, riding, getting down, and so on. This implies that he can turn himself into anything, that he is perfect master of himself. It shows his absolute freedom. All these acts are not to be judged from the objective point of view. We have to go down into the inner life of the master himself and experience the going out of these activities from him. He has nothing to do with objectives, he just goes out. What he wants to do he does.

Coming out of the inner consciousness of the master, what is expressed as riding is riding. When it is connected with the outer environment it is dismounting; dismounting shows connection or relationship with environment. . . . [21] Hampered on all sides, we can never be absolutely free. We talk so much of freedom, of empty space, of being altogether free in movement, but really there is no freedom. Freedom is free when it has something that makes it unfree. Freedom is possible only in the world of infinity. Freedom is not in time. Therefore, when he talks of becoming an ass or horse he is absolutely free, though he may be working in any capacity. This is Zen *praṇidhāna.*

In trying to master Zen and become an enlightened man, [one needs to know] there is a triple body in Buddhism: Buddha, Dharma, the brotherhood. A monk asks a master about the three separately, beginning with Buddha. "Where is Buddha?"

Master: "At the crossroads." Where the roads cross each other is where the busiest city life takes place, and in city life the busiest human life takes place. This does not necessarily mean Buddha has to be in a city—it can be fullest activity anywhere.

Monk: "Where is Dharma?"

Master: "This Dharma is in a village full of the inhabitants to be contained in three families." It is the smallest possible village and must be remote.

So Buddha is in the busiest place, Dharma is in the most remote place in the mountains. Dharma is found everywhere, even in the remotest parts of human habitation. Buddha is everywhere, right in the midst of the city.

Monk: "Where is the brotherhood?"

Master: "They are working on the farm, cultivating the ground, plowing in the earth."[22]

So in these answers there is no reference whatever to abstract doctrine; there is just life itself in all human fields of activity, not conceptualized at all. Buddha is a holy being and a man working as ourselves. Dharma is working in the remotest part of the world, not as in books; Dharma is found anywhere, everywhere. The brotherhood works on the farm, strenuously plowing the fields. So Zen explains *praṇidhāna* in this way, not by explaining abstract problems. This also illustrates the Chinese aspect of Zen, for the Chinese speak about life, not generalizations. Indians will not say such things, these things being typically Chinese and not Indian. This is the Zen life of *praṇidhāna*, not necessarily kneeling before God and offering prayers. Zen men do not try to obtain objects beyond our attainment, but their daily life is attaining, is *praṇidhāna* in the most practical way.

Another monk asks, "What is the primary man?" This man means this divine consciousness, or divine personality, or man as not yet come down into the created world, man in his original essence—what kind of man is he? What is he? This is the same as asking, "What is Buddha?"

The master's answer is rather short, never discursive, always terse. In the most practical and concise way, without generality or conceptualization, the answer just comes out of himself as primary man: "My face is covered with dust, and wind blows over it." A breeze blows over one's full face covered with dust, this is a literal translation of his statement.[23]

After working he now enjoys a breeze blowing over his body. This is primary man; he is not hidden beyond creation, he works right out before everyone. Wind blows over the dust covering the whole face. This is Zen *praṇidhāna,* not properly praying in a room or in some closet. It is not hidden in the closet of Christ; it is not inward but in action, in useful expression of action.

The idea is this: This enlightened man does not stay contemplating highly abstract philosophical problems or ideas. He goes into the village and works as hard as a donkey, so his face and body are covered with dust and all kinds of dirt. Then a breeze blows over him. When we speak of eternal self, we think of something that sits back in consciousness and serenely contemplates the world. But Zen goes out into the crossroads to work, into the midst of all those hurry-scurries. Zen is not at the crossroads not knowing which way to turn, but simply at the busiest place. This is the Zen way of practicing *praṇidhāna.*

Other answers to this question of Buddha include these:

"*Jōjō sōsō.*" Everything in the world, actual life as we go on, is all confused.[24]

"Today we reap, we cut rice. Tomorrow I carry fuel. This is the Buddha's work."[25]

"In this grinding or polishing of rice, the millstone goes round and round."[26] In China they have big millstones that are turned round and round by an ox or cow; so rice is polished.

Turning around this way, life goes on this way all the time—this is Buddha. We just go around, and actions themselves come out. I think the best way to interpret Zen life is as *praṇidhāna.* It is significant that China emphasized daily life and manual labor, this coming out especially to me as I go over Zen texts. So this idea of returning to practical life is not new, for Zen started from the very beginning the practice of all forms of manual labor; and this manual labor has always been much encouraged. But full conscious development of this side of Zen was only made two or three hundred years after Bodhidharma, as Zen grew to become more conscious of this practical side. At the same time this literal way of expressing it developed to give literal expression to Zen experience, rather than to put it in philosophical terms of right and left horns. These things are more or less dialectical, the dialectical coming along with many other aspects of Zen experience in the Song dynasty.

In Zen monasteries they specify four items of universal *praṇidhāna*. They generally recite these after each service, after each lecture or sermon given by the master, after each meal, and after reading the sutras:

> All beings, however limitless, I vow to carry across;
> My evil passions, however inexhaustible, I vow to destroy;
> The Dharma teachings, however innumerable, I vow to study;
> The Buddha way, however peerless, I vow to attain.

In the first vow "save," though frequently used, is not quite a proper translation of *do* [*du*; *uttaraṇam* (coming out)], which literally means "to cross over" the stream of *saṃsāra*, not "to save [*uttāraṇam* (rescuing)] ." All there is, *sarvasattva,* however innumerable, is to be helped over the stream of birth-and-death. They cannot be numbered, being so many—this characterizes each of these items of *praṇidhāna.*

Purely from the Zen viewpoint, neither bad nor good passions are to be distinguished. From the purely Zen point of view, the enlightened man has gone beyond these terms of opposites, so there really are no evil passions. But as we come down to this world of relativity we have good and bad. These passions may be numberless, but they vow to extinguish them all. This is also a contradiction, for to be means to have these opposites, one struggling against another.

This universal *praṇidhāna,* we see, begins with all beings, these being innumerable, while evil passions in the second vow are individual. The first *praṇidhāna* is concerned with beings or things; the second with oneself. This is to be especially noticed: Buddhist life begins with otherness, not oneself; there is altruism rather than ego. One is not to get enlightenment for oneself but to see others enlightened. It is necessary to get enlightenment oneself to do this. When a bodhisattva sees so much suffering and misery going on in the world, his sympathy is moved; he wants to save those suffering beings. Buddhist life starts here. Next evil passions are controlled, so the work will be free from selfish interests.

There also cannot be so many teachings, there being just one absolute teaching that can be mastered right away. We think that in learning certain things learning is done once for all, but this learning goes on; it is eternal learning, eternal practicing. To have one thing separated from another thing means cutting totality into pieces. When one thing is mastered the second can be mastered, but when the whole is mastered once for all, the whole is whole; therefore, it can be divided and mastered one by one. The whole is mastered all at once, but at the same time this mastering goes on infinitely. Things are in unity or totality actually.

Every one of the four items we have seen to be characterized by limitlessness. The first is literally boundless. The second is inextinguishable. The third is immeasurable. The fourth is nothing higher than. Everything is negatively stated because everything we see in this world is limited. But these *praṇidhāna* go beyond these sense limitations.

The Bodhisattva Samantabhadra and the Zen master have ten vows, ten *praṇidhāna* we might say, that are practically the same as these four universal *praṇidhāna*. In these ten, every one has this *kokū* [*xukong*], emptiness, or space as I generally translate it, for *kokū* is just sky, or space in the modern conception, though they did not have this idea of space in those ancient days. In fact, space is still a moot question. Philosophers do not know how to define the idea of it. It is something objectively existing, it can never be exhausted. We cannot stay like this, we would like to go beyond. Astronomers know so many stars and galaxies, but we cannot stop there. Our telescopes cannot be said to exhaust whatever is to be seen in the heavens, for the telescope is limited itself, and human ingenuity cannot put a limit to the universe.

As far as our mentality works, we have limit. But otherwise we cannot be limited. As space is unlimited, Buddhists say, so are nonsentient beings. We, the sentient, are simply limited because our senses are limited. It is still possible that we will come to have another sense besides our present five. In case we have something else, we will come to discover something else: all will not be limited to five. However precise, instruments and measures apply to sense discrimination, and intellect is based on these sense experiences.

I do not know whether this picture of the universe as infinite is in harmony with modern physics, but physics nowadays is limited by our own sense experience. Modern science does not dare to speculate, it just stays with sense experience; and the infinite idea does not go very well with sense experience. However, I am told that Einstein has an equation for the universe that has it finite, but beyond sense understanding, and that there is no contradiction between it and what I have said here.

The thing is this: when we talk about these things, the very nature of the symbol limits anything we may ask about infinity. Only *prajñā*-intuition can comprehend infinity—when mental activities are not at the level of relativity.

So the Buddhist idea is that beings sentient and nonsentient are not limited, nor are our possibilities. "Possibility" is not a good term—whatever is going on in our consciousness. We seem to be able to pick up beyond the boundaries—national, social, worldly, cosmic. This consciousness is not only what manifests on the surface of consciousness, but through this consciousness we reach the unconscious.

The Dharma teachings of the third vow are not necessarily limited to teachings expounded in the sutras or shastras. They can be broadened into a kind of scientific study of reality, not only of teachings directly called Buddhist. Globally speaking, our scientific knowledge is also part of Buddhist teachings, as is everything really, including psychological experience. This teaching changes all the time; whatever hypotheses we formed a hundred years ago are now abandoned. It does not matter very much, for when they change they change, and we go on. There are different ways of interpreting reality—and this changing goes on all the time. Scientific studies are always welcomed by Buddhists, and from the broad viewpoint everybody is a Buddhist.

Enlightenment experience, or the "Buddha way," of the fourth vow is to be distinguished from particular experience. As we know, this enlightenment is the fundamental experience underlying all experiences. This fundamental enlightenment experience, therefore, is something that cannot be exhausted. If it is capable of exhaustion, an experience is one of particular experiences, not fundamental experience. "However difficult in fact *praṇidhāna* is to attain, no-attainment is attainment"—I interpret this vow this way. To attain the unattainable means eternal striving for attainment.

As this emptiness of space is inexhaustible, so are all beings. As long as all beings are inexhaustible, their karma, work, or activity will never be exhausted. And not only activities, the desires behind them are also inexhaustible. So we will go on eternally like this and eternally strive. We like to think we will reach Utopia eventually. But time is always fleeing, never staying. We eternally strive to bring into being the heavenly kingdom, but this kingdom will never stay with us; striving can never be brought to an end, it is always going on. In the relative way of thinking, we like to think it will come and stay, but no such static state will ever come. Staying quiet, unmoving, will never be attained. When it comes, Nirvāṇa, perfect nothingness, will be left.

The doctrine of this unlimitedness comes out in the Zen masters, who have working intuition, from their being engaged in daily life in practical *praṇidhāna*. According to the Kegon Sutra, Samantabhadra has these ten *praṇidhāna*:

1. To revere all the Buddhas. According to Kegon, the universe is full of Buddhas. On every piece of hair there is an innumerable, infinite number of Buddhas. Every atom is Buddha: the one who wants to bow to Buddha is Buddha. In relative terms Samantabhadra puts all infinity together as one Buddha; he wants to bow to him.
2. To praise all the Buddhas. Samantabhadra wants to be constantly praising all the Buddhas.
3. To make extensively all kinds of offerings to the Buddhas, especially what may be termed "moral offerings" (*dharmapūjā*). This is a kind of paying homage. Praise is more verbal, while homage entails actual offerings.
4. To repent all sins ever committed by himself. By confession a man wants to clear himself of all karmic hindrances that might be in him.
5. To be sympathetically joyful over whatever merits are acquired by others. This also includes sympathy for bad luck, or catastrophe. It is used in two senses: the personal and what the person undergoes.
6. To ask the Buddha to revolve the Wheel of the Dharma. This also includes preaching the doctrine, which is taking place all the time.

7. To ask the Buddha to stay on living in this world. This is to see Buddha living among us all the time, not just once in a while.
8. To be always learning from the life of the Buddha. There must be chances to learn from the Buddha, to come under his spiritual influence, to discipline oneself under his leadership.
9. To look after the spiritual welfare of all beings. This one is quite characteristic of Buddhism: compliance with all beings, what they do, and so on. Samantabhadra leads them in accordance with their capacities, their abilities to understand truth, and in conformation with their *karma*.
10. To turn all his merits towards the promotion of goodness and the suppression of evils. This is also characteristic of Buddhism. Whatever merit one has accumulated is to be transferred to other beings, so they can share, so they can be equally enjoyed by other people. He does not mention bad things being transferred. Merit is transferred not only to individuals, but also to the general store of good. Good stocks are to be stored up, as in a bank I suppose—I do not know how they do this. From absolute subjectivity all these things make no sense, but as long as we live here they are full of meaning apparently.[ix]

When a reference was made above to the stream of consciousness the Zen master has attained, or strives to attain—either way—I said he refers to the place, the physical surroundings in which Zen is. Sometimes it is not just the physical surroundings—in these

ix. For these vows see SLS, 230–231; those of a bodhisattva entering the first stage are given on 222–223.

practical examples you may see what I mean. For instance: "What is the field of mind, or stream of consciousness, the Zen master enjoys?"

This did not happen so much in the early days of Zen. A question is asked, then reference is made to surroundings or environment. It is possible that the question was asked by a monk when night was coming on. The master answered as if night were already advanced. When it is very late, the Chinese say "deep." This does not refer to the darkness of night, but to its being far advanced. "Deep" may refer to white also.[27]

Another question follows soon after the first: "Who is the person in this environment who appreciates it?" Who is right in it? Who is the man in it?

Master: "The tiger cries, and the monkey roars." Monkeys and tigers are frequent in the mountains, so this came from the actual surroundings, I suppose.[28]

Another type of question is, "What is your *gocara* (i.e., field of activity)?"

"You just see and understand it yourself, you do not have to ask."

"Who is the man in it?"

Master: "What, what!"[29]

This is more subjective, we might say. It is not quite questioning, "What? What?" It is questioning and yet wondering: mysterious is the way God works; we cannot penetrate it. At the same time it is appreciating without knowing what one is doing, that kind of "what," a most important point, "Let thy will be done," *laissez-faire*. The subject is in a way defined, "just this." The object is "What, what!" There is no living there, in this division. That alone is not enough: social communication must take place, one working on the other, certain dynamics must go on. That is the third question, "If a visitor comes, what will you do?" How do you express that mutuality? What is mutual living together, communal life? The answer is, "Have a cup of tea."[30] This is courtesy, the social way, even if the country is suffering famine; whatever things there are, give them away in an altruistic deed. All this takes place in personal, everyday life, but expanded to include all there is. That is what is characteristic of Zen, and people do not understand that. It is very difficult to make really clear.

Another question is, "What is *kore,* what is your *kore*?" *Kore* is "this," *shako* (*zhege*) is "just so," "just this."

A master's answer is, "When a breeze passes through pine needles, the pine needles rubbing against each other give a sound not like that through leaves."[31] Japanese people and poets enjoy the sound of these needles very much.

There is an old story of a Chinese Buddhist scholar called Dōshō (Daosheng, d. 434) who was intuitively certain, before the introduction in China of the *Mahāparinirvāṇa Sūtra* in its complete text, that all things are endowed with buddha nature. This was disputed very much by the other scholars and could not be decided until the remaining part of the text came from India. Dōshō, the young revolutionary, said it did not matter about the text, for Buddha himself teaches that everything is endowed with buddha nature, there being no exception whatever. This did not please the others, and Dōshō had to leave. He made a sermon on his understanding of the sutra and delivered it in the mountains, where there were only rocks to hear. When he said that all beings are endowed with buddha nature, the rocks themselves began to nod.[x] So, "when the breeze passes through the pines, the stones are not touched." This simply reads, "How pleasant are the pine needles rubbing against each other when a breeze passes through them!"[32]

The next question is, "Who is the man?"

---

x. SZ,195.

Master: "If I plant vegetables or I raise fruit trees, wild fruit trees, I provide the monks with fruit and vegetables."

This man was not idly listening to the pine needles, but he was also practical. He works to do society a service, we might say, [with] fruit and vegetables, entertaining passing monks and other travelers.

This monk did not stop there; he said, "I thank you very much."

Master: ["How do they taste?"][33]

Subject and object were not mixed at first. There was just a description of surroundings.

"What is [your] *gocara*?"

"Straight in front of you runs [the stream] eastward."

"How about the man?"

"Come in and you will see him."[34]

"At night I hear water running through the bamboo grove at the back of this cottage. During the day I see the clouds arising from the mountain before the cottage."[35] This simply means water is heard, and so on.

Another *mondō* begins, "What is your life?"

"Bamboo chopsticks and earthenware." Bowls of rough clay are meant.

Monk: "When an important visitor comes, how do you treat him?" That is, bamboo chopsticks and rough bowls may not be good enough.

Master: "No different treatment."[36]

This is the practical life shown in Zen books. It is nothing but practical demonstration of Zen *praṇidhāna*. Zen monks refer so much to practical life; Zen expresses itself in this way.

The dualistic way of seeing things goes all through Chinese thought, Daoism excepted. Confucius sees things in two parts, and the Chinese have a dualistic conception of reality, shown in *yang* and *yin*, for example. They considered this human world to be divided into two layers, above and below, and the Chinese poet spends much time and thought on striking a couplet including the two. One of the best known of these has already been quoted: "*shang qiu puti, xia hua zhongsheng*" (*jōgu bodai, geke shujō*), "On the one hand seek enlightenment, on the other convert all beings."[37]

Christians do not have this help for others as Buddhists have it. I would like to emphasize this point: Christians do not like to help one another, I'm afraid. When they try to help others they appeal to God. If they see people in need and themselves lack money to help they pray to God for them, on their behalf. But Zen feels that we work all together. In Buddhism there is some kind of prayer, but in that case the Buddhist doctrine of karma may come in. At the same time I do not ask God's help for a man in need, but I want to help him somehow. I do this by asking that whatever merit I have accumulated, or may accumulate in future, all be dedicated to him; and that he be relieved of his bad karma in a future life, if such is not possible in his present life. Buddhism puts more thinking into its desire to help, while the Christian has an emotional response.

In the couplet, it is better not to distinguish a first and a second part, for either may come first or second. The two are so intertwined that the other comes along if one does. To get others enlightened means to get oneself enlightened, and vice versa. This idea runs through different Buddhist sects, for example Shin, the opposite teaching of Buddhism to Zen.

Zen emphasizes self first, Shin the other first. But this other and this self are not to be relatively interpreted. The Shin idea of "other power" is not to be understood in opposition to "self power," nor is self to be put forth in opposition to other, for not-self is self, self is not-self. In the Shin doctrine of other power Amida is supposed to be standing on the other side, the objective recollection of the self, not the psychological, superficial self. And self as understood by Zen is at the opposite extreme of the relative self. Therefore, the Zen self corresponds to the Shin Amida. Amida made a pilgrimage to get all people enlightened, though Shin is not supposed to teach the doctrine of enlightenment but that of being born in the Pure Land. When more closely examined, however, the object of birth in the Pure Land is to obtain enlightenment there, not to stay in it. The Pure Land is supposed to be more congenially constructed, so enlightenment is not so difficult to obtain there. They do not have to wait until sometime after their birth: the very time they are born in the Pure Land, enlightenment takes place.

Amida made as a condition for his own enlightenment that all beings be born in the Pure Land he would create. So his enlightenment and our being born in the Pure Land are simultaneously attained. When Amida attains we attain, when we attain Amida attains; we are born in the Pure Land, therefore he attains enlightenment and [satisfying] his enlightened condition comes about by our being born in the Pure Land.

Some Shin people, the less orthodox ones, say, "Amida attained his enlightenment and we are assured of being born in the Pure Land, so what is the use of being a Shin follower? Regardless of what we do, the established fact is that we are to be born in the Pure Land—what is the use of desiring to be so born?" But this is not the man who has really experienced enlightenment, or being born in the Pure Land. Amida has established it so that each individual attains enlightenment himself. When he attains it, he is sure of Amida's having attained it. Amida's attaining is not just a matter of record in a book but is to be experienced personally by each individual. It is not just depending on other power; other power works through him.

Therefore, Zen's idea of attaining and helping to attain are not to be divided. One brings the other. Our speech always divides one thing into two. This is inevitable, I suppose, for language is meant for communication: one is to speak, one is to hear. At the same time, there is no absolute truth individually. The individual gains meaning when others are in existence; one individual has no meaning. When we speak of one, this one brings others along—not just humans, but all the universe, or cosmos. We often forget this and try to subject nature to our will. Nature does not submit, often to the confusion of our minds.

Now this *praṇidhāna* is the *karuṇā* aspect of enlightenment. This is, of course, a contradiction; *prajñā* goes beyond *karuṇā,* and yet *karuṇā* is in *prajñā.* There is no *prajñā* unless it works out into *karuṇā;* and *karuṇā* is possible because of *prajñā.* This circle is to be obtained. And on account of *karuṇā* and *prajñā* coming out of *praṇidhāna* this kind of *praṇidhāna* is divided.

As long as moral life is concerned, it always has tracks, for it tries to attain certain ends. And it can be tracked by these footprints. But this having an intention, or object, before one is not *prajñā,* nor *praṇidhāna.* Zen *praṇidhāna* is simply looking to the infinitely expanding future. This is the eternal, infinitely fulfilling prayer of *praṇidhāna.* Zen does not really have other kinds of *praṇidhāna.*

The Zen idea of *praṇidhāna* is not just wishing to save all beings nonsentient and sentient. As we see in the history of Zen in China, Zen emphasizes this doctrine of work, instead of just contemplation or meditation or practicing some kind of yoga. Not only this, but the monk's time is used in daily labor, in work sometimes considered below the dignity of a yogin or *rishi* in India. Baizhang, the founder of Zen monasteries in China, said, "A day of no working is a day of no eating."[38] As Zen was developed by the practical people of China, it naturally values very much the meaning of manual labor. Not only were the monks employed but also the masters took part with them. The monasteries were most democratic: master and disciples exchanged *mondō* while working together. These we have seen to be more or less metaphysical discussions—not discussions, really, just *mondō.* While working they exchanged *mondō,* and this working is itself Zen expression of *praṇidhāna* according to my own interpretation. By working they demonstrated their understanding of reality. Reality is expressed not only in the words or gestures exchanged but also—and principally, I like to say—in the working, in the bodily demonstration of legs, arms, etc. So this is Zen *praṇidhāna.*

In short, *praṇidhāna* is man. In other words, it is the human situation, which is at the same time being and nonbeing. The human situation consists in becoming: being plus nonbeing. Being and at the same time nonbeing, this is the human situation in which we find ourselves—and *praṇidhāna* naturally flows out. What makes *praṇidhāna* possible is the human situation.

This contradiction in which we are is no other than *praṇidhāna.* "To be" is the absolute present in which past and future are contained. The absolute present is not just the present itself, but at the same time it contains in it the past and the future. Both come out of it. So we can say man is and is not.[39] "To be" and "not to be" are becoming—and this is *praṇidhāna. Praṇidhāna* means that which it wishes not to be.

Wishing is not unnatural; it comes spontaneously out of ease itself. *Praṇidhāna* is possible when "to be" and "not to be" exist simultaneously, yet in time sequence. There is no *praṇidhāna* if they just exist simultaneously. So "to be" and "not to be" also exist in time sequence, and *praṇidhāna* comes out. "Going out" is future. *Praṇidhāna* is at once present and future, because present is not just present; it is present because of future and past. We can say future is future because of present. Present is what we have and feel. Past has meaning only when it is in the present. Past wants to be itself by becoming the present, by being in the present. Past is past only by being in the present; past always orients itself in the present. This present implies future, so future is *praṇidhāna.*

Praṇidhāna is history that is not yet finished. *Praṇidhāna* is not the history of the past, therefore, as we generally understand history, but history yet to be written, of the future man is going to write. History in the real sense is not written and all closed up; it is in the making and never completed. We often think history is finished, but it is not; we are always writing it all the time. History and *praṇidhāna* never come to an end. *Praṇidhāna* is eternal, never completed, eternal "prayer."

Praṇidhāna by its very nature is unattainable. Yet because and in spite of this unattainability there is continuous, perpetual, never-ending *praṇidhāna.* So life itself is *praṇidhāna, praṇidhāna* is human life. This is the reason even a bodhisattva has his own *praṇidhāna*; and we are all bodhisattvas having our own *praṇidhāna.* This *praṇidhāna* is altogether purposeless; it has no track, no circumference whatever. This is the gist of Zen: purposeless *praṇidhāna*, continuous, no interruption whatever, no limitation, no intermission, no track, altogether purposeless—for purpose belongs to time. When time is taken away there is no purpose whatever. This purpose is time; therefore, this time is purpose.

The Kegon Sutra in the part devoted to Samantabhadra has a chapter devoted to his *caryā,* generally translated *gyō* in Japanese and understood to mean "practice," "discipline." But the best way to translate it is "life": a human being living the life of Samantabhadra, riding on an elephant, representing the *karuṇā* aspect of enlightenment. Living a life of love, according to Christian terminology, is meant. The life of Samantabhadra, therefore, is in constant *praṇidhāna*, and his life is a *praṇidhāna* that has no ending whatever.

When they [all the bodhisattvas] talk of the interminability or unattainability of Samantabhadra's *praṇidhāna*, which is also our own *praṇidhāna*, it is compared to empty space. Indians and some scientists today think that the emptiness of space, *ākāśa*, may be extinguishable, that it may be time for this emptiness to be annihilated. But sentient and nonsentient will have no ending whatever. As all these things have no end, so our *praṇidhāna* has no end. Furthermore, this emptiness of space may come to nonexistence someday, but *praṇidhāna* will never come to a finish.

Praṇidhāna is will itself, will to be understood in its broadest and most fundamental sense. Astronomers talk of the heavenly bodies and say that they may all be destroyed someday, but will interpreted in human terms will never come to an end. Will ever strives to articulate, to live. This will, as I have said, has a much deeper sense than the biological given to it by Schopenhauer. As long as this will remains blind, human life cannot go any further than animal life, for which no history is possible; history is only possible for humans.

So this will, instead of remaining blind and unconscious, wants to live and become conscious of itself. When this consciousness is realized, this is enlightenment. So the enlightenment experience that Buddha realized after six years of moral and intellectual trials, this experience is no more than will becoming conscious of itself. Will always tries to become conscious of itself, and this becoming conscious is enlightenment. So we can say that human consciousness is the eternal striving of will to become conscious of itself. When the unconscious comes out into the field of consciousness, we can say that will has attained its ultimate end. In modern psychological terminology, the unconscious forever strives to become conscious of itself. So enlightenment is unconscious consciousness, or conscious unconsciousness. Aśvaghoṣa and other Mahāyāna thinkers speak quite frequently of *mushin* [*wuxin*] or *munen* [*wunian*]. *Munen* is not just separated from *nen* [*nian*; thought, thinking] but free from *nen* and at the same time having *nen*: the unconscious becoming conscious of itself, this is what constitutes enlightenment experience.

In terms of life, life is constant striving. Unconsciously the unconscious strives to become conscious of itself; it constantly strives for self-expression. This inevitably involves frustration, so life is a series of frustrations. We all ultimately die, but there is no such thing as death as long as life and will are concerned. Death is only individual. Philosophers, who are afraid of death, talk of the meaninglessness of human life, but they are all talking in individual terms. As long as they cannot go beyond these, they cannot get rid of fear, they cannot understand Samantabhadra's life of *praṇidhāna.*

In terms of society *praṇidhāna* is the human situation as one finds oneself in society, *en soi* and *pour soi*; it is handy to use these terms of Sartre here. Philosophers are apt to see men facing and fighting each other. They talk so much about frustration because they want to fight. When defeated, one feels frustrated; then death puts an end to it.

But Buddhist *praṇidhāna* does not keep man separated from what is not himself. *En soi* is at once *pour soi.* These two are not taught by Buddhists as fighting against each other. Intuitively one is impossible without the other. They are one and the same, identical. It is only due to the human way of thinking to see reality in a dichotomous way.

As the human way goes on, the two will fight. The individual, in fact, is no individual without what is not individual: we can talk of individual only when there is not-individual. So the individual is as much an illusion as the superindividual is. The individual transcends himself by identification with what is not-individual. But self-identification is not separate from individuality, either. Individuality always strives to get out of itself, for this self means conceptuality, which is bondage, not freedom. The individual cannot be free as long as he is in individuality.

This is why Communism takes hold, but this fascination must not involve making ourselves slaves to the whole. In this case the individual becomes smaller than the whole, the whole larger than the individual. Indeed, we must be always looking about, not to get caught in another snare in getting away from the first. We always construct these traps and get out of one into another. Man is forever destined to remain in a state of slavery, it seems.

As I think of it now, modern man talks so much of this idea of freedom, yet he does not understand what it means.[xi] There is no such thing as individual freedom. As long as man remains individual he has no freedom. Only when the individual negates himself does he begin to have freedom. When the Japanese wanted to translate "liberty" in Mill's book *On Liberty*, which was translated into Japanese eighty years ago, there was nothing corresponding to it in Japanese or Chinese. Finally one word corresponding to "liberty" was found, *jiyū* (Chinese *ziyou*), a most expressive term. "Liberty" implies conditionality, to be free from something. It implies that something binds, to be free from it being liberty. But *jiyū* had no such sense, though it is now used in this way. Working by itself, it has no such negative meaning in it. It is affirmative with nothing negating it. It means "autonomous," but not something that works quite automatically, not the "automatic" that reminds us of mechanical working. *Jiyū* is originally a Buddhist term used to characterize the nature of *ātman*. In addition to "autonomous," it is "self-mastery," "depending only on oneself," corresponding to the Buddhist *ātman*; "one's self," "essence," "nature," "the principle of life," "the abstract individual," "the whole person considered as one."

In an article comparing Schweitzer and Radhakrishnan, a quotation from Radhakrishnan includes this phrase, "the eternal life of the spirit, working itself out unconsciously and spontaneously."[xii] With this "unconsciously and spontaneously" *jiyū* may be compared, but spontaneous does not quite correspond to *jiyū*. Schweitzer uses

xi. See D. T. Suzuki, "Freedom of Knowledge in Chinese Buddhism," *Middle Way* 31 (1956): 12–18, also referred to above.

xii. C. W. M. Gell, "Schweitzer and Radhakrishnan a Comparison," *The Hibbert Journal* 51 (1952–53): 234–241; 355–365; see p. 241 particularly.

"supra-ethical," a clumsy word, in his struggle to express what he has realized in himself. "Spontaneously ethical life" would be a better term, according to the author. Ethics does not have *jiyū*; *jiyū* does not belong to the realm of ethics, which always constrains and has something binding in it. Radhakrishnan's "unconsciously and spontaneously" is much better. But *ātman* in its original sense is much more effective, I think.

Jiyū belongs to ultimate reality itself. As long as individuals are concerned, there is no *jiyū*, no liberty for them. We just imagine we have liberty, for as long as the individual wants to exercise freedom he comes into conflict with others. So the individual is hedged around by musts, oughts, shoulds. We do not realize it, but we cry for liberty because the individual has something in him beyond individuality that wants to assert itself, supreme *ātman* or *jiyū*.

This term *jiyū* is noteworthy from the standpoint of Buddhist thinking; without Buddhist literature we could not find this term—neither in Confucianism nor in Daoism is there such an idea. They may have something vaguely corresponding to it, but not the so exactly expressed idea of *jiyū*, for *jiyū*, liberty in the real sense, belongs to ultimate reality, to God himself. Indians identified it with supreme *ātman*. And when this identification takes place there takes place the unification or identification of freedom and necessity. Then freedom is necessity, necessity is freedom. When this unification is realized, enlightenment experience takes place. In other words, we might say that enlightenment experience is the realization that freedom is necessity, necessity is freedom: the two contradictory ideas are unified. This is not to be understood in a dialectical sense, for it is a matter of direct experience, of direct intuition.

When God created the world, he did this out of his free will. In sheer emptiness there was nothing to oppose this exercise of free will; and even when he has the world, he abides in absolute emptiness, in absolute freedom. We individuals think we are not free, and so we do not attain liberty. This world God created is God himself, and God is the world. This necessity and freedom, that is, the identification of the two contradictory ideas, is best expressed in a well-known Zen *mondō:*

A master was asked by a monk, "When the whole world"—Buddhism has a system or scheme of worlds that really has no bounds—"comes to an end, does this also come to an end?" "This" is something beyond individual existence. He does not say God, ultimate reality, ultimate truth, One Mind, *ālaya-vijñāna*—simply "this."

Master: "Yes."

Monk: "There is supposed to be freedom from such limitations." Puzzled: "Why?" is what he is asking.

Master: "Because it is identical with the universe."[40] But this identification is not to be understood in the objective sense. In an objective sense we think we see the universe in which we are. Objectively "this" is identical with the universe. But the destruction of the universe does not concern this absolute subjectivity. Therefore, objectively it seems destined to destruction.

Another master said, " 'This' does not go to destruction with the destruction of the universe."

Monk: "Why?"

Master: "Because it goes along with it, it is in conformity with it, it does not contradict it."[41]

Here the master emphasizes that this is subjective, not objective, conformity of psychological experience. His idea is that of absolute subjectivity, which is also the absolute present, metaphysically speaking. The absolute present goes along with destruction and no-destruction. The absolute present goes along with absolute subjectivity, where this real freedom is necessity, necessity is freedom. When this takes place, necessity, karma, causality go together.

Freedom negates karma; causality is *praṇidhāna. Praṇidhāna* comes out of causality, which binds everything up, with no escaping, and *praṇidhāna* comes out of this chain. This is where *praṇidhāna* is freedom.

Because of this freedom we transcend ourselves. When the individual is identified with society or environment we think individuality is lost, but individuality is really asserted when it transcends individuality. This transcendence is what is most important in interpreting *praṇidhāna.* When we know what *praṇidhāna* means, we transcend ourselves, and this is freedom. When history is considered, all that is close to the present is karma, causality, unchangingness. But the absolute present implies not only the present but the past and future, and because of the future coming out there is *praṇidhāna.* We are able to make any *praṇidhāna*; we are not committed to our individual limitations if we transcend individuality and become really free. Freedom is appreciated only when we have *praṇidhāna* well understood.

There is no difference in Zen and Zen *praṇidhāna. Praṇidhāna* is the dynamic aspect of *yū.*[42] The cosmic *yū* is not independent of the human *yū.* The cosmic comes out into the human *yū.* As it comes out, either love or hate can be used of it, yet humanly it is somehow love or compassion.

But when we use a term once, we ossify it; the term loses flexibility—one concept cannot be used for another. There is really a fusion of contradictory ideas here. We love when we feel love, and we hate when we feel hate, between individuals. When individualities are transcended, the individual expresses himself not as an instrument of "self-individuality"—I do not know what word to use for it; when this takes place the absolute subject knows neither hate nor love. "Hate" and "love" are terms we try to interpret relatively. As long as subjectivity is concerned, we cannot talk of love and hate—anything will do. The lower levels of intuition have to speak of hate, love, etc.; they cannot help it. From here we cannot go up to understand a higher level, though we can come down to understand the lower level. Most people do not live on the higher plane. In reality there are no levels, of course, but it is better to talk as if there were.

Good and bad apply only to moral life. In the ultimate sense there is neither good nor bad, freedom being the activity of godhead. When godhead works on freely there is no good or bad; when we interpret we call one good, another bad. But when it comes out of the godhead freely we cannot say good or bad. We who are not beyond the level of particulars talk about good and bad. When we talk of absolute, nothing human is present. When we talk of human it is no more absolute.

If we stay on the level of the absolute there is no love, no hate. In response to conditions, what comes down to this level we are on turns into good or bad. This causality itself comes out of this absolute *subjectum*. Karma is subjective, humanness is subjective. When karma subjectivity goes into human subjectivity, there is this eternal longing for good, or love. But this works through ignorance, and there is hate, or discord. We cannot get rid of discord eternally; it is a kind of Zoroastrian conflict. But good will finally win.

Ignorance moves in the body of original enlightenment; because of ignorance there is original enlightenment. This ignorance is beyond our human interpretation—and our troubles come out of this, where both love and hate are. *Praṇidhāna* is the outcome of ignorance. But ignorance is not possible without original enlightenment, original enlightenment is not possible without ignorance. And because of cosmic will there is human will. Human will is a mixture of ignorance and enlightenment. The *subjectum* is at once cosmic and human.

The absolute plane has no opposites, yet when we are dead to this world we cry and sympathize. Cosmic will goes out in terms of compassion because cosmic will is good, we have to say, I suppose. We can't escape the concept of the devil, personal or otherwise. The rise of consciousness is angelic and at the same time demonic.

As I have said, Buddhist *praṇidhāna* has no special, definite object to obtain. It is objectless movement, objectless working of *prajñā*. *Prajñā* is the static aspect of enlightenment; *karuṇā* is just the opposite, its dynamic aspect. So *prajñā* corresponds to being, and *karuṇā* will be becoming. But being is becoming, becoming is being—the two are one in *praṇidhāna*. So we understand why *praṇidhāna* has no special object to attain. But this is not "purposelessness" in the ordinary sense of "moving on but not attaining at all." Yet if Buddhist *praṇidhāna* has any definite object to realize it will not be unceasing *praṇidhāna*.

We may ask ourselves, "If *praṇidhāna* works without any interruption, constantly with no interval, how can we become conscious of it?" When things go on uninterruptedly there is no possibility of any thought, of any consciousness getting into it. When we cannot reflect on it, when there is no time interval, it is the same as not having it at all. When we speak of Buddhist *praṇidhāna*, therefore, there must be something there that makes us conscious of *praṇidhāna*. Time must cut into timelessness, in other words. But how does timelessness turn into time? This is a great problem and a great contradiction; all our thought goes into fighting it. We try to fight out this contradiction on the intellectual plane, but we forget that in the contradiction itself there is no contradiction if we do not stay away from it. When we live in what we think to be contradictory, the contradiction itself disappears. And the disappearance of the contradiction is experienced in this enlightenment that Buddha is said to have had so long ago. I will illustrate with this very short sermon given by a Zen teacher:

"To know, no knowing. Knowing and yet not-knowing." This is the gist of Zen experience. It is known most clearly and most transparently—and yet when we begin to say, "It is there," it is no more there, so it is also no-knowing.

At the same time it is two and one, two yet one. Yet in this 1 one does not cling to 1. When we say 1 we think 1 is enough. We are so used to 1 standing by itself, yet it is no more 1 but 2. So there is knowing, yet no-knowing. This is a way to experience enlightenment. Ontologically it is not-2 and 1, and no clinging to this 1. This is a contradictory dictum.

Another interesting thing in this connection comes from a sutra. "Knowing and seeing," this phrase we come across from the very beginning of Buddhist history. Knowing is not enough; they always say they see too. While seeing is actually experienced, knowing is more or less indirect and mediated. Knowing and seeing are very much in evidence in the sutra. So we take them as expressing one idea, not two, in Chinese.

If we establish or erect knowing, this is the origin of ignorance. But when we have this experience of knowing and seeing, this knowing and seeing cannot be expressed in terms of intellect. Zen says that "I know" means "I do not know," so knowing means not-knowing. When anything specially distinguishes knowledge as knowledge then it ceases to be universal knowledge; it turns into particular knowledge, instead of being pure knowledge. It turns into knowledge of some special object. So knowing is the origin of ignorance.

If there is no knowing, no seeing, there is Nirvāṇa. This knowing and seeing is to be understood as knowing-seeing, as one experience, for there is no dividing it. In this experience of knowing-seeing, if we have anything we know, we see, this knowing-seeing experience comes down onto the plane of relativity, and knowing-seeing will be lost. Therefore, I know, yet I do not know; I see, yet I do not see. When this is experienced, this is Nirvāṇa.

But a man before he became a regular Zen teacher read the sutra this way—and his reading helped him to enlightenment experience: "When knowing and seeing is established, if one says there is such a thing as knowing and seeing, I know this is the origin of ignorance." Practically, this comes to the same thing. "Where there is knowing and seeing, there is no knowing and no seeing"—the opposite of the first line. "When there is no seeing, no knowing," or when there is no knowing-seeing, "then I see. This is no other than Nirvāṇa."

When knowing-seeing is established, I know this is the origin of ignorance. When there is no knowing-seeing I see this is Nirvāṇa. It finally comes to the same thing. When someone said to him, "This is no ordinary way of reading it, it is against the ordinary way," he answered, "It does not matter. Grammars I understand. Sometimes such a thing happens."

Shinran, founder of the Shin sect, also had a reading altogether different from the ordinary one, in *Sukhāvatīvyūhasūtra, The Sutra of Eternal Life.*[xiii] This is the way to read a sutra. In taking the text as it is ordinarily understood we sometimes cling to the sutra too much. Instead of our reading it, the sutra makes us its slave. Letters kill, the spirit frees—as has been said many times.

Every bodhisattva has his *praṇidhāna.* Each one of us is a bodhisattva, so we have our own *praṇidhāna* each to carry out in our own way. One *praṇidhāna* of the bodhisattva in question is this: "My *praṇidhāna* is to be in compliance or conformity with all beings. Being in conformity with all beings, I will strive to bring them to enlightenment." In striving to do for his fellow beings, this would-be bodhisattva goes out of himself. This going out of himself and trying to

xiii. Suzuki, "The Shin Sect of Buddhism," 245–246; p. 276ff.

do something for others makes him already a bodhisattva, we might say. Merging into each other, becoming into being, being into becoming, is an intellectual contradiction. But when this is actually realized there is no contradiction. We go on being and at the same time we become. This state is going out of ourselves. This *praṇidhāna* literally means to go out in conformity with [others].

We just say "all Beings" in a most general way, but this bodhisattva specified them. According to this interpretation this universe, physical and spiritual, and all the space occupied by this universe are included; and any inhabitants there may be on the stars, and also everywhere in space where there are worlds where some beings may be living—all are included. But if such beings are in existence they may be different from us. There are considered to be four ways of birth: from a mother body, from an egg, from moisture, from transformation. In all beings are the four elements on which they depend: earth, water, fire, air.

All these different beings may have all kinds of physical bodies, shapes, lengths of life, names, mentalities, desires; all kinds of will, movement, dignity, posture; all kinds of dress, diet, villages, towns, cities; they also include heavenly or celestial beings. Eight different classes are named: human beings, nonhuman beings, those having two or four or more legs, colored, uncolored, with thought, without thought, neither with nor without thought.

This bodhisattva is in compliance with all these beings. When among four-legged beings, he becomes like one of them. He will become a god when he works among gods. He speaks all kinds of languages. He serves these beings, administers to them, is a bodhisattva toward them as to his own parents, teacher, master. He makes no difference between all of these and Buddha. In case of disease he is a good physician; he is a good guide to the lost, a treasury to the poor, and so on. This Bodhisattva uniformly benefits all beings, he respects them uniformly. He tries to gladden them as if he were trying to please all the Buddhas. He does it because of his great *karuṇā* mind, which constitutes buddhahood and tathāgatahood.

This great mind works in response to the needs of all beings. Because of great compassion there grows in all beings what is known as *bodhicitta* [the mind for attaining awakening]. This *bodhicitta* awakes in all beings in response to the great compassionate mind that Buddha has. When it opens it calls out responses from all beings. *Bodhicitta* is the mind moving toward enlightenment, so the enlightened mind in all beings comes to the stage of activity in response to the great *karuṇā* mind. By awaking this *bodhicitta* in all beings, they come finally to attain enlightenment.

In a great desert is a big tree. When it gets water, leaves, branches, flowers, amd fruit grow up in rhapsody. So the growth of the enlightenment tree is something like this. The roots of this enlightenment tree are in all beings, all beings constitute the roots of this tree. The bodhisattvas are the flowers and fruits of this tree, so what nourishes it is water of the great *karuṇā citta,* the great compassionate mind. When all beings are thus benefited they are able to bring out flowers and fruit as bodhisattvas or buddhas. Therefore, enlightenment depends on all beings.

We can speak about enlightenment on account of the existence of all beings. If the experience is only *prajñā* it is not enlightenment. Because of ignorance it is enlightenment, and because of original enlightenment there is ignorance. Because of this ignorance there is the awakening of mind to enlightenment. Aśvaghoṣa, as we know, speaks of the different kinds of enlightenment before ultimate enlightenment is reached. So here is the same thing in the Kegon Sutra. Ignorance in the first part of the *Awakening* is a noetic expression, but in the Kegon Sutra ignorance becomes all beings, it represents the *karuṇā* aspect.

Even the attainment of enlightenment is not necessary at all. *Praṇidhāna* works just because we live on this plane of relativity, in ignorance. But there is actually no ignorance; ignorance is what we create, nothing else. We are all bodhisattvas, with the possibility of developing into fully enlightened buddhas conscious of enlightenment. Between a cat that becomes conscious of herself as a cat—if such could be—and a cat that has no consciousness of herself as a cat there is a great difference. We are all cats, in fact.

Praṇidhāna is connected in idea with *pariṇāmanā, ekō* [*huixiang*] being its literal translation into Chinese. *Pariṇāmanā* means turned around and moving this way, literally "change," "transformation," "changing into." *Pariṇāmanā,* or *ekō,* is very much used in Buddhism, the idea being especially characteristic of Mahāyāna thought. In the earlier form of Buddhism the *pariṇāmanā* idea does not occur as far as I know, but it is very important later.

Pariṇāmanā is the same as Christian vicarious atonement. Buddhists supply the necessary principle to make the idea of vicarious atonement possible: somebody substituted for somebody else. The idea of substituting is present, though there is no actual substitution; what is underneath is the possibility of substituting one thing for another. If one thing can be turned into another, this implies something common to the two. One may not be able exactly to replace the other, but there is something common to them. *Pariṇāmanā* is not exactly this potential substitution; it is turning over one's merit, especially, which comes out of one's deeds. This good karma is dedicated, or turned about, to the general stock of merit, so enlightenment will become easier, so that everybody can draw benefit of it for himself or herself. It is a kind of savings bank system. We may not do it consciously, yet when we do something good the whole universe seems glad to see it. There is correspondence between self and general environment, or we could not have this instinctive feeling aroused in every one of us. Moral teachers call it conscience, yet find it hard to explain where it comes from.

But it is explained in *ekō,* where karma turns toward the general source of merit to make enlightenment easier. We put our karma into the general stock, and the general stock by itself turns about and gives out from its own reservoir to all beings. We dedicate our merit to the general stock, and the general stock by our own movement spreads over all beings, mechanically moving from one to another.

This *pariṇāmanā* idea is especially emphasized in the Shin sect, though in a somewhat different way. Shin devotees talk of the Pure Land and our being born in it after death or while living. They do not wish to go to the Pure Land to stay, but [wish] to come back into this world. They go for themselves, for conditions are more favorable for obtaining enlightenment there than in this world. Conditions are unfavorable here; sometimes they find it impossible to realize enlightenment here. But one can arrange to be born in the Pure Land if one believes in Amida. This belief consists in pronouncing his name, calling on him for help, though "help" is not a very good term for it. Amida does everything, self does nothing, so help does not really exist. Amida is helping himself in the logical extreme, by saving all beings. Also, the Christian God by sacrificing his only son saves man and helps himself.

To help self to save self is altogether unnecessary from the relative viewpoint; it is like putting one roof over another roof, as Japanese say. But this is what we all do; there is nothing new under the sun, including the sun itself. So Amida helps himself by having all beings born in the Pure Land. The Pure Land is not a good abode where good beings enjoy blessings to eternity—this would be the height of ennui, so tiresome we could not stand this state of things. The Pure Land is a kind of station where humans go, and as soon as they go there they attain enlightenment. To be born in the Pure Land means to attain enlightenment. This birth and attaining take place together, at the same time; they are not two different events succeeding one after the other: birth *and* enlightenment.

Thereafter those souls, or ourselves, come back right away to this world. But it is really senseless to say "come back," as if the Pure Land were not the same as this world. There is actually no going from one place to the other. At the same time and place, now and here, birth and enlightenment take place. "Come back to this world" is just a figure of speech. However, this coming back to this world is a form of *pariṇāmanā*, or transference. This is the Shin way of explaining the double form of *pariṇāmanā*, its two forms of movement. It is significant that Shin emphasizes the *praṇidhāna* idea so much; it is really based on and made up of this idea. And *praṇidhāna* has so much to do with *pariṇāmanā*.

Amida makes *praṇidhāna* to save all beings, and every bodhisattva has his *praṇidhāna*—in each case coming out of his own being. Therefore, it is sincerity itself, sincerity having a much deeper meaning in China and Japan than in the West. As this *praṇidhāna* comes out of the very being, this ultimate reality itself makes the bodhisattva's *praṇidhāna*. This *praṇidhāna*, therefore, goes over all beings, and all beings are recipient to *praṇidhāna* as they respond in their own way.

As Buddhist cosmology is ontological, Buddha stands opposite all beings, and this dichotomy makes up the main framework of Buddhism. All beings include all things that are in existence, all nature as a whole, nature including humans. Ordinarily we say nature and humans, for nature in Western history of thought stands in such contrast to humans. Nature is considered so hostile to humanity. When humans want to do good, nature interferes and does what they do not desire: cyclones, floods, earthquakes, and so on may come. But the Western way of thinking of humans as the center of the cosmos is highly egocentric. The *homo sapiens*-centric idea naturally comes with the personal God idea.

As "all beings" in Buddhism includes everything, *praṇidhāna* affects everything. *Praṇidhāna* works on the dog; the dog is affected by Samantabhadra's *praṇidhāna*, for example. The dog has his own wants satisfied in his own way, not in the human way, and he responds to *praṇidhāna* in the dog's way. Human beings are of various sorts socially, physically, mentally—we are so diverse. No two are identical, all are different. Each has his own way of thinking, desiring, and so on. Many general things apply and many particular.

In an army each individual does not count; all are so many parts of force, or power, or mathematical units. There is regimentation, organization; individuals are just numbers, they do not count as human beings. So states do not care about sacrificing humans if this is needed to overcome the opponent. But in *praṇidhāna* this is not so. Each individual has his own personality, and according to this personality *praṇidhāna* works. This is the Buddhist way of explaining the *praṇidhāna* idea.

I have this way of thinking in connection with the Kegon idea of reality; how mathematicians would agree is another thing: 0, 1, 2, 3, 4,. . . . Ordinarily zero does not mean anything, and 1 is always 1. But I understand that zero is needed, otherwise we can do no counting—God created this world out of nothing, to infinity. We cannot just go from 1 to 2. 1 + 1 = 2, this ought to be so mathematically, but it can never be two unless one 1 moves to the other 1 and the other 1 moves to the first 1: $1 \leftrightarrows 1 = 2$. 1(a) affects 1(b), and 1(b) affects 1(a). There is an interfusion, an interpenetration, no-obstruction, as the Kegon Sutra says. This addition is impossible without this inner relationship within each number.

Zero contains all numbers in it, all numbers come out of zero. But God did not say a word just once; he is always saying it, so 1 always comes out of zero and 2 comes from 1 and so on—or this world does not come into existence. When we go on like this zero = infinity, infinity = zero.

This is at the base of Buddhist thought, also of *praṇidhāna* and *pariṇāmanā.* And this is, I think, a most important idea. Metaphysically expressing this, you will say the unlimited, absolute nothing, or limitlessness itself is because of 0, 1, 2, 3, 4, . . .

God wished to see himself in himself, so God created the world. And God succeeded in seeing himself reflected in the creation. The creation reflects God in the same way God reflects creation: there is mutual reflection. In Buddhism they have the idea of mirrors. Two mirrors, brightly shining, stand opposite each other; there are no shadows, no reflections between the two; both are brightly polished. When "all things" are brought between the mirrors, the mirrors reflect the multiplicity of things. But there is no image on either when the two mirrors are just standing opposite each other.

When the mirrors are rid of ignorance, or defilement, and thoroughly penetrate into the very source of all things, they identify themselves with original enlightenment. The whole universe, infinitely divided, still is reflected in infinite mind as if there were no diversification. When original mind in its absolute purity reflects the world of multiplicities, the world of multiplicities loses its multiplicity and becomes pure oneness, as if there were no diversity. And this condition is reflected in the mirror of original enlightenment—but this is not exactly so. We want to have the multiplicity of things level off, nothing to be left. In this condition we think we embrace ultimate reality, original enlightenment, something out of this world, erasing all traces of diversity and becoming one with the absolute, with God.

But this is not the way of it. It is not so important whether Buddhism transcends this or that, but this is not the way one will come to realization. I would like to have all these things abolished. From the point of enlightenment experience is the way we have to think. And this world of multiplicities, just as it is—dog is dog, cat is cat, all individuals are retained just as they are—this aspect of reality just as all things are is oneness. Manyness remains as manyness, not a particle of this manyness changes, yet this manyness, just as it is, is oneness. This is the most important thought needed to explain reality. The idea of duality is so contaminating that it is very difficult for us to comprehend that one is many, many is one. We are apt to say that many vanishes, then one comes. But manyness, or many, is left there: manyness is one, one is manyness. This, I must emphasize, is important.

Kegon philosophy does not ignore manyness at all; it starts from manyness, from 1, 2, 3, . . ., all these numbers are there. One pervading something runs through them. But when I say one thing pervades I have already gone out of reality. Yet as long as we have to use language we cannot avoid this. So Japanese wisely say that we must insert another wedge to get one wedge out.[43] This process infinitely repeated is the perpetual curse humanity has to endure; but it is really no curse.

The Kegon Sutra starts from manyness and goes on to no-obstruction, no-interference. As Kegon starts from manyness, it goes on to say each number contains others and the others contain 1: zero = infinity, infinity = zero. Zero is taken as corresponding to emptiness, while infinity corresponds to suchness. Suchness is the manyness side of things. Emptiness is the zero side of reality. Therefore, zero = suchness, suchness = zero. Suchness, affirming things as they are, is forgotten in constant movement. No transformation, no change, no becoming is inertia or Nirvāṇa. But Nirvāṇa is really becoming, not being. So suchness always implies becoming. Therefore, becoming = being, being = becoming, another important idea in the Kegon and other Mahāyāna sutras.

This is the outcome of *prajñā*-intuition, and as I have repeatedly said, *prajñā*-intuition is not the intuition of individual things or of individual things added to make a whole. *Prajñā*-intuition takes the whole as it is, and also each individual thing that makes up the whole. So the whole and its units are not separate, and vice versa. All things are composed in the wholeness of things in the same way that zero = infinity and each number is in every other number, moving back and forth, which we call addition or interpenetration. This *prajñā*-intuition, therefore, does not need many words or movements to express itself. Just one word or one gesture of the body, or the body itself, is enough.

In Zen we know there is something of the practical. When a single object is completely identified with a subject, object and subject become one, there issues from this identification a certain experience when a certain thing takes place. Subject and object are completely one; it is not just ordinary unification or identification—from this state enlightenment comes and all things are taken in in their totality, not individually as chair, table, etc. But when this totality is grasped, these things come along not as individuals but totalistically. This chair is chair because of table, you, me, everything. It cannot start all by itself. When subject and object are one there is no individual anywhere anymore, but all knowledge takes place, all the universe comes along with this chair. Psychologically speaking it may be a narrowing down.

So reality has two aspects: emptiness, suchness. Emptiness is zero, and *prajñā*, suchness, is infinity, *karuṇā*:

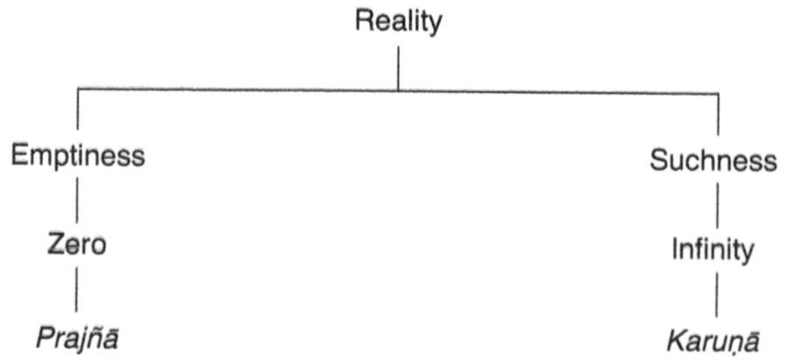

Of course I do not know whether the mathematicians will come around to my view or not; that is another thing. But I am convinced, I *know* this is.

Seeing the flower, seeing the morning glory, this is also *praṇidhāna*. *Praṇidhāna* comes out of suchness. If suchness were static, no *praṇidhāna* would be possible. But becoming is being, being is becoming—and *praṇidhāna* comes out. In the Kegon Sutra *prajñā* is the mother of all buddhas. Therefore, we can say so of all beings. *Prajñā* corresponds to emptiness and zero, so zero is the mother of all numbers and God created the world out of nothing.

This nothing, emptiness, *śūnyatā*, zero is not to be objectively, scientifically comprehended. All things belong in the realm of absolute subject. When we talk of subject this subject also brings in object. But we cannot talk of absolute object, for we are the subject itself, and all things come in by the senses of the subject. In *prajñā*-intuition, the absolute subject is realized; and we realize that this subject is not just the subject we place opposite the object—it is also the object itself. Yet in this absolute subject there is no subject, no object: this is emptiness. This is also shown in the two mirrors standing against each other above, there being no reflection, nothing between the two. Yet in this idea of having nothingness between, this nothingness is also in the way.

I have talked of *pariṇāmanā* as if it were something coming out of the dead, as leaving a track, as carrying over into the general stock; but this is a very bad way to explain it. *Praṇidhāna* and *pariṇāmanā* are in one in this becoming, and no track is left. We who are so used to reason in a dualistic way, we are apt to think of something always leaving something behind; this comes from our incurring an addiction to the dichotomous way of reasoning. But the beginningless ignorance of Aśvaghoṣa is better if rightly comprehended. The trouble comes from not rightly comprehending it.

Because of beginningless ignorance we can talk of original enlightenment, and because of original enlightenment we can talk of beginningless ignorance. In this mutual working one upon the other of original enlightenment and beginningless ignorance no track is left. If any track is left, any footstep, any mark, any defilement, then original enlightenment can never become beginningless ignorance, and beginningless ignorance can never be original enlightenment. But neither stage leaves a mark. *Pariṇāmanā* in fact is nonexistence, is nonsense. But out of this nonsense of no track left, or this circle without circumference, this universe has come out. There is no shadow between the two mirrors: one is original enlightenment, the other beginningless ignorance. One who makes *praṇidhāna*, one affected by *praṇidhāna*—between these two there is no track of one having been affected by the other, no track of one affecting the other.

In the same way, birth in the Pure Land and coming back into this world of defilement has no track, there is no way to trace it. No such things exist between the two events. Being born in the Pure Land is coming back here, coming back here is remaining in the Pure Land. We carry the Pure Land along with this world of Dharma; the Pure Land is a reflection of this world. Each affects the other, or neither affects the other.

This is not the result of thinking, it is just so. In the suchness idea there is this *shako* [*zhege*], "just so-ness," "thisness," "suchness." This does not mean taking things as they are this moment but taking things as they move on forever. Constant becoming is not static. Constant becoming does not just stop at one place and make all movement impossible. It moves eternally, the zero that contains all things. And when one finger is raised, all is seen dancing on the end of this finger.

According to the Kegon Sutra one pore contains three thousand chiliocosms [of buddha lands], this being equal to infinity mathematically stated. So becoming is being, endless, constant becoming. In Christian terms we would say the world is constantly created. That is, God does not create the world and stop his working there, but God is creating the world constantly; it never stops becoming.

Yet becoming itself is being; this is suchness. To come to the realization of this experience we must realize this absolute subject, *sarvasattva-citta* in Aśvaghoṣa—*citta* being Mind with a capital M here, the Mind of all beings. Or it may be better to say all-beings-Mind. Otherwise, you may understand the mind existing individually in each being. But being as a whole is this Mind.

If nature abhors a vacuum, Zen abhors words and concepts. Our mind works constantly along conceptual lines, and we think concepts are real things. They are in a way, but not real as concrete things are. Zen would have us move from mind to Mind, to *sarvasattva-citta.*

CHARACTER GLOSSARY

baishu (*hakuju*) 柏樹
Baizhang Huaihai 百丈懷海
Bankei Yōtaku 盤珪永琢
Banzan Hōshaku (C. Panshan Baoji) 盤山寶積
Bao'en Yuan Xingchong 漳州報恩院行崇
benyuan (*hongan*) 本願
Biyan-lu 碧巌録
bu jue 不覚
Caoshan Benji 曹山本寂
Chan 禅
chanding 禪定
Changsha Jingcen (J. Chōsa Keishin) 長沙景岑
Chanlin Baoxun 禪林寶訓
Channa (*Zenna*) 禪那
chantang (zendō) 禪堂
chongchong wujin (*jūjū-mujin*) 重重無盡
Chōsa Keishin (J. Changsha Jingcen) 長沙景岑
Chou I (*Zhouyi*) 周易
Ciming Chuyuan 慈明楚圓
Dabeiyuan (J. Daihi-in) 大悲院
Dahui Pujue Chanshi yulu 大慧普覚禅師語録
Dahui Zonggao 大慧宗杲
Daihi-in (C. Dabeiyuan) 大悲院
Daitō Kokushi 大燈國師

daiyū (*dayong*) 大用
daiyū genzen (C. *dayong xianqian*) 大用現前
Damei Fachang 大梅法常
Danyuan (Danyuan Yingzhen) 耽源應真
Dao (*Tao*) 道
Daosheng (Dōshō) 道生
Dasheng qixing-lun 大乘起信論
dayong (J. *daiyū*) 大用
dayong xianqian (J. *daiyū genzen*) 大用現前
Dentō roku (C. *Chuandeng lu*) 傳燈録
dianxin (J. *tenshin*) 點心
ding 定
dengchi 等持
do (C. *du*) 度
Dōshō (C. Daosheng) 道生
du (J. *do*) 度
Duofu heshang of Hangzhou 杭州多福和尚
Ejaku (J. Kyōzan Ejaku; C. Yangshan Huiji) 仰山慧寂
ekō (C. *huixiang*) 迴向
Enō (C. Huineng) 慧能
Famen 法門
Fayan School (Fayan-zong; J. Hōgen-shū) 法眼宗
Fayan Wenyi 法眼文益
Fazang 法藏
Fenglin (J. Hōrin) 鳳林
Fenyang Shanzhao 汾陽善昭
Foguang, Chan master (Foguang chanshi) 佛光禪師
Foxin school 仏心宗
Foxing lun 佛性論
foyuxin 仏語心
Fu Fazang Yinyuan zhuan 付法藏因緣傳
Fuke (J. Puhua) 普化
Fushan Fayuan 浮山法遠
Fuyō (*Fuyō kyō*; C. *Puyao jing*) 普曜
Gaoan Dayu 高安大愚
gong'an (J. *kōan*) 公案

Guannan Daochang 關南道常
Guangxiao Huijue 光孝慧覺
Guanxi Zhixian 灌谿志閑
Gutei (Juzhi) 俱胝
Chongke guzunsu yulu 重刻古尊宿語録
gyō 行
Hakuin Ekaku 白隠慧鶴
hakuju (*baishu*) 柏樹
Hannya (*Panruo*) 槃若
Heshan Wuyin 禾山無殷
Hiranuma Kiichirō 平沼騏一郎
Hōgen School (J. Hōgen-shū, C. Fayan-zong) 法眼宗
hongan (*benyuan*) 本願
Hongren 弘忍
Hōrin (C. Fenglin) 鳳林
Huayan Sutra (Huayan jing; J. Kegon gyō) 華嚴經
Huiji (Yangshan Huiji; J. Kyōzan Ejaku) 仰山慧寂
Huineng (Enō) 慧能
huixiang (*ekō*) 迴向
i (C. *yi*) 異
I Ching (*Yijing*) 易経
Imakita Kōsen 今北洪川
innen (C. *yinyuan*) 因縁
Isan (Isan Reiyū; C. Weishan/Guishan Lingyou) 偽山靈祐
ishiki 意識
isshin (C. *yixin*) 一心
jijin (J. *sokkon*) 即今
jimingzi (J. *keimyōji*) 計名字
jing (J. *kyō*) 境
Jingde Chuandeng-lu 景德傳燈録
jingjin 精進
jinglü 静慮
Jitsu sai (J. *jissai*; C. *shiji*) 實際
jiujing jue 究竟覚
jiyū (C. *ziyou*) 自由
jōgu bodai, geke shujō (C. *shangqiu puti, xiahua zhongsheng*) 上求佛道下化衆生

jōjō sōsō (C. *raorao congcong*) 擾擾匆匆
jū (C. *zhu*) 住
jūjū-mujin (C. *chongchong wujin*) 重重無盡
Juzhi (Gutei) 俱胝
Kegon Sutra (Kegon gyō; C. Huayan jing) 華厳経
keimyōji (C. *jimingzi*) 計名字
Kenshū Shobi (C. Qianzhou Chuwei) 虔州處微
kōan (C. *gong'an*) 公案
kokū (C. *xukong*) 虚空
kyō (C. *jing*) 境
Kyōgen Chikan; (C. Xiangyan Zhixian) 香嚴智閑
Kyōzan (Kyōzan Ejaku; C. Yangshan Huiji) 仰山慧寂
lao er wugong (J. *rōshite kō nashi*) 勞而無功
lukou 路口
Linji (J. Rinzai) 臨濟
Linji Yixuan (J. Rinzai Gigen) 臨濟義玄
Liuzu Dashi fabaotang-jing 六祖大師法寶壇經
Longjishan Shaoxiu 竜済山紹修
Luohan *heshang* (J. Rakan Oshō) 羅漢和尚
Luohan *heshang* of Zhangzhou 漳州羅漢和尚
Maming (J. Memyō) 馬鳴
Mazu Daoyi 馬祖道一
Memyō (C. Maming) 馬鳴
mie (J. *metsu*) 滅
metsu (C. *mie*) 滅
Minghua (J. Myōke) 明化
mō (C. *wang*) 妄
mondō 問答
Monju (C. Wenshu) 文殊
Moshan-ni Liaoran 末山尼了然
Mugai Nyodai 無外如大
Mujaku *zen-ni* 無著禪尼
munen (C. *wunian*) 無念
mushin (C. *wuxin*) 無心
Myō-e Shōnin 明恵上人
Myōke (C. Minghua) 明化

Nanquan Puyuan 南泉普願
nanso 軟蘇・軟酥
nen (C. *nian*) 念
nian (J. *nen*) 念
Niaoke 鳥窠
niu (J. *gyū*) 牛
okage de genki desu お陰で元気です
oya (C. *qin*) 親
Panruo (J. Hannya) 槃若
Panshan Baoji (K. Banzan Hōshaku) 盤山寶積
Puhua (J. Fuke) 普化
Puyao jing (*Fuyō kyō*) 普曜經
Qianzhou Chuwei (J. Kenshū Shobi) 虔州處微
qin (J. *oya*) 親
Qingrui 清鋭
Qingshui 清稅
Rakan Oshō (C. Luohan *heshang*) 羅漢和尚
raorao congcong (J. *jōjō sōsō*) 擾擾匆匆
randeng 然灯
Randeng Rulai 然灯如来
Rinzai (C. Linji) 臨濟
Rinzai Gigen (C. Linji Yixuan) 臨濟義玄
Rokuso dangyō 六祖壇經
rōshite kō nashi (C. *lao er wugong*) 勞而無功
saisei itchi 祭政一致
sanmei 三昧
sanmodi 三摩地
satori 悟
Sekitō Kisen (C. Shitou Xiqian) 石頭希遷
shako (C. *zhege*) 這个
shangqiu puti, xiahua zhongsheng (J. *jōgu bodai, geke shujō*) 上求佛道下化衆生
sheng (*shō*) 生
shiji (*J. jitsu sai; jissai*) 實際
shin (C. *xin*) 心
shin (C. *zhen*) 真
Shin (Jōdo-shinshū) 淨土眞宗

Shintai (C. Zhendi) 眞諦
Shishuang Xingkong 石霜性空
Shitou Xiqian (J. Sekitō Kisen) 石頭希遷
shō (C. *sheng*) 生
sho (C. *xing*) 性
Shobi (J. Kenshū Shobi; C. Qianzhou Chuwei) 虔州處微
Shōmatsu (Shōma) 庄松
Shoushan Shengnian 首山省念
shūshu (C. *zhiqu*) 執取
Shūhū Myōchō 宗峰妙超
Sijia Yulu 四家語録
sō (*so-o*) 然う, 想
sokkon (C. *jijin*) 即今
suifen jue 随分覚
tada shako (C. *zhi zhege*) 只這個
Tao (C. *Dao*) 道
tenshin (C. *dianxin*) 點心
Tianlong (Tianlong heshang) 天龍（天龍和尚）
Tiansheng Guangdeng-lu 天聖廣燈録
Tianyi Yihuai 天衣義懐
Tōa shin chitsujo 東亜新秩序
Touzi (Touzi Datong) 投子大同
Unmon Bun'en (C. Yunmen Wenyan) 雲門文偃
ushi (*gyū*, C. *niu*) 牛
wang (J. *mō*) 妄
Weishan Lingyou (J. Isan Reiyū) 偽山靈祐
Wenshu (J. Monju) 文殊
wumen 無門
Wumenguan 無門關
wunian (J. *munen*) 無念
Wu-tai Shan 五臺山
Wuxue Zuyuan 無學祖元
wuxin (J. *mushin*) 無心
Xiangyan Zhixian (Kyōgen Chikan) 香嚴智閑
xiangsi jue 相似覚
Xiantong 咸通

xin (J. *shin*) 心
xing (*shō*) 性
Xingyan Xuanjiao 行言玄覺
Xuansha Shibei 玄沙師備
Xuefeng Yicun 雪峯義存
xukong (J. *kokū*) 虛空
Yakusan (Yakusan Igen; C. Yaoshan Weiyan) 藥山惟儼
Yang 陽
Yangshan Huiji (J. Kyōzan Ejaku) 仰山慧寂
Yaoshan Weiyan (J. Yakusan Igen) 藥山惟儼
Yantou Quanhuo 巖頭全豁
Yexian Guisheng 葉縣歸省
yi (J. *i*) 異
Yijing (*I Ching*) 易経
Yijiaojing-lun 遺教經論
Yin 陰
yinyuan (J. *innen*) 因緣
yixin (J. *isshin*) 一心
yong (J. *yū*) 用
you (J. *yū*) 幽
yū (C. *you*) 幽
yū (C. *yong*) 用
Yuanwu Keqin 圜悟克勤
Yunju Qingyang 雲居清錫
Yunmen guang lu 雲門廣録
Yunmen Wenyan (J. Ummon Bun'en) 雲門文偃
zendō (*chantang*) 禪堂
Zenna (Channa) 禪那
Zhangqing Huileng 長慶慧稜
Zhangzhou 漳州
zhao *shangzuo* 招上座
Zhaozhou Congshen 趙州從諗
Zhaozhou lu 趙州録
zhege (C. *shako*) 這个
zhen (*shin*) 真
Zhendi (J. Shintai) 眞諦

Zhengfayanzang 正法眼藏
zhenzi 枕子
zhi zhege (J. *tada shako*) 只這個
Zhikai of Yangzhou (Yangzhou Zhikai) 揚州智愷
zhiqu (*shūshu*) 執取
Zhouyi (*Chou I*) 周易
zhu (J. *jū*) 住
zixinxian 自心現
ziyou (J. *jiyū*) 自由
zong 宗
Zongmen wuku 宗門武庫
Zongmen tongyao 宗門統要
Zutang ji 祖堂集

ACKNOWLEDGMENTS

In editing *Spreading Indra's Net* and writing the introduction, I have received ongoing support, for which I am grateful, from the Matsugaoka Bunko, D. T. Suzuki's archive in Kita-Kamakura, Japan. In particular, the head business administrator, Ms. Ban Katsuyo, and the archive director, Ishii Shūdō, have allowed me access to manuscripts and permissions necessary to produce this volume. In editing *Spreading Indra's Net*, I benefited greatly from the annotations to the Matsugaoka Bunko edition of the Columbia University Seminar Lectures that was edited by Shigematsu Sōiku and Tokiwa Gishin. Their deep knowledge of the Zen tradition and painstaking annotation of the Matsugaoka edition made it possible for me to track down most of the exact line references to the Zen literature cited by Suzuki.

My work on this book also has benefited from the generous assistance of many librarians, archivists, and scholars at Duke University Libraries, the Columbia University Rare Book and Manuscript Library, the Rockefeller Archive Center, the Trustees Archive and Research Center in Massachusetts, the Yale Sterling Memorial Library Manuscripts and Archives, the University of Memphis Institute of Egyptian Art and Archaeology, the Boston Psychoanalytic Society and Institute, and the Archives of American Art. I am extremely grateful to Norman Waddell for notifying me about the location of Elizabeth Thomas's notebooks and Bekku Masanobu, Mihoko Okamura's husband, for allowing me to use those documents for this project.

While working on *Spreading Indra's Net* I have received generous financial support from my home institution, Duke University, as well as the National Humanities Center and Fulbright IIE Japan fellowships. This has allowed me to do the research travel, source collection, and writing required.

I am deeply thankful to Dr. Jeffrey Nicolaisen, then a PhD student at Duke, for his invaluable editorial assistance converting Suzuki's manuscript into a Microsoft Word document and rendering the romanizations into standardized styles. I also have received valuable input from the two readers of the manuscript, Dr. Steven Heine and a second reader, who remains anonymous. They, along with members of the editorial board at Columbia University Press and my editor, Wendy Lochner, provided helpful advice for improving the quality and readability of this book, particularly the introduction. My research also has benefited from the insights of numerous people familiar with D. T. Suzuki's life and legacy. These include my two late friends, Mihoko Okamura and Jacob Needleman, as well as James Dobbins, Iwamoto Akemi, Kay Larson, and Roger Lipsey.

My wife, Elaine, used her keen editorial eye to help me write a better introduction. Her insistence that I bring into view all those unacknowledged actors whose support, friendship, and work made D. T. Suzuki's stay in New York in the 1950s a pivotal event in global religious history was an essential intervention. With that point in mind, I thank her, Zina, and Chris for the advice, inspiration, support, and good cheer that buoyed me as I worked for many years editing this book.

NOTES

INTRODUCTION

1. Columbia University Central Archive, "Goodrich L. Carrington," Box 394, Folder 18. Romanization as in the original, Wade-Giles, orthography.
2. A. W. Sadler, "In Remembrance of D. T. Suzuki," *Eastern Buddhist*, New Series, 2, no. 1 (1967), 198. A. W. Sadler was a graduate student at Union Theological Seminary enrolled in the first semester of Suzuki's course; his recollections include quotes that differ slightly from the manuscript version of the lectures, cited in note 3.
3. Richard M. Jaffe, "D. T. Suzuki's Columbia University Seminar Lectures Manuscripts: February 5 and February 7, 1952." *Matsugaoka Bunko kenkyū nenpō* 36 (2022): 8. Huayan (J. Kegon) Buddhists take as their principal sutra the *Avataṃsaka sūtra*, known in its Chinese translation as the *Huayan jing* or, in Japanese, the *Kegon gyō*. That title often is rendered in English as the "Flower Garland Sutra." In his lectures, Suzuki inconsistently used both the Japanese and Chinese pronunciations of the sutra and the school of Buddhism that revolved around its interpretation. Here I have tried to use the English, "Flower Garland," as much as possible.
4. Sadler, "In Remembrance of D. T. Suzuki," 198–200. Horace L. Friess in the Department of Philosophy at Columbia described the course in a letter to Chadbourne Gilpatric, May 23, 1952. Rockefeller Archive Center (hereafter, RAC), Subseries 200r, Box 310, Folder 2875.

5. Arthur Danto, "Upper West Side Buddhism," in *Buddha Mind in Contemporary Art*, ed. Jacquelynn Baas and Mary Jane Jacob (Berkeley and Los Angeles: University of California Press, 2004), 54. Danto received his PhD in philosophy in 1952 and began teaching at Columbia that year. He does not state when his observations about Suzuki's seminar were made.
6. Margaret Rioch, "Memories of Dr. Daisetz Suzuki," *Eastern Buddhist*, New Series, 2, no. 1 (1967): 191.
7. John Cage, *Silence: Lectures and Writings*, 50th anniversary ed. (Middletown, CT: Wesleyan University Press, 2011), 262 (Kindle).
8. Lundsford P. Yandell, "Death: The Moon Sailing," *Eastern Buddhist*, New Series, 2, no. 1 (1967): 201–202.
9. Cage, *Silence*, 32 (Kindle ed.). In *Zen and Japanese Culture*, Suzuki translates *yū* as "cloudy impenetrability." See Suzuki, *Zen and Japanese Culture* (New York: Pantheon, 1959), 220n2.
10. "People Are Talking About," *Vogue*, January 15, 1952, 98.
11. Parenthetical page references in the introduction refer to the text of the lectures in this book.
12. Mihoko Okamura-Bekku, "Telephone Conversation Concerning D. T. Suzuki," interview by author, August 4, 2020. Information about Thomas's move to Mississippi in "Egyptologist, Book Donor to MSU Dies," *Commercial Appeal* (Memphis, TN), November 30, 1986. I thank Norman Waddell for telling me about the presence of the notebooks in the Okamura residence and Mihoko's husband, Bekku Masanobu, for allowing me to use those documents for this book.
13. Catharine Roehrig, "Elizabeth Thomas," Women in Old World Archaeology, https://www.brown.edu/Research/Breaking_Ground/results.php?d=1&first=Elizabeth&last=Thomas. In particular, see the PDF biography of Thomas by Barbara Leosko that is attached to the website.
14. Elizabeth Thomas, *The Royal Necropoleis of Thebes* (self-pub., Princeton, [NJ], 1966).
15. "Thomas, Elizabeth | Theban Mapping Project," http://thebanmappingproject.com/glossary/thomas-elizabeth. Barbara S. Lesko, "Elizabeth Thomas (1907–1986)," Women in Old World Archaeology, https://web.archive.org/web/20060512105845/http://www.brown

.edu/Research/Breaking_Ground/results.php?d=1&first=Elizabeth &last=Thomas.

16. Elizabeth Thomas to D. T. Suzuki, May 30, 1952, Elizabeth Thomas papers, University of Memphis Institute of Egyptian Art and Archaeology.
17. Daisetz Teitaro Suzuki, *Zen and Japanese Culture* [rev. and enl. 2nd ed.] (New York: Pantheon, 1959); Suzuki, *Zen Buddhism and Its Influence on Japanese Culture*. See the letter, Suzuki to Thomas, December 25, 1956, SDZ 38: 458, for comments on her editing of the manuscript for *Zen and Japanese Culture*.
18. Elizabeth Thomas to D. T. Suzuki, April 16, 1961, Elizabeth Mary Thomas Papers, University of Memphis Institute of Egyptian Art and Archaeology.
19. Thomas letters to Mihoko Okamura, November 10, 1957, and March 5, 1958, Mihoko Okamura Papers.
20. The manuscript, for example, contains footnotes for D. T. Suzuki, *Mysticism: Christian and Buddhist* (London: Allen and Unwin), 1957.
21. Thomas notebook VII, 955 verso–964 verso.
22. For details of Suzuki's life, see James Dobbins, "D. T. Suzuki," *Oxford Biographies Online*, 2022; and "D. T. Suzuki: A Brief Account of His Life," *Eastern Buddhist*, Third Series 2, 2 (2022): 1–83; SWS 1: xix–xxxvi; SWS 2: x–xxi.
23. For recent speculation about Beatrice's profound influence on Suzuki, see James C. Dobbins, "D. T. Suzuki Scrutinized: Reflections and Hypotheses," *Eastern Buddhist* 4, no. 1 (2024): 89–113.
24. SWS 1: xxiv.
25. Richard M. Jaffe, "D. T. Suzuki and the Two Cranes: American Philanthropy and Suzuki's Global Agenda," in *Beyond Zen: D. T. Suzuki and the Modern Transformation of Buddhism*, ed. John Breen, Fumihiko Sueki, and Shōji Yamada (Honolulu: University of Hawai'i Press, 2022), 137.
26. D. T. Suzuki, "The Zen Sect of Buddhism," *Journal of the Pali Text Society*, 1907, 84. On the invention of linkages between Zen and *bushidō*, see Oleg Benesch, *Inventing the Way of the Samurai: Nationalism, Internationalism, and Bushidō in Modern Japan* (Oxford: Oxford University Press, 2014), 139.
27. Jaffe, "D. T. Suzuki and the Two Cranes," 138.

28. Robert Sharf, "The Zen of Japanese Nationalism," *History of Religions* 33, no. 1 (1993): 1–43.
29. Professor Moriya Tomoe presented samples of Suzuki's letters to Senzaki Nyogen concerning the Nanking Massacre during an online meeting of the Tobei Zen Benkyōkai, April 3, 2022, and discussed Suzuki's attempts to obtain news of the event from non-Japanese sources.
30. Kemmyō Taira Satō, "D. T. Suzuki and the Question of War," *Eastern Buddhist* 39, no. 1 (2008): 88. Suzuki wrote this in a letter to his friend,Yamamoto Ryōkichi, February 10, 1940, SDZ 37: 1–2.
31. See Brian Victoria, "Zen as a Cult of Death in the Wartime Writings of D. T. Suzuki 死の信仰としての禅 鈴木大拙、戦時下の著述," *The Asia-Pacific Journal: Japan Focus*, August 2, 2013, https://apjjf.org/2013/11/30/brian-victoria/3973/article. Victoria sees Suzuki's article as evidence of his support for the Japanese war effort but admits, "As in many other instances of his wartime writings . . . Suzuki maintains a studied ambiguity that makes it impossible to state what he was referring to." In addition, we do not know on what basis Suzuki submitted the article to the *Kaikō kiji*. Was it voluntary, or did he feel compelled to contribute an article, whatever his feelings about the war?
32. "Chisei busoku no Nihonjin," SDZ 33: 7. The essay was originally published in the journal *Teisai ronri* in September 1945.
33. See the letters from Charles Moore to Charles W. Morris, January 17, 1950, and from Chadbourne Gilpatric to Charles W. Morris, March 21, 1950, RAC, Subseries 200r, Box 430, Folder 3702.
34. Chadbourne Gilpatric Interview with D. T. Suzuki, March 8, 1950; Letter from Chadbourne Gilpatric to D. T. Suzuki, March 21, 1950, RAC, Subseries 200r, Box 430, Folder 3702.
35. Charles Fahs, "Interview, Ryūsaku Tsunoda," May 1, 1950, RAC, Box 430, Subseries 200r, Folder 3702.
36. Suzuki, "The Development of Buddhist Thought in China" (Columbia University, March 1, 6, and 8, 1951), unpublished manuscript A97, Matsugaoka Bunko.
37. Suzuki to Chadbourne Gilpatric, April 27, 1952, RAC, Subseries 200r, Box 310, Folder 2875.
38. On the dedication of *Zen Buddhism and Its Influence on Japanese Culture* to Charles Richard Crane, see Jaffe, "D. T. Suzuki and the Two Cranes," 133–155.

39. These events are detailed in a letter from Cathalene Parker Bernatschke to Ruth Shipley in the U.S. Passport Office, May 22, 1952. Boston Psychoanalytic Society and Institute, Karen Horney Papers, Box 11, Folder 5. Cathalene, who had remarried and taken the surname Bernatschke, wrote to Shipley to help Horney obtain a passport to travel to Japan with Suzuki; Cornelius; and Horney's daughter, Brigitte. The quotation of Suzuki's book is in Karen Horney, *Our Inner Conflicts: A Constructive Theory of Neurosis* (New York: Norton, 1945), 163.
40. Horace L. Friess to Chadbourne Gilpatric, March 23, 1953, RAC, Subseries 200r, Box 310, Folder 2875.
41. Thomas, notebook VII, 960.
42. Yandell, "Death: The Moon Sailing," 202.
43. Chadbourne Gilpatric Interview with D. T. Suzuki, March 8, 1950, RAC, Series 200r, Folder 3702.
44. Kay Larson, *Where the Heart Beats: John Cage, Zen Buddhism, and the Inner Life of Artists* (New York: Penguin, 2012), 242 (Kindle). Larson derives Cage's description from the documentary film *Cage/Cunningham: A Film*, dir. Elliot Caplan (West Long Branch, NJ: Kultur, 2006).
45. Cage, *Silence*, 32; 262 (Kindle).
46. Michael Goldberg, "Interview with Dr. Albert Stunkard," D. T. Suzuki Documentary Project Collection, 2003–2010, http://library.duke.edu/digitalcollections/rbmscl/suzukidt/inv/.
47. Friess to Gilpatric, May 23, 1952, RAC, Subseries 200r, Box 310, Folder 2875.
48. Fazang (643–712). The "Record of the Transmission of the Lamp" was composed in 1004 CE. The most widely circulated edition of the *Record of Rinzai* dates from 1120.
49. See "Introduction," in SWD 1: xl–xli.
50. Cage, *Silence*, 266 (Kindle).
51. Jikai Fujiyoshi, "Daisetz Suzuki and Shin'ichi Hisamatsu," *Eastern Buddhist*, New Series, 2, no. 1 (1967): 195.
52. H. J. (Harold John) Blackham, *Six Existentialist Thinkers* (London: Routledge & K. Paul, 1952) (Kindle).
53. On the prominent place of "freedom" in American intellectual life during the 1950s, see Louis Menand, *The Free World: Art and Thought in the Cold War* (New York: Farrar, Straus, and Giroux, 2021), particularly the preface (Kindle).

54. Suzuki elaborates on both Kyōgen and Rakan Oshō on pp. 79; 125 and 167.
55. SWS 1: 209. Orthography as in the original text, which was published in the *Middle Way* in 1964.
56. The title of the text, *Dasheng qixin lun,* supposedly translated into Chinese by Śikṣānanda, was translated into English by Suzuki as *Açvaghosha's Discourse on the Awakening of Faith in the Mahāyāna* in 1900. Multiple variant English translations have been published since, most of them based on the supposed Chinese translation that was attributed to Paramārtha. The *Gandavyūha* circulated separately before being incorporated into the *Avataṃsaka Sūtra.* (See note 3 above for information about the various translations of this title.) In the most widely used Chinese translation of the composite text of the *Avataṃsaka Sūtra*, the *Gandavyūha* became the "Ru fajie pin," that is, "Entering the Dharma Realm" chapter. The chapter describes the monk Sudhana's visit with fifty-three Buddhist teachers in his quest for awakening.
57. For a complete English translation of the *Huayan jing*, see Thomas F. Cleary, *The Flower Ornament Scripture* (Boston: Shambhala, 1993). Cleary translated Śikṣānanda's Chinese translation of the text, *Dafangguang fo huayan jing* (T. 279), which is the most complete version in Chinese.
58. A useful translation and thorough introduction to this text is John Jorgensen, et. al, *Treatise on Awakening Mahāyāna Faith*, Oxford Chinese Thought (Oxford: Oxford University Press, 2019), https://login.proxy.lib.duke.edu/login?url=https://academic.oup.com/book/32223, 7–8. See also Peter Gregory, "The Problem of Theodicy in the 'Awakening of Faith,'" *Religious Studies* 22, no. 1 (1986): 63–78.
59. See Gregory, "The Problem of Theodicy," 73.
60. D. T. Suzuki, *Acvaghosha's Discourse on the Awakening of Faith in the Mahâvâna* (Chicago: Open Court, 1900). Suzuki writes about Fazang's commentary on pp. 40–41.
61. For example, see Hu Shih, "Ch'an (Zen) Buddhism in China Its History and Method," *Philosophy East and West* 3, no. 1 (1953): 3–4.
62. D. T. Suzuki, "Zen: A Reply to Hu Shih," *Philosophy East and West* 3, no. 1 (1953): 26.

63. EZB 3: 1–185. Both the *Daśabhūmika* (*Shidi jing*; J. *Jūjikyō*) and the *Gaṇḍavyūha* (*Ryu fajie bin*; J. *Nyū hokkai bon*) circulated as influential, independent texts as well as chapters incorporated into the composite Flower Garland Sutra.
64. "Gendai ni okeru Kegon shisō no igi," SDZ 22: 148; *Essence of Buddhism*, SWS 4: 213–215. See also Ishii Kōsei, "Kegon Philosophy and Nationalism in Modern Japan," in *Reflecting Mirrors: Perspectives on Huayan Buddhism*, ed. Imre Hamar (Wiesbaden: Harrassowitz, 2007), 332–333, on Suzuki's efforts to use Kegon philosophy as the basis for the construction of a democratic postwar Japan.
65. Suzuki, "The Development of Buddhist Thought in China," enl 6. (Suzuki divided the page numbering into three sections based on the content of the lectures: "Sadd"; "enl"; and "Keg," based on the topic of the lecture.
66. Robert Michael Gimello, "Chih-Yen (智嚴, 602–668) and the Foundations of Hua-Yen (華厳) Buddhism" (PhD diss., Columbia University, 1976), 23.
67. Suzuki wrote about the relationship between the universal and the individual as described in Flower Garland Buddhism as early as 1934. See EZB 3: 66–67.
68. For an explanation of the relationship between *ālayavijñāna* and *tathāgatagarbha* in the *Awakening of Faith*, see Peter N. Gregory, *Tsung-Mi and the Sinification of Buddhism* (Princeton, N.J.: Princeton University Press, 1991), 180–181.
69. AFM 78.
70. Gregory, "Theodicy in the *Awakening of Faith*," 78. Romanization of Chinese as in the original. *Huatou* (J. *watō*) are crucial phrases in koan that are used as subjects of concentration in Zen practice.
71. EZB 3: 1–185.
72. Suzuki letter to Ruth Fuller Sasaki, January 14, 1954, SDZ 38: 7–8.
73. Rick Fields claims Crane insisted the lectures be open to the public but provides no source. Rick Fields, *How the Swans Came to the Lake: A Narrative History of Buddhism in America*, 40th anniversary ed. (Boston, MA: Shambhala, 2002), 196.
74. Matthew Hedstrom, *The Rise of Liberal Religion: Book Culture and American Spirituality in the Twentieth Century* (Oxford and New York: Oxford

University Press), 2013 (Kindle;n.p.), chapters 2, 3, 4. Sales figures for Merton's book are in "The Mountain," *Time*, April 11, 1949.

75. Leigh Eric Schmidt, *Restless Souls: The Making of American Spirituality* (Berkeley: University of California Press, 2012), 285 (Kindle).
76. Steve Antinoff, *Reports from the Zen Wars: The Impossible Rigor of a Questioning Life* (New York: Counterpoint, 2016), 43–44 (Kindle).
77. Albert Stunkard, "Suzuki Daisetz: An Appreciation," *Eastern Buddhist*, New Series, 36, no. 1/2 (1964): 192–228.
78. Goldberg, "Interview with Dr. Albert Stunkard.".
79. Goldberg, "Interview with Dr. Albert Stunkard."
80. Carolyn Brown, *Chance and Circumstance: Twenty Years with Cage and Cunningham* (New York: Knopf, 2007), 22.
81. Goldberg, "Interview with Dr. Albert Stunkard."
82. In an interview with Dr. Jack Rubins conducted in 1976, Harte recalls Horney attending several of the meetings. According to Harte, the group included Harold Kelman, Ōtani Kōshō, Kondō Akihisa, Mihoko Okamura, and Richard DeMartino, and they met approximately fifteen times. The earliest mention of the meetings in Suzuki's diaries is in January 1953; however, that is more than a year after Horney's death, so Harte's recollections of the seminars in the Rubins interview probably are inaccurate. See "B. Joan Harte Interview" by Jack L. Rubins, November 6, 1976, Karen Horney Papers, Yale University, Series Accession 200–M–091.
83. On the founding of Pantheon Books and Bollingen publications, see Menand, *The Free World*, 72 (Kindle).
84. William McGuire, *Bollingen: An Adventure in Collecting the Past* (Princeton, NJ: Princeton University Press), 1982.
85. Edith Schloss vividly describes the community of artists in downtown Manhattan in Edith Schloss and Mary Venturini, *The Loft Generation: From the De Koonings to Twombly: Portraits and Sketches, 1942-2011* (New York: Farrar, Straus and Giroux: 2021).
86. A handwritten postcard announcing the lectures is in the Phillip Pavia Papers, Rose Library, Emory University, Collection 981, Box 1, Folder 11.
87. Ibram Lassaw, Transcript of Oral History Interview with Ibram Lassaw, August 26, 1968, Archives of American Art, p. 86.

88. Larson, *Where the Heart Beats*; Ellen Pearlman, *Nothing and Everything: The Influence of Buddhism on the American Avant-Garde, 1942–1962* (Berkeley, CA: Evolver Editions: Distributed by North Atlantic Books, 2012).
89. Larson, *Where the Heart Beats*, 186; 259; 444.
90. Friess to Gilpatric, May 23, 1952, RAC, Subseries 200r, Box 310, Folder 2875.
91. Stanley Cavell, *Little Did I Know: Excerpts from Memory* (Stanford, CA: Stanford University Press, 2010), 264. Kaplan was one of Cavell's early, influential philosophy mentors. Abraham Kaplan, *The New World of Philosophy* (New York: Random House, 1961).
92. Ayako Sairenji, "From Ethnic Church to Multi-Cultural Congregation: The Transformation of a Japanese-American Buddhist Church," (M.A. thesis, Drew University, 2002), 71–73.
93. Daisetz T. Suzuki, *Friday Night Talks with D. T. Suzuki, On Shin Buddhism, Shinran, and Saichi*, ed. Edythe Vassall (New York: American Buddhist Study Center, 2022).
94. SWS 2:236–239.
95. Richard M. Jaffe, conversation with Mihoko Okamura, December 19, 2022.
96. "D. T. Suzuki's English Diaries," *Annual Report of Researches of Matsugaoka Bunko*, March 27, 1953.
97. Mihoko has written extensively about Suzuki in Japanese, and to a lesser extent in English. See, for example, Okamura Mihoko 岡村美穂子 and Ueda Shizuteru 上田閑照, *Omoide no kobako kara: Suzuki Daisetsu no koto* 思い出の小箱から:鈴木大拙のこと, Tōei Sensho 29 (Kyoto: Tōeisha, 1997). There is an extensive interview with Mihoko by Michael Goldberg in D. T. Suzuki Documentary Project Collection, 2003–2010, June 19, 2003. Some of the above information is based on several conversations I had with Mihoko Okamura via telephone and in person in Kyoto during 2021–2022.
98. A menu for Aki Dining Room is available in the Culinary Institute of America Menu Collection, http://ciadigitalcollections.culinary.edu/digital/collection/p16940coll1/id/13304/rec/1.
99. Jaffe, conversation with Mihoko Okamura, December 19, 2022.
100. Scott A. Mitchell, *The Making of American Buddhism* (New York: Oxford University Press, 2023), 134–135.

101. An excellent overview of the renewed interest in Japanese culture and the growth of US-Japan exchange in the post–World War II era is found in Michael R. Auslin, *Pacific Cosmopolitans: A Cultural History of U.S.-Japan Relations* (Cambridge, MA: Harvard University Press, 2011), 169–217. The instances cited above are mentioned by Auslin on pp. 182 and 189.
102. See, for example, Suzuki's 1954 speech, "The Spirit of Shinran," SWS 2: 237–240, and his 1962 "Open Letter to President Kennedy and Premier Krushchev," , SWS 3: 227–229.
103. Alexander Soper, "Review of Zen and Japanese Culture," *Artibus Asiae* 23, no. 2 (1960): 140.
104. Michael Goldberg, "Interview with Mihoko Okamura," February 13, 2005, D. T. Suzuki Documentary Project Collection, 2003–2010.
105. Dorothy Norman, *Encounters: A Memoir* (New York: Harcourt Brace Jovanovich, 1987), 205.
106. These statements are based on my conversations with Mihoko Okamura once or twice per year, in person in Kyoto and by telephone, from 2007 until her death in June 2023. During a telephone conversation on April 26, 2022, Okamura told me that before she met Suzuki, her parents' disharmonious marriage and her own self-doubts had left her feeling depressed. Suzuki's diaries for 1952–1956 detail the increasing frequency of her visits and all the ways she assisted him.
107. Jacob Needleman, *What Is God?* (New York: J. P. Tarcher/Penguin, 2009), 26–36 (Kindle).
108. Telephone interview with Jacob Needleman, June 9, 2021. Needleman (1934–2022), was my undergraduate major advisor in religious studies at San Francisco State University.
109. Elizabeth Thomas to D. T. Suzuki, May 30, 1952, Elizabeth Thomas papers, University of Memphis Institute of Egyptian Art and Archaeology.
110. "D. T. Suzuki's English Diaries," January 7, 1953.
111. Thomas, notebook V, 794–792, in reverse order. On the practice of *nanso*, see Hakuin, "Hakuin's Yasenkanna," trans. Norman Waddell, *The Eastern Buddhist* 34, no. 1 (2002): 113.
112. John Cage, "Questions," *Perspecta* 11 (1967): 71.
113. Larson, *Where the Heart Beats*, 77 (Kindle). The lecture, which is listed in the catalogue of the Harry Ransom Center at the University of Texas

at Austin as "Zen and Dada," is Nancy Wilson Ross, "The Symbols of Modern Art" (Cornish School, 1938), Nancy Wilson Ross Papers, 1913–1986, Harry Ransom Center.

114. Cage, *Silence*, xxx, cited in Larson, *Where the Heart Beats*, 77.
115. Calvin Tomkins, "Figure in an Imaginary Landscape," *New Yorker* (November 28, 1964): 86–88.
116. Calvin Tomkins, "Figure in an Imaginary Landscape," *New Yorker* (November 28, 1964): 88.
117. Richard Kostelanetz, *Conversing with Cage* (New York: Routledge, 1987), 42–43.
118. Cage, *Silence*, 262.
119. Marilyn Belford and Jerry Herman, eds., *Time and Space Concepts in Art* (New York: Pleiades Gallery, 1980), 6.
120. Ibram Lassaw, "Ibram Lassaw (1913–) Papers" (Microfilm, Washington, D.C., n.d.), Archives of American Art, Microfilm Reel N69/129. The section on Suzuki's seminars is found in the notebook dated March 5, 1954–May 6, 1955. That portion begins on p. 533 of the microfilm reel.
121. Lassaw, notebooks, May 12, 1954, Frame #536.
122. Lassaw, notebooks, March 26, 1954, Frame #538.
123. Lassaw, notebooks, March 26, 1954, Frame #538.
124. Lassaw, notebooks, April 9, 1954, Frame #541.
125. Irving Sandler, Tape Recorded Interview with Ibram Lassaw, August 26, 1968, Archives of American Art, Transcript, p. 60. Lassaw said almost the exact same thing to Nancy Heller in 1974. See Nancy Gale Heller, "The Sculpture of Ibram Lassaw" (PhD diss., New Brunswick, NJ, Rutgers University, 1982), 172.
126. Henry Bugbee, The *Inward Morning; A Philosophical Exploration in Journal Form* (State College, PA: Bald Eagle Press, 1958; Athens: University of Georgia Press, 1999), 89 (Kindle).
127. Bugbee, *Inward Morning*, 89.
128. Philip Kapleau, ed., *The Three Pillars of Zen: Teaching, Practice, and Enlightenment* (New York, Harper & Row, 1965), 219.
129. Danto, "Upper West Side Buddhism," 54.
130. Ethan Kleinberg, *Generation Existential: Heidegger's Philosophy in France, 1927–1961* (Ithaca, NY: Cornell University Press, 2005), 67.

I

1. This is a reference to the eight types of *vimokṣa* (*gedatsu* 解脱) that are associated with the attainment of the four states of dhyanic concentration. See the *Princeton Dictionary of Buddhism*, 972; 1080. [RMJ]
2. Thomas notes that she did not record the seven synonyms.
3. Kyōgen Chikan (C. Xiangyan Zhixian; d. 898). See Randolph S. Whitfield, trans., *Records of the Transmission of the Lamp* (Norderstedt, Germany: Books on Demand, 2016), 3: 88; *Jingde chuandeng lu* T2076_.51.0284a09–11. For details, see Suzuki's explanation in chapter III (p. 62). Rakan Oshō of Shōshū (C., Luohan Heshang of Zhangzhou; n.d.). See Whitfield, *Records*, 3: 122; *Jingde chuandeng lu* T2076_.51.0288c23. For details, see the story of Rakan Oshō in chapter 3.
4. Changsha Jingcen (d.u). See Thomas Cleary, trans., *The Blue Cliff Record* (Boulder, CO: Prajñā Press, 1978), 269; *Biyan lu* T2003.48.017 4b03–07.
5. Thomas did not record the title of the sutra, which was left blank in the "Columbia Seminars Manuscript." Shigematsu and Tokiwa in the Matsugaoka edition of the lectures suggest that Suzuki was referring to the *Puyaojing*, the Chinese translation of the *Lalitavistara* (Extensive Play), a third- or fourth-century CE account of the life of the Buddha. [RMJ]
6. The next paragraph on page 21 is filled with interlinear suggestions from Thomas and is garbled. I have deleted the problematic paragraph, as much of the same content is repeated in the following paragraph. The text of the manuscript continues on pp. 21a–22. [RMJ]

II

1. Yunmen Wenyan (864–949). See *Yunmen Kuangzhen Chanshi guang lu*, T1988_.47_0560b17–18.
2. Imakita Kōsen (1816–92), Suzuki's first Zen teacher at Engakuji.
3. Yantou Quanhuo (828–87). See Whitfield, *Records*, 4: 139; *Jinde chuandeng lu*, T2076_.510327a05–07.

4. According to his autobiography *Itsumade-gusa,* Hakuin Ekaku (1685–1768), upon hearing a temple bell while doing *zazen* at a temple in Echigo district, said he realized Yantou was "alive and well." See Norman Waddell, trans., *Wild Ivy: The Spiritual Autobiography of Zen Master Hakuin* (Boston and London: Shambala, 2001), 26.
5. Kichijōten (Śrī Mahādevī/Mahāśrī), the goddess of good fortune, and her sister, Kokuanten (Kalārātri), the goddess of misfortune.
6. The passages cited by Suzuki are from the *Linji yulu.* An English translation by Ruth Fuller Sasaki, with extensive notes by the editor, can be found in Thomas Yūhō Kirchner, ed., *Record of Linji* (Honolulu: University of Hawai'i Press, 2009), 265–266. See also Linji Yixuan (?–866), *Zhenzhou Linji Huizhao Chanshi yulu,* T1985_.47.0502a08–13. The passages from Linji that follow below in the text, up to "This is called attaining the *dharma,*" are all from the aforementioned passage in the *Record of Linji.*
7. This is a reference to Devadatta. According to some traditional accounts, because of Devadatta's evil actions against the Buddha and the sangha, he was swallowed up by the earth and fell into Avīci hell for 100,000 eons.
8. Suzuki is referring to Xuansha Shibei (J. Gensha Shibi; 835–908), who trained with Xuefeng Yicun (J. Seppō Gison; 822–908). See Andrew E. Ferguson, *Zen's Chinese Heritage: The Masters and Their Teachings* (Boston: Wisdom, 2000), 272; Whitfield, *Records,* 5: 33; *Jingde chuandeng lu,* T2076_.51.0344a06–07. According to the *Zutang ji* (CBETA 2023.Q4, B25, no. 144, p. 487a10–14), Xuefeng one day called to him, "Brother Bei, you have never been to various masters; why not go out to have a look around?" When called thus four times, Xuansha realized how anxious Xuefeng was for him to travel, made his preparations, left the temple, and on reaching the top of the mountain, stumbled on a rock, when he abruptly attained a great awakening. Later he cried out involuntarily, "Bodhidharma had never come; the second patriarch did not transmit [the dharma]." [S&T, 52, note 13]
9. That is, the question concerning why Bodhidharma came to China.
10. That is, the question to Linji about the nature of nonattainment. [RMJ]

11. A dialogue between Caoshan Benji (840–901) and a monk named Qingshui in *Wumenguan*, case 10. See Robert Aitken, trans., *Gateless Barrier* (San Francisco: North Point Press, 1991), 70. The source is the record of Caoshan in the *Jingde chuandeng lu*, T2076_.51.0336a26–28; Whitfield, *Records*, 4: 197.
12. Hōrin (C. Fenglin, dates unknown). Suzuki's sentence in the manuscript was incomplete, ending with "he said," I have completed the sentence based on the note in Kirchner, ed., *Record of Linji*. There are several versions of the line, but the only one that begins with "he [Linji] said" continues with "Who says he is away?" See Kirchner, ed., *Record of Linji*, 336. [RMJ]
13. "Myōke" (C. Minghua) was inserted into the manuscript. [S&T, 52, Note 18–1] The source is the same as in the above note. See Kirchner, ed., *Record of Linji*, 334–335; *Jingde chuandeng lu*, T1985_.47 .0506b07–09.
14. A dialogue between Puhua (J. Fuke, dates unknown) and Linji. Kirchner, ed., *Record of Linji*, 291–293; *Jingde chuandeng lu*, T1985_.47.0503b03–09. Puhua (J. Fuke, dates unknown). The rest of the story that follows below, up to "I see he is a real one," is based on this source.
15. Zhaozhou Congshen (778–897). James Green, trans., *Recorded Sayings of Zen Master Joshu* (Boston: Shambala, 2001), 15–16. *Zhaozhou Zhenji Chanshi yulu* in the *Chongke guzunsu yulu*, CBETA 2023.Q4, X68, no. 1315, p. 77c1–4.
16. Here Thomas interpolated "in the master's mind," but it probably should be "in the monk's mind."
17. Page 22 of the manuscript is missing, so this dialogue was unfinished in the manuscript. The remainder of the dialogue is found in the commentary to case 47 in the *Book of Serenity* (C. *Congrong lu*; J. *Shōyōroku*).

> Chan Master Huijiao went to Fayan's place; Fayan asked, "Where have you recently come from?" Huijiao said, "Zhaozhou." Fayan said, "I hear Zhaozhou has a saying, 'The cypress tree in the yard'—is it so?" Huijiao said, "No." Fayan said, "Everyone who's been around says a monk asked him about the meaning of Chan and Zhaozhou said, 'The cypress tree in the yard'—how can you say no?" Huijiao

said, "The late master really didn't say this; please don't slander him."

See Xingxiu, *Book of Serenity*, trans. Thomas Cleary (Boston: Shambhala, 1998), 197–198; *Congrong lu* T2004_.48.0256c26–0257a01. Note that Suzuki is following traditional Zen commentaries on this case from the *Mumonkan*. See, for example, the commentaries on case 37 in Aitken, *Gateless Barrier*, 226–228, and Shibayama Zenkei, *Zen Comments on the Mumonkan* (New York: New American Library, 1974), 265–271.

III

1. See, for example, Philip B. Yampolsky, trans., *Platform Sutra of the Sixth Patriarch* (New York: Columbia University Press, 1967), 135–136. Suzuki writes at length on the topic in Suzuki, *Zen Doctrine of No-Mind* (1949; reprint, London: Rider and Company, 1958), 46ff. See also the section on *dhyana* and *prajñā* in *Liuzu Dashi Fabaotang-jing* T2008_.48.0352c12–0353b6.
2. Here "*prajñā* is *dhyāna* is *prajña*" is corrected to "*prajñā* is *dhyāna*." [S&T, 68, note 2]
3. At this point in the text Thomas inserts the following lengthy etymological comment about *prajñā*: §*Prajñā* is a combination of two Sanskrit words, the prefix *pra-* and *jñā*. Among the dictionary meanings given these words are the following: *pra-*: before, in front; pre-eminently, excessively; *jñā*, the verb: to know, become acquainted with; perceive, apprehend, understand, experience; investigate; ascertain; *jña*, the noun: a wise and learned man; *prajñā*, the verb: to know, understand; to distinguish, discern; to become aware of, find out, discover; the causative verb form, *prajñāpayati*, to show or point out (the way); *prajñā*, the noun: wisdom, intelligence, understanding; discernment, discrimination, judgement. In its Buddhist use and in its combination with English intuition, *prajñā* includes most of these definitions and is impossible to translate by a single word, or even by several words. *Pra-* perhaps corresponds more closely to the German *Ur-*, "primal," than to any English word, but without sufficient emphasis upon the

emphatic connotation of *pra-*. The usual English translation of the noun *prajñā* is "wisdom." "Primal all-apprehending awareness" is perhaps a better rendering of the sense, but it is better left untranslated.§

4. Suzuki mistook the page number for the verse number. "*Dhammapada* 123" has been changed here to "*Dhammapada* 191." [S&T, 68, note 3] Suzuki appears to have cited S. Radhakrishnan *Dhammapada* (Oxford: Oxford University Press, 1950), for translations of the Pāli terms for the Noble Eightfold Path.
5. Luohan, *Heshang* of Zhangzhou (ninth century). See Whitfield, *Records*, 3: 122; *Jingde chuandeng lu* T2076_.51.0288c17–28. Suzuki also referred to Luohan *Heshang* (Rakan Oshō) in chapter 1, p. 15: "Rakan Oshō saw the rising sun." See Whitfield, *Records*, 3: 122; *Jingde chuandeng lu* T2076_.51.0288c17–28. Whitfield translates the line, "I saw the sun in its wholeness for the first time."
6. Suzuki recounts the full story of Kyōgen/Xiangyan's awakening in EZB 1: 242–243 [227–228].
7. *Dhammapada* 254 reads, "There is no path in the sky, there is no recluse (adopting the Buddhist path) outside (of us)." See Radakrishnan, *Dhammapada*, 139.
8. Suzuki is quoting Whitehead, who states, "Religion is what the individual does with his own solitariness." See Alfred North Whitehead, *Religion in the Making* (New York: Macmillan, 1926), 16. Thanks to Michael Quick for this reference. [S&T 68, note 7]
9. Suzuki alludes to Guanxi Zhixian's (d. 895) dialogue with Moshan-ni Liaoran. See Whitfield, *Records*, 3: 122; *Jingde chuandeng lu* T2076_.51.0289a01–13. Suzuki's loose translation differs from Whitfield's more literal translation in several places.
10. Heshan Wuyin (J. Kazan Muin; 884–960) comments on the above case, "How did he get there?" See T2076_.51.0289a06. [S&T, 69, note 9–5]
11. Concerning Jinhua Shan Juzhi (J. Chikan Gutei; d.u.), see EZB 1, 35, note 2 [22, note §]. The story is also found in the *Jingde chuandeng lu*. See Whitfield, *Records*, 3: 118–119; T2076_.51.0288a23–0288b11. Gutei became famous for his "one-finger Zen," as Suzuki describes below.

12. Suzuki is citing comments on the "one finger" by four masters from the end of the section on Juzhi in the *Jingde chuandeng lu*, including Xuansha, referred to as X by Thomas in the manuscript. See Whitfield, *Records*, 3: 119.

IV

1. Manura (C. Manuluo) was the twenty-second patriarch of Chan. This verse is in his brief biography in the *Jingde chuandeng lu*. See Whitfield, *Records*, 1: 120–122; T2076_.51.0214a24–25. In this passage, Suzuki translates the character *yū* (C. *you* 幽), which literally means deep or secluded, as "serene."
2. Suzuki translates the character *yū* (C. *you* 幽) as "cloudy impenetrability" in D. T. Suzuki, *Zen and Japanese Culture* (New York: Pantheon, 1959), 220, note 2. The compound *yūgen* he translates as "beyond intellectual calculability." He interprets the term *yūgen* as synonymous with *myō*, "wondrous" or "mysterious." [RMJ].
3. There is a missing word in the sentence of the manuscript in this sentence.
4. Daitō Kokushi (National Teacher), Shūhū Myōchō (1282–1337). [S&T, 105, note 11] Suzuki translates the entire verse in *Manual of Zen Buddhism*, 179.

   Buddha and Fathers cut to pieces—
   The sword is ever kept sharpened!
   Where the wheel turns,
   The void gnashes its teeth.

5. Duofu *Heshang* of Hangzhou (J. Tafuku; n. d.). See Whitfield, *Records*, 3: 115; *Jingde Chuandeng-lu* T2076_.51.0287c15–18.
6. The manuscript version has "*a priori*" instead of "*aporia*," but the latter word makes more sense as an equivalent of "impasse."
7. Suzuki recounts Xiangyan's koan about a man hanging from a branch over a precipice in various places. See EZB 1, 277–278 [263] and EZB 2, 217–218 [196], for example. The story is found in Whitfield, *Records*, 3: 91; *Jingde chuandeng lu*, T2076_.51.0284b21–25, as

well as case 5 of the *Wumenguan*, for example in Aitken, *Gateless Barrier*, 38–45.

8. Suzuki inserted a note in the text referring to "Essays II, 240." The actual reference is found in EZB I: 257–258, note 1 [241–242, note *].
9. In Raymond Bernard Blakney, trans., *Meister Eckhart* (New York: Harper and Brothers, 1941), Blakney notes that he is translating the word "*vünkelīn*" on 326, note 8, as "spark."
10. This story is found in Dahui's *Zongmen wuku*, which states,

> Yexian Guisheng (dates unknown, a *dharma*-heir of Shoushan Shengnian [926–93]), was a severe and dry master, and the monks were in awe of him. Two masters, Fushan Fayuan (991–1067) and Tianyi Yihuai (993–1064), when still studying *Chan*, came to attend Master Yexian for practice. They happened to come on a cold, snowy day. Yexian cursed and scolded to drive them away. He even splashed water on them at night to make their clothes wet. The other monks all got angry and left; only Fayuan and Yihuai, arranged the sheets and clothes and kept sitting through the night. Yexian scolded them, and said, "You will not leave, so I shall strike you." Fushan approached the master and said, "We two came thousands of miles to practice Chan with you. How could we be driven away with a ladle of water splashed upon us? Even if you strike us down, we won't leave." Yexian laughed, and said, "You two must practice Chan with me; go stay in the monastery." Then he asked Fushan to serve as head cook. *Dahui Pujue Chanshi zongmen wuku*, T1998B.47.0944a12–19. [S&T, 106, note 15 translation revised by RMJ]

11. See above, chapter II, note iii.
12. Suzuki is alluding to the story of the dragon king's daughter transforming into a bodhisattva, when denigrated by Śāriputra for being hindered by birth as a woman. See Leon Hurvitz, trans., *Lotus Blossom of the Fine Dharma (The Lotus Sūtra)*, rev. ed. (New York: Columbia University Press, 2009), 183–185.

13. A reference to Xuansha Shibei (J. Gensha; 835–908). See Cleary, *Blue Cliff Record*, 565–566; *Biyan lu*, T2003_.48.0212c08–14.
14. Cleary, *Blue Cliff Record*, 566; *Biyan lu* T.2003._48.0212c15–23.
15. C. *zhege*, literally, this one or this.
16. This story appears in a comment to case 4 of the *Blue Cliff Record*. See Cleary, *Blue Cliff Record*, 24; *Biyan lu*, T2003.48.0143c06–07. The term *tenshin* (C. *dianxin*) is more commonly known in its Cantonese pronunciation, *dimsum*, referring to snacks or refreshments. The word "*dian*" in "*dianxin*," however, can mean to ignite, rather than punctuate, and *xin* means "mind," so "*dianxin*" could be interpreted as igniting/refreshing one's mind.
17. See Augustine, *Confessions*, trans. E. B. Pusey (1907; reprint, London: J. M. Dent & Sons, 1957), 262. Augustine writes, "What then is time? If no one asks me, I know: if I wish to explain it to one that asketh, I know not . . ."
18. Suzuki discusses the Sanskrit term *praṇidhāna* (C. *guan*; J. *gan*) at length in chapter 6. He variously translates the term as "vow" and "prayer." For Suzuki's discussion of the term, see his translation, *Shinran's Kyōgyōshinshō: The Collection of Passages Expounding the True Teaching, Living, Faith, and Realizing of the Pure Land* (Oxford and New York: Oxford University Press, 2012), 20–22.
19. See Burton Watson, trans., *The Vimalakirti Sutra* (New York: Columbia University Press, 1997), 86–87; *Weimo jing*, T475_.14.0547c.
20. *Pariṇāmanā* (J. *ekō*; C. *huixiang*) means dedication of one's merit to another. In particular it refers to the dedication of one's merit to the achievement of buddhahood in order to liberate all beings.

V

1. *Dasheng qixinlun*, T1666_.32.0575a04–0583b16, trans. Paramārtha; T1667_.32.0583b22–0591c21, trans. Śikṣānanda. Suzuki published a translation of the Śikṣānanda version early in his career. See AFM. In the seminar Suzuki quoted from AFM. The asterisk indicates that the Sanskrit title, **Mahāyāna-śraddhotpāda śāstra*, is a hypothetical reconstruction of the title from the Chinese, *Dasheng qixinlun*. No Sanskrit version of the text exists. Most contemporary

scholars believe the śāstra was composed in China. (See the introduction to this volume for more about the *Dasheng qixin lun*'s authorship.)

2. See AFM, 62–65. In Chinese and according to a more recent English translation, these four stages are (1) *bujue* (nonawakening), (2) *xiangsijue* (semblance awakening) (3) *suifenjue* (partial awakening), and (4) *jiujingjue* (final awakening). See John Jorgensen et al., trans., *Treatise on Awakening Mahāyāna Faith*, Oxford Chinese Thought (New York: Oxford University Press, 2019), 73–74.
3. *I-Ching* in the more familiar Wade-Giles translation of this title.
4. The manuscript has "fifth century," which has been corrected to "around the middle of the sixth century," as Suzuki writes in his translation of the *Dasheng qixin lun*: "the present one came from his pen on the tenth day of September, A.D. 554." [S&T, 162, note 9]
5. The Śikṣānanda version has "*yiqie zhongsheng xin*" (*sarvasattvacitta*), "the mind of all sentient beings," while the Paramārtha version has simply "*zhongsheng xin*" (*sattvacitta*), that is, "mind of sentient beings." [S&T, 165, note 14, modified by RMJ]
6. Suzuki does not give any equivalent to "*yū*," apparently a romanization of a Japanese character.
7. Kyōgen Chikan (C. Xiangyan Zhixian; d. 898) (C. Xiangyan Xiangshu?~898). See above, chapter III, footnote v.
8. These five exchanges occur between Guishan/Weishan Lingyou (771–853) and Yangshan Huiji (807–83). See Whitfield, *Records*, 2: 259–260; *Jingde chuandeng lu*, T2076._51.0265b29–0265c04. Suzuki omits the last line of the dialogue;, Guishan's final comment after Yangshan's remark, "Are you asking about this?"is, "This is really how a king goose selects milk [from water.]" [S&T, 168, note 21]
9. Clinging *zhiqu* (J. *shūshu*) and the imputation of names, *jimingzi* (J. *keimyōji*). Suzuki had "*kia suyo je*" in the typed manuscript. See Fazang's *Dasheng qixin lun yiji* (Commentary on the *Qixin-lu*), where he states, "What is called aging aspect means two things: 1. clinging, and 2. imputation of names" (*yan yi-xiang er zhe, yi zhiqu-xiang, er jiming-zi-xiang*), T1846._44.0257b25–26. The Chinese rendering *yi*, for change, does not convey the meaning of aging and death connoted by the original Sanskrit term *jarā*. [S&T, 165 note 25, modified by RMJ]

10. 1. *bujue* (J. *fukaku*; nonenlightenment), 2. *xiangsijue* (*sōjikaku*; enlightenment in appearance), 3. *suifenjue* (J. *zuibunkaku*; approximate enlightenment), 4. *jiujingjue* (J. *kukyōkaku*; ultimate enlightenment) (T1667.32._0585a16–22). See note 2 above for more recent translations of the four stages of awakening.
11. *vijñāna* (C. *shi*; J. *shiki*); *manovijñāna* (C. *yishi*, J. *ishiki*); and *manas* (C. *yi*; J. *i*).
12. An allusion to *Blue Cliff Record*, case 1. See Cleary, *Blue Cliff Record*, 6; *Biyan lu*, T2003_.48.0140a17–0141b26, which recounts the dialogue between Emperor Wu of Liang and Master Dharma. To the emperor's question, "What is the ultimate principle of the holy truth?" the master replied, "Vast emptiness and nothing holy." To this remark the compiler put a comment, "I thought it was a thing of some worth. The arrow passed to Korea. It's all clear." *Eastern Buddhist* (New Series) 1, no. 1 (September 1965): 10. The English translation is Suzuki's. The comment, "*jian guo Xinluo*" (The arrow has passed Silla; T2003_.48.0141a02), seems to be the source of the present expression. [S&T, 174, note 47, modified by RMJ]
13. Touzi Datong (819–914). See Whitfield, *Records*, 4: 94; *Jingde chuandeng lu*, T2076_.51_0319c17–18. Suzuki inaccurately quotes Touzi's last retort, "Truly deceitful words." Suzuki cites a more accurate version of the story in *Zen Buddhism: Selected Writings of D. T. Suzuki*, ed. William Barrett (Garden City, NY: Doubleday, 1956), 225–226.
14. Zhaozhou Congshen (778–897), when asked by Yanyang Shanzhao (n.d.), "How is it when a man brings nothing with him?" Zhaozhou responded, "Throw it away." EZB 1, 175 [162] as well as *Dahui Pujue Chanshi yulu*, T1998A.47_0938c01–02. See also James Green, trans., *Recorded Sayings of Zen Master Joshu* (Boston: Shambala, 2001), and Ferguson, *Zen's Chinese*, 179.
15. This is a continuation of the previous story about Zhaozhou and Yanyang. See EZB 1, 175 [162] as well as *Dahui Pujue Chanshi yulu*, T1998A.47_0938c02–04. See also Green, trans., *Recorded Sayings of Zen Master Joshu* and Ferguson, *Zen's Chinese Heritage*, 179.
16. Qianzhou Chuwei (J. Kenshū Shobi; dates unknown). See Whitfield, *Records*, 2: 278; *Jingde Chuandeng-lu* T2076_.51.0269a12–15.
17. Also known as Muzhou Daoming (J. Bokushū Dōmyō; n.d.). See Whitfield, *Records*, 3: 134; *Jingde chuandeng lu*, T2076_.51.0291b05–08. See also

Ferguson, *Zen's Chinese Heritage*, 160. Suzuki's translation of the story differs slightly from those of Ferguson and Whitfield.

18. Here, Thomas inserts the following comment into the lectures: "§A *gāthā* by one of the early Zen masters (probably eighth century), [Banzan Hōshaku] a disciple of Mazu, has this: 'Mind is like the moon, round, perfect'—this corresponding to One Mind. 'The ten thousand things are swallowed up, taken into the moon itself,' etc.—Unfortunately, I did not get this down well enough to include and have been unable to find it published so far. If you will supply it, probably the comments I have will fit in. Some of them follow, of course not entirely in proper context.§" The master, Banzan, is C. Panshan Baoji (720–814). See Whitfield, *Records*, 2: 186; *Jingde chuandeng lu*, T2076_.51.0253b15–17. See also Ferguson, *Zen's Chinese Heritage*, 100.
19. *Chongke guzunsu yulu, Muzhou Heshang*, CBETA 2023.Q4, X68, no. 1315, p. 36c21–22.
20. Green, trans., *Recorded Sayings of Zen Master Joshu*, 101; see also *Dahui Pujie Heshang yulu*, T1998A.47.0893c12–13.
21. C. *chongchong wujin*; J. *jūjū-mujin*: a technical term describing the complete, endless interdependence of all phenomena. This is the interpretation of dependent origination in the Huayan (J. Kegon) school.

VI

1. C., Danxia Tianran (739–824).
2. An allusion to the European Christian aphorism that "God is an infinite sphere whose center is everywhere and circumference nowhere." The expression was widely used by such authors as Alain de Lille, Meister Eckhart, and Blaise Pascal. By the fifteenth century, "sphere" had become "circle." See Otto J. Brendel, *Symbolism of the Sphere: A Contribution to the History of Earlier Greek Philosophy*, Etudes Préliminaires Aux Religions Orientales Dans l'Empire Romain; t. 67 (Leiden: Brill, 1977), 29 and 29n35.
3. An interlinear, handwritten note suggests that *prajñā* should be *karuṇā* in this sentence.
4. The dialogue occurs between Wufeng Changuan (J. Gohō Jōkan; n.d.) and an anonymous monk. See Whitfield, *Records*, 2: 269; *Jingde*

chuandeng lu, T2076_.51.0267b05–07. See also Ferguson, *Zen's Chinese Heritage*, 123.

5. See Whitfield, *Records*, 2: 269; *Jingde chuandeng lu*, T2076_.51.0267b02–05. See also Ferguson, *Zen's Chinese Heritage*, 123.
6. See Whitfield, *Records*, 2: 269; *Jingde chuandeng lu*, T2076_.51.0267b07–10. See also Ferguson, *Zen's Chinese Heritage*, 123.
7. Shishuang Xingkong (J. Sekisō Seikū; n. d.). The literal question was: "What was the meaning of [Bodhidharma's] coming from the west? The cleric's response to Shishuang's second question more literally was: "Recently in the Hunan district Master Chang has appeared in the world; he has been engaged in idle back-alley chatter." See EZB 2, 219–220 [198]; Whitfield, *Records*, 2: 269–270; *Jingde chuandeng lu*, T2076_.51.0267b11–14.
8. Yangshan Huiji (J. Kyōzan Ejaku; 807–83) and Danyuan Yingzhen (J. Tangen Ōshin; n.d.). See EZB, 2, 219–220 [198]; Whitfield, *Records*, 2: 270; *Jingde chuandeng lu*, T2076_.51.0267b14–16.
9. Weishan Lingyou (aka Guishan Lingyou, J. Isan Reiyū; 771–853). See EZB 2, 219–220 [198]; Whitfield, *Records*, 2: 270; *Jingde chuandeng lu*, T2076_.51.0267b16–18.
10. EZB 2, 198/220; Whitfield, *Records*, 2: 270; *Jingde chuandeng lu*, T2076_.51.0267b18–19. Suzuki translates the aforementioned passage in *Essays* cleaving more closely to the original text: "Under Tan-yüan, I got the name, while under Wei-shan I got the substance."
11. Whitfield, *Records*, 2: 275; *Jingde chuandeng lu*, T2076_.51.0268b7–9.
12. Whitfield, *Records*, 2: 275; *Jingde chuandeng lu*, T2076_.51.0268b10–13. The text states the monk was Yangshan Huiji (J. Kyōzan Ejaku).
13. The version of the *Jingde chuandeng lu* used by Suzuki differs slightly from the Song version contained in T. 51. In the version Suzuki used, apparently from the Koryŏ canon, the text has a pillow (C. *zhenzi*), whereas the Taishō version has (C. *wuwu*) that is, "nothing." The typewritten manuscript has mistakenly "A pillar" instead of a pillow. There are other minor variations between the source for Suzuki's translation and that of the other versions of the text. [S&T, 236, notes 22–23, modified by RMJ]
14. The text Suzuki mentions in footnote vi was translated into Japanese based on a manuscript written by Suzuki in English. The citation is

"Kyokutō bunka shijō ni okeru Bukkyō shisō no yakuwari," in *Ajia bunka no sai ninshiki: Ajia Bunka Toshokan kaikan kinen ronbun shū,*" ed. Ajia Bunka Toshokan (Tokyo: Asahi Shinbun Sha, 1957), 31–62. See also SDZ, 22: 165–194.

15. Guangfa Dashi Xingqin of Fuqing, Quanzhou. See Whitfield, *Records*, 6: 172; *Jingde chuandeng lu*, T2076_.51.0401b28–0401c01. Whitfield mistakenly interprets the term *randeng* to mean lighting a lamp, whereas Suzuki translates it as *Randeng Rulai*, Dipaṃkara (Maker of Light), the buddha before Śākyamuni.
16. From the *Yunmen guang lu*, T1988_.47.0554c02. Yunmen Wenyan (J. Unmon Bun'en; 864–949). The Chinese reads, "*dayong xianqian bucun guize.*" The phrase appears frequently in Zen texts. See, for example, case 3 of the *Blue Cliff Record*, where the pointer to the case reads, "The Great Function appears without abiding by fixed principles." Cleary, *Blue Cliff Record*, 18, and *Biyan lu* T2003_.48.0142c05.
17. This phrase, in Chinese, "*you tui zhou wu lu, lao er wu-gong,*" is from the *Zhuangzi*, "Tianyun" (Revolution of Heaven) chapter. In James Legge's translation, the sentence reads, "To seek now to practice (the old ways of) Zhou in Lu is like pushing along a boat on the dry land. It is only a toilsome labour, and has no success." See "Chinese Text Project," https://ctext.org/zhuangzi/revolution-of-heaven.
18. Zhaozhou Congshen is the master in this dialogue. See Whitfield, *Records*, 3: 54; *Jingde chuandeng lu*, T2076_.51.0278a–0278b01.
19. Shōmatsu, usually called Shōma, 1799?–1871. Suzuki discusses Shōma's experiences at length in *Daisetz Teitaro Suzuki and Taitetsu Unno, Buddha of Infinite Light,* (Boston New York: Shambhala Publications in association with the American Buddhist Academy ; Distributed in the U.S. by Random House, 1997), 35–37. See also "Shūkyō keiken no jijitsu" (The Actual Facts of Religious Experience), published in 1943. SDZ 10: 1–129.
20. An allusion to the words of Changsha Jingcen (J. Chōsha Keishin; d. 868). The dialogue in the *Jingde chuandeng lu* reads:

> A monk asked: "Nanquan has passed away; where will he go?"
> The master said: "In an eastern house he will become a donkey; in a western house he will become a horse."
> The monk said, "What do you mean by that?"

The master said. "If you need to ride, ride; if you need to dismount, dismount."

See Whitfield, *Records*, 3: 29–30; *Jingde chuandeng lu*, T2076_.51.0274b22–24. [S&T, 239, note 31]

21. The manuscript has several lacunae that render two sentences between "environment" and "Hampered" difficult to interpret, so I have deleted the incomplete sentences. [RMJ]
22. In the *Jingde chuandeng lu*, there is a dialogue in which Linxi Jingtuo *Heshan* of Yingzhou was asked about the Buddha and the Dharma. See Whitfield, *Records*, 6:73–74; *Jingde chuandeng lu*, T2076_.51.0386b29–0386c2. No mention of the sangha is made in that exchange, however. [S&T, 239, note 33]
23. This is a dialogue between Linxi Jingtuo and an unnamed monk. See Whitfield, *Records*, 6: 73; *Jingde chuandeng lu*, T2076_.51.0386b27.
24. C. *raorao congcong*. The Later Zhaoqing *Heshang* of Quanzhou was asked,

"What is the essence of the Buddhist teaching?"

The master said, "In noisy tumult and hasty confusion, the morning cockcrow and the evening bells."

See Whitfield, *Records*, 6: 53; *Jingde chuandeng lu*, T2076_.51.0383c21–22.

25. This seems to be an allusion to the dialogue between a monk and Yining Longjing Lun *Chanshi* of Guangzhou.

"What is the Buddha?"

The master said, "He diligently ploughs the fields."

"I don't understand."

The master said, "Early morning, collecting grain."

See Whitfield, *Records*, 6: 66–67; *Jingde chuandeng lu*, T2076_.51.0383c14–15.

26. This is probably an allusion to the dialogue between Chan Master Zhangzhou Bao'en Yuan Xingchong and a monk.

> "'What is the meaning of the Buddha-dharma?'
>
> 'The pestle for pounding, the millstone for grinding,' replied the master."

See Whitfield, *Records*, 6: 51; *Jingde chuandeng lu*, T2076_.51.0383c01–02.

27. A monk asked Chan Master Ziling Wei, "What is Ziling's field of activity (*kyōgai/gocara*)?" The master said, "With the quiet illumination of lamplight, the night is already deep." See Whitfield, *Records*, 6: 137; *Jingde chuandeng lu*, T2076_.51.0396a14–15.
28. The same monk asked, "How is the person in your field of activity?" The same master said, "Monkeys cry and tigers roar." See Whitfield, *Records*, 6: 137; *Jingde chuandeng lu*, T2076_.51.0396a15–16.
29. A monk asked Yanqing Guixiao, "What is your range of action?" The master said, "Carefully watch." The monk, "How is the man in this range of action?" The master, "Do you know?" Whitfield, *Records*, 6: 136; *Jingdeng chuandeng lu*, T2076_.51.0396a03–04. Suzuki mistakenly inserted, "What, what?" which is the reply by Shizang Huiju in the next story.
30. A dialogue between a monk and Shizang Huiju of Dingzhou:

> Someone asked, "How is the temple?" The master said, "Simply this." The monk asked, "How is the man in the temple?" The master said, "What? What?" The monk asked, "Should you see a guest suddenly come, how will you treat him?" The master said, "Please take tea."

See Whitfield, *Records*, 5: 180; *Jingdeng chuandeng lu*, T2076_.51.0366b22–24.

31. An allusion to a dialogue between a monk and Master Hengyue Nantaisi Zang.

> A monk asked, "I've come all the way, seeking instruction from the master; please, Master, accept me."
>
> The master said, "No door separates you."
>
> The monk asked, "How is Nantai's realm of activity (*kyōgai*)?"

The master said, "When the pine wind blows, the stones are not touched; Below a solitary peak, it's difficult to align a rampart."

See Whitfield, *Records*, 6: 125; *Jingdeng chuandeng lu*, T2076_.51.039 4c04–06.

32. The manuscript has, "when the breeze passes through the pines, *do not find stone.*" Following the dialogue in note 31, I have changed this to "the stones are not touched."
33. Master Zang's dialogue continues:

"How is the man in the realm of your activity?"

The master said, "In front of the cliff I plant wild fruits and receive visitors."

"In that case, let me thank you for your offerings."

The master said, "How do they taste?"

See Whitfield, *Records*, 6: 125; *Jingdeng chuandeng lu*, T2076_.51.039 4c06–08. In the manuscript, the final response by the master was left blank.

34. This is a dialogue between Cangxi Lin of Langzhou and an unnamed monk.

A monk asked "What is Cangxi's range of activity?" The master said, "In front a river runs due east."

"What is Cangxi's family's style?"

The master said, "Enter, then you will see."

See Whitfield, *Records*, 6: 90; *Jingdeng chuandeng lu*, T2076_.51.03 90a15–17.

35. The dialogue between Huizhen Guangwu and an interlocutor reads,

"What is the environment on Mt. Shuangfeng?"

The master said, "At night listening to the stream run in the bamboo behind the hermitage; during daytime watching clouds arise [from] the mountain in front."

See Whitfield, *Records*, 6: 64; *Jingdeng chuandeng lu*, T2076_.51.03 85b09–10.

36. A dialogue with Ximingyuan Chen of Quanzhou reads:

> A monk asked, "What is the style of the master's house?"
> The master said, "Bamboo chopsticks and earthen bowls."
> The monk said, "If you happen to have an important guest coming, how would you entertain him?"
> The master said, "With pickles and rice."

See Whitfield, *Records*, 6: 55; *Jingdeng chuandeng lu*, T2076_.51.03 84a18–20.

37. As noted by S&T (244, note 49), Suzuki alludes to Zhiyi (538–97), who writes in the *Mohe zhiguan*, "There is no *bodhi*-wisdom in passionate afflictions and no passionate afflictions in *bodhi*-wisdom; this is what is inferred from the Four [Noble] Truths [understood as] arising-and-perishing—the arousing of *bodhicitta* as seeking the path of the Buddha above and saving sentient beings below." See Paul Swanson, trans., *Clear Serenity, Quiet Insight: T'ian T'ai Chih-I's Mo-ho chih-kuan* (Honolulu: University of Hawai'i Press, 2018), 1: 170. See also *Mohe zhiguan*, T1911_.46.0006a17–19. See also the introduction, p. 52, for Suzuki's thoughts about the use of this phrase by contemporaneous Zen Buddhist masters.
38. A saying attributed to Baizhang Huaihai (J. Hyakujō Ekai; 749–814). See, for example, *Chixiu Baizhang qinggui*, T2025_.48.1119b02.
39. The next sentence in the manuscript is incomplete, so I have elided it. The typescript, including an interlinear comment by ET, reads, "Is" is present, "is not" is [being]§beginning? becoming?§.
40. Suzuki is citing a dialogue between Dasui Fazhen (J. Dazui Hōshin; 834–919) and an unnamed monk.

> "A monk asked Zen Master Dasui, 'When the aeonic fire engulfs everything is *this* annihilated or not?' Dasui said, 'Annhilated.' The monk said, 'Then it is annihilated along with everything else?' Dasui said, 'It is annihilated along with everything else.' "

See Whitfield, *Records*, 3:103; *Jingdeng chuandeng lu*, T2076_.51.02 86a16–18.

41. See *Xingxiu, Book of Serenity,* 135, for the dialogue between Longji Shan Shaoxiu and an unnamed monk. See also the dialogue in the *Jingde chuandeng lu*.

> "A monk asked Longji the same question. Longji said, 'Not destroyed.' The monk asked 'Why is it not destroyed?' Longji said, 'Because it is the same as the universe.' "

See Whitfield, *Records*, 6: 168; *Jingdeng chuandeng lu*, T2076_.51.040 1a10–12.

42. In the manuscript, Suzuki does not make clear which *yū/yu* he has in mind. ET queries the author in the typescript, "§meaning of yu here is what exactly?§ From the context, it appears Suzuki intends "*yū*," "function," which also is part of the compound "*daiyū*," cited above in the text.

43. This aphorism is found in the *Laṅkāvatāra Sūtra*. See LS, 83: "Since beginningless time, the ignorant are found transmigrating through the paths, enwrapped in their attachment to existence; as a wedge is induced by another wedge, they are led to abandonment [of their wrappage]." See also *Lengqie abaduoluo bao jing*, T0670_.16.0491c20.

BIBLIOGRAPHY

ARCHIVAL MATERIAL CONSULTED

Archives of American Art
Columbia University Central Archives
Elizabeth Mary Thomas Notebooks, Bekku-Okamura Mihoko Papers, D. T. Suzuki Museum, Kanazawa, Japan
Elizabeth Mary Thomas Papers, University of Memphis Institute of Egyptian Art and Archaeology
Michael Goldberg, *D. T. Suzuki Documentary Project Collection, 2003–2010*
Karen Horney Papers, Boston Psychoanalytic Society and Institute
Karen Horney Papers, Yale University Library Manuscripts and Archives
Matsugaoka Archive
Rockefeller Center Archive
Trustees of Reservations Archive (Massachussetts)

PUBLISHED SOURCES

Auslin, Michael R. *Pacific Cosmopolitans: A Cultural History of U.S.-Japan Relations*. Cambridge, MA: Harvard University Press, 2011.

Belford, Marilyn, and Jerry Herman, eds. *Time and Space Concepts in Art*. New York: Pleiades Gallery, 1980.

Benesch, Oleg. *Inventing the Way of the Samurai: Nationalism, Internationalism, and Bushidō in Modern Japan*. Oxford and New York: Oxford University Press, 2014.

Blackham, H. J. (Harold John). *Six Existentialist Thinkers.* London: Routledge & K. Paul, 1952. Kindle.

Brown, Carolyn. *Chance and Circumstance: Twenty Years with Cage and Cunningham.* 1st ed. New York: Knopf, 2007.

Bugbee, Henry. *The Inward Morning: A Philosophical Exploration in Journal Form.* State College, PA: Bald Eagle Press, 1958.

Cage, John. "Questions." *Perspecta* 11 (1967): 65–71.

Cage, John, and Kyle Gann. *Silence: Lectures and Writings.* 50th anniversary ed. Middletown, CT: Wesleyan University Press, 2011. Kindle edition.

Danto, Arthur C. "Upper West Side Buddhism." In *Buddha Mind in Contemporary Art*, ed. Jacquelynn Bass and Mary Jane Jacob, 49–59. Berkeley and Los Angeles: University of California Press, 2004.

Dobbins, James C. "D. T. Suzuki: A Biography." Oxford Research Encyclopedias: Religion, September 3, 2022. https://doi-org.proxy.lib.duke.edu/10.1093/acrefore/9780199340378.013.1106.

——. "D. T. Suzuki: A Brief Account of His Life." *Eastern Buddhist*, Third Series, 2, no. 2 (2022): 1–83.

——. "D. T. Suzuki Scrutinized: Reflections and Hypotheses." *Eastern Buddhist* 4, no. 1 (2024): 89–113.

Fields, Rick. *How the Swans Came to the Lake: A Narrative History of Buddhism in America*, Fortieth Anniversary Edition. Boston: Shambhala, 2022.

Gimello, Robert Michael. "Chih-Yen (智儼, 602–668) and the Foundations of Hua-Yen (華嚴) Buddhism." PhD diss., Columbia University, 1976.

Gregory, Peter. "The Problem of Theodicy in the 'Awakening of Faith.'" *Religious Studies* 22, no. 1 (1986): 63–78.

——. *Tsung-Mi and the Sinification of Buddhism.* Honolulu: University of Hawai'i Press, 1991.

Hakuin Ekaku. "Hakuin's Yasenkanna." Trans. Norman Waddell. *The Eastern Buddhist* 34, no. 1 (2002): 79–119.

Harootunian, Harry. "Post-War America and the Aura of Asia." In *The Third Mind: American Artists Contemplate Asia, 1860–1989*, ed. Alexandra Munroe, 45–55. New York: Guggenheim Museum: D.A.P./Distributed Art Publishers distributor, 2009.

Hedstrom, Matthew. *The Rise of Liberal Religion: Book Culture and American Spirituality in the Twentieth Century.* Oxford and New York: Oxford University Press, 2013. Kindle edition.

Heller, Nancy Gale. "The Sculpture of Ibram Lassaw." PhD diss., Rutgers University, 1982.

Hu, Shih. "Ch'an (Zen) Buddhism in China Its History and Method." *Philosophy East and West* 3, no. 1 (1953).

Ishii, Kōsei. "Kegon Philosophy and Nationalism in Modern Japan." In *Reflecting Mirrors: Perspectives on Huayan Buddhism*, ed. Imre Hamar. Asiatische Forschungen. Wiesbaden: Harrassowitz, 2007.

Jaffe, Richard M. "D. T. Suzuki and the Two Cranes: American Philanthropy and Suzuki's Global Agenda." In *Beyond Zen: D. T. Suzuki and the Modern Transformation of Buddhism*, ed. John Breen, Fumihiko Sueki, and Shōji Yamada, 133–155. Honolulu: University of Hawaiʻi Press, 2022.

James, William. *The Varieties of Religious Experience: A Study in Human Nature*. New York: Longmans, Green, 1902.

Kapleau, Philip, ed. *The Three Pillars of Zen: Teaching, Practice, and Enlightenment*. [1st U.S. ed.]. New York: Harper & Row, 1965.

Kleinberg, Ethan. *Generation Existential: Heidegger's Philosophy in France, 1927–1961*. Ithaca, NY: Cornell University Press, 2005.

Kostelanetz, Richard. *Conversing with Cage*. New York: Routledge, 1987.

Larson, Kay. *Where the Heart Beats: John Cage, Zen Buddhism, and the Inner Life of Artists*. New York: Penguin, 2012. Kindle edition.

Menand, Louis. *The Free World: Art and Thought in the Cold War*. New York: Farrar, Straus, and Giroux, 2021.

Mitchell, Scott A. *The Making of American Buddhism*. Oxford and New York: Oxford University Press, 2023.

Munroe, Alexandra, and Solomon R. Guggenheim Museum. *The Third Mind: American Artists Contemplate Asia, 1860–1989*. New York: Guggenheim Museum: D.A.P./Distributed Art Publishers distributor, 2009.

Needleman, Jacob. *What Is God?* New York: J. P. Tarcher/Penguin, 2009.

Norman, Dorothy. *Encounters: A Memoir*. San Diego: Harcourt Brace Jovanovich, 1987.

Okamura Mihoko 岡村美穂子 and Ueda Shizuteru 上田閑照. *Omoide no kobako kara: Suzuki Daisetsu no koto* 思い出の小箱から：鈴木大拙のこと. Tōei Sensho 29. Kyoto: Tōeisha, 1997.

Pearlman, Ellen. *Nothing and Everything: The Influence of Buddhism on the American Avant-Garde, 1942–1962*. Berkeley, CA: Evolver Editions, 2012. Kindle edition.

"People Are Talking About." *Vogue*, January 15, 1952, 98.

Rioch, Margaret J. "Memories of Dr. Daisetz Suzuki." *Eastern Buddhist*, New Series 2, no. 1 (1967): 191–193.

Sadler, A. W. "In Remembrance of D. T. Suzuki." *Eastern Buddhist*, New Series 2, no. 1 (1967): 198–200.

Sairenji, Ayako. "From Ethnic Church to Multi-Cultural Congregation: The Transformation of a Japanese-American Buddhist Church." M. A. thesis, Drew University, 2002.

Sandler, Irving. Tape-recorded Interview with Ibram Lassaw, August 26, 1968. Archives of American Art.

Satō, Kemmyō Taira. "D. T. Suzuki and the Question of War." *Eastern Buddhist* 39, no. 1 (2008): 61–120.

Schloss, Edith, and Mary Venturini. *The Loft Generation: From the De Koonings to Twombly: Portraits and Sketches, 1942-2011*. New York: Farrar, Straus and Giroux, 2021.

Sharf, Robert. "The Zen of Japanese Nationalism." *History of Religions* 33, no. 1 (1993): 1–43.

Soper, Alexander. "Review of Zen and Japanese Culture." *Artibus Asiae* 23, no. 2 (1960): 139–140.

Stunkard, Albert. "Suzuki Daisetz: An Appreciation." *Eastern Buddhist*, New Series, 36, no. 1/2 (1964): 192–228.

Suzuki, D. T., trans. *Acvaghosha's Discourse on the Awakening of Faith in the Mahâvâna* (Chicago: Open Court, 1900).

——. "D. T. Suzuki's English Diaries." *Annual Report of Researches of Matsugaoka Bunko*, 2005–.

——. *Studies in the Lankavatara Sutra*. London: George Routledge & Sons, Ltd., 1930.

——. *Zen Buddhism and Its Influence on Japanese Culture*. Kyoto: Eastern Buddhist Society, 1938.

——. *Living By Zen*. Tokyo: Sanseido, 1949.

——. *Zen Doctrine of No-Mind*. London: Rider and Company, 1949; reprint, 1958.

——. *Essays in Zen Buddhism (First Series). His Complete Works*. London, New York, Published for the Buddhist Society by Rider, 1949.

——. *Essays in Zen Buddhism (Second Series). His Complete Works*. London, New York, Published for the Buddhist Society, London by Rider, 1950.

——. *Essays in Zen Buddhism (Third Series). His Complete Works*. London, New York, Published for the Buddhist Society by Rider, 1953.

——. *Studies in Zen*. A Delta Book, 1955.

——. *An Introduction to Zen Buddhism. Complete Works*. London: Published for the Buddhist Society, London, by Rider, 1957.

——. *Manual of Zen Buddhism. Complete Works*. London; New York: Published for the Buddhist Society : Rider and Co., 1950.

——. *Mysticism: Christian and Buddhist*. London: Allen and Unwin, 1957.

——. "Zen: A Reply to Hu Shih." *Philosophy East and West* 3, no. 1 (1953).

——. "The Zen Sect of Buddhism." *Journal of the Pali Text Society*, 1907, 8–43.

Suzuki, D. T., trans. *The Lankavatara Sutra*. London: George Routledge & Sons, 1932.

Suzuki Daisetsu 鈴木大拙. "Chisei busoku no Nihonjin" 知性不足の日本人. SDZ 33: 6–12.

Suzuki, Daisetz T. *Friday Night Talks with D. T. Suzuki, On Shin Buddhism, Shinran, and Saichi*. Ed. Edythe Vassall. New York: American Buddhist Study Center, 2022.

Suzuki, Daisetz Teitaro. *Selected Works of D. T. Suzuki, Volume I: Zen*. Ed. Richard M. Jaffe. Berkeley: University of California Press, 2015.

——. *Selected Works of D. T. Suzuki, Volume II: Pure Land*. Ed. James C. Dobbins. Berkeley: University of California Press, 2015.

——. *Selected Works of D. T. Suzuki, Volume III: Comparative Religion*. Ed. Tomoe Moriya and Jeffrey Wilson. Berkeley: University of California Press, 2016.

——. *Selected Works of D. T. Suzuki, Volume IV: Buddhist Studies*. Ed. Mark L. Blum. Berkeley: University of California Press, 2020.

——. *Zen and Japanese Culture*. [Rev. and enl. 2nd ed. New York]: Pantheon, 1959.

——. *Zen Buddhism: Selected Writings of D. T. Suzuki*. Ed. William Barrett. Garden City, NY: Doubleday, 1956.

Suzuki, Daisetz Teitaro. *Daisetz Teitaro Suzuki's Columbia University Seminar Lectures*. Ed. Sōiku Shigematsu and Gishin Tokiwa. Kamakura: Matsugaoka Bunko, 2016.

Suzuki, Daisetz Teitaro, and Taitetsu Unno. *Buddha of Infinite Light*. Boston; New York: Shambhala Publications in association with the American Buddhist Academy, 1997.

Thomas, Elizabeth. *The Royal Necropoleis of Thebes*. Self-pub., Princeton, NJ, 1966.

"Thomas, Elizabeth | Theban Mapping Project." http://thebanmappingproject.com/glossary/thomas-elizabeth.

Tomkins, Calvin. "Figure in an Imaginary Landscape." *New Yorker* (November 28, 1964): 64–128.

Xingxiu. *Book of Serenity*. Trans. Thomas Cleary. Boston: Shambhala, 1998.

Yandell, Lundsford P. "Death: The Moon Sailing." *Eastern Buddhist* 2, no. 1 (1967): 200–207.

INDEX

Absolute Mind (*zhenru*; *shinnyo*): *Awakening of Faith* on, 29; consciousness and, 232; contradiction and, 191; ignorance and, 32, 232; *isshin* and, 195, 212, *213*, 224; Lassaw's notes on, 57; Mahāyāna Buddhism and, 182–185; *munen* and, 208–209, *208*, 210; original enlightenment and, 31, 33, 212, 218, 224; perfect enlightenment and, 207, 208; potential movement and, 26, 195, 197, 203–204, 210–211, 212, 216–217, 225; pure consciousness and, 219–220; stages of Mind and, 195–196; storehouse consciousness and, 29, 184, 197; suchness and, 30, 303. *See also* bifurcation of Mind

absolute present (*sokkon*; *jijin*): consciousness and, 139, 141, 148, 149; duality and, 137; Eckhart on, 151–159; Eckhart's two eyes and, 157–159; enlightenment and, 161, 163–164, 168; freedom and, 286–287; intellect and, 140, 229; intuition and, 134–135; *mondō* and, 167–168, 229–230; *munen* and, 209, *209*; Nirvāṇa and, 147; past and future and, 168–170; practicality of Zen Buddhism and, 161–162; *prajñā* and, 34; *prajñā*-intuition and, 134, 141; *praṇidhāna* and, 170, 258, 260, 280–281; space and, 134, 137, 140, 158, 168, 170, 171; stages of enlightenment and, 209–210, 228–230, 335*n*12; *yū* and, 142–143; as zero consciousness, 149–151, 152, 159–161, 170

absolute subject, 4

ākāśa, 281

Aki Dining Room, 46

Akizuki Ryōmin, 10

ālaya, 205, 225, *225*, 227–228, 231

ālayavijñāna (storehouse consciousness), 26, 29, 30, 184, 197, *205*, 206–208, 225
Althusser, Louis, 62
American Buddhist Academy, 45
Amitābha (Amida) Buddha, 35, 57, 85, 278
ananta, 244
anantagocara (*kyō*; *jing*), 244, 245, 336*n*2
animals, 75–76, 81, 97, 98, 105, 119, 144
Antinoff, Steve, 39
apada, 243–244
aporia, 162
approximate enlightenment, 198, 202, 207
Araki Eikichi, 47
Arendt, Hannah, 38
Aron, Raymond, 62
asceticism, 73–74
Aśvaghoṣa, 27, 157, 173. *See also* *Awakening of Faith in the Mahāyāna*
Ataka Yakichi, 11, 16
ātman. *See* self
attachment (*zhiqu*; *shūshu*), 171, 197
Auerbach, Ellen, 42, 43
Auerbach, Walter, 42
Augustine, St., 169, 179, 333*n*17
awakening. *See* Buddha's enlightenment; enlightenment; stages of enlightenment
Awakening of Faith in the Mahāyāna (**Mahāyānaśraddhotpādaśastra*; *Dasheng qixin lun*) (Aśvaghoṣa), 173, 320*n*56; Columbia seminar content and, 3, 20, 25–27, 29, 30, 31–32. *See also* Mind; original enlightenment; stages of enlightenment

Baizhang Huaihai, 36, 238, 279
Banzan Hōshaku, 336*n*18
Barrett, John D., Jr., 42
Bataille, Georges, 62
Beauvoir, Simone de, 22, 102
becoming: creativity and, 260; in Flower Garland Sutra, 302–303; intuition and, 233; *karuṇā* and, 34, 289; Nirvāṇa and, 299; *pariṇāmanā* and, 301; *prajñā*-intuition and, 117; question/questioner and, 223; senses and, 205; *shako* and, 302; time and, 136, 169, 222, 280. *See also* becoming/being; birth-and-death; impermanence
becoming/being: absolute present and, 142, 170; absolute vs. relative self and, 101; bifurcation of Mind and, 224; intellect and, 223; *praṇidhāna* and, 289, 292, 300; substance and, 192; suchness and, 4, 303; time and, 222
being. *See* becoming/being
Bhagavad-Gītā, 201
bhūtakoṭi (*jitsu sai*; *shiji*), 248
bifurcation of Mind, 26, 29–30; *Awakening of Faith* on, 26, 182, 183–185, 195, 204; *munen* and, 209; *praṇidhāna* and, 246; pureness and, 217; question/

questioner and, 223–224; stages of enlightenment and, 208–209, *208*, 212–213, 216, 222–224; storehouse consciousness and, 26, 30, 225; time and, 222
birth (*jāti*; *sheng*; *shō*), 196, 197
birth-and-death (*saṃsāra*; *xin shengmie*): *Awakening of Faith* on, 182; becoming and, 30; bifurcation of Mind and, 26, 30, 182, 183, 184–185, 195, 204; as Buddha's koan, 22–23, 72, 74, 78, 85; ego and, 93, 145–146; emancipation from, 70, 71, 97; everyday experience and, 161; *karma* and, 96–97; question/questioner and, 147; time and, 157
Blackham, H. J., 22, 102–103, 231–232
bodhicitta, 293
Bodhidharma, 106–108, 109–111, 114, 168, 327*nn*8–9
bodhisattva ideal, 176, 269. *See also karuṇā*
bodhisattvas, 200, 202
Bollingen Foundation and Series, 41–42
Brown, Carolyn, 2, 40–41, 43
Brown, Earle, 42, 43
buddhahṛdaya, 67
buddha nature (*buddhatā*), 226–227, 275
Buddha's enlightenment, 25, 71–72; centrality of enlightenment and, 71; creator and, 85, 86–87; dissolution and, 85–86; duality and, 72; early Buddhist accounts of, 90–91; expressions of, 85–90; fellow beings and, 83–84; Flower Garland Buddhism and, 1, 220; infinite/finite and, 72–73, 90; intellect and, 73, 74–75, 76; *karuṇā* and, 131; moral discipline and, 73–74, 76; Nirvāṇa and, 87, 88–89; passivity and, 82; personal experience and, 87–88; *prajñā* and, 115, 119, 131; *praṇidhāna* and, 99; pure experience and, 82–83; question/questioner and, 74–77, 80, 132; *samādhi* and, 23, 77, 78–79; *sarvasattva* and, 71; self and, 70–71; sense experience and, 79–80; stages of, 77–79; time and, 133; tracklessness and, 89–90; will and, 3–4, 86; Zen practice and, 22–24
Buddhist meditation practices, 57–58, 60. *See also dhyāna*
Buddhist Philosophy and Its Effects on the Life and Thought of the Japanese People (Suzuki), 12
Bugbee, Henry Greenwood, Jr., 44, 51, 58–59
bushidō, 12, 48

Cage, John, 2; artistic community and, 43; artistic work of, 55–56; on Flower Garland Buddhism and, 56–57; psychoanalysts and, 41; seminar experiences, 3, 21, 49, 53–55; on Suzuki's teaching style, 17, 18–19, 50, 56

Cambridge Buddhist Association, 61
Cangxi Lin, 341*n*34
Carus, Paul, 9, 24, 26
caryā (*gyō*), 281
Cassard, Frances, 7
causation, 227–228, 231, 287
Cavell, Stanley, 323*n*91
change (*jarā*; *yi*; *i*), 196, 198, 220, 222–223, 224, 334–335*n*9. *See also* impermanence
Changsha Jingcen (Chōsa Keishin), 81, 338–339*n*20
Chengguan, 28
Chin the Elder, 215–216, 221
Christianity: absolute present and, 154, 156, 157; *anantagocara* and, 336*n*2; consciousness and, 141, 149; creativity and, 258–259; creator and, 86, 97, 110, 178–179, 303; desire to help and, 277; everyday experience and, 161–162; faith and, 70; grace and, 127; morality and, 256; *munen* and, 210; parents and, 249n; *pariṇāmanā* and, 295; personality in, 177–178; prayer in, 255, 257; Pure Land and, 166; risk and, 121; salvation in, 261; sin in, 176, 240; unconsciousness and, 101; vicarious atonement and, 294. *See also* Eckhart, Meister; God
citta (*xin*; *shin*) (mind; consciousness), 149, 182, 303
clairvoyance, 119–120
Claremont Colleges, 15
the Club, 43
Coe, Robert, 43
Cold War, 47, 48
collective unconscious, 228
Columbia seminars, 1–4; artists and, 42–43, 57; attendee motivations, 50–51, 52–53, 54–55; challenging nature of, 49, 56; content of, 20–21; cultural context of, 37–38; dynamic nature of, 62–63; early suggestions for, 11; funding of, 16–17; influence on Bugbee, 58–60; interlaced Western material in, 21–22; Japanese culture fascination and, 47–48, 61; Japanese/Japanese American community and, 44–45; Kapleau's experience of, 60–61; Lassaw's notes on, 49–50, 57–58; manuscript origins, 4–5, 6–8; philosophy field and, 43–44; postwar Japan meetings and, 39–40; psychoanalysts and, 40–41, 321*n*73; spiritual seekers and, 38–39, 54–55; Suzuki's teaching style and, 17–20, 50–52, 56
compassion. *See karuṇā*
Confucianism, 114, 185, 195, 276–277, 285
consciousness: Absolute Mind and, 232; absolute present and, 139, 141, 148, 149; active nature of, 98–99; creativity and, 143–144; duality and, 137–138; enlightenment and, 123, 126,

150, 166, 244, 258, 282; enlightenment in appearance and, 201; experience and, 138–139, 141, 149; infinite, 244, 246, 256, 336*n*2; *karma* and, 199–200; *mondō* and, 109–110; *nen* as unit of, 208, 210; perfect enlightenment and, 202, 203, 206; personality and, 100; *praṇidhāna* and, 289; pure, 217–220; question/questioner and, 140, 147–148; rejection of, 101; senses and, 205; stages of enlightenment and, 215, 217–219, 231–232; time and, 148–149, 156, 159, 202n; will and, 282. *See also* storehouse consciousness
contradiction, 185–189, 191, 239, 289–290
Crane, Cathalene Parker, 16, 17, 319*n*39
Crane, Charles Richard, 11, 12, 16, 321*n*73
Crane, Cornelius, 16–17, 37
creativity, 143–144

"Dada and Zen" (Ross), 54
Dahui, 332*n*10
daiyū (*dayong*), 258, 259, 260
Daiyū genzen, 258–259
Danto, Arthur, 2, 44, 62
Danyuan, 251
Daoism, 276, 285
Daśabhūmika (*Shidi jing*; *Jūjikyō*), 27, 321*n*63
Dasui Fazhen, 343*n*40
death. *See* birth-and-death; impermanence
de Kooning, Elaine, 43
de Kooning, Willem, 43
delusion, 31, 196, 203–204
DeMartino, Richard, 17, 39, 49, 322*n*82
dependent origination (*jūjū mujin*), 228, 336*n*21
despair, 241–242, 246
Devadatta, 327*n*7
Dhammapada, 3, 85–86, 87n, 88–89, 118, 126, 145, 243–244
dharma, 28, 108, 110–111, 157–158, 178, 182. *See also* suchness; Three Marks of Existence
dhyāna (meditation), 67–68, 78n, 115, 117
Diamond Sutra (*Kongōkyō*), 57, 168
Dienes, Sari, 38, 43
differentiation. *See* bifurcation of Mind
Dipaṃkara Buddha, 253–254
discrimination, 198
divine consciousness/unconsciousness, 259–260, 266
Dōshō (Daosheng), 275
drugs, 79n
duality: Buddha's awakening and, 72; in Chinese culture, 276–277; consciousness and, 137–138; ethics and, 242; human situation and, 283; language and, 216; parents and, 249n; sin and, 176, 241; time and, 139–140
Duchamps, Marcel, 38
Duofu, 162

Eastern Buddhist, 11
East-West Philosophers' Conference, 14
Eckhart, Meister, 21; on absolute present, 151–159; on agent in the soul, 185–188; contradiction and, 185–189, 239; on enlightenment, 163; on godhead, 184; on spark, 164; training and, 165; on two eyes, 157–159, 176, 178, 179; on will, 152–153, 178
ego (*manas*): birth-and-death and, 93, 145–146; moral discipline and, 73, 74; senses and, 167; stages of enlightenment and, *205*, 206, 207. *See also* egolessness; self
egolessness (non-*ātman*), 144, 145–146, 147, 201
Eightfold Path, 118
Einstein, Albert, 270
emancipation, 68, 70
Emerson, Ralph Waldo, 201
emptiness (*śūnyatā*; *kong*): *li*/*shi* and, 28; *prajñā* and, 300, 301, *301*; stages of Mind and, 195–196; subject/object identification and, 300; Zen Buddhism and, 181. *See also* Absolute Mind
Engakuji monastery (Kita-Kamakura), 9, 13
enlightenment: absolute present and, 161, 163–164, 168; *aporia* and, 162–163; *Awakening of Faith* on, 31–32; *bodhicitta* and, 293; centrality of, 71; consciousness and, 123, 126, 150, 166, 244, 258, 282; contradiction and, 289–290; despair and, 241–242, 246; drugs and, 79n; as experience, 70–71, 121–122, 124–125, 132; fellow beings and, 83–84, 85; freedom and, 285; Huineng and, 238; intuition and, 127; *karuṇā* and, 141; knowing-seeing and, 290–291; need for re-experience and, 99–100; objective verification and, 139; *prajñā* and, 115, 132; *prajñā*-intuition and, 122; pure experience and, 82–83; Pure Land (Shin) Buddhism and, 85, 166, 167, 278, 295–296; question/questioner and, 141; sense experiences and, 79–81, 111, 126, 127, 161, 167, 327*n*8; sin and, 241; as stage of awakening, 30; subject/object and, 162, 163; suchness and, 160–161; Suzuki's *satori* experience, 23–25; time and, 133; totality and, 144; tracklessness and, 89–90, 243–245; training and, 164–166; transmission and, 107–108; unconsciousness and, 127–128; zero consciousness and, 160–161, 331*n*4. *See also* Buddha's enlightenment; original enlightenment; stages of enlightenment
enlightenment in appearance, 198, 200–202, 207
en-soi (in itself), 22

Eranos Lectures, 41–42, 45–46
Essays on Zen Buddhism (Suzuki), 11
ethics, 242–244, *243*, 245–246, 285
everyday experience, 127–131, 193–195, 247. *See also* practicality of Zen Buddhism
Existentialism, 22
experience: consciousness and, 138–139, 141, 149; enlightenment as, 70–71, 121–122, 124–125, 132; enlightenment as personal, 87–88; everyday, 127–131, 193–194, 247; *karuṇā* and, 132; philosophy and, 103–104, 121–122, 139; pure, 82–83; vs. science, 102–103; Zen Buddhism and, 235–236

face to face encounter, 18–19
faith: Christianity and, 70; intuition and, 113, 121; *prajñā* and, 120; *praṇidhāna* and, 248; sin and, 240, 241, 248
Fayan, 114, 328–329*n*17
Fayan (Hōgen) school, 181
Fazang, 20, 26, 28, 181, 196, 197
Feldman, Morton, 40–41
Fields, Rick, 321*n*73
first awakening (*shijue*), 33–34, 174, 175, 176, 177–178, 179–180, 236–237, *236*
Flower Garland (Kegon/Huayan) Buddhism: *Awakening of Faith* and, 26; Buddha's enlightenment and, 1, 220; Cage's notes on, 56–57; Columbia seminar content and, 20; dependent origination in, 228, 336*n*21; development of Chinese Buddhism and, 34; importance of Flower Garland Sutra in, 315*n*3; interpenetration in, 4, 28–29; postwar writing on, 15–16; *praṇidhāna* and, 34–35, 297–299; Zen Buddhism and, 25, 28, 181. *See also* Flower Garland Sutra
Flower Garland Sutra (*Avataṃsaka Sūtra*; *Huayan jing*; *Kegon gyō*): Absolute and multiplicity in, 28–29; becoming and, 302–303; bifurcation of Mind and, 236–237, *236*; on Buddha's enlightenment, 220; Columbia seminar content and, 3, 25; development of Chinese Buddhism and, 28, 236; Fayan (Hōgen) school and, 181; on first awakening, 236–237, *236*; *Gandavyūha,* 25, 27, 35, 320*n*56, 321*n*63; on ignorance, 293; importance of, 315*n*3; on Indra's net, 4; on *li* and *shi,* 28; *mondō* and, 32, 35, 221; postwar peace and, 27; on *prajñā,* 300–301; on *praṇidhāna,* 272–273, 281–282; Zen Buddhism and, 236
Ford Foundation, 47
freedom, 22, 72, 84, 264–265, 284–288
Friess, Horace L., 17, 19–20, 44, 49
Froebe-Kapteyn, Olga, 41
Fromm, Erich, 2, 41, 48–49

Gakushuin University, 10

Gandavyūha (*Ryu fajie bin*; *Nyū hokkai bon*), 25, 27, 35, 320*n*56, 321*n*63. *See also* Flower Garland Sutra

Gate of Hell (*Jogokumon*), 47

Gensha, 167

genzen (*xianqian*), 260

Gilpatric, Chadbourne, 14, 18

Gimello, Robert, 28

God: absence in Buddhism, 177; absolute present and, 151–152; absolute vs. relative self and, 98; Bugbee on, 59–60; consciousness and, 100, 109, 144; contradiction and, 186–187, 188–189; as creator, 97, 106–107, 110, 134, 138, 151–152, 233, 258, 285–286, 298, 303; duality and, 178; Eckhart's two eyes and, 178; ego and, 145–146, 147; Incarnation and, 121; as Mind, 195; philosophy and, 70; *prajñā* and, 179–180; *praṇidhāna* and, 257–258; question/questioner and, 76; risk and, 121; sin and, 240; suchness and, 184, 185, 189; will and thought and, 152–153. *See also* Christianity; godhead

godhead, 86, 174, 175, 177, 178, 184, 288

Goodrich, Carrington, 16, 17

Graves, Morris, 54

Gregory, Peter, 32

guṇa, 170

Gurdjieff movement, 42, 51

Guston, Phillip, 2, 43

Gutei (Juzhi), 129–131

Hagakure, 48

Hakuin Ekaku, 53, 327*n*4

Harp of Burma, The (*Biruma no tategoto*), 47

Harte, B. Joan, 41, 322*n*82

Hasegawa Saburo, 43

Heard, Gerald, 39

Hedstrom, Matthew, 38–39

Hegel, Georg Wilhelm Friedrich, 62, 102

Hegeler, Edward, 9

Hengyue Nantaisi Zang, 341*n*31

"here now". *See* absolute present

Herrigel, Eugen, 48

Hīnayāna Buddhism, 71, 131–132

Hiranuma Kiichiro, 40

Hirose Seiichi, 45

Hiroshima and Nagasaki bombings, 48

Hisamatsu Shin'ichi, 21, 61

Hongren, 237

Horney, Karen, 16, 41, 319*n*39, 322*n*82

huatou (*watō*), 321*n*70

Huayan Buddhism. *See* Flower Garland (Kegon/Huayan) Buddhism

Huijiao, 114, 328–329*n*17

Huineng (Enō), 35–36, 115, 237–239

Huizhen Guangwu, 342*n*35

hungry ghost ritual, 262–263

Hu Shih, 27

Huxley, Aldous, 39

ignorance (*avidyā*): Absolute Mind and, 32, 232; consciousness and, 149; as disturbance, 177; first awakening and, 33, 34, 175, 176; knowing-seeing and, 291; original enlightenment and, 33–34, 174–175, 288, 293, 302; *praṇidhāna* and, 288, 293–294; stages of enlightenment and, 174–175, 198, 200, 207, 212, 214–215, 232, 293
Imakita Kōsen, 9, 40
impermanence (*anityatā*; *mie*; *metsu*), 144, 145, 146–147, 196–198
Incarnation, 121
Indian philosophy, 70
infinite/finite, 72–74, 90, 116–117, 135–136, 239–240
innen, 227–228, 231
Institute of Current World Affairs, 11
intellect: absolute present and, 140, 229; bifurcation of Mind and, 223; Buddha's enlightenment and, 73, 74–75, 76; Eckhart on, 178; enlightenment in appearance and, 200–201, 207; language and, 81, 185; limits of, 126; *mondō* and, 226–227; *prajñā* and, 116, 117–118, 135, 145; question/questioner and, 223; self and, 96; stages of enlightenment and, 223
interpenetration (*shishi wuai*; *jiji muge*), 4, 28–29, 35, 72, 118–119, 297, 351. *See also* subject/object
Introduction to Zen Buddhism, An (Suzuki), 11
intuition, 127, 134–135, 231, 233. *See also* *prajñā*-intuition
Inward Morning, The (Bugbee), 58–59
Isan (Weishan Lingyou), 125–126, 192–194, 334*n*8
isshin, 195, 212, *213*, 224
Iwamura, Jane, 61

James, William, 10, 21
Japanese-American internment, 44, 45
Japanese/Japanese-American community, 44–47
Japanese war role, 12–14, 40, 48, 318*n*31
Japan Society, 47
Jaspers, Karl, 22
jiyū (*ziyou*), 284
Jōdo Shin (True Pure Land) Buddhism. *See* Pure Land (Shin) Buddhism
Johns, Jasper, 43
Jung, Carl, 41
just this (*tada shako*) (*zhi zhege*), 245, 302

Kalama, Alara, 72
Kant, Immanuel, 228
Kaplan, Abraham, 44, 323*n*91
Kapleau, Philip, 39, 40, 60–61
karma: birth-and-death and, 96–97; freedom and, 286–287; impermanence and, 198; *pariṇāmanā* and, 294–295; stages of enlightenment and, 199–200, 225; subjectivity and, 288

karuṇā (compassion): *bodhicitta* and, 293; Buddha's enlightenment and, 131; Eckhart's two eyes and, 176; enlightenment and, 141; first awakening and, 175, 177–178, 236–237, *236*; in Flower Garland Buddhism, 34–35; ignorance and, 174; original enlightenment and, 33–34; *praṇidhāna* and, 246, 279, 281; in Pure Land (Shin) Buddhism, 131–132; Samantabhadra Bodhisattva and, 34, 35, 176, 236, *236*, 281; self and, 101; stages of enlightenment and, 217; suchness and, 300, *301*; in Zen Buddhism, 35–36, 237, 247
Kegon/Huayan Buddhism. *See* Flower Garland (Kegon/ Huayan) Buddhism
Kelman, Harold, 322*n*82
Keyserling, Hermann von, 12
Kichijōten (Śrī Mahādevi/Mahāśri), 327*n*5
Kierkegaard, Søren, 22, 121, 239, 240, 241
knowing-seeing, 290–291
kōan (*gong'an*): Buddha's enlightenment and, 22–23; *huatou* and, 321*n*70; infinite/ finite and, 135–136; stages of enlightenment and, 215; Suzuki's Zen practice and, 23–24
Kojève, Alexandre, 62
kokū (*xukong*), 269–270
Kokuanten (Kalārātri), 327*n*5
Kondo Akihisa, 41, 322*n*82
Kyōgen (Xiangyan Zhixian), 23, 25, 79, 125–127, 161
Kyōzan (Yangshan), 192–194, 334*n*8
Kyōzan Ejaku, 214–215. *See also* Kyōzan

Lacan, Jacques, 62
Lalitavistara Sutra (*Puyaojing*), 326*n*5
language: Mind and, 185; *prajñā*-intuition and, 119, 135; senses and, 80–81; stages of enlightenment and, 216, 219, 221–222; time and, 136; *yū* and, 143. *See also* intellect
Laṅkāvatāra Sūtra (Ryōgakyō), 57, 104, 119, 181, 343*n*43
Laozi, 114
Larson, Kay, 43, 54
Larson, Lois, 43
Lassaw, Ibram, 43, 49–50, 57–58
Legend of Musashi, The (*Miyamoto Musashi*), 47
Lévi-Strauss, Claude, 38
liberty. *See* freedom
li/shi, 28
Living by Zen (Suzuki), 59
Loft Generation, 42–43
Long, Lois, 43
love. *See karuṇā*
Low, Jackson Mac, 43

Mahāparinirvāṇa Sutra, 275
Mahāyāna Buddhism, 71, 132, 173, 181, 182–183, 294. *See also* *Awakening of Faith in the Mahāyāna*
Majjhima Nikāya, 86–87

Making of American Buddhism, The (Mitchell), 46–47
Mañjuśri Bodhisattva (Monju; Wenshu), 34, 35, 36, 176, 236, *236*, 237, 250
manovijñāna (*ishiki*) (mental-perception), 204, 205, *205*, 206, 207
Manual of Zen Buddhism (Suzuki), 11
Manura, 233
Matsumi Kanemitsu, 43
meditation (*dhyāna*), 67–68, 78n, 115, 117. *See also* Buddhist meditation practices
Mellon, Mary, 42
Mellon, Mary Conover, 41
Mellon, Paul, 41
Menand, Louis, 22
Merton, Thomas, 39
Mexican Psychoanalytic Society, 49
Mill, John Stuart, 284
Mind, 25–26, *196*; contradiction and, 185–188; everyday experience and, 193–195; godhead and, 184; manifestation and, 195–197; stages of, 196–198; substance and, 189–193, 195–196; Will and, 26. *See also* Absolute Mind; bifurcation of Mind
Mitchell, Elsie, 61
Mitchell, Scott, 46–47
mokṣa, 68, 326*n*1
mondō (*wenda*; Zen dialogues), 111–114; absolute present and, 167–168, 229–230; animals and, 105, 119; *Awakening of Faith* and, 32; Bodhidharma and, 106–108, 109–111, 114, 168, 327*nn*8–9; complementary, 192–193; consciousness and, 109–110; ethics and, 245–246; everyday experience and, 105, 128–131, 162, 193–195; faith and, 113; Flower Garland Sutra and, 32, 35, 221; freedom and, 286; ignorance and, 214–215; infinite/finite and, 135–136; manual labor and, 105, 279–280; perfect enlightenment and, 204; practicality of Zen Buddhism and, 114, 125, 328–329*n*17; *praṇidhāna* and, 248–254, 261–262, 338–339*n*20; self (*ātman*) and, 251–252; stages of enlightenment and, 213–216, 226–227, 229–230; substance and, 189–193; time and, 253–254
moral discipline, 73–74, 117
Morris, Charles W., 14
Mu koan, 24
munen (*wunian*): Absolute Mind and, 208–209, *208*, 210; consciousness and, 282; Huineng on, 239; *praṇidhāna* and, 259; stages of enlightenment and, 203, 207, 208–209, *208*, 210–211, 217–218; time and, 156; zero consciousness and, 149–150
mushin (*wuxin*), 149, 239, 259, 282
Myō-e Shōnin, 257
Mysticism: Christian and Buddhist (Suzuki), 21

Nanking Massacre (1938), 13
nanso (soft butter visualization), 53

Nazi Germany, 12

Needleman, Jacob, 51–52, 61

nen (*nian*) (unit of consciousness), 208–209, *208*, *209*, 210, 213–214. *See also munen*

New Thought movement, 10

New World of Philosophy (Kaplan), 44

New York Buddhist Church, 44, 45

Niaoke, 257

Niebhur, Reinhold, 59

Nirvāṇa, 87, 88–89, 144, 146, 147, 224, 291

nonego. *See* egolessness

nonenlightenment. *See* ignorance

nonobstruction (*lishi wuai*; *riji muge*), 28, 35, 299

Norman, Dorothy, 2, 42, 43, 50

no-self, 144, 145–146, 147

Nyogen Senzaki, 13

occultism, 42

Okamura, Frank, 45

Okamura, Mihoko, 4, 5, 45–46, 49, 50–51, 322*n*82

Okamura, Reiko, 5, 45, 46

Okamura, Toshimi Nishikubo, 45, 46

One Mind. *See* Absolute Mind

On Liberty (Mill), 284

Open Court Publishing, 9–10, 26

original enlightenment (*benjue*), 173–180; Absolute Mind and, 31, 33, 212, 218, 224; as devoid of characteristics, 173–174; duality and, 175, 177–178; Eckhart's two eyes and, 176, 178, 179; first awakening and, 33–34, 176; ignorance and, 33–34, 174–175, 288, 293, 302; *prajñā* and, 33–34, 174, 180; pureness and, 217; stages of enlightenment and, 173–175, 211–213, *213*

Ōtani Kōshō, 322*n*82

Otani University, 10, 13

Our Inner Conflicts (Horney), 17

Pantheon Books, 41

parāvṛtti (turning back), 218

pariṇāmanā (*ekō*; *huixiang*), 171, 294–296, 301, 302

Pavia, Phillip, 43

Pearlman, Ellen, 43

perennialism, 10, 21

perfect enlightenment, 198, 202–203, 206–207, 208

personality, 100, *100*, 132, 167, 177–178

philosophy, 69–70, 103–104, 121–122, 138, 139

Platform Sutra of the Sixth Patriarch (*Rokuso dangyō*), 115, 238–239

postwar Japan, 27, 39–40

pour-soi (for itself), 22

practicality of Zen Buddhism: absolute present and, 161–162; manual labor and, 35–36, 37, 105, 238, 247, 267, 279; *mondō* and, 114, 125, 328–329*n*17; *praṇidhāna* and, 35–36, 37, 254–255, 263–264, 265–268, 275–276, 279–280, 339*n*24, 340*n*26; subject/object identification and, 300

prajñā (wisdom), 85; absolute present and, 34; Buddha's

enlightenment and, 115, 119, 131; centrality of, 178; Eckhart's two eyes and, 176; emptiness and, 300, *301*; enlightenment and, 115, 132; etymology of, 329–330*n*3; experience and, 141; faith and, 120; first awakening and, 33, 175, 178, 179–180, 236–237, *236*; infinite/finite and, 116–117; intellect and, 117–118, 135, 145; Mañjuśri Bodhisattva and, 34, 35, 36, 176, 236, *236*; original enlightenment and, 33–34, 174, 180; *praṇidhāna* and, 279; stages of enlightenment and, 217; suchness and, 117, 300; thought and, 153; Three Marks of Existence and, 145; wholeness and, 115–116. *See also* *prajñā*-intuition

prajñā-intuition, 115–121; absolute present and, 134, 141; becoming and, 117; clairvoyance and, 119–120; as discipline, 117–118; emptiness and, 301; enlightenment and, 122; faith and, 241; infinity and, 117, 270; interpenetration and, 118–119; language and, 119, 135; question/questioner and, 132, 223–224; speculative reason and, 120–121; wholeness and, 299–300

Prajñā Parāmitā Sutra (*Hannyakyō*), 57, 181, 236

praṇidhāna (*hongan*; *benyuan*): absolute present and, 170, 258, 260, 280–281; all beings and, 296–297; Bodhidharma question and, 107; bodhisattva ideal and, 291–293; Buddha's enlightenment and, 99; causation and, 287; consciousness and, 289; creativity and, 258–259, 260; divine unconsciousness and, 259–260; everyday experience and, 247; Flower Garland Buddhism and, 34–35, 297–299; Flower Garland Sutra on, 272–273, 281–282; four vows, 35, 268–272; freedom and, 264–265, 287; human situation and, 280, 282–283; hungry ghost ritual and, 262–263; ignorance and, 288, 293–294; individuality and, 283–284, 287; infinite nature of, 248, 255, 256, 257, 268–269, 270–272, 279, 281–282, 338*n*16; *karuṇā* and, 246, 279, 281; *mondō* and, 248–254, 261–262, 338–339*n*20; morality and, 256; *pariṇāmanā* and, 171, 294–296, 301, 302; personality and, 297; practicality of Zen Buddhism and, 35–36, 37, 254–255, 263–264, 265–268, 275–276, 279–280, 339*n*24, 340*n*26; prayer and, 255–258, 281; in Pure Land (Shin) Buddhism, 246–247, 254; as purposeless, 281, 289; suchness and, 300–301; ten vows and, 269–270; tracklessness and, 301; will and, 153, 282; *yū* and, 258; in Zen Buddhism, 35–37, 246–247, 268

Pratyekabuddhas, 200

prayer, 255–258
precepts, 201–202, 243
present. *See* absolute present
pṛthagjana, 199
psychoanalysts, 40–41, 48–49
psychology, 189
pure consciousness, 217–220
Pure Land, 57, 85, 243, 261, 278, 295, 302
Pure Land (Shin) Buddhism: enlightenment and, 85, 166, 167, 278, 295–296; ethics and, 243; *karuṇā* and, 35, 131–132; other power in, 277–278; *pariṇāmanā* and, 295–296; *praṇidhāna* and, 35, 246–247, 254; *Sukhāvatīvyūhasūtra* and, 291; Suzuki's American Buddhist Academy lectures on, 44–45; tracklessness and, 302
pūrvapraṇidhāna, 247

Quanzhou, 339*n*24
question/questioner: bifurcation of Mind and, 223–224; Buddha's enlightenment and, 74–77, 80, 132; consciousness and, 140, 147–148; enlightenment and, 141; *prajñā*-intuition and, 132, 223–224

Radhakrishnan, 244, 284, 285
Rakan Oshō, 23, 25, 79, 124, 166
Rambova, Natacha, 42
Rashomon, 47
Rauschenberg, Robert, 43
Record of Rinzai, 20
"Record of the Transmission of the Lamp [Compiled in] the Jingde Era," 20
Reinhardt, Ad, 2, 43
Religious Book Club, 39
Rinzai (Linji), 106, 107, 109, 110, 111–113, 167, 327*n*10
Rinzai (Linji) School, 258
Rioch, Margaret, 2
risk, 120–121
Rochester Zen Center, 40, 60
Rockefeller, John D., 3rd, 47
Rockefeller Foundation, 14–15, 47
Ross, Nancy Wilson, 42, 54
Rossetti, Christina, 21, 94–96

Sadler, Arthur W., 7, 17
Śākyamuni. *See* Buddha's enlightenment
samādhi: Buddha's enlightenment and, 23, 77, 78–79; difficulty of understanding, 68–69; Eightfold Path and, 118; interpenetration and, 118–119; Suzuki's experience of, 24–25; vs. Zen Buddhism, 68–69
Samantabhadra Bodhisattva (Fugen; Puxian), 34, 35, 36, 176, 236–237, *236*, 269, 272, 281
Sāṃkhya school, 72
saṃsāra, 22, 86, 204–205, 224. *See also* birth-and-death
Samurai, 47
samurai. See bushidō
San Francisco Zen Center, 53
Śāriputra, 171
Sartre, Jean-Paul, 22, 62, 283

sarvadharma, 178
sarvasattva, 71, 178, 179, 182, 268, 303
Sasaki, Ruth Fuller, 11
satori: *prajñā* and, 134; stages of enlightenment and, 216; Suzuki's experience of, 23–25; time and, 133. *See also* enlightenment
Saunders, Kenneth, 11
Schmidt, Leigh, 39
Schneider, Herbert W., 17
Schopenhauer, Arthur, 86, 282
Schweitzer, Albert, 284–285
science, 102–103, 271
Sekitō (Shitou), 189–191
self (*ātman*): absolute vs. relative, 98, 99, 100–101; Buddha's enlightenment and, 70–71; as burden, 94–96; compassion and, 101; desire for, 93–94, 97–98; intellect and, 96; *jiyū* and, 284, 285; Pure Land (Shin) Buddhism and, 277–278; Zen Buddhism and, 248, 251–252, 277–278
self-nature (*svabhāva*), 233
senses: enlightenment and, 79–81, 111, 126, 127, 161, 167, 327*n*8; limits of, 270; stages of enlightenment and, 205, *205*, 206–207
Seven-Storey Mountain (Merton), 39
shako, 168, 170, 302
Shaku Sōen, 9, 10, 24
Sharf, Robert, 13
Shin Buddhism. *See* Pure Land (Shin) Buddhism
Shinran, 291
Shishuang Xingkong, 251
Shizang Huiju, 340*n*30
Shobi (Chuwei of Qianzhou), 214–215
Shōma, 261–262
Śikṣānanda, 26, 320*n*56
sin, 176, 240–241, 248
Six Existentialist Thinkers (Blackham), 22
sō, 172
Society for International Cultural Relations (Kokusai Bunka Shinkōkai), 12
Soper, Alexander, 48
space: absolute present and, 134, 137, 140, 158, 168, 170, 171; breaking of, 131*n*4, 160; *prajñā* and, 117; *praṇidhāna* and, 269–270, 281
speculative reason, 120–121
Spinoza, Baruch, 183n
Śrāvakas, 200
stages of enlightenment (*fanliu siwei*; *honru shi'i*), 30–31, 33–34, 198–233, 334*n*2, 335*n*10; Absolute Mind (*zhenru*; *shinnyo*) and, *208*; absolute present and, 209–210, 228–230, 335*n*12; *ālaya* and, 206–207, 225, *225*, 227–228, 231; approximate enlightenment, 198, 202, 207; bifurcation of Mind and, 208–209, *208*, 212–213, 216, 222–224; buddha nature and, 226–227; causation and, 227–228, 231; consciousness

stages of enlightenment (*continued*) and, 215, 217–219, 231–232; enlightenment in appearance, 198, 200–202, 207; ignorance and, 174–175, 198, 200, 207, 212, 214–215, 232, 293; intuition and, 231, 233; *karma* and, 199–200, 224–226; *mondō* and, 213–216, 225–227, 229–230; *munen* and, 203, 207, 208–209, *208*, 210–211, 217–218; *nen* and, 208–209, *208*, *209*; original enlightenment and, 173–175, 211–213, *213*; perfect enlightenment, 198, 202–203, 206–207, 208; potential movement in Mind and, 203–204, 216–217, 225; pure consciousness and, 217–220; senses and, 205, *205*, 206–207; storehouse consciousness and, 206–208; will and, 216–217

storehouse consciousness (*ālayavijñāna*), 26, 29, 30, 184, 197, *205*, 206–208, 225

Stunkard, Albert, 2–3, 17, 19, 39, 40, 41

subjectivity (*smṛti*), 199, 288

subject/object: absolute present and, 137, 139, 148, 161; approximate enlightenment and, 202; Buddha's enlightenment and, 73, 74, 76, 78, 80, 82, 89; consciousness and, 138, 148; enlightenment and, 162, 163; enlightenment in appearance and, 201; ethics and, 242, *243*; ignorance and, 200, 232; intellect and, 96; language and, 80; *mondō* and, 114, 214, 215, 249, 276; objective verification and, 139; perfect enlightenment and, 203, 208; practicality of Zen Buddhism and, 300; senses and, 205; stages of Mind and, 197, 198; storehouse consciousness and, 207; suchness and, 118; time and, 140; will and, 216. *See also* duality; interpenetration; question/questioner; *samādhi*

substance, 189–193

suchness (*tathatā*; *xin zhenru*): Absolute Mind and, 30, 303; awakening and, 31; *Awakening of Faith* on, 182; becoming/being and, 4, 303; bifurcation of Mind and, 26, 29–30, 182, 183–185, 195, 204; enlightenment and, 160–161; *karuṇā* and, 300, *301*; perfect enlightenment and, 203; *prajñā* and, 117, 300; *praṇidhāna* and, 300–301; *samādhi* and, 118; *shako* and, 302; stages of enlightenment and, 199, 203; zero consciousness and, 161. *See also* Absolute Mind; bifurcation of Mind

Sukhāvatīvyūhasūtra, 291

śūnyatā. *See* emptiness

supreme enlightenment. *See* perfect enlightenment

Suzuki, Beatrice Erskine Lane, 10–11, 13

Suzuki, Daisetz Teitarō: background and education, 8–9; criticisms of, 21, 27, 48, 62; groups meeting with, 39–40, 322*n*82; health issues, 40; Japanese war role and, 12–14, 48; marriage, 10; Open Court Publishing employment, 9–10, 26; postwar career, 14–15; *satori* experience of, 23–25; teaching style of, 17–20, 50–52, 56; writing of, 10–12, 13; Zen practice of, 8, 9, 10, 22–24
Sze, Mai-mai, 42, 43

taṇhā (craving), 86
Tanka, 243
Taraknath Das Foundation, 15
tathāgatagarbha (matrix of the buddhas), 29, 30, 184
theodicy, 32
Theosophy, 10, 42
Thomas, Elizabeth Mary, 5–8, 18, 49, 50, 52–53, 57, 60
Three Marks of Existence, 144–147
Three Pillars of Zen (Kapleau), 60–61
Tianlong, 130
time: becoming and, 136, 169, 222, 280; bifurcation of Mind and, 222; consciousness and, 148–149, 156, 159, 202n; duality and, 139–140; enlightenment and, 133; impermanence and, 146–147; *mondō* and, 253–254; space and, 137. *See also* absolute present
timelessness, 144
Tobey, Mark, 54
Tokusan, 168–169, 170
Tomkins, Calvin, 54, 55
Touzi Datong, 213, 335*n*13
tracklessness, 89–90, 243–245, 301, 302
transmission, 107–108
triple body, 265–266
two eyes, 157–159, 176, 178

Uddaka Ramaputta, 72
unchanging state (*sthiti*; *zhu*; *zū*), 196
unconscious consciousness. *See* storehouse consciousness
unconsciousness, 101, 127–128, 259. *See also munen*
Union Theological Seminary, 14
universal mystic experience, 108–109
Unmon (Yunmen), 97, 167
Upaniṣads, 164, 201

Van Itallie, Theodore, 39, 40
Varieties of Religious Experience, The (James), 10
Victoria, Brian, 318*n*31
Vimalakīrti, 171
Virtual Orientalism (Iwamura), 61
Voltaire, 22, 166, 261
vow. *See praṇidhāna*

Weishan, 251–252
Whitehead, Alfred North, 127
"Who Shall Deliver Me?" (Rossetti), 94–96

will: Buddha's enlightenment as, 3–4, 86; Eckhart on, 152–153, 178; freedom and, 285–286; ignorance and, 33; *karuṇā* and, 34, 176; Mind and, 26; original enlightenment and, 176; *praṇidhāna* and, 153, 282; stages of enlightenment and, 216–217; stages of Mind and, 197
Wolff, Helen Mosel, 38, 41
Wolff, Kurt, 38, 41
words. *See* language
Wordsworth, William, 101
World Parliament of Religions (1893), 9
Wu (Emperor of Liang), 335*n*12

Ximingyuan Chen, 342*n*36
Xuansha Shibei (Gensha Shibi), 327*n*8
Xuefeng Yicun (Seppō Gison), 327*n*8

Yandell, Lundsford P., 2, 17, 18, 50
Yangshan, 251
Yanqing Guixiao, 340*n*29
Yanyang Shanzhao, 335*n*14
Yijing, 177
Yining Longjing Lun, 339*n*25
Yogācāra Buddhism, 26, 207, 254
yū (*you*), 3, 142–143, 184, 233, 258, 287

Zen and Japanese Culture (Suzuki), 6, 12, 42, 48
Zen and the Art of Archery (Herrigel), 48
Zen Buddhism: as ahistorical, 27; ethics and, 242–244, *243*, 245–246; etymology of, 67; experience and, 235–236; Fayan (Hōgen) school, 181; Flower Garland Buddhism and, 25, 28, 181; Huineng and, 237–239; hungry ghost ritual, 262–263; Japanese teachers of, 21, 61; *karuṇā* in, 35–36, 237, 247; *munen* and, 210; personal crisis and, 50; philosophy and, 69–70; *prajñā* and, 131, 176, 237, 247; *praṇidhāna* and, 35–37, 246–247, 268; as realizing absolute subject, 4; religion and, 69, 125; Rinzai (Linji) School, 258; vs. *samādhi*, 68–69; *satori* as central to, 216; self (*ātman*) and, 248, 251–252, 277–278; Suzuki's practice of, 8, 9, 10, 22–24; training methods in, 165–166; Western practitioners, 11, 61, 63. *See also mondō*; practicality of Zen Buddhism
Zen Buddhism and Its Influence on Japanese Culture (Suzuki), 11–12, 16
Zendō (Zen Way), 10
zero consciousness, 149–151, 152, 159–161, 170, 331*n*4. *See also* absolute present
Zhangzhou Bao'en Yuan Xingchong, 340*n*26
Zhaozhou, 114
Zhaozhou Congshen, 335*n*14, 338*n*18
Zhiyi, 342*n*37
Ziling Wei, 340*n*27
Zongmi, 28

GPSR Authorized Representative: Easy Access System Europe, Mustamäe tee 50, 10621 Tallinn, Estonia, gpsr.requests@easproject.com

www.ingramcontent.com/pod-product-compliance
Lightning Source LLC
LaVergne TN
LVHW041208250326
834689LV00022BA/175/J
* 9 7 8 0 2 3 1 1 9 2 8 6 6 *